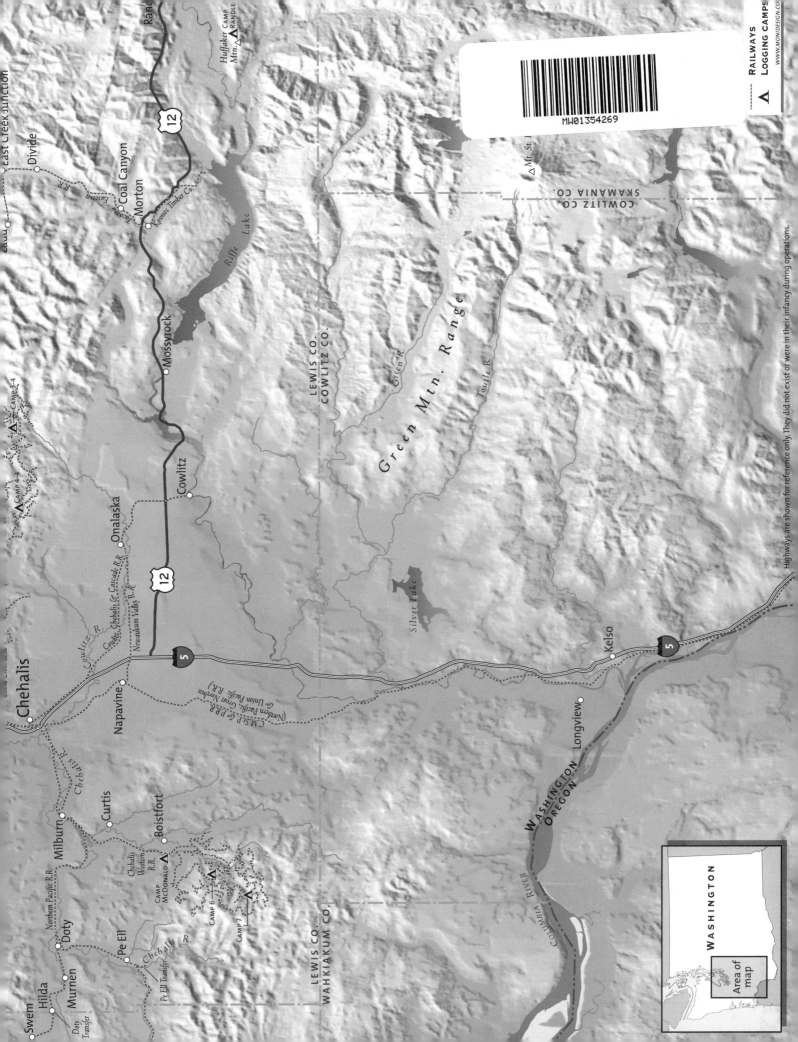

Logging Railroads of Weyerhaeuser's Vail-McDonald Operation

Including the Chehalis Western and the Curtis, Milburn & Eastern

Frank W. Telewski
Scott D. Barrett

PUBLISHED BY
Oso Publishing Company
P.O. Box 1349
Hamilton, MT 59840 USA
(800) 337-3547
www.osorail.com

Library of Congress Cataloging-in-Publication Data

Telewski, Frank W., 1955-
　　Weyerhaeuser's Vail and McDonald logging railroads / Frank W. Telewski, Scott Barrett.
　　　　p. cm.
　　Includes bibliographical references and index.
　　ISBN 1-931064-05-9
　　 1. Weyerhaeuser Company--History. 2. Logging railroads--Washington (State). I. Barrett, Scott, 1952-   II. Title

TF24.W2T45 2004
385.5'4'09797--dc22

2004058117

First edition, first printing.

Copyright 2005 by Oso Publishing Company

All rights reserved. No part of this book may be reproduced or transmitted by any mechanical or electronic means, including photocopying, scanning or digitizing, or any other means, without written permission from the publisher, except for purposes of critical review.

Printed and bound in the United States of America

Manuscript Editor: Teri Bicknell
Production Editor: Lynda Rygmyr
Indexer: Lynne Grimes
Design: James D. Kramer, Kramer Design Services, Everett, WA 98208
Cartographer: Monika Petroczky

Table of Contents

Preface and Acknowledgments v

Introduction vii

Chapter 1: The Beginning of the Skookumchuck Operation: 1924-1929 1

Chapter 2: Into The Woods: 1927-1929 29

Chapter 3: The Great Depression into the Vail Woods: 1930-1934 59

Chapter 4: Crossing the Skookumchuck: 1934-1942 71

Chapter 5: The Genesis of the Chehalis Western and Columbia Construction Quarry 107

Chapter 6: The Chehalis Western and Camp McDonald: 1937-1945 121

Chapter 7: The Transition Years at Vail-McDonald: 1943-1953 149

Chapter 8: Vail-McDonald: 1954-1961 179

Chapter 9: The Pe Ell Years: 1961-1975 197

Chapter 10: The Curtis, Milburn and Eastern: 1973-1980 229

Chapter 11: End of the Milwaukee Road As We Knew It: 1977-1980 243

Chapter 12: The Chehalis Western: 1980-1992 263

Chapter 13: Requiem for a Logging Railroad Giant: 1992-1995 297

Appendix I: Vail-McDonald Camp Locations 307

Appendix II: Rolling Stock and Equipment 308

Appendix III: Steam Locomotives at Vail-McDonald including the Chehalis Western 321

Appendix IV: Weyerhaeuser-Vail; Chehalis Western; and Curtis Milburn & Eastern
Diesel Locomotives 326

Appendix V: Bridge Data on Vail Operation Logging Railroad from 1940 331

Appendix VI: Bridges and Stations Along the Chehalis Western Mainline 333

References 335

Index 344

Dedication

We dedicate this book to our parents, James F. and Rosalie F. Barrett and Fred F. and Madeline E. Telewski. And to my (Scott's) older brother Jim. Finally, we wish to dedicate this book to all the Weyerhaeuser employees who worked at the Vail and Camp McDonald Tree Farms, and the Everett Mills.

Preface and Acknowledgments

Our work on a book documenting Weyerhaeuser's Vail-McDonald Operations in western Washington actually started in the early 1980s as an initial interest of mine in modeling a logging railroad. At the time I was working as a tree improvement researcher for Weyerhaeuser's Southern Forest Research Center in Hot Springs, Arkansas, while co-author Scott Barrett was working for the Chehalis Western Railroad. We didn't know each other at the time and it would be another decade before we would team up to write this book. While working for Weyerhaeuser, I was influenced by two colleagues, Dr. Michael Greenwood and Dr. William Carlson. Mike is, in addition to being a fine tree physiologist, an avid model railroader working in N scale. Bill, also an innovative tree physiologist, has a strong passion for the history of the Pacific Northwest as his family roots harken back to the early settlement of the area and involvement in the timber industry. In the summer of 1980, model railroading, forest history and the timber industry came together for me as a concept for a future model railroad layout. A few years later I first visited Weyerhaeuser Archives at Federal Way in Washington and met Archivist Megan Moholt. At the time, I began to dig into the photographic collection and found photographs of Weyerhaeuser's Baldwin locomotive #111, a 2-6-6-2 semi-saddle tank engine and Pacific Coast Shay #5. I fell in love with the engines and knew I had to model the operation where they once ran. I ordered copies of some of the old photographs and mentioned to Megan that these would be for my modeling projects and possibly a "future book" on the history of Vail.

Years passed and I build a few models based on Vail prototypes. Finally, in the early 1990s I began to give serious thought to designing and building a layout now that I finally acquired a house with a full basement and lots of room to build. At the time, some of my modeling friends introduced me to John Ozanich, a locomotive engineer who works for the Grand Trunk Western. Jack is also an avid model railroader and builder of the Atlantic Great Eastern, a world-class HO scale model railroad layout here in Michigan. He runs his model railroad like the prototype, with a dispatcher, train orders and clearances. An entirely new era of modeling opened up to me and I became very interested to know how a logging railroad would have operated its trains. If I was going to model a logging railroad and operate it, I wanted to get it right. At this time, the Internet and E-mail were becoming commonplace. I knew Clark McAbee as the editor of *Tall Timber Short Lines* magazine (TTSL) and he suggested I contact Scott Barrett, a TTSL author, given my interest in the Vail-McDonald operation.

On October 17, 1997 Scott and I began to exchange information regarding the logging railroads of Vail-McDonald. Scott, being third generation in a logging railroad family, along with his father Jim senior, were able to answer just about every question I had regarding the design and operation of the logging railroad. After a short period of time and a visit to western Washington, Scott and I formally teamed-up to write this book. Over the ensuing years, we spent many days driving on rough logging roads and walking old railroad grades, visiting and verifying the location of logging camps and rail lines in the woods. We poured over archival records at Weyerhaeuser with the help of Megan Moholt as well as the collections of the John Labbe, Martin Hansen, Thurston County Historical Society, University of Washington and the Whatcom Museum. We also were fortunate to sort through the many boxes of papers collected by the Barrett family, especially by Scott's brother Jim to begin piecing together the story of the men, women and equipment which worked the woods for over 7 decades. Scott was fortunate to interview numerous former Weyerhaeuser employees and their family members to obtain first-hand accounts, experiences and information regarding the history of Vail-McDonald. Unfortunately, many of these "old-timers" passed away during the production of this book and were unable to see the finished product. We are honored to preserve their memories in this volume.

The effort to produce this book would not have been possible without the help of so many people. Scott's family, especially Jim F. Barrett, Sr., and Rosalie Barrett (Scott's mother) for providing volumes of oral history related to this project. Also to Jim Barrett, Jr. Scott's older brother who saved volumes of precious historical documents from destruction and provided countless miles of transportation while we investigated the Vail woods operation. Unfortunately, Jim passed away in the summer of 2004 before seeing this work published. Without Megan Moholt and the access she helped provide to Weyerhaeuser's historical records, this book would not have been possible. We are indebted to the assistance of Martin Hansen, John Labbe, John Henderson, John Taubeneck, Ken Schmelzer, Lyle Spears, Jim Shaw, John Cummings, Jim Whaley, Bob and Colleen (George Hales' daughter) Pallett, Rick and Suzanne Nelson, Kristopher Johnson, Peter Replinger, George Cummings, Jeff Johnston, and Dennis McClure for providing access to their personal and family photographic collections and making copies of their materials available to be presented here. John Taubeneck also provided information regarding locomotive and equipment rosters for Vail-McDonald. Rick Beaber was most helpful in providing both photographs and information related to the fleet of former Milwaukee Road steel log cars purchased by the Chehalis Western. Former and current Weyerhaeuser employees, Roy West, Bob Gehrman, Frances Neumen, Paul LeRoy, Floyd Canfield, Ted Ward, Richard Hussey, Fred Toby, Bob Pettit, Bill Johnson, Rick Nelson, Dennis McClure, John Kell, Ken Lentz, Lisa Boire and Landis Roher for providing personal insight and/or access to Weyerhaeuser lands and field records (section maps, aerial photographs and old railroad maps). Bob Chatwood Sr., former employee of Frank Lambertson's tie mill provided valuable information on this aspect of the operations and Allen Miller, former Milwaukee Road agent who worked at Western Junction and Chehalis provided information related to the joint Milwaukee Road-Weyerhaeuser operations and provided a copy of the Vail dispatchers map. Gina Blum of the Washington State Department of Natural Resources (DNR) provide access to the Weyerhaeuser files left at South Bay and permitted us to document and measure the remaining structures at the old log dump. The Washington State DNR also provided numerous aerial photographs used to verify the location and layout of Vail-McDonald trackage and reloads. Ellie Worsham and Harold Cooper of the Cowlitz River Valley Historical Society were helpful in locating old Weyerhaeuser reloads in Lewis County. Jack Anderson of the Mt. Rainier Scenic Railroad, provided access to their extensive collection of former Weyerhaeuser equipment and access to the former Weyerhaeuser Mineral reload. Thanks also to Jeff Jewel of the Whatcom Museum for providing access to their extensive photo collection. Chris Blomquist of the University of Washington Map Collection provided access to the U.S. Army 1945 photographic mosaic sheets. We also thank Diana Rivera of the Michigan State University Map Library for providing Corps of Engineers, U.S. Army topographic maps circa 1949, Jeff Wilson for technical support, Tyler Whitcomb for information on Western Junction and Dan Cozine for providing access to his personal map collection. We also wish to thank Susan Barrett, Jill Grimes, John Altshool, Dave Rygmyr, Megan Moholt, and John Taubeneck for reading and editing early versions of this book. Last but certainly not least, we thank our wives, Jill Grimes (Telewski) and Susan Barrett for their unwavering support, encouragement and patience with us during the years of research and writing.

Introduction

The story of Weyerhaeuser timber operations and logging railroads does not begin or end with the Vail–Camp McDonald Operation. The logging operation documented in this book is one of many affiliated with the Weyerhaeuser family name that existed throughout the Midwest, Inland Empire of Idaho, Pacific Northwest, and South. Frederick Weyerhaeuser began the long association between his family and the timber industry shortly after his immigration to the United States from Germany by purchasing a joint share in a Rock Island, Illinois, lumber mill. The mill would later bear the name Weyerhaeuser and Denkmann.

Bell-Nelson Mill in Everett purchased by Weyerhaeuser in 1902 was an old circular saw mill which would be replaced by a complex of mills over the course of the next 85 years. —Weyerhaeuser Archives

VIII LOGGING RAILROADS OF WEYERHAEUSER'S VAIL-McDONALD OPERATION

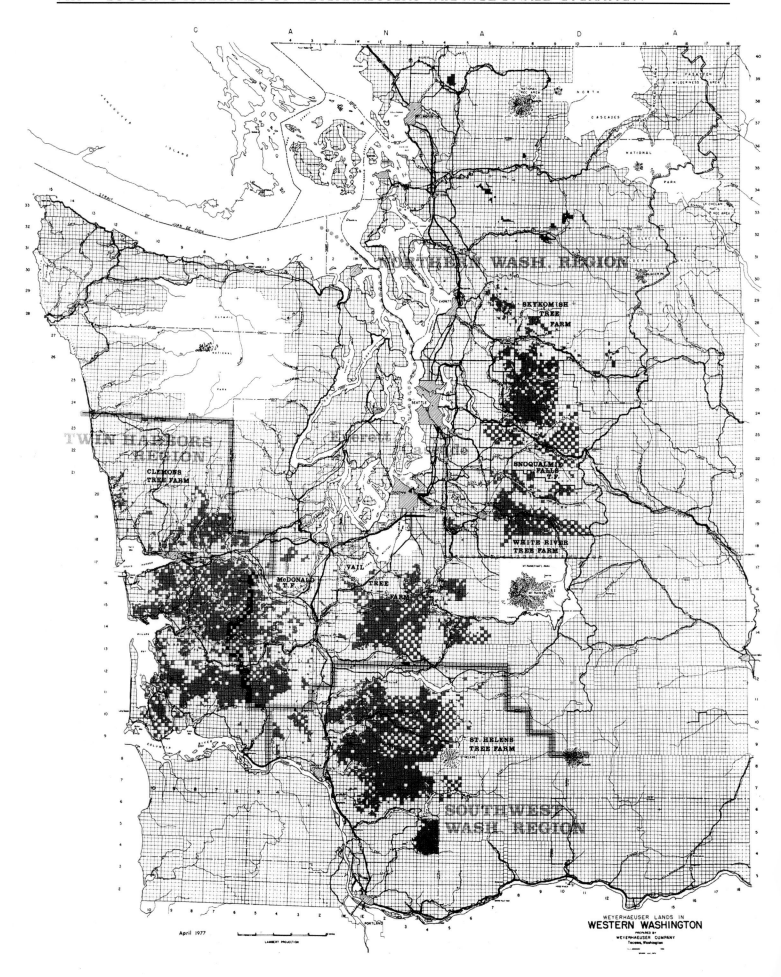

The original Bell-Nelson mill, located on the Everett waterfront facing Puget Sound, became Weyerhaeuser Timber Company's Mill A. Photographed here around 1906, the sawmill operated until 1936 when it was converted to a sulphite pulp mill. The sulphite mill was converted to a thermo-mechanical pulp mill in 1975 and remained in operation until December 1980. —Weyerhaeuser Archives

As demand for timber increased during the second half of the 19th century, the supply of standing timber grew increasingly remote from the waterways used to transport logs to mills. The growing availability of railroads and locomotives gave rise to the idea of moving logs from the woods to river landings or directly to mill ponds. This was attractive to the timber industry because of its cost-effectiveness.

Mr. Weyerhaeuser's first involvement with a logging railroad occurred in 1881 when he and Denkmann acquired shares in the Shell Lake Lumber Company located at Shell Lake, Wisconsin. To facilitate the harvest of white pine timber, the Shell Lake Lumber Company founded a narrow-gauge logging railroad in 1881, the Crescent Springs Railroad, which was also Wisconsin's first logging railroad. Mr. Weyerhaeuser must have been impressed with what a railroad could offer in terms of harvesting timber when water was not available for driving logs. Late in 1882, Mr. Weyerhaeuser incorporated the standard-gauge Chippewa River and Menomonie Railway to harvest his own timber holdings in Chippewa Valley, Wisconsin. The railroad began to move logs in 1883. Following the lead of the Crescent Springs Railroad and Chippewa River and Menomonie Railway, Weyerhaeuser and his partners would eventually establish more than two dozen logging railroads in six states to harvest timber and bring it to the mills.

By the end of the 19th century, the white pine timberlands of Wisconsin and Minnesota were almost depleted, leading Weyerhaeuser and his partners to look toward the South and Pacific Northwest for future timber supplies. Participation in the Coast Lumber Company (1898–1903) and the founding of the Sound

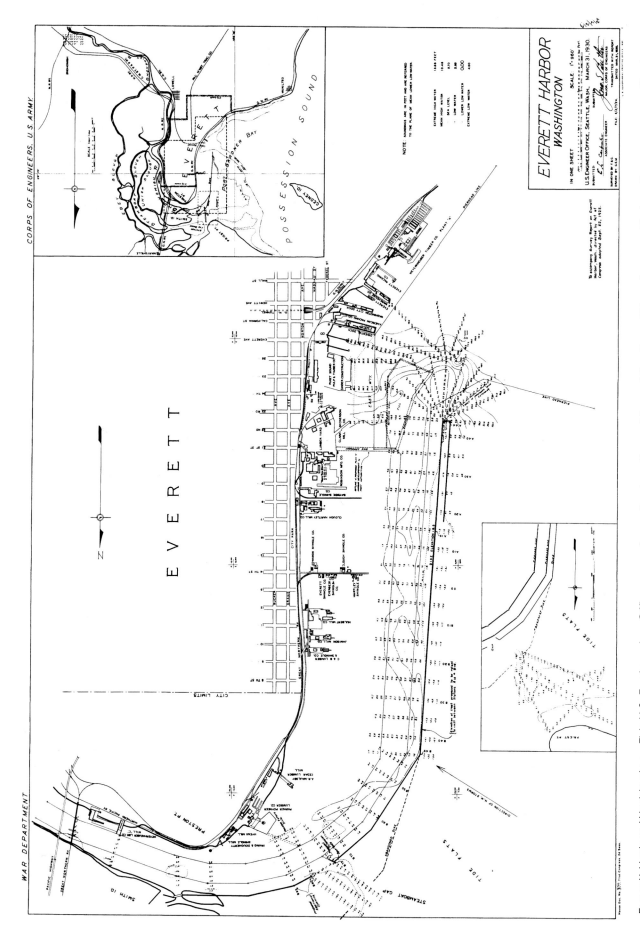

Everett Harbor, Washington. This U.S. Engineering Office map shows the locations of two of the three Weyerhaeuser Timber Company sawmills at Everett as they existed on March 31, 1930. Mill A is located along the Puget Sound waterfront; Mill C is located just above Preston Point along the bank of the Snohomish River. Mill B was located just to the east of Mill C (north on this map is to the left) on the other side of the Great Northern tracks and the Pacific Highway. —Frank W. Telewski Collection

Weyerhaeuser's Mill B, located near the mouth of the Snohomish River, was dedicated on April 29, 1915 and launched the Weyerhaeuser Timber Company as a major supplier of finished lumber, with 1000 employees and producing over one million board feet of lumber per day. Seen here in an aerial view from 1928, the mill is ready to receive shipments from the Vail operation. —Brubaker Aerial Surveys, Weyerhaeuser Archives

Timber Company organized in late 1899 were Weyerhaeuser's first ventures in the Puget Sound area. By far the biggest news to hit the lumber industry was in 1900 when the Weyerhaeuser office announced the purchase of 900,000 acres of timberland from the Northern Pacific Railway. Weyerhaeuser and his partners had arrived in the Pacific Northwest in a big way.

The new company's incorporators proposed naming the landholdings the Weyerhaeuser Timber Company, which was adopted over the protests of Frederick Weyerhaeuser. On February 9, 1900, the directors ratified the appointment of George S. Long as manager of the company. Long established headquarters in the Northern Pacific Building in Tacoma and would later play a significant role in shaping not only the future of this new company, but also that of the lumber industry in the Pacific Northwest.

Initially, the company's objective was to consolidate and evaluate land holdings. In 1901, George S. Long purchased pieces of land from the Northern Pacific in the Grays Harbor–Thurston County district west of Mount Rainier and in Clarke and Cowlitz counties. The land held stands of timber ranging from 50,000 to 100,000 feet an acre.

In 1902, the fledgling Weyerhaeuser Timber Company purchased its first sawmill in the region. The Bell-Nelson Mill Company's mill, located on Puget Sound near the mouth of the Snohomish River in Everett,

Mill B was build to handle the large, old growth logs that were common during the first half of the 20th century. Here a sawyer begins cutting a large log on the mammoth headrig (band saw) in 1940. —Juleen Studio, Weyerhaeuser Archives

Miles of narrow gauge industrial tracks were used to shuttle lumber from Mill B to finishing mills and seasoning yards. —Juleen Studio, Weyerhaeuser Archives

The finished product is loaded into waiting boxcars at Mill B's massive covered loading shed. —Juleen Studio, Weyerhaeuser Archives

Washington, contained old circular saws, a planer, and a small kiln, all of which required rebuilding. The mill relied on logs supplied from company-owned operations such as the Maple Valley Timber Company, Sound Timber Company, Cherry Valley Timber Company, and later the Siler Timber Company, as well as purchases from other timber companies located along the headwaters of the river. After the mill was rebuilt, it began turning out a little less than 40 million feet of lumber a year. By 1906–07, the Everett Mill had cut more than 82 million feet of lumber, reflecting an exceptional demand, partially the result of the San Francisco fire and an earthquake in Valparaiso.

Milling and manufacturing lumber were the future for Weyerhaeuser, drawing upon its vast forest reserve for raw materials. But the company's main activity during the first decade of the 20th century was land acquisition and the sale of timber to local manufacturers. In Thurston County, Weyerhaeuser sold timber to Turvey Brothers Lumber, Skookumchuck Lumber, Mutual Lumber, and other concerns in the district. During the early years, while the company consolidated land holdings and evaluated its position in the region, the actual manufacturing of lumber was a secondary activity. Weyerhaeuser built or acquired additional sawmills during the first half of the 20th century, including Snoqualmie Falls and White River (Enumclaw, Washington), as well as the large mill operations at Longview, Washington, and Klamath Falls, Oregon.

On April 29, 1915, a party of Weyerhaeuser executives gathered in Everett to inaugurate the new Mill B, constructed on the shores of the Snohomish River. George S. Long himself threw the switch of the big mill chain, signaling the expansion of manufacturing at Everett and the opening of one of the largest and most up-to-date sawmill plants in the United States. Mill C, a third mill that specialized in sawing only hemlock, was opened in November 1924. Increased production capacity of the new mills at Everett placed a strain on timber supplies. For the Everett Mill complex to continue operations, let alone expand, a source of logs was necessary. To address the need for logs, in 1928 Weyerhaeuser opened a new logging operation southeast of Olympia in Thurston County.

Originally named Skookumchuck, the new logging operation was later renamed Vail, after the company town and headquarters camp, which itself was named after a local family who sold the land occupied by the new town to Weyerhaeuser. The headquarters camp was complete with shops for servicing locomotives, rail cars, and logging machinery, as well as providing lodging and support for the woods and railroad crews.

Opening the new logging operation became the responsibility of Minot Davis, Lloyd Crosby, and Walter Ryan. The operation was furnished with both newly purchased equipment and used equipment from other Weyerhaeuser logging railroads that had completed operation. Locomotives and camp cars were obtained from Cherry Valley Timber Company, Clarke County Timber Company, and eventually the

Mill B grew substantially over the decades as can be seen in this aerial photograph from 1971. Notice the Pacific Highway located in the lower right hand corner of the photograph is now a four lane divided highway. The mill remained in operation until early 1980. —*Western Ways, Inc., Weyerhaeuser Archives*

Siler Logging Company—all Weyerhaeuser-affiliated operations. The new Skookumchuck logging railroad would run from the mountainous slopes west of Mount Rainier north to a log dump at South Bay on Puget Sound. Logs were then rafted on the sound to the mills at Everett. The Vail operation would give Weyerhaeuser access to 4 billion feet of reserved timber and would supply the Everett mills with about two-thirds of the required logs. After the Vail railroad was completed, Lloyd Crosby moved on to build the logging railroad at Klamath Falls, turning over the early field operations at Vail to Ronald A. McDonald.

Timber output from the Vail operation was supplemented a decade later by the opening of Camp McDonald west of Chehalis, Washington. Named for Ronald A. McDonald, this new operation harvested an additional 260 thousand acres of timber to supply the demands of the Everett mills. To move the logs from the forests south of the Boisfort Prairie, a logging railroad was constructed from Camp McDonald south into the woods. Weyerhaeuser incorporated the Chehalis Western Railroad, which became joint owner of a portion of the Vail and Camp McDonald logging lines, to move the logs from Camp McDonald to South Bay. Camp McDonald and the Chicago, Milwaukee, St. Paul and Pacific Railroad were connected at Chehalis, and an agreement was established that gave the Chehalis Western running rights on Milwaukee trackage from Chehalis Junction to Western Junction. At this point, the log trains transferred to jointly owned Chehalis Western and Weyerhaeuser trackage for the final run north to South Bay. The two separate land holdings had a log dump and a mission in common, supplying logs to the Everett Mill complex. Shortly after Weyerhaeuser founded the first certified tree farm at its Clemons operation in 1941, the two opera-

This is Mill C one year after it opened in November 1924, specialized in sawing hemlock. —*Weyerhaeuser Archives*

Mill C was located just west of Mill B where the Pacific Highway and Great Northern tracks crossed the Snohomish River. The mill was eventually closed in January 1977. —Brubaker Aerial Surveys, Weyerhaeuser Archives

Vail, Weyerhaeuser's headquarters camp for the Skookumchuck District was built in 1927 providing housing for the camps staff, and was home to the locomotive shops, car shops, dispatcher's office, general office and company store. —Aero-Marine Photos, Weyerhaeuser Archives

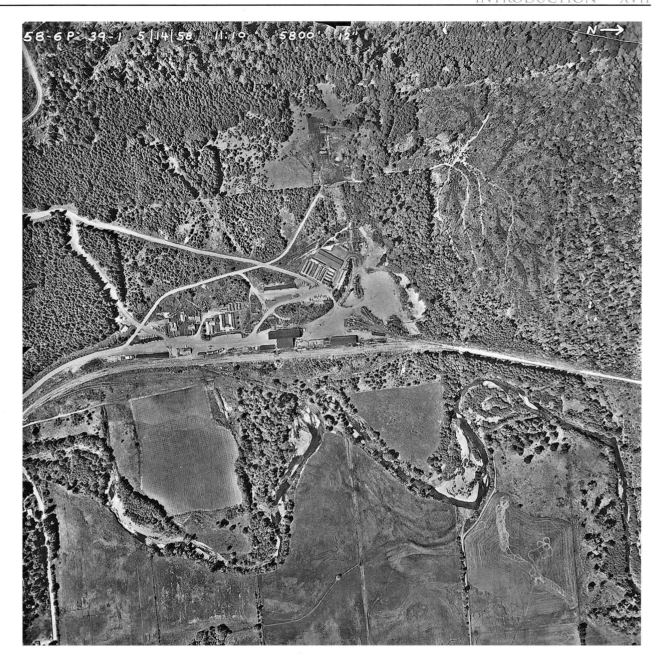

Established in 1938, Camp McDonald provided access to an additional 260,000 acres of timber for the Everett Mills. Seen here in an aerial view taken in the 1950s, the general layout of the headquarters camp has changed little with the exception of the addition of a large seed extraction facility located to the left of the tail track of the wye. —*Weyerhaeuser Archives*

tions were certified as tree farms (Vail on September 28, 1942; McDonald on October 10, 1943) and were frequently referred to in the singular as the Vail-McDonald Tree Farm.

From the late 1950s through the early 1970s, large old-growth logs from the Vail-McDonald Tree Farm were being replaced by an abundance of smaller, second-growth logs. To accommodate these logs, Weyerhaeuser built a small log mill, Mill D, which operated at Everett from 1965 to 1971. Mill D was then replaced by the more modern Mill E, which cut the second-growth logs until 1984.

The Chehalis Western vanished briefly late in the 1970s after Weyerhaeuser established the Curtis, Milburn and Eastern Railroad. It was born again out of necessity when the Milwaukee Road abandoned its western lines and the Curtis, Milburn and Eastern was retired by Weyerhaeuser to a paper railroad. The new Chehalis Western assumed control of the old Milwaukee Road tracks from Chehalis to Tacoma and from Tacoma south to Morton, the old Tacoma Eastern Line, as well as the former Curtis, Milburn and Eastern tracks west of Chehalis.

A change in markets, closure of the last lumber mill (Mill E) at Everett, and a diversion of logs to export led to the eventual abandonment of the South Bay log dump in 1984 and a focus on the extended run to the Tacoma Sort Yard and the Port of Tacoma. Eventually, the entire railroad operation was terminated in early 1994. The Vail-McDonald Tree Farm still existed as of the Weyerhaeuser Company's centennial celebration in 2000, but the chores once conducted by rail had been completely replaced by the diesel logging truck. Most of the original Vail logging railroad had been scrapped, and the shop buildings at Vail were razed in the mid-1990s. The shop buildings at Camp McDonald were demolished decades earlier. At the start of the 21st century, only a small portion of logging railroad trackage at Western Junction and Skookumchuck linking the original Milwaukee Road remained intact, as did most of the original Milwaukee Road Line once owned by the Chehalis Western. The new Chehalis Western shops at Western Junction faced an uncertain future.

A hundred years after Weyerhaeuser established a western empire built of timber, little remains of the once vast railroad empire that supported the industry. Equipment, operations, and personnel changed over the life of this logging railroad operation, but the mission of moving logs by rail remained a constant for more than 65 years. This is the story of the logging railroads of the Vail-McDonald operation.

Next page: Weyerhaeuser's Skookumchuck operation, later known as the Vail operation operated a 30 mile mainline railroad stretching from five miles south of the company town of Vail northward to the waters of Puget Sound via South Bay. The Skookum Chuck Ry., as it was known during the early days also interchanged with the Northern Pacific's Prairie Line at Wetico and with the Milwaukee Road at Skookumchuck. The mainline also crossed two other Northern Pacific tracks but did not connect with them. —Map redrawn and modified from original by Frank W. Telewski

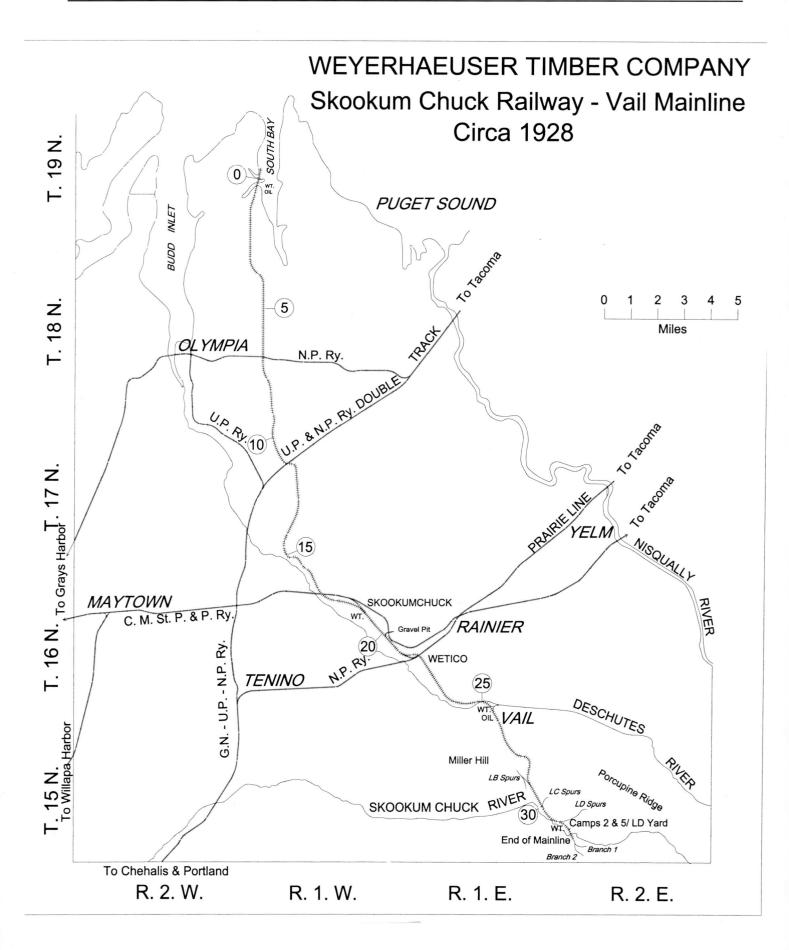

CHAPTER 1

The Beginning of the Skookumchuck Operation: 1924–1929

Weyerhaeuser's additional land acquisition of 1901 from the Northern Pacific Railway included 100,000 acres of land within the watersheds of the Skookumchuck, Deschutes, Newaukum, and Nisqually Rivers in Thurston, Pierce, and Lewis Counties, approximately 31 miles southeast of Olympia, Washington. Eventually, the total amount of company-owned timberlands in the region would approach 400,000 acres.

Logs being dumped into South Bay by the steam jammer. —Kenneth S. Brown, Weyerhaeuser Archives

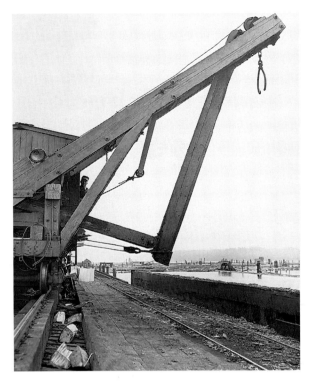

Close-up view of the steam jammer that ran on a level, parallel track to the tilted unloading track, which was tilted towards the water.

— Kenneth S. Brown, Weyerhaeuser Archives

The land was fairly mountainous, characterized by steep slopes and rich forests with elevations ranging from 464 feet to over 2,700 feet above sea level. The forests contained approximately 75 percent fir, 12½ percent hemlock, and 12½ percent cedar, with a stand average of between 57,000 and 60,000 feet per acre.

The Weyerhaeuser Timber Company initially named the land holdings Skookumchuck Camp after the Skookumchuck River that flowed through the heart of the district. Company plans to open up the Skookumchuck district at the south end of Puget Sound as a source of timber for the Everett mills became a reality between 1924 and 1926 when the Weyerhaeuser Timber Company secured a 30-mile right-of-way from the proposed log dump and booming grounds at Woodward Bay south to the Skookumchuck River watershed. Directed by Weyerhaeuser's logging railroad construction engineer Lloyd Crosby and led by chief surveyor G. M. Upington, a survey team began to lay out the new logging line the second week of July 1926, and quickly completed surveying 20 miles of the proposed 31-mile standard-gauge logging railroad main line. By August 1926, the survey work was completed and the right-of-way was ready to be graded.

Anticipating construction of the railroad, Lloyd Crosby, representing the Weyerhaeuser Timber Company, secured permission on September 20, 1926, from the Thurston County Board of Commissioners to construct grade crossings for the Skookumchuck Railway main line over county roads.

The main line needed to cross the Deschutes River, and in December 1926 Lloyd Crosby proposed the crossing be made with two 41-foot steel spans supported by a pier in the center of the river. F. R. Titcomb wrote to Crosby requesting a set of plans for the proposed crossing so that they could request bids

A Cruising Crooner

The Crosby family settled early in the Puget Sound area. Lloyd Crosby found work with the Weyerhaeuser Timber Company as a logging railroad engineer and was responsible for designing and supervising right-of-way construction. He began work on the Weyerhaeuser-affiliated Clemons Lumber Company logging lines around Grays Harbor in the 1910s and 1920s. Among his most notable efforts were the Skookumchuck Railway and the logging railroad for Weyerhaeuser's Klamath Falls, Oregon, operation. Years before the Weyerhaeuser Timber Company sent Lloyd Crosby to survey the right-of-way for the Skookumchuck Railway in Thurston and Lewis counties, each section of land owned by the company was cruised. This was a mapping process in which the land was surveyed and an inventory of timber recorded. In some cases, suggestions for the potential routing of a logging railroad were made. Enter Lloyd Crosby's cousin, Harry Lillis Crosby, born the fourth child of Harry Lowe Crosby and Catherine Helen "Kate" Crosby on May 3, 1903, at their home on 1112 North J Street, Tacoma, Washington. Harry took a summer job with the Weyerhaeuser Timber Company in 1920 and worked with a survey crew on mapping and inventorying some of the scattered land holdings that would become part of the Vail-McDonald operation. In July 1920, Harry cut his knee badly with an axe while working in the woods near Westdale. By the fall, recovered from his injury and ready for college, Harry Crosby entered Gonzaga University. After graduation, he went on to achieve fame as the world-renowned crooner "Bing" Crosby.

THE BEGINNING OF THE SKOOKUMCHUCK OPERATION: 1924-1929

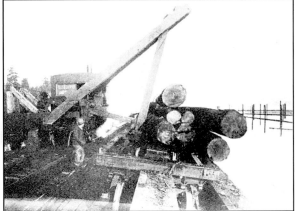

SOMETHING NEW IN LOG UNLOADERS

Weyerhaeuser Timber Co., at South Bay, near Olympia, Wash., has been testing out an improved type of log unloader, designed by A. H. Onstad, the company's engineer. Motive power is obtained from the engine of a Marion shovel, with special gearing to speed it up. A large arm, under control of the operator, equipped with a claw tip at the end, extends outward shoving the logs off the car. The shift from one car to another can be made in eight seconds. Absolute safety is claimed

The newly designed steam jammer by Weyerhaeuser engineer A. H. Onstad was feature news in *The Timberman* when it was introduced to the logging community.

Once the logs were dumped into the water, they were sorted and arranged into rafts by small boom boats. Once a raft was assembled, it was towed to Everett by a larger tugboat. —Weyerhaeuser Archives

WEYERHAEUSER TIMBER COMPANY

Section 12   Township 15 N   Range 1 E

40	40	40	40
40	40	40	40 1929
32 1928 11 Swamp	5 Swamp 16 3	37 SLV 1957	40
1	31	40 18 22	40

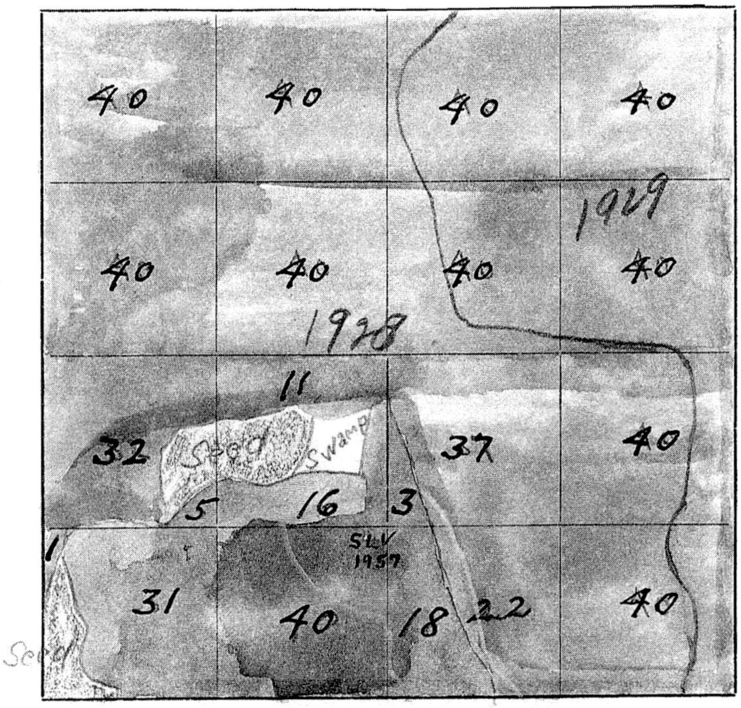

Acreage Logged

Total to date   March 1, 1932 — 503 Acres

Actual Acreage — 513.5

Total to Jan. 1, 1939 (113.0) — 616.0 Acres

All Logged

Examined _____ 19___

By _____

Form 13 2m 1-31 Ray

Weyerhaeuser Timber Company cruiser's section map showing logged-off areas and the date they were cut. The majority of this section was cut in 1928–1929. The form also shows the suggested location or actual location for rail lines. In this case, this section holds part of the LC line and the mainline (marked on this map as the BR. 10).

BASE MAP SYMBOLS

- ┼┼┼┼┼ Railroad
- ⊢⊣⊢⊣ Abandoned railroad
- ＝＝＝＝ Summer road
- ▬ ▬ ▬ ▬ Improved road
- ▬▭▬▭▬ Graveled public road
- ▬▬▬▬ Paved road
- ▭▭▭▭ Plank road
- ── ── Trail
- ･･･････ Telephone line
- ■ Building, in use
- ✕ Building, abandoned
- ▲ Guard station
- ⬟ Headquarters station
- ◬ Lookout station
- ◆ Known section corner
- ▶ Known ¼ corner
- ⌶ Bridge
- ⊥ Locked or guarded gate

FUEL TYPE LEGEND

Extreme : X (red)
High   : H (orange)
Medium : M (blue)
Low   : L (green)

Rate of spread: first letter, solid color, principal factor listed on second line of symbol

Resistance to control: second letter, border color, principal factor listed on third line of symbol

Fuel type boundary: ─o─o─

Boundary of examination within section _____

FUEL TYPE AND BASE MAP

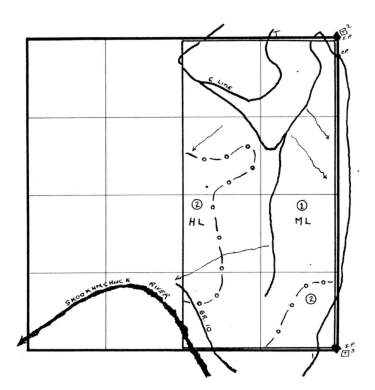

Route of Examination

Map Scale:
_____ inches per mile

Fuel Map Key	Fuel Type	Acres	SNAGS No. per Acre	Range in Diam. & Ht.	COMMENTS AND SUGGESTIONS
1	ML	257.0	1	10" x 40'	
2	HL	58.0	1	10" x 40'	
		320.0			

The Skookumchuck District was located west of Mt. Rainier. The forests contained approximately 75 percent fir, 12½ percent hemlock and 12½ percent cedar, with a stand average of between 57,000–60,000 feet per acre. On a clear day, Mt. Rainier was visible from just about any ridge or hilltop as can be seen in this early Clark Kinsey photograph. Looking east towards the mountain that appears in the distance, the Skookumchuck river canyon lies directly below. Visible in the lower right is a thin ribbon of rails, part of the Weyerhaeuser's Vail logging railroad. —Clark Kinsey, Rainier Historical Society

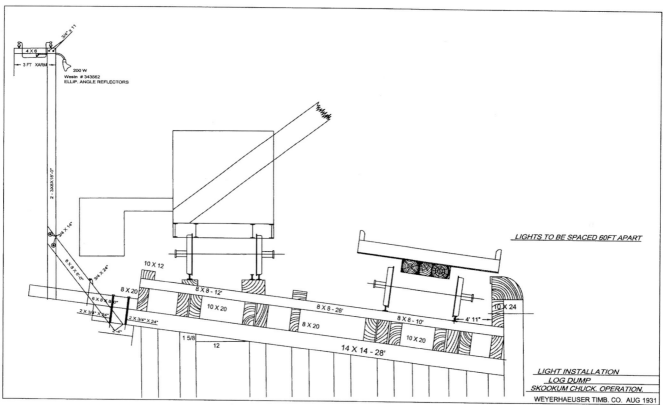

The log dump at South Bay held two tracks, one for log cars and the other for a steam jammer that would dump the loads into the waters of South Bay. The entire deck of the trestle was sloped towards the water, which tilted the log cars for unloading. The jammer's track was leveled using a stringer. Lights were installed at the dump in the summer of 1931 to facilitate unloading after dark. —Weyerhaeuser Archives, redrawn by Frank W. Telewski

This later aerial photograph of South Bay provides an excellent view of the two-way boom created in Henderson Inlet, just beyond the mouth of Chapman Bay. Boom sticks, very long logs cut specifically for this purpose, separate the sorting areas to the left and right of the dumping grounds. In the sorting area the logs are arranged by species, grade and size. In the boom, the sorted logs are bound together to create sections of a raft. A completed raft ready for shipping to Everett appears in the upper right hand corner of the photo at the mouth of Woodward Bay. —Weyerhaeuser Archives

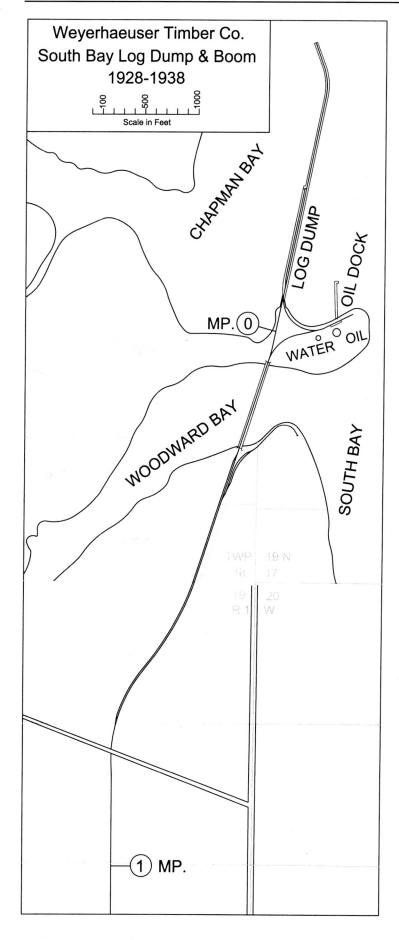

from the United States Steel Corporation for a single 80-foot span and the two 41-foot spans. Titcomb favored the construction of a wooden span, stating: "...I am much inclined to believe that the wooden span would be the more satisfactory." Titcomb's preference for wood prevailed, and it wasn't until decades later that Weyerhaeuser rebuilt the bridge with the central pier supporting two steel spans.

Track laying on the main line was proposed to start in October 1926, but apparently little progress was made until 1927. Early in 1927, the *Timberman* reported the purchase of a track-laying machine from the Long-Bell Lumber Company that was shipped to Rainier for construction of the logging railroad. The delivery of the track-laying machine coincided with the purchase of 3,500 tons of new 70-pound rail for main line use from the United States Steel Corporation, slated for a March delivery. The new railroad was named the Skookumchuck Railway, and by early 1927 the surveyed right-of-way, including logging spurs, was reported to have exceeded 55 miles in length and was nine months ahead of contract.

The Weyerhaeuser Timber Company secured a site for a log dump and boom at the north end of the railroad right-of-way in Puget Sound, on Henderson Inlet's Chapman Bay. The site for the boom and log dump required deep water regardless of tidal fluctuations and shelter from the wind. On November 2, 1926, Weyerhaeuser filed an application to construct a trestle, log dump, and boom in Henderson Inlet with the U.S. Department of War. The Army Corps of Engineers approved the application on November 30, 1926. As track laying progressed northward along the graded main line toward its terminus in Henderson Inlet, equipment and

Left: Track layout at South Bay log dump and booming grounds as it appeared from 1928–1938 —Weyerhaeuser Archives, redrawn by Frank W. Telewski

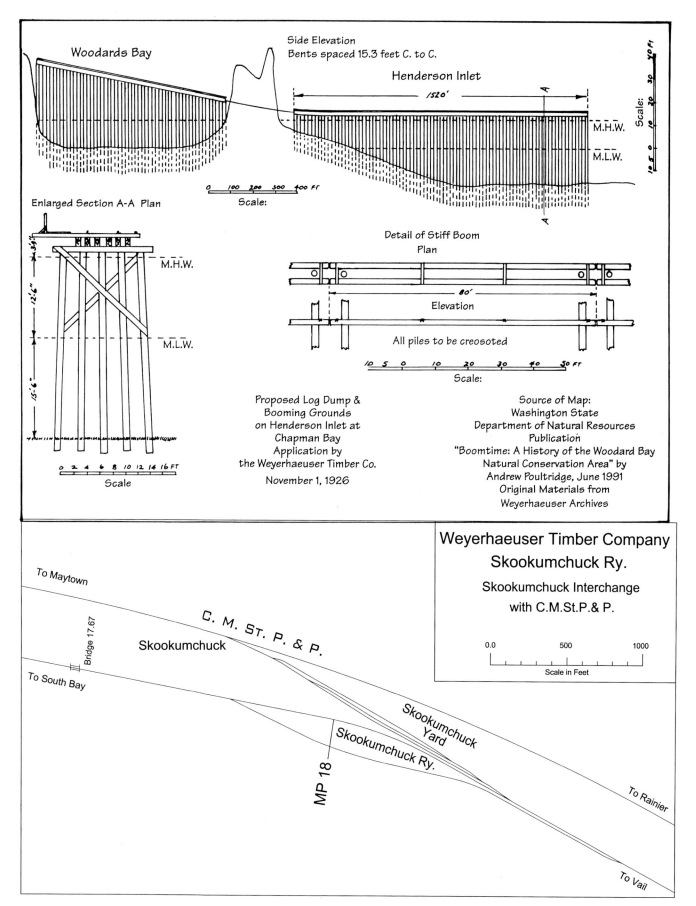

The Skookumchuck Ry. interchanged with the Milwaukee Road at Mile 18 and was named Skookumchuck. The interchange included a three-track yard and a siding. —Weyerhaeuser Archives, redrawn by Frank W. Telewski

materials were transported for the construction of the trestle across the mouth of Woodward Bay, and the unloading pier extended into Chapman Bay.

Construction on the pier was initiated on September 15, 1927, with the arrival of several carloads of equipment, a pile driver, and men. The pier of the log dump held two parallel tracks and was originally designed to be 2,020 feet in 1927. The unloader track was 1,550 long, and the brow log opposite the unloader track was 900 feet long. The brow log protected the trestle and rail from the impact of logs as they were dumped from the trestle into the water. It would require replacement about every 18 months. Under contract with the timber company, the Hart Construction Company extended the tail track 448 feet, with the addition of 22 bents in the summer of 1928. The log dump track was tilted toward the water to facilitate the unloading process. Mr. A. H. Onstad, the timber company's engineer, designed the wood-

Rolling Down to the Sea

The line from Vail to South Bay can best be visualized as a long, gentle roller coaster ride from beginning to end with a few flat spots in between. Imagine being at the throttle of a locomotive as you enter the grade heading north out of Vail, moving downhill until your train crosses the Deschutes River Bridge. After the bridge, the grade levels off and becomes more even. Passing milepost 23 (MP 23), the track is straight for almost a mile until your train starts climbing a gentle grade and begins to curve under the State Route 507 underpass and the former Northern Pacific Railway (Burlington Northern) underpass as the train passes the interchange track at Wetico. It is always a good idea to keep an eye on the switch stand and track at Wetico because you never know when there might be rail cars sitting in the wrong place. Once, a Weyerhaeuser steam engine pulling a train of loaded cars collided with a Northern Pacific train at this point, even though there was a derail at the Weyerhaeuser end of the Wetico interchange track.

After the curve straightens out at Wetico, the track is straight for a long ways as it crosses the Old Military Road and Waldrick Road and starts to dip and curve into the Milwaukee interchange track at MP 18. Once again, it is a good idea to keep an eye on the high switch stand and check for any railroad cars that have been inadvertently pushed or rolled out onto the Vail main line. The grade starts to climb gently toward the Milwaukee overpass as it rounds the curve at MP 18 and reaches the crest of the grade at the overpass as the track curves again.

After crossing the Milwaukee overpass, the grade slopes sharply downhill again as it passes through Western Junction and curves slightly before reaching the Waldrick Road crossing. Then, after crossing Stedman Road, the track curves back and forth past the Deschutes River. Over the years, Weyerhaeuser dumped lots of riprap near MP 15 to prevent the river from washing out the tracks at this location. Flooding was always a problem. Water from Tempo Lake and from the swamp ran off into the river through a culvert under the track. After a short, straight stretch past a farm crossing near MP 14, the track starts to drop again until leveling out around MP 13. Passing through the two crossings and the curve at MP 13, the grade climbs again until it reaches MP 12, when it descends and curves under the Burlington Northern/Northern Pacific Railway underpass. The underpass at MP 11 sits in a swamp, so keeping the grade from washing out was another continuous task. The track levels out again as it straightens out and passes the long siding at MP 10. It starts a gentle bend over the Yelm Highway before curving again through MP 9.

The track straightens out as it crosses Herman Road and curves and climbs gently past Chambers Lake, crossing over the top of Elizabeth Avenue in Lacey, Washington. After reaching the Northern Pacific Railway (Burlington Northern) overpass, the track is straight for a long ways as it dips and climbs over Pacific Avenue in Lacey, and later I-5 and Martin Way. After passing the short siding at MP 5½, the track descends sharply and bottoms out as the track passes through the Pleasant Glade Road crossing. It starts to climb gently again and curves back and forth through the South Bay and Schinke Road crossings, where it heads straight for the water at South Bay. The track dips and climbs a little as it passes through farm land past the long siding at MP 1½ (which was added later in the operation) and crests at the Woodard Bay Road overpass as the track descends sharply past the run-around siding. The grade finally levels out as it passes by the upper switch of the lower wye, and the loads of logs drift onto the long bridge for unloading.

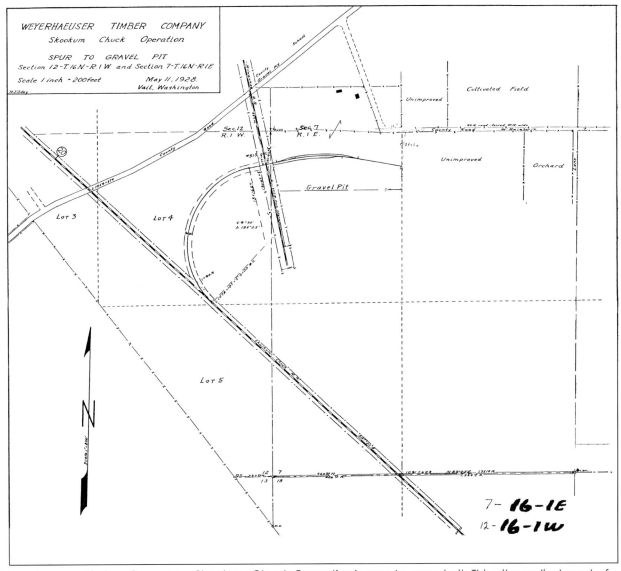

Weyerhaeuser Timber Company, Skookum Chuck Operation's spur to gravel pit. This pit supplied most of the ballast used in the construction of the logging railroad for over two decades. To access the pit, Weyerhaeuser trains had to cross the Milwaukee Road's tracks. The track layout within the pit would change over time to accommodate mining. This is the original layout of the pit on May 11, 1928. — Weyerhaeuser Archives

fueled, steam-powered log unloader, also called a jammer, and had it built from an old Marion steam shovel. The jammer was capable of unloading seven to eight cars per minute. In later years, the timber company would refer to the log dump as South Bay. South Bay required periodic dredging to keep the booming grounds deep enough during low tides to float the logs. Dredging occurred about every three years.

The "as-built" design of the log dump had deviated from the plans originally approved by the Army Corps in 1926. Originally designed as a one-way log boom with all sorting and storage to the north, Weyerhaeuser altered the design to include sorting and storage facilities to both the north and south, making a two-way boom. This improved design took full advantage of the sheltered location and deep water. Unfortunately, by deviating from the originally approved design, the facility as built was deemed illegal. To rectify the issue, the company got the support of Representative Albert Johnson of Olympia, who drafted legislation in congress to authorize the modified construction of the South Bay log dump. On March 1,

1929, by an act of congress (H.R. 15382, Public No. 879, 70th Congress), the construction of the trestle, log dump, and boom in Henderson Inlet by the Weyerhaeuser Timber Company was officially legalized.

To support the operations at the log dump, South Bay also contained a small boom camp composed of an office building, a bunkhouse for the boom crew, supply sheds, a cookhouse, and a dining hall. Several small boats were used in the boom to sort and position logs into the rafts for movement to the Everett mill. South Bay was also an oil terminal for the timber operation. Oil and diesel that fueled the locomotives, skidders and other equipment for the Vail operation arrived via a General Petroleum Corporation tanker and were transferred to a 50,000-barrel oil storage tank or delivered in 55-gallon drums. Empty oil tank cars were brought to the bay, filled, and returned to the woods along with the log loads and returning empty skeleton log cars. The oil storage and terminal facility was located on the tail track of the wye at South Bay.

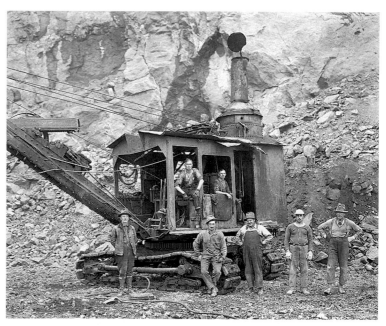

Working a rock cut along the Vail rail line using a steam shovel. —Clark Kinsey, Weyerhaeuser Archives

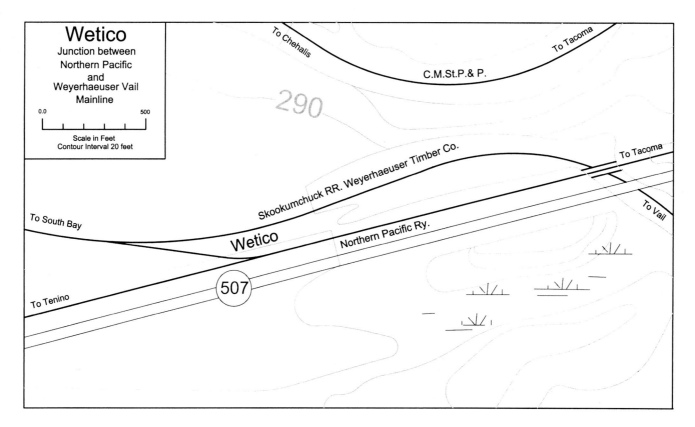

Skookumchuck Ry. interchange with the Northern Pacific was named Wetico. —USGS topographic map, USGS aerial photo redrawn by Frank W. Telewski

Construction crews used cedar poles harvested from Weyerhaeuser land to build trestle in the Vail woods. —Clark Kinsey, Weyerhaeuser Archives

General trestle designs used by Weyerhaeuser at Vail. —*Weyerhaeuser Archives*

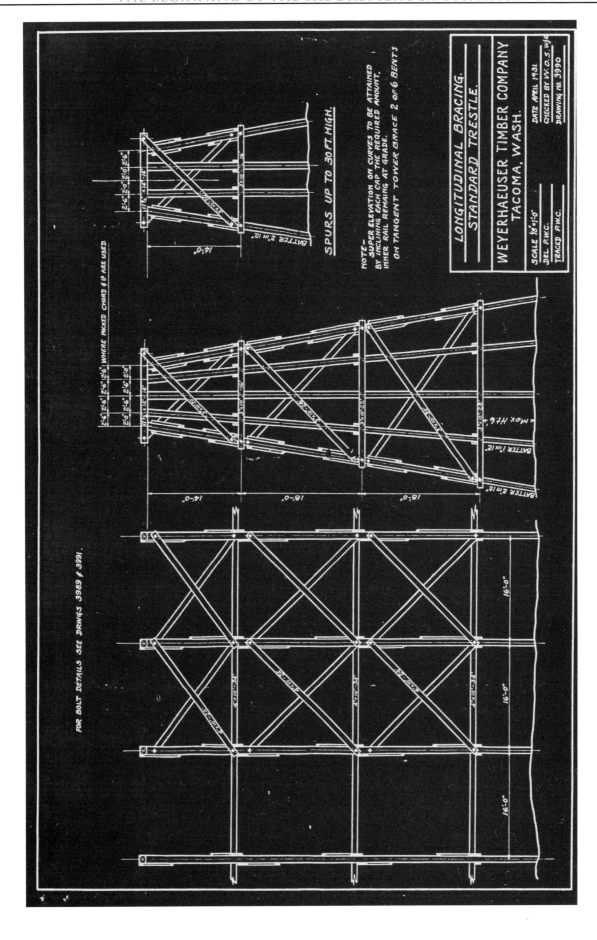

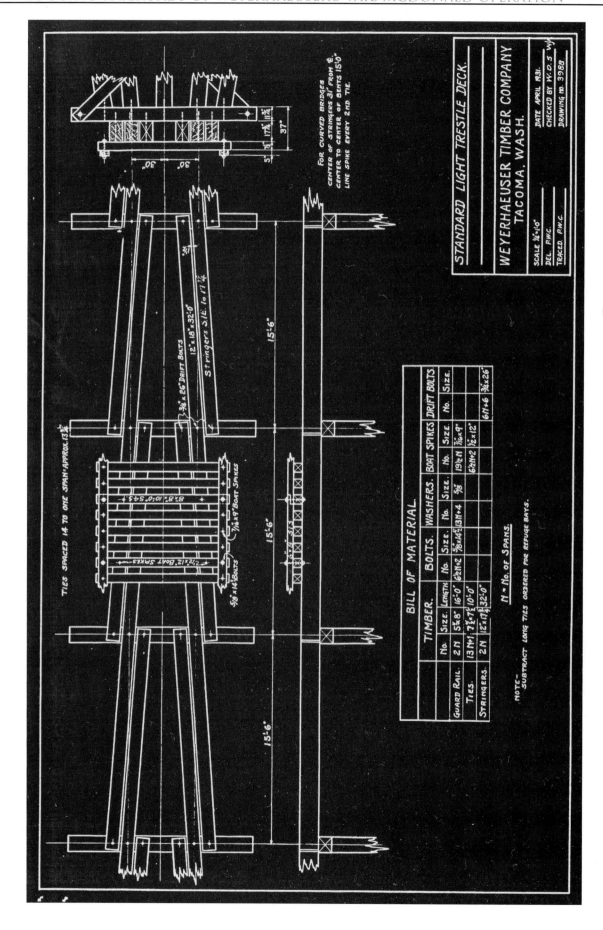

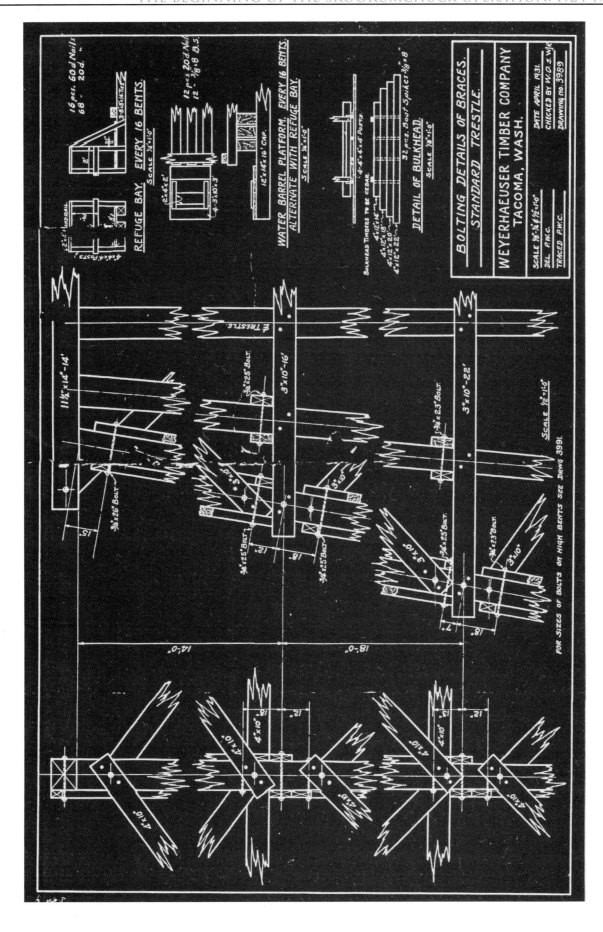

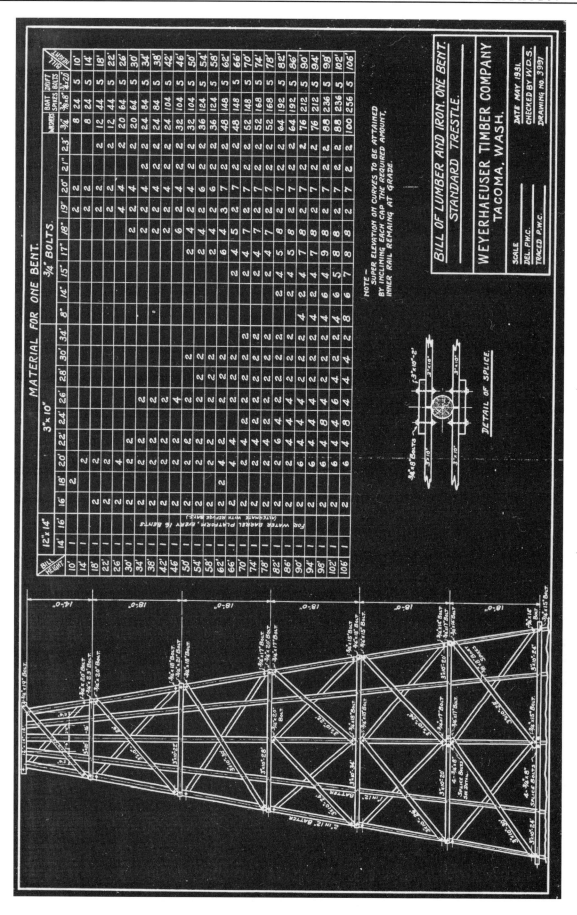

THE BEGINNING OF THE SKOOKUMCHUCK OPERATION: 1924-1929

A track crew lays down new rails at Vail. The ties were not treated and were referred to as "buckskin" ties for their light color. —Darius Kinsey, Whatcom Museum

The new railroad main line was completed late in 1927 with 70-pound rail, a maximum grade of two percent, No. 7 and No. 9 turnouts, and curves confined to six degrees between South Bay and Vail Headquarters Camp, a distance of 25.7 miles. The main line would extend an additional six miles south of Vail, which was also the company town, and into the Skookumchuck watershed to a point known as LD Yard and the high bridge crossing of the Skookumchuck River. Sidings and the tracks at Headquarters were laid using 56-pound rail.

When it was built in 1927, the logging railroad main line interchanged with the Chicago, Milwaukee, St. Paul and Pacific's fourth subdivision of the Coast Division 6.6 miles west of Rainier at what was originally named Weyerhaeuser Spur and later renamed Skookumchuck by the Milwaukee Road. This would be the location of the steel structure crew's camp in 1927 (the first location for Camp 2). The Skookumchuck Railway also interchanged with the Northern Pacific's Prairie Line 1.8 miles west of the town of Rainier at Wetico. In the early days, this interchange facilitated the shipment of pilings from Rainier to Weyerhaeuser's Longview operation and receipt of materials shipped to Vail from Weyerhaeuser's retired Clarke County Railway, as well as a host of supplies shipped over the Northern Pacific to Vail.

The railroad was constructed by both Weyerhaeuser crews and contractors, including Railroad Contracting Company of Aberdeen, Washington; Pearson and Larson Company and Strong & MacDonald Construction Company, both of Tacoma, Washington; Allen Engineering Company, and J. L. Smith. Allen Engineering was contracted for the grading north of the Pacific Highway toward Puget Sound, while J. L. Smith employed 40 men working on a grading contract at Fir Tree (just north of the Skookumchuck interchange). Railroad Contracting Company cleared and graded the rights-of-way south of Vail, whereas Pearson and Larson were contracted to build Vail Camp and grade the roadbed south to Mulqueen. Weyerhaeuser had contracted with Strong & MacDonald to lay steel, ties, and frogs as well as build the viaduct that crossed the Pacific Highway and the Northern Pacific tracks at Johnson's Hill.

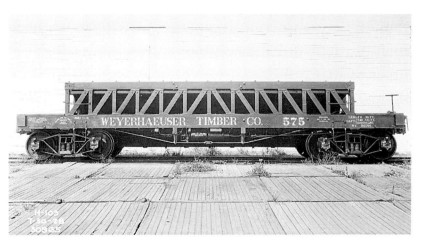

Pacific Car & Foundry builder's photo of a Rogers Ballast car for Weyerhaeuser's Vail operation. —PACCAR, Inc., Ken Schmelzer Collection

Top: Looking across the Vail yard tracks at the town of Vail. The dispatcher's office is on the left and the camp office and company store is on the right. —Weyerhaeuser Archives

Center: The crew of Frank Lambertson's tie mill pose for Clark Kinsey's camera in 1938 along with the mill in the background and their new 1938 Ford truck. Not only did the mill supply ties for railroad construction, but also provided slab wood to keep camp buildings warm.
—Clark Kinsey, Weyerhaeuser Archives

Bottom: Frank Lambertson's tie mill was located on the 20 line in the mid 1930s. The mill was originally powered by a gasoline engine and was upgraded with a Caterpillar diesel engine in 1934. The diesel engine is visible to the left side of the mill.
—West Coast Lumberman, Jan 1935

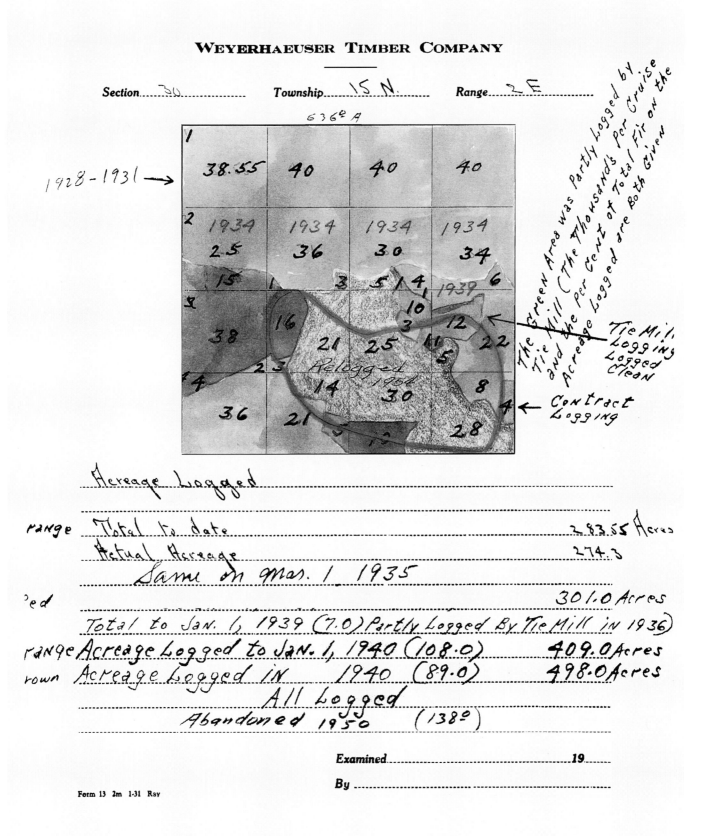

Section map showing location of tie mill logging in 1936. —Weyerhaeuser Archives

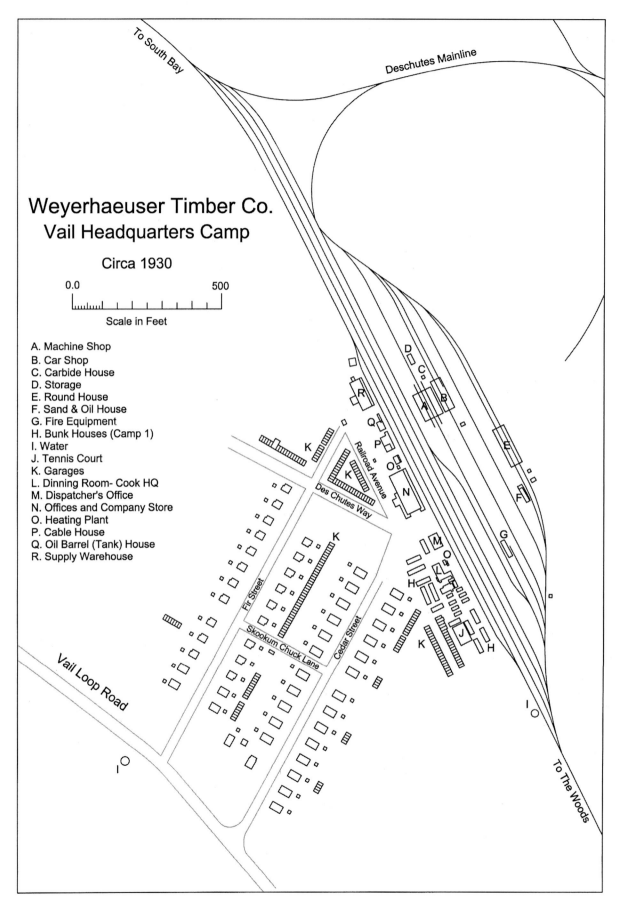

General layout of Vail Headquarters Camp as it appeared around 1930. —*Weyerhaeuser Archives, redrawn and modified by Frank W. Telewski*

Company houses under construction in Vail around 1927. Notice the railroad spur running down the center of the street that allowed loads of lumber to be delivered right to the "door" of the new houses. —Clark Kinsey, Weyerhaeuser Archives

Lloyd Crosby purchased rail for the rail line from Weyerhaeuser's Cherry Valley Railroad, which was in the process of abandonment, from the Milwaukee Road, Northern Pacific, and steel distributors such as United States Steel Corporation and Hofius Steel in Seattle. The Pacific Coast Forge Company supplied spikes, bolts, plates, and other construction materials. The steel gang used the lighter 56-pound rail from Cherry Valley for sidings and the tracks at Headquarters. Crosby also purchased bridge timbers from Weyerhaeuser's Everett Mill as well as from local lumber companies, including the Mutual Lumber Company of Tenino, and shipped

The company store was the center of activity at Vail and was the largest building in town which wasn't dedicated to servicing equipment. —Francis Neuman Collection, Rainier Historical Society

The shop crew poses outside two of the major machine shop buildings at Vail. Both buildings were equipped with overhead cranes supported by sturdy timber construction. —Clark Kinsey, Weyerhaeuser Archives

over the Northern Pacific to Wetico. Under Crosby's direction, crews harvested poles and cedar piles from company property, which were used in the construction of the various trestles, bridges, and culverts along the right-of-way. With regard to trestle construction, Lloyd Crosby commented in a letter to George S. Long: "We are using a great many cedar piles, which we are getting out from our own timber. Without going into details, we are saving about 35 percent over purchasing from a pole company. We will not be able to secure enough cedar on Section 27-17-1W, and in prospecting around we find some available cedar piles on North of Section 25-17-2W… We believe we can secure enough there for all the trestle work between Chambers Prairie and the bay, and would haul them directly from the ground to the various bridge sites." Section 27 is one mile north of the Skookumchuck interchange, and Section 25 is about 1.5 miles west northwest of Offut Lake.

As early as October 1926, F. R. Titcomb recommended to Lloyd Crosby the installation of "…two or three (portable) mills going in there as soon as you reasonably can." The portable mills cut lumber and ties that were used in the construction of the logging railroad or sold to other railroads. Wood ties were a significant expense to a logging railroad. Timber used in the production of ties was less timber that could be sold and converted into lumber for sale by the company. Conserving timber resources while producing ties was a high priority for Lloyd Crosby. In a letter updating George S. Long on progress on the Skookumchuck Railway, Crosby wrote: "We expect to use approx. 180,000 ties prior to actual logging operations." He went on to explain that, "by bucking to eight feet, we gain all of the taper in the log. We are paying $10.59 for no. 1 ties and $7 for no. 2 delivered to the right-of-way. The market price for these ties is $16, and as we have no freight or handling expense, we believe we will save considerably on tie cost." Although the company owned the timber, each operation was set up as a cost center. Therefore, even though Crosby could produce ties using the company's portable mills or cedar piles using its own timber, there was still a cost for production, including the cost of the timber. Crosby used an additional measure to ensure large, valuable trees were not used in tie production; he writes, "we are not cutting trees over 32 inches stump dia., and believe we can contract later to truck loggers to load out the large trees to the railroad at a very reasonable price." The ties originally used on the Skookumchuck were untreated and were referred to as "buckskin" ties. In an additional effort to conserve timber used to manufacture ties, a low-grade tie used on spurs was made from the thin logs from treetops and saplings. These ties usually had bark on at least one side. By February 1927, a total of four tie mills were reported in operation, employing 15 men each.

Later on in the operation, contractor-operated tie mills located along the railroad also cut ties using local timber. At one time, several portable tie mills were operating, supplying ties for the expanding rail lines south of Vail. Frank Lambertson owned and operated several portable tie mills, supplying both ties and firewood for the growing woods operation. One of the mills owned and operated by Lambertson was located deep in the woods above the Skookumchuck River in late 1929. This mill was equipped with a 32-inch top saw and 52-inch bottom saw originally powered by a gasoline engine. The tie-length logs were brought to the mill by truck, and the finished ties were loaded onto 40-foot truss rod flat cars for transport to the site of track laying. Lambertson's crew cut slab wood into short lengths, which were used to heat camp and shop buildings. The firewood was loaded onto a special wood car, a modified flat car with a wood crib constructed on top and transported by rail wherever firewood was needed.

Later in 1936, Lambertson's tie mill was reported to be the first mill in the country to be re-powered with a Caterpillar diesel engine. The conversion was reported to have increased cutting capacity from 316 ties per eight-hour day to 600 ties.

Weyerhaeuser Timber Company's track crew ballasted and surfaced the finished track. The track crews got the ballast from a glacial river gravel pit at MP 20, which consisted of rounded river rock from a half-inch up to six inches in diameter. The pit was located across the Milwaukee Road main line east of Skookumchuck where the Vail spur crossed the Milwaukee Road main line at grade. When entering the pit by train, the crews had to stop at the crossing and call the dispatcher's office located near Skookumchuck for clearance to cross the Milwaukee main. The crew would then place red fusees on the Milwaukee rail to the east and west, and align the two stop gates across the Milwaukee Line. Once clear of the crossing, they realigned the gates across the ballast pit spur track, and removed the fusees from the Milwaukee track.

This inside view of one of the shop buildings provides excellent interior detail. Notice that the machinery was all belt driven from a central pulley drive shaft in the early days before the introduction of individual electric motors.
—Clark Kinsey, Weyerhaeuser Archives

This is an early view of Vail Headquarters Camp. Company housing can be seen in the foreground, while the locomotive and car shops can be seen in the background. The offices, company store and dispatcher's office were also located in Vail. —Clark Kinsey, Peter J. Replinger

This process was repeated when the loaded ballast train was ready to proceed back to the Skookumchuck Railway main line.

In 1927, Vail was built as a new company town three miles south of Rainier. Pearson and Larson Company and Walter G. Scheel of Tenino were contracted by Lloyd Crosby to construct the Vail Camp buildings. The contractors purchased kiln-dried lumber from the Everett mills for use in constructing the buildings and bunkhouses. Vail served as the headquarters camp for the Skookumchuck operation, and eventually the name Vail replaced the name Skookumchuck. The company town initially consisted of 14 five-room timber houses, six six-room bungalows, and 21 four-room houses built on site for the crew. There was also a two-story Dutch Colonial house for superintendent R.A. McDonald, as well as three shop buildings, a company store and office, dispatcher's office, dining hall, heating plant, garages, and supply warehouses. During the construction of the houses, the section crew installed a rail spur that ran up the street so that flat cars containing construction materials could be unloaded right at the building site. Families began to move into the houses during the third week of January 1928. Mr. Walter Scheel built four additional six-room and six additional five-room houses at Vail in June 1928. Eventually, the number of houses would increase to 61. Later on, 13 bunkhouses, a guesthouse, meeting hall, and showers were added to support single men working for the company.

The town was named Vail after the Vail family, whose ranch numbered some 800 acres in the district, and who sold Weyerhaeuser the land on which the town was built. The Vails were also instrumental in securing rights-of-way for the new logging railroad Lloyd Crosby and G. M. Upington, chief surveyor, were developing. Both were grateful for the family's assistance. In an article published in Weyerhaeuser's employee magazine in April 1951, Lloyd Crosby reminisced: "Upington, present chief engineer of Klamath Falls Branch, had surveyed the proposed town site and was engaged in making a plat of it. As he was preparing to place a title on his map I came into his office and started looking over the plat. Upington turned to me and said, 'Lloyd, what are we going to name this town site?' Just then Billy Vail walked into the office, which gave me the idea. Why not name the town site 'Vail' after Billy? He had been our good friend in securing the right-of-way and particularly Mrs. Vail, who was so friendly in our right-of-way negotiations. She did not, however, sign the deed until we purchased her the best cook-stove she could find in the mail order catalog to go along with the money."

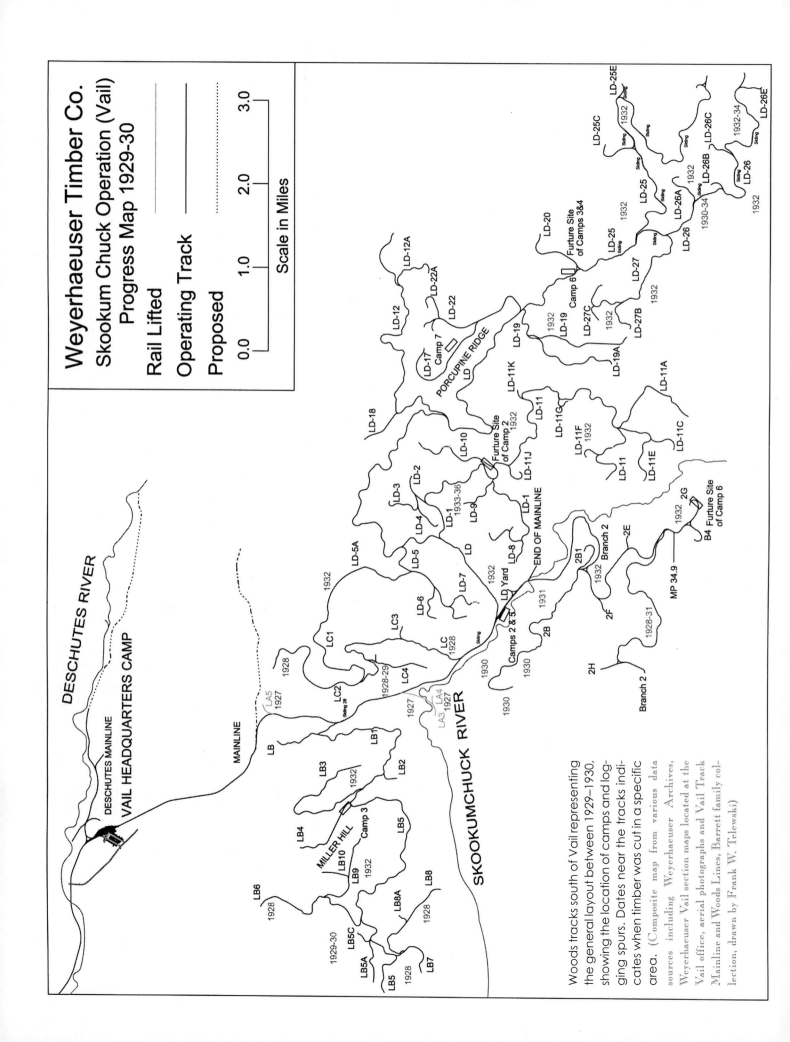

CHAPTER 2

Into the Woods: 1927–1929

When it began operating, Vail consisted of eight major camps: Vail (Headquarters Camp or Camp 1), six woods camps, and a boom camp at South Bay. Camps 2 and 3 were rail camps that housed the Cherry Valley camp cars. The cars, built in 1918, were 60 feet long by 14 feet wide and were set on trucks for movement by rail.

The first location for Camp 3 was on the B4 spur just below the summit of Miller Hill. A typical rail camp for Vail, it was composed of former Cherry Valley camp cars. In the foreground can be seen an early open crew car fashioned from a flat car, which provided no protection from the weather, and the filers shack, perched on a PC&F skeleton log car. —Clark Kinsey, Weyerhaeuser Archives

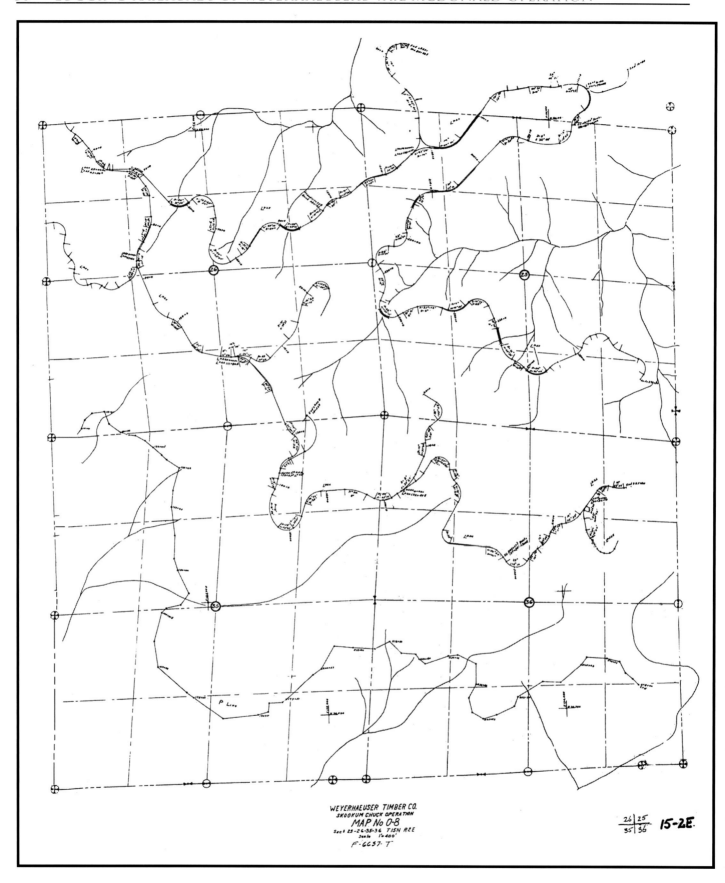

Weyerhaeuser Timber Co. Skookum Chuck Operation engineering map #0-8 showing the proposed location of tracks, bridges, sidings and spurs along the LD line. This section shows the LD25 and LD26 logging lines and their respective spurs. —*Weyerhaeuser Archives*

An Ohio "Loggers Special" crane is called into work clearing debris along the rail line. —Clark Kinsey, Weyerhaeuser Archives

Additional camp buildings were soon needed for the Vail operation, and in January 1927 F. R. Titcomb sent Lloyd Crosby plans for bunk houses used by the West Fork Logging Company. Titcomb included written instructions with the plans: "Mr. Murray uses 40-foot bunk houses of this same construction." "I presume that we will want to ship our kiln dried 2×4s and our 1×4 or 1×6 8-ft pieces, which we are now talking of for the purpose of bunk houses, out of our Everett Stock…" Titcomb preferred to use kiln-dried lumber: "Personally I would like to use dry dimension in so far as possible in the construction of our bunk houses as this would decrease the probability of cracks in our plaster and thereby give us a better constructed building."

The lumber used to build the bunk houses was shipped, along with the materials used to build the shops at Vail from Everett. The 14×10–foot bunk houses and additional 10×20–foot and 10×24–foot support buildings used for Camps 4, 5, and 6, were built at Vail in 1927 and 1928. Because these structures were not built on rail trucks, they were moved by picking up the structure with a locomotive crane and loading it onto a log or flat car for rail transport to a campsite deep in the woods. To provide stability for moving, the smaller buildings were constructed on a frame of 12-inch diameter logs, similar to that used for donkey skidders. Hence, these movable camp buildings were referred to as skid shacks. The larger 40-foot–long buildings were constructed on two 8"×12" timbers rather than an under frame of logs. Camp 4 was a combination camp, composed of a few Cherry Valley camp cars and bunk houses. The camp was composed of six camp cars and 38-man bunkhouses. Two washhouses and two warehouses were also built on site. The buildings for Camp 4 were constructed at Vail in July 1928. Camp 6 was composed of six camp cars built at Vail and moved to Porcupine Ridge late in August 1928. The camp cars served as the cookhouse, eating quarters, general office, and commissary.

Camps 2, 3, and 4 were logging camps, and Camps 5 and 6 were the railroad construction camps. Late in 1929, a third railroad construction camp for the steel gang, Camp 7, was established. This is documented in timber company correspondence from 1929 to 1931 regarding camp expenses and accounting. Camp 7 was located somewhere along the LD Line on Porcupine Ridge in 1929. Camps 6 and 7 ceased to exist at Vail by the mid-1930s, and the designations of Camp 6 and Camp 7 would not be used again until after the opening of the McDonald branch of the operation in 1938 and 1940, respectively.

South of Vail, the main line first followed the course of the Deschutes River before crossing through a small gap into the Skookumchuck River drainage. Once the main line crossed the gap into the Skookumchuck watershed, it gave rise to a number of spur lines that ran up into the mountains. Over 30 miles of spur track had been laid before the first logs were shipped to South Bay. This portion of the logging railroad main had a grade from four to four and a half percent, with maximum curvatures of 22 degrees. The spurs had grades of five to six percent and curves up to 32 degrees. Railroad construction required a total of five shovels—P&H diesels and Bucyrus-Erie steam-driven shovels. Two Ohio locomotive cranes were also dedicated to construction work. Track crews replaced switch stands in the woods with ground throws given that the switch stands could accidentally be removed by passing log trains.

The construction of spurs into the woods progressed at a rapid pace between 1927 and 1928. The first logging spurs were initially designated using letters: Line B (LB) branched off the main line and switch-backed up Miller Hill; Line C (LC) wound its way up the Run Creek drainage farther up the main line; and Line D (LD) branched northeastward about a mile further south, following the drainage of Laramie Creek and up to Porcupine Ridge. Spurs off the lettered lines were designated with a number such as B1, B2, C1, C2, D1, D2, etc. There is some evidence of an LA Line, a rather short spur off the main line just beyond Branch 6.

> **Warring Waitresses Wreck Weyerhaeuser Eating Place**
>
> The following account of camp life was first published in the *Tenino County Independent* on July 6, 1928. When the story came out, Camp 2 was located, along with Camp 5, at LD Yard above the Skookumchuck River, three miles southeast of Vail:
>
> *War broke out in the lunch room at Camp 2 near Vail, Monday when five waitresses indulged in a free-for-all. Lunch buckets, thermos bottles and other convenient articles filled the air, together with various feminine forms of depreciation. Fortunately the bombardment was feminine so that the casualties were confined to one girl, who happened to get in the way of a flying thermos bottle from the hand of an infuriated blonde.*
>
> *According to popular report, the lunchroom was a total wreck after hostilities ceased. Immediately afterward, two blonds thought to be vanquished (anyway, they vanished) packed their clothes and walked three miles to headquarters at Vail, where they drew their pay and proceeded to move on.*
>
> *Nobody seemed to know the cause of the skirmish, although several volunteered solutions. The most logical of which was that one blonde decided she didn't like the color of one of her coworker's flaming red hair.*

A rail line referred to as the Deschutes Mainline was built along the south bank of the Deschutes River and originated from the tail track of the wye at the north end of the Vail yards. The Deschutes Mainline joined up with the abandoned road bed of the old Lindstrom-Handforth Lumber Company logging railroad after crossing the Vail Loop Road. It is not clear how far Weyerhaeuser extended this track along the old right-of-way. There were at least two spurs which were used to harvest timber to the north and east of Vail. Another logging spur which would become known as Branch 6 was first proposed by Minot Davis to F. R. Titcomb in a letter dated February 21, 1929. The proposed spur would access timber the company owned in Sections 31 and 32 of Township 16 North, Range 2 East which needed to be harvested by August 16, 1931. Davis wrote: *I believe we can develop this country very easily by building easterly from our main line across the S1/2 of Section 36, Twp. 16 North, Range 1 East, and I believe that we should inves-*

Vail Headquarters in the early days of 1928. This is a very busy photograph showings lots of operating detail. Two strings of Cherry Valley camp cars are set-up in the Vail yard providing temporary housing and services until Vail's buildings and bunkhouses were completed. Meanwhile a train of loads begins to head north followed by caboose #711 and at least two empty oil tank cars, which will be filled at South Bay. A second train, headed by Mikado #103 is ready to depart for the woods with a string of empty log cars. Clark Kinsey stood on the water tank at the south end of the Vail yard to capture this photo. — Clark Kinsey, MSCUA, University of Washington Libraries, UW4930

The LD yard was also the location of Camps 2 and 5 in late 1929. Collectively known as LD Camp, Camp 2 was composed of Cherry Valley camp cars seen here to the left and Camp 5 consisted of skid shacks and is on the right hand side of this photo. The LD line branched off to the left and climbed up to Porcupine Ridge. —Clark Kinsey, Peter J. Replinger

Camp 4 was the largest of woods camps at Vail. It is highly likely that this is the first location of Camp 4 taken during the very early days of the Vail operation. The 3-spot Shay is ex-Cherry Valley #3 and now Weyerhaeuser's Vail three spot. The tank car on the siding has not yet been re-lettered W. T. Co. and is still bares the reporting marks for Cherry Valley (C.V.). The next time Camp 4 was relocated, it would be joined by six camp cars. —Clark Kinsey, MSCUA, University of Washington Libraries, UW4942

tigate the possibility of building such a spur with the idea that we shall probably want to log this timber before the expiration of the time limit. Very likely we might also want to log a portion of Sections 5 and 6 in Twp. 15, Range 2 East, to this same spur, but in general I imagine we would not want to extend this spur any further to the east, unless it should develop that some portion of Section 33, Twp. 16 North, Range 2 East, or of Section 4, TWP. 15 North, Range 2 East could be logged to this spur more economically than to another spur which would connect with our proposed Deschutes River main line.

The LB Line climbed Miller Hill and was served by Camps 3 and 4. The first location of Camp 3 was on LB4, just as it crossed Baumgard Creek at a point immediately below the summit of Miller Hill. The first two locations for Camp 4 have yet to be discovered.[1] After the completion of logging on Miller Hill by 1932, Camps 3 and 4 were moved to the LD Line. Here they joined Camp 6 and served this line as a joint camp, known as "Spike Camp," approximately 10 miles from the main line on LD20. Logging along the LD spurs was completed by 1936. Camps 2 and 5 were initially located on the main line, south of the LD Line turnout at milepost 31 at LD Yard, and were called "LD Camp." The crew of Camp 2 at LD Camp finished logging the LC Line by 1929. With the removal of timber from LC complete, Camp 2 was moved to a site on LD10 shortly after October 1929.

The main line continued southwest of LD siding and crossed the Skookumchuck River, spanning the deep canyon on a 420-foot long, 96-foot high wood bridge built in 1927. After the main line crossed the river, it split and gave rise to two branches: Branch 1 (later renamed Branch 10) followed the

Skookumchuck River, crossing the river again about a mile above the first crossing; and Branch 2, which climbed the steep grade west of the Skookumchuck.

Weyerhaeuser's railroad construction camp at Vail was named Camp 5, and smaller grading camps were designated A and B. Contractors Strong & MacDonald also had small tent camps located close to major construction projects, usually at the large trestles they were responsible for building. They also used a small light rail system for grading. Trestles were built from cedar timber harvested locally on Weyerhaeuser property. Each bent was composed of five cedar poles. Two types of trestle deck configuration were employed, one for heavy use and one for light spur use. Once an area had been logged completely, the rails were lifted by the steel gang and moved to a new location where track construction was taking place.

The survey crew's camp was in charge of the steel gang and the grading and clearing crews. Headed by Vail's civil engineer, Robert Alexander, the survey crew mapped the location of the railroad grades several miles ahead of all other activity. Pack donkeys and men on foot carried food and supplies into the woods. Mr. Alexander reminisced on his retirement in 1951 about one experience surveying grades deep in the Vail woods: "Our camp on the 42 Line in 1929 was known as Hoodoo Camp. First, a fire sent the crew scrambling one night. Then a storm knocked a tree across the packer's shelter, but his donkeys had already jumped the corral and bolted. When the packer rounded up his donkeys and returned with a broad

More Deadly Than War

Too often, those of us who never grew up in or around a community of loggers, let alone lived or worked in a logging camp, tend to romanticize a life working in the tall timber. It's easy to do. The fresh air, hard work, hearty meals in the dining hall, the smell of fresh cut fir and wood, coal, and oil smoke, the hiss of steam, call of whistles, and the throbbing of a geared locomotive all conjure images of the logging industry and the pleasures of living and working in the woods. But this was no easy life. Instead, it was one filled with uncounted dangers. The steam equipment was huge and scalding hot, hand saws and axes sharp, the trees and logs huge and heavy, sometimes crashing to earth in unexpected directions; forest fires could spread without warning, and danger is always associated with the operation of any railroad. Safety in the woods was emphasized, but fatigue, accidents, and sometimes pure carelessness took their toll on the workers. In 1924, *The Timberman* reported, "Fatalities among loggers average 20.1 per 1,000, according to labor department statistics. Their occupation is considered the most hazardous in the United States." The book, *More Deadly Than War: Pacific Coast Logging 1827-1981*, by Andrew Mason Prouty, builds upon this statistic and describes the perils of working in the woods, placing the life into a more realistic context for anyone interested in this profession or period in history.

Life in the Vail woods was no exception to the dangers associated with Pacific Coast logging or any logging, for that matter. The local county newspaper, The *Thurston County Independent*, chronicled many of the accidents, injuries, and deaths that occurred over the years at the Skookum Chuck operation. One of the more common causes of injury or death was loggers being pinned under or between logs. Falling trees didn't always fall where fallers planned. Logs brought to the landing or loaded on log cars were a constant danger. Logs slipping from chokers or tongs would roll unexpectedly, crushing anything and anyone who happened to be in the way. Swaying tongs, choker hooks, and heavy cables also posed a danger to workers at landings. The heat and steam escaping from donkey engines, loaders, and locomotives were a steady source of severe burns. From the start of logging until the end of 1929, 12 men were reported to have been injured, and five lost their lives in woods-related accidents. One simple invention, the hardhat, would significantly reduce death and injuries when it was introduced into the woods.

It is often said among railroaders that "railroad rules are written in blood." Logging railroads were as subject to this saying as any, and the railroad at Vail had its share of accidents. The first was the derailment of a locomotive in February 1928, but fortunately no one was killed in that incident. In a less fortunate case, a worker was crushed to death by a log train when he fell off the tender of a Vail locomotive in August 1928. In November 1928, one of the Washington Iron Works tree skidders tipped over when the car it was on jumped the track near Camp 3. Again, fortunately, no one was injured. Another railroader was injured when his speeder was hit by a car at a grade crossing in 1929.

Camp 4 from the far end. —Weyerhaeuser Archives

smile on his face, we knew that his hidden jug had also come through safely." A couple of near accidents followed the fire and wind storm. Mr. Alexander continues, "I was working at the drafting table in the office tent when an axe cut its way through the canvas and sailed by me near enough to make me jump and swear. An amateur axeman had been cutting wood." A second accident involved the camp cook, Art Slack, who was demonstrating that his revolver was unloaded and proceeded to shoot two holes in the floor, narrowly missing the spectators. These events cinched the name "Hoodoo" for the camp. Mr. Alexander would continue to survey not only the Vail woods but also the woods of the McDonald operation, including the headwaters of the Chehalis River south of Pe Ell.

In 1927, two older Weyerhaeuser operations completed logging their respective lands and shut down. The first was the Cherry Valley Timber Company, located in King County near Stillwater on the Snoqualmie River. The Cherry Valley Timber Company was founded in 1912 as part of a merger between Weyerhaeuser interests in the Snoqualmie River Valley and the Cherry Valley Logging & Railway Company. The second was the Clarke County Timber Company, located in southern Washington in the watershed of the Columbia River. The Clarke County operation was created in 1903 to salvage timber left in the wake of the Yacolt burn of 1902. As a result of the closure of these two operations, a large portion of the railroad equipment at Vail was purchased from the Cherry Valley and Clarke County logging railroads.

The second location for Camp 4, before it was moved to Porcupine Ridge, has yet to be determined. This camp was a combination of Cherry Valley camp cars without a clerestory and skid shacks built at Vail. —Clark Kinsey, Weyerhaeuser Archives

The first woods operations location for Camps 2 and 5 was along the mainline just above the junction with the LD branch, which headed up to Porcupine Ridge. This location was also a major marshaling point for loaded and empty log cars brought up from Vail and was named LD yard. Because of the location near LD yard and the LD branch, the two camps were jointly referred to as LD Camp. The rail camp composed of Cherry Valley cars is Camp 2. Camp 5 was composed of skid shacks.

—Clark Kinsey, Weyerhaeuser Archives

Late in 1927, no fewer than 24 Cherry Valley camp cars were moved via rail from Carnation to Kirkland on the shores of Lake Washington, loaded onto barges, and towed through the Lake Washington Ship Canal and Ballard Locks to Puget Sound, where they were towed to South Bay. There they were lifted onto the track of the log dump and moved to the woods south of Vail where they would serve as Rail Camps 2 and 3. One of the Cherry Valley bunk cars was retained at South Bay, where it served house workers at the log dump. In 1927, a total of five locomotives were purchased from Cherry Valley for the Vail operation. These included #1, a 2-truck Shay (c/n 2030); #2, a 3-truck Shay (c/n 3090); #3, a 2-truck Shay (c/n 2671); #5, a 2-truck Shay (c/n 486); a Baldwin 2-8-2 #101 (c/n 39787); and a Baldwin 2-8-2 #104 (c/n 52192). The #5 was sold to Weyerhaeuser's Longview operation in 1928. Two steel frame 7,000-gallon oil cars and three wooden-frame 6,000-gallon oil cars were also transferred to Vail from Cherry Valley.

Moving Day. When the Cherry Valley Timber Company closed up its operations, the majority of its equipment was shipped, via rail to and then by barge on Puget Sound, reaching South Bay where they were again placed on rails for the trip south to Vail. Here a string of camp cars and two locomotives head out across the flats of the Snoqualmie River on their way to Puget Sound. The cars in the foreground lack clerestories, some of these camp cars were used in Camp 4 and Camp 6 at Vail. The cars in the background have clerestories. These camp buildings were used in Camps 2 and 3 at Vail as well as around Vail where they served as storage and temporary housing until more permanent buildings were completed. —Darius Kinsey, Weyerhaeuser Archives

The closure of the Clarke County Timber Company provided two rod locomotives in 1927; a Baldwin 2-8-2 #102 (c/n 37496), a Baldwin 2-8-2 #103 (c/n 37539), and an assortment of spare parts, cables, blocks, and cook house materials. Shortly after their transfer to Vail, the #3, #102, and #104 spots were transferred to the newly open Klamath Falls operation in Oregon. In 1928 and 1929, four additional locomotives were purchased new to supplement the roster of used locomotives at Vail. This included the #4, a 3-truck Heisler (c/n 1573) purchased from Heisler dealer Whitney Engineering Company; the second #5, a Pacific Coast Shay (c/n 3316) from Shay dealer Hofius Steel & Equipment Company; Baldwin compound mallet 2-6-6-2T with semi-saddle tanks #110 (c/n 60561); and a

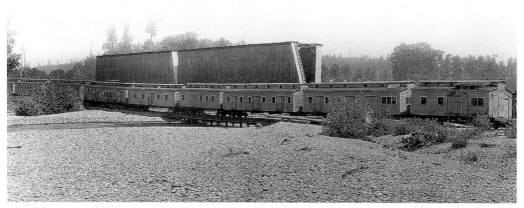

A string of Cherry Valley camp cars with clerestories passes a covered bridge on the Milwaukee Road's line along the Snoqualmie River as they head towards Puget Sound and eventually to Vail. —Darius Kinsey, Weyerhaeuser Archives

Weyerhaeuser Timber Company's 1-spot, a two truck Shay built in November 1907 as Stillwater Lumber Company's #1, came to Vail via the Cherry Valley Timber Company, where it served as their #1. —Al Farrow, Martin E. Hansen Collection

Cherry Valley Timber Company's 2-spot poses for its builder's photograph at the Lima Locomotive Works, Lima, Ohio, in August of 1920. The 3-truck shay was transferred to Vail along with four other locomotives in 1927, where it kept its road number and served as Vail's 2-spot. —Lima Locomotive Works, Frank W. Telewski Collection

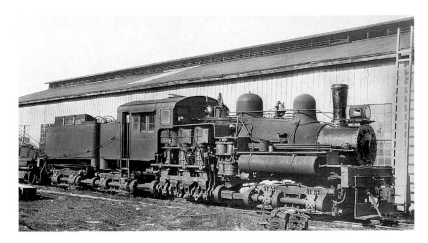

After 23 years of service, the 2-spot rests next to the locomotive shop at Vail. It's April 14, 1943, and the engine is nearing the end of the road, as it would be scrapped in November of that year. —Al Farrow, Frank W. Telewski Collection

Built by the Baldwin Locomotive Works as Cherry Valley Timber Company #101 in 1913, this logging Mikado was sent to Vail when Cherry Valley closed down. The locomotive, like its sister Mikados, made the daily run of loads and empties between Vail and LD siding to South Bay. Here it poses with its crew at LD siding, a square water tank stands in the background. —Darius Kinsey, Martin E. Hansen Collection

A little smaller than its sister Mikado #101 from Cherry Valley, #104 had 44-inch drivers and was lighter in weight. Built by Baldwin Locomotive Works in 1919 as Cherry Valley Timber Company's 4-spot, it was the second Mikado sent to Vail from Cherry Valley. Here it poses with its crew and a load of giant Douglas fir logs at the north end of LD yard just as the train passes Camp 2. This engine wouldn't serve very long at Vail as it was shipped south to Weyerhaeuser's Klamath Falls operation in 1929. —Darius Kinsey, Martin E. Hansen Collection

Baldwin simple mallet 2-6-6-2T with semi-saddle tanks #111 (c/n 60811). No more additions would be made to this roster until 1935.

Also in 1927, the Vail shop crew built a gasoline-powered pile driver with a 4,000-pound hammer. This pile driver was used to build the South Bay log dump trestle and subsequent trestles and bridges in the woods. Lloyd Crosby was responsible for purchasing the railroad equipment. In March 1927, he took delivery of three 8,000-gallon steel under frame tank cars from Hofius Steel & Equipment Company. He purchased an additional four 8,100-gallon tank cars from Hofius in April. Crosby ordered 200 42-foot skeleton log cars with 10-foot bunks and 30-inch wide sills, several steel-moving flat cars, and several wooden-framed Rogers type ballast cars from Pacific Car and Foundry Company in 1927. He purchased an additional 50 skeleton log cars in 1928, and also acquired seven truss rod flat cars from the United Commercial Company and five wooden Pullman cars from the Northern Pacific Railway. Ex-Puget Sound Electric Railway interurban car #504 was also purchased in 1927 and was assigned #718 at Vail. The passenger cars and interurban car were used to ferry crews from camps to the sides. An additional seven wood Oregon Electric Railway interurban cars and three ex-Northwest Traction interurban cars were acquired after 1936, replacing the wood Pullman cars, which were wearing out.

In February 1927, Mr. Titcomb first proposed to Mr. Crosby a numbering system to designate the class of railroad equipment: "I would suggest that we number our flat cars starting with 401, the thought being in my mind that in that way we will designate the class of equipment and decrease the possibility of confusion later on when we are operating and speaking of specific cars. I specified that the oil tank cars should start with No. 501. It would be my thought that we number our skeleton cars starting with No. 101, the thought being that we could use the figures 1 to 20 for locomotives and speeders..." This numbering system was adopted by the Vail operation with one modification; skeleton log car numbering began with the #1, and locomotives and speeders were numbered separately, reusing the numbers from 1 to 120.

With the survey work and construction of the main line and initial logging spurs at Vail completed by the end of 1927, George S. Long requested that Lloyd Crosby transfer to Klamath Falls and begin the layout and construction of a logging railroad to harvest Weyerhaeuser's large Ponderosa pine holdings in southern Oregon. Crosby responded to Long's letter, stating the following: "I will be very pleased to go to Klamath Falls, or any where else you might want me to go. We are winding up all of the details now that I have to tend to personally, and I cannot think of anything that should bother Mr. Ryan or Mr. McDonald after Jan. 1st [1928]. Mr. McDonald came yesterday [December 8, 1927] and Mr. Ryan will be here Monday, so I believe I will be ready to leave by Jan. 1st." He closed his letter with, "I feel certain that Mr. McDonald will be able to start logging in volume very shortly." Thus, as of the end of 1927, the Vail operation became the complete responsibility of Ronald McDonald, who had transferred from the Cherry Valley Logging Company.

Actual movement of logs from the woods to Puget Sound was projected to start in January 1928, and traffic was anticipated

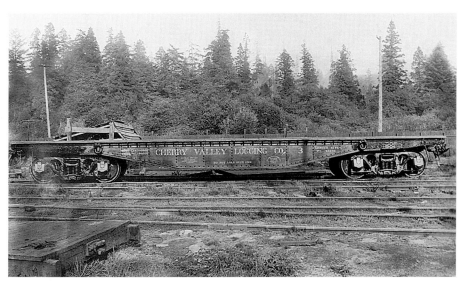

One of the Cherry Valley Logging Company Pacific Car & Foundry moving cars that were transferred to the Vail operation in 1928. —PACCAR Inc., John Henderson Collection

to be two trains of 50 to 60 cars per day, with an eventual projected total of 140 cars per day. The first load of logs was dumped into South Bay on February 2, 1928, from a train of 39 cars. However, timber had already been cut and shipped from the Vail Operation. One of the first shipments of timber from the new operation was a load of fir pilings sent to Weyerhaeuser's Longview Branch on December 30, 1927, which was under construction and set to start operations by 1929. Ties cut by the portable mills were also sold to the Longview operation and to the Milwaukee Road. Additional pilings and boom sticks were shipped to South Bay for the construction of the booming grounds and dump trestle.

Logging in the Vail woods proceeded in an orderly fashion. When Ronald McDonald designated an area to be logged, the first activity was the removal of timber in which the Weyerhaeuser Timber Company had no interest. This was done by contractor loggers who would remove fir poles, pilings, and cedar poles. Fir poles and pilings were harvested by the K & K Timber Company of Everett and cedar poles by the National Pole Company of Everett. The poles were up to 120 feet in length and were dragged out of the woods using a special cast iron "cone," which was fixed to the end of the pole by three hooks and a line attached to a ring on the tip of the cone. The long poles were loaded onto swivel bunk log cars. Shorter poles were shipped on Great Northern steel 50-foot flat cars (67000–67549 series), and steel 52-foot flat cars (65000–65499 series). Weyerhaeuser train crews set the cars out at Wetico for interchange, and the Great Northern, which had running rights over the Northern Pacific's Prairie Line, shipped the loads to National Pole Company's Everett facility. K & K rafted its poles from South Bay to Everett. After the contractors finished their work, the area was logged clean by Weyerhaeuser crews.

During the early days of logging at Vail, the operation was essentially a steam show with 16 steam donkeys, two Washington diesel donkeys, and one Clyde Iron Works gasoline donkey. The main logging units consisted of two big Washington Iron Works steam skidders (#1 and #2). The Clyde gasoline yarder was used exclusively for cold decking. The Washington steam and Washington diesel engines were also used in high-lead, cold decking operations. Vail employed considerable cold decking due to the rough terrain and as a method to reduce the cost of railroad construction. The cold decks were not allowed to remain for long periods of time, especially during fire season, due to the potential fire hazard they presented.

The Vail operation was very active in the fall of 1929, operating a total of eight sides, five of which were cold decks, out of three woods camps. Camp 2 was the most active, with one Washington tree skidder side, one high lead swinging out cold deck, and one cold deck

First Logging Train Wreck at Vail

The Morning Olympian and later the *Olympia News* and *Thurston County Independent* reported the first logging train wreck of the Vail operation. The accident occurred on Saturday, February 18, 1928, late in the afternoon at Skookumchuck yard near the site of the first Camp 2, at the interchange with the Milwaukee Road main line. Locomotive #101 hit an open switch in the yard, derailing the engine and three log cars. The accident was believed to have been caused by some schoolboys who had been playing with the unlocked switch and left it in the half open position. Three of the four-man crew escaped injury by leaping from the train. Joe Sensa, fireman, Otto Stolp, conductor, and Arthur Nelson, brakeman, were unhurt. The engineer, Richard Vorn, received cuts and bruises when the engine plowed into a bank of soft dirt. He was returned to Vail after receiving first-aid treatment at the scene of the accident. The locomotive fell on the engineer's side of the cab, with the tender doubled up alongside with two of the three log cars. Local residents reported the whistle valve was locked open by the impact, and as *The Morning Olympian* reported, "...the engine shrieked and wailed like some giant animal in distress as the steam escaped." William Erndart, assistant superintendent in charge of clearing the wreckage, reported traffic on the logging line was resumed on Sunday, February 19, after the equipment was removed and the track repaired. This was the third wreck the #101 had been involved in, the first at the Vail operation. The two previous accidents occurred when the locomotive worked at Cherry Valley. Although damaged in the accident, the locomotive and cars were repaired and returned to service.

Originally built by the Baldwin Locomotive Works in 1912 for Weyerhaeuser's Twin Falls Logging Company as their #102, this Mikado was transferred to Vail in March of 1927. At Vail it would be the first of three engines to share the number 102. Similar in size to #104, it too was transferred to Klamath Falls after only briefly serving at Vail. In this rare photo, #102 rests near Camp 2 at LD yards, sporting a very fresh coat of paint and lettering. Of particular interest here is the color of the lettering on the tender. It is neither white nor silver, but in the black and white image appears to be a shade of gray, suggesting a different color. Also notice the multicolored Weyerhaeuser Timber Company logo which had a dark gray green inner circle surrounded by a lighter gray green outer circle separated by a ring of black. Comparing the shades of gray, could the lettering have also been a dark gray green? —Darius Kinsey, Martin E. Hansen Collection

LD yard must have been a popular place to photograph locomotives. Here #103, recently transferred from Weyerhaeuser's Twin Falls Logging Company poses with its crew. Originally built by the Baldwin Locomotive Works as Twin Falls' #101 in 1913, the engine was renumbered as Vail's 103 since there already was a #101 at Vail. This photograph provides an interesting view of the unusual river rock ballast used at Vail in railroad construction.

—Darius Kinsey, Martin E. Hansen Collection

Weyerhaeuser ordered a small fleet of 3 truck Heislers in the late 1920's for their various woods operations. Most saw service in the Inland Empire serving such operations as Potlatch. The 4-spot, built in November 1927 was delivered directly to Vail. The engine is 10 years old in the 1937 photograph taken at Vail and still has its original lettering scheme. —Al Farrow, Martin E. Hansen Collection

side producing 45,000 feet of timber daily. The two diesel donkeys were cold decking at Camp 3. At Camp 4, a Washington tree skidder side, one high lead and two cold deck sides were in operation.

On October 26, 1929, 150 delegates from the Pacific Logger's Congress were the guests of the busy Weyerhaeuser Timber Company operation at Vail. It was the first time in years that an actual field trip to a logging show was scheduled as part of the congress. The delegates drove by automobile to Vail where they boarded a special train that took them to Camp 2 at LD yards for lunch. Afterward, the train carried the visitors to the scene of operations, where they observed one of the Washington Iron Works tree-rigged skidders hauling logs out of a deep canyon. The group witnessed the yarding and loading of logs with an Ohio locomotive crane along the right-of-way of a woods spur. After the tour, the guests were served a turkey dinner at Camp 2.

Left: Ads for Heisler featured Weyerhaeuser's #4 which served at Vail in *The Timberman* (November 1930)

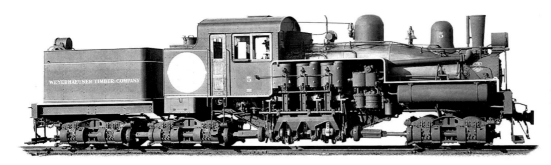

Vail's 5-spot, a Pacific Coast Shay, poses in this builder's photo at the Lima locomotive shops on 2-16-28. —Lima Locomotive Works, Weyerhaeuser Archives

Another locomotive portrait taken at the north end of LD yard, this time of Vail's 5-spot, a Pacific Coast Shay built new for the operation in February 1928. The locomotive had the largest Weyerhaeuser Timber Company logo ever used on a engine at Vail, and was the two-tone green, black and white design used on many of the engines at Vail in this early period. This engine was the second 5-spot at Vail, the first one was a 2-truck Shay which was transferred from Cherry Valley and then shipped to Longview in January 1928. —Darius Kinsey, Martin E. Hansen Collection

The West Coast Lumberman, covering the visit by the Logger's Congress, reported "The railroad equipment consists of eight oil burning locomotives, three of which are Shays, and one Heisler. All repair work is done in the company's very complete shops at Vail. There are 250 Pacific Car & Foundry Co. skeleton logging cars, and a number of flat cars equipped with swivel bunks for carrying loads of fir and cedar poles. Thirty-three ballast cars are used in railroad construction and upkeep, and 10 flat cars and two cabooses." Each of the three logging camps was equipped with a water tank car for fire protection and one 200,000-pound capacity and one 120,000-pound capacity Pacific Car & Foundry moving car to transport

Hofius Steel & Equipment Co. featured Weyerhaeuser's #5, Pacific Coast Shay in their ad in *The Timberman*.

Vail's #110 was featured in this Baldwin Locomotive Works ad in *The Timberman* in 1928.

Timber in which the Weyerhaeuser Timber Company had no interest, such as cedar poles, were harvested by contractor loggers. Here, Weyerhaeuser Timber Company's #104 hauls an Ohio Logger's Special crane and a string of Great Northern flat cars loaded with cedar poles for the National Pole Company of Everett. —Wrays Studio, Francis Neuman Collection, Rainier Historical Society

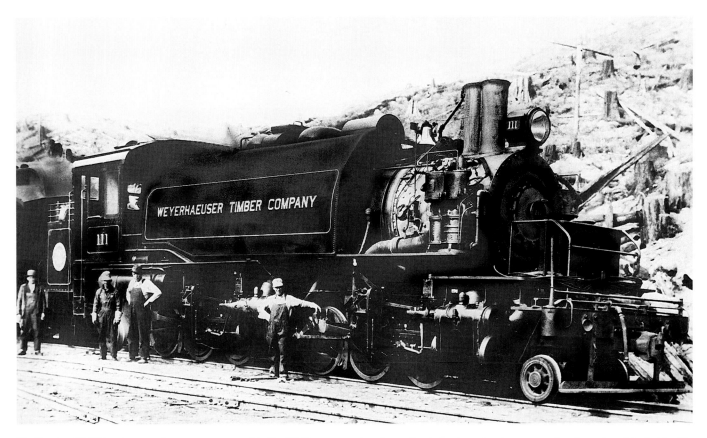

Similar to #110 in size and appearance, Vail's #111 was a simple articulated or single-expansion logging Mallet built by the Baldwin Locomotive Works in May 1929. The two distinguishing features which separated this engine from compound Mallets was the twin smoke stacks and both front and rear steam cylinders were the same size. Poised with its crew at the north end of LD yard and a string of ex-Northern Pacific wooden passenger cars in tow, the #111 was captured in original lettering scheme on October 26, 1929 leading a tour of Vail for the Twentieth Pacific Logging Congress. —Weyerhaeuser Archives

Weyerhaeuser purchased five wood passenger cars from the Northern Pacific as crew cars, transporting logging and construction crews to and from camps and to and from Vail for weekend leaves. These cars were also used to ferry delegates from the Twentieth Pacific Logging Congress for their tour of Vail and its logging operations in October 1929.

—Weyerhaeuser Archives

A High Lead rigged spar tree with two steam donkey engines loading PC&F log cars at a landing or setting near Camp 3. The donkey on the left is the duplex and the one on the right is the yarder, which brings the logs to the landing.
—Clark Kinsey, Weyerhaeuser Archives

Loading logs using donkey engines. Here the landing crew has just released the tongs from a log placed on the railroad car while another member of the crew releases a choker used to drag the log to the landing. —Clark Kinsey, Weyerhaeuser Archives

Left: Although Vail was primarily a steam operation in the late 1920s to mid 1930s, Weyerhaeuser did experiment with some gasoline and diesel technology. Here the Clyde gasoline donkey is employed in a cold decking operation. —Clark Kinsey, Weyerhaeuser Archives

Below: Another donkey setting, here clearly showing the larger yarder engine and the smaller duplex with High Lead rigging. —Clark Kinsey, Weyerhaeuser Archives

INTO THE WOODS: 1927-1929

Another internal combustion engine used at Vail since its opening in 1928 was diesel. Here a sled mounted Washington Iron Works diesel donkey is set up at a landing in the Vail woods. —Darius Kinsey, Whatcom Museum of History and Art

Prior to the arrival of the mammoth tower skidders, the largest units at Vail were two rail-mounted Washington Iron Works tree rig skidders. Most of the donkey engines were built on wood sleds or skids and could pull themselves through the woods or were loaded onto donkey moving cars and hauled by rail to a new setting. The large Washington Iron Works skidders were mounted on railroad trucks and remained on the rails and could do the work of two smaller donkey engines. The crew of skidder #2 take a break to pose for the camera before loading their next car. —Clark Kinsey, Weyerhaeuser Archives

A Washington Iron Works tree rig skidder loading logs with a duplex. Each skidder setting commonly had at least two tank cars. One for oil and one for water. Water cars were commonly filled from water tanks in the woods or via a pipe fed by a local spring run to the tank car. Oil cars had to be taken to South Bay to be filled. —Clark Kinsey, Weyerhaeuser Archives

donkey engines to new sides. Two Washington Iron Works tree skidders were purchased new in February and July 1929. Numbered #1 and #2, the skidders both required four-truck Pacific Car & Foundry cars of 54-foot and 56-foot lengths, respectively. Both of these skidders would eventually be converted to diesel power and used as transfer machines into the 1970s.

Two early photos identified as Camp 4 by Clark Kinsey show two different camps. Several attempts have been made by the authors to verify the early locations of Camp 4 in the Vail woods prior to Camp 4 at Spike Camp on Porcupine Ridge. Robert Gehrman, formerly with Vail Reforestation and Land Department, believes a Camp 4 was located west of the peak of Miller Hill. James F. Barrett, former Vail-McDonald railroad employee who began working at Vail in 1935, said that there was only one camp on Miller Hill (Camp 2). James Barrett's father, Lawrence Barrett, worked on Miller Hill and is the source of his information. Additionally, Mr. Barrett also cites timekeeper Leo Riley, who came from Cherry Valley when the operation moved to Vail. Mr. Riley also ran the 1 spot when he wasn't working as a timekeeper and related to Mr. Barrett that there was just one camp on Miller Hill. Future detailed field surveys may resolve this mystery.

Another view of one of Vail's two Washington Iron Works tree rig skidder. —Clark Kinsey, Weyerhaeuser Archives

Weyerhaeuser Timber Company Entertains Congress Delegates at Vail

Left to right - 1. Ohio locomotive crane yarding logs along the right of way. 2. R.A. McDonald, resident manager of Vail. 3. Washington Iron Works tree skidder. 4. Camp 2, where delegates were entertained at luncheon. 5. Make-up yard at Vail, where trains start on journey to tidewater. 6. Baldwin Mallet locomotive which hauled delegates from Vail to scene of logging. 7. William M. Ehrengart, assistant logging superintendent. 8. Eighty-ton Shay locomotive starting from woods with 22-car train. In the picture are Arthur Grandstrom, foreman of Camp 2; Charles McKay, second brakeman; Roe Malone, engineer; C.R. Vickery, fireman. —*The Timberman*, November 1929

Vail's Ohio Logger's Special crane was featured in Ohio Locomotive Crane Company's ad published in *The West Coast Lumberman* in 1931.

Baldwin Locomotive Works featured #111 in their October 1929 ad in *The Timberman*.

Pacific Car and Foundry supplied wood skeleton cars as featured in this ad from the *West Coast Lumberman* for a number of Weyerhaeuser's operations including Vail.

A Washington Iron Works tree rig skidder rigged with a High Lead system. —Clark Kinsey, Weyerhaeuser Archives

Pacific Logging Congress
WHISTLE SIGNAL CODE

HIGH LEAD SIGNALS

ONE SHORT	Go ahead on main line
ONE SHORT	Stop
TWO SHORT	Come back on haulback
THREE SHORT	Come ahead easy on main line
TWO SHORT AND TWO SHORT	Come back easy on haulback
FOUR SHORT	Slack the main line
TWO SHORT AND FIVE SHORT	Slack the haulback
THREE SHORT AND TWO SHORT	Tight line
THREE MEDIUM	Hooktender. Followed by three short, calls in crew
TWO LONG AND THREE SHORT	Donkey doctor
THREE LONG AND TWO SHORT	Climber
THREE LONG	Locomotive for switching
FOUR LONG	Foreman
TWO LONG AND ONE SHORT	Oil
ONE LONG	Stop oil
TWO LONG	Water
ONE LONG	Stop water
SIX LONG	Man hurt, locomotive and stretcher
FOUR LONG AND SIX SHORT—REPEAT	Fire
SUCCESSION OF SHORTS	Danger, blasting at landing
ONE LONG AND ONE SHORT	Starting and quitting

LOCOMOTIVE SIGNALS

FOUR LONG	Foreman
FIVE LONG	Section crew
SIX LONG—REPEAT	Man hurt, stretcher
FOUR LONG AND FOUR SHORT—REPEAT	Fire

BUTT RIGGING SIGNALS AT TREE

TWO SHORT	No choker
THREE SHORT	Strawline
TWO SHORT AND ONE SHORT	One choker
TWO SHORT AND TWO SHORT	Two choker
ONE SHORT AND TWO SHORT	Bull choker

The above Logging Whistle Signal Code has been adopted by the Whistle Committee of the Pacific Logging Congress as standard for Pacific Coast Logging Operations

Whistle signal codes used in high lead operations.
—*The Timberman*, February 1930.

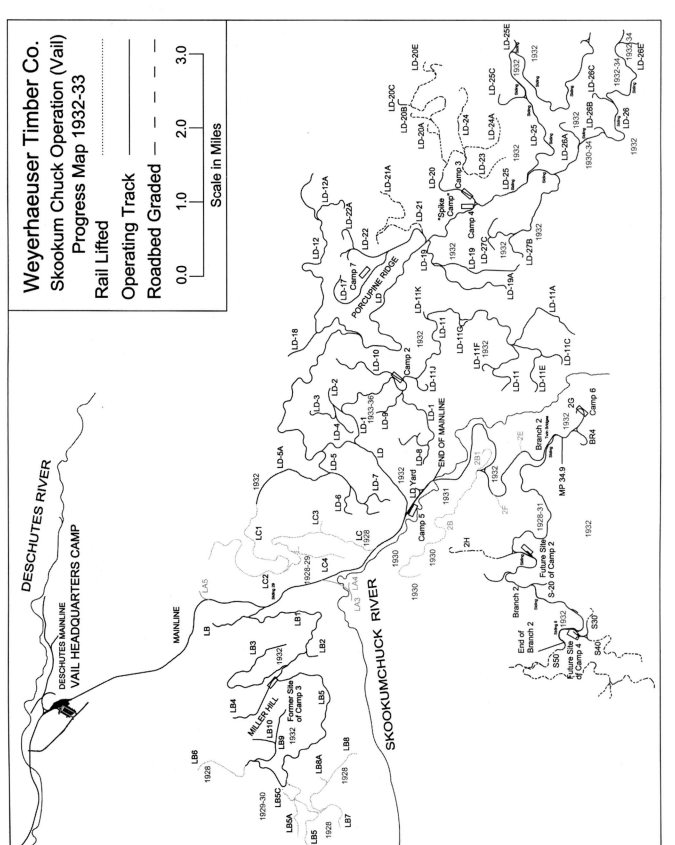

Woods tracks south of Vail representing the general layout between 1932 and 1933, showing the location of camps and logging spurs. Dates near the tracks indicates when timber was cut in a specific area. —Composite map from various data sources including Weyerhaeuser Archives, Weyerhaeuser Vail section maps located at the Vail office, aerial photographs and Vail Track Mainline and Woods Lines. —Barrett Family Collection, drawn by Frank W. Telewski

CHAPTER 3
The Great Depression into the Vail Woods: 1930–1934

The stock market crash of October 1929 and the resulting Great Depression influenced all aspects of the forest products industry for many years, including Weyerhaeuser's operations. The reduced demand for timber resulted in periodic shutdowns of the woods and mill operations, slowing the shipment of logs from Weyerhaeuser's timberlands. The demand for forest products bottomed out in 1933 and began to rebound by 1934, but overall West Coast lumber production and employment in the woods never fully recovered until the start of World War II. Because the Vail Operation was opened up with the sole intent of supplying logs for Weyerhaeuser's Everett mill complex, it was tied to market fluctuations, which influenced mill activities. As went the demand for logs at Everett, so went operations at Vail. Mill A of Weyerhaeuser's Everett complex was idled shortly after the start of the Depression and did not resume full production until mid-1933. Mill B faced periodic closures up until 1933. As a result, Vail fared in the early years of the Great Depression little better than most West Coast logging operations.

Speeders served a number of functions on the woods rail lines. They would ferry small amounts of supplies, bring mail to the woods camps, bring out injured workers and shuttle a variety of crews from camps to work sites. Here a Vail rigging crew taking a short break to pose next to their speeders at Vail. Miller Hill can be seen in the background. —Clark Kinsey, Weyerhaeuser Archives

The steep slopes of the Vail operation presented many challenges to harvesting. Here a Washington Iron Works tree rig skidder rests on the top of the ridge. Trees are felled and bucked to log-lengths, chokers set and hauled to the top of the hill where they were loaded onto log cars. —Clark Kinsey, Weyerhaeuser Archives

Operations at Vail during the year after the market crash were initially affected only marginally. The July 4, 1930, issue of *The Thurston County Independent* declared employment prospects were good in the county, with the logging operations at Vail resuming on July 15 after a two-week shutdown for the July 4 holiday. In 1930, Ronald McDonald had purchased a load of 62 ½–pound rail once used on the Santa Fe. Railroad construction that year was focused along the 2H and 18 to 20 Line spurs and their branches, as well as the beginning of the 30 and 40 Line spurs. In late 1930 to early 1931, Vail was reported to be operating six sides, employing 800 men. The equipment inventory included four rod locomotives (#101, #103, #110, and #111) and four geared locomotives (#1, #2, #4, and #5), 250 skeleton log cars, 10 flat cars, two moving cars, seven tank cars, two loco cranes, one gas shovel, four diesel shovels, seven speeders, two tree rigged Washington skidders, nine Washington loaders, and 24 donkey engines. On November 8, 1930, Mr. McDonald wrote the Hofius Steel & Equipment Company, stating that he needed between 12 to 15 track miles of 60-pound rail for 1931. An additional 24 miles of railroad were laid that year, most of it on the 30 Line and the 50 Line.

However, one year later, the Vail logging operation faced serious cutbacks and was idled on June 29, 1931, for an extended July 4 break. In August, Ronald McDonald spoke to Mr. French at the Everett mills about starting up operations at Vail in September. On the 22nd, Mr. F. R. Titcomb responded that discussions regarding reopening were taking place and that they would need to "...determine definitely what we are up against for these operations as it applies to our log supply." He went on to write, "My personal feeling is that we should not start up before the rainy season or at least before the 10th of September, if this is at all practical." Logging activities did resume on September 7, 1931, with 85 loads shipped to South Bay. With the opening of camps, a crew of 600 men reported back to work—150 at Camp 2, 180 at Camp 3, 150 at Camp 4, and 50 graders at Camp 7.

Railroad expansion continued early in 1931, and the majority of grading took place on the 30 Line. However, the pace of activity could not be maintained, and by October 31, the crew employed at the Vail Operation was reduced to 463 men. On November 5, the prospect of maintaining any production began to fade, and Mr. Pettingill wrote with regard to employment at Vail, "If operating December 1st [1931], we estimate a payroll of 350 men." Camp 4 shut down on November 3, and on November 27 Mr. Pettingill confirmed the worst: "Word was just received that logging operations are to cease Saturday night, November 28th." In the closing days of 1931, his charge was to finish up the year-end inventories of the camps, warehouse, and shop before turning out the lights for the next four months.

The Economic History of the West Coast Lumber Industry 1926 to 1937

(Table by West Coast Lumbermen's Association, Industrial Facts Department)

Year	Production Million Feet	Percent of Capacity Used	Percent of Capacity Idle	Gross Value Production	No. of Employees Average Per Year	Average Wage Per 8/Hr Day	Estimated Daily Payroll
1926	10,411	72.8	27.2	$215,700,000	75,617	$5.03	$380,355
1927	9,988	69.9	30.1	$197,200,000	72,545	$5.09	$369,254
1928	10,182	71.2	28.8	$196,300,000	73,351	$5.22	$382,892
1929	10,377	72.0	28.0	$214,100,000	74,756	$5.26	$393,216
1930	7,638	47.9	52.1	$135,900,000	56,000	$5.14	$287,840
1931	5,368	33.6	66.4	$72,700,000	37,228	$4.16	$154,868
1932	3,090	19.8	80.2	$35,500,000	33,000	$3.43	$113,190
1933	4,653	30.2	69.8	$67,700,000	40,059	$3.60	$144,312
1934	4,276	29.6	70.4	$73,700,000	42,000	$4.63	$194,460
1935	4,766	35.4	64.6	$82,400,000	45,000	$4.89	$220,050
1936	6,357	47.1	52.9	$124,000,000	48,000	$5.34	$256,320
1937	6,323	46.8	53.2	$139,100,000	48,000	$5.99	$299,500

Weyerhaeuser's tower skidder #3 is rolled out of Washington Iron Work's Seattle shops prior to the attachment of its steel spar and loading boom. — *Washington Iron Works, Ken Schmelzer Collection*

Fire and Ice

Camp closures were a common occurrence in the woods, and the shutdowns were not necessarily the result of poor economic conditions such as those brought on by the Great Depression. Camps were traditionally closed for the holidays, usually for about two weeks at the end of the year for Christmas and New Year's and for about two weeks around July 4. On rare occasions, when there was high market demand, some camps would open early, just after Christmas. Such was the case for Camp 3 during the holiday season of 1936. On the other hand, heavy snows during the winter and any combination of extremely low humidity, high temperatures, and wind during the summer fire seasons often curtailed woods operations, and such weather conditions could prolong the normal two-week holidays.

Fire season in the Pacific Northwest usually occurred in conjunction with the dry summer months of July, August, and September. During fire season, crews were called to the woods during the early morning hours before dawn, completing their day's work by midday. Known as the "hoot owl shift," the crews could work in the forest while it was still relatively cool and moist. The first fire reported at the Vail Operation occurred during September 1928. It started in the cut-over lands near Camps 2 and 3 but didn't burn much of the merchantable timber before the flames were extinguished.

Abnormally light spring rains created a significant fire danger in 1929. During the summer, Vail camps were closed for a six-week period from July to mid-August. September brought fire again in 1930, with a blaze in standing timber reported near Camp 6. The summer of 1934 proved to be another serious fire season. Record low humidity was recorded in late August, and several fires were reported in Thurston County. One of the fires was in Weyerhaeuser timber near Reichel Lake southeast of Vail. An unusual period of low humidity in May 1935 resulted in an early fire season and a 10-acre blaze south of Vail. By mid-July, the Vail woods were closed to entry. No fires were reported again until July 1938, when winds and low humidity brought the fire hazard to a dangerous level. Another fire in the Reichel Lake area broke out and spread from 40 acres on July 19 to over 100 acres the following day. The fire was brought under control with the help of CCC workers from the local CCC camp near Rainier. High temperatures and low humidity during the summer of 1939 again raised the fire hazard, closing logging operations throughout western Washington. Fortunately for Weyerhaeuser, no fires were reported in the Vail woods.

Several examples of severe low temperatures or heavy snow were reported by *The Thurston County Independent*. The cold winter weather of early 1930, with temperatures of 12 degrees below zero reported on January 20 and a foot of snow at Camp 2, kept Vail camps closed. Seven inches of snow covered the ground in Rainier, and more sub-zero temperatures were measured on January 31. The woods operation did not start again until February. Snow returned early in November, with 14 inches reported on the ground at Camp 3 and 20 inches at the upper two camps, resulting in the closure of these camps until March of the following year.

In later years, as the woods camps were moved farther up into the mountains, winter weather became more of a problem. In 1937, Camp 2 was located along the 42 Line, and on January 29, 51 inches of snow were reported on the ground and additional snow was forecast, bringing the total amount to five feet. An extended winter shutdown occurred in 1938 when the camps were closed from before Christmas 1937 until March 1938. Snow closed Vail down again in early February 1939, with 14 inches at Vail, over four feet at Camp 2, 40 inches at Camp 3, and 30 inches at Camp 4.

Logging did resume on April 1, 1932, when 300 men returned to the woods camps. In the depth of the Depression and in response to the reopening of the Vail operation, Minot Davis, who was manager of Weyerhaeuser Timber Company's woods and logging department, stated that the reopening of the camps was "largely out of consideration of the needs for employment of the men since there was a long list of men to be taken care of". However, with an increasingly weakened economy, operations at Vail could not be sustained, and a fourth prolonged shutdown occurred from June 1932 until June 1933. During the periods when Vail was idle, Weyerhaeuser purchased logs on the open market to supply the mills still operating at Everett.

The attempt of the administrative staff, especially Mr. Ronald McDonald of Vail, to accommodate workers during this long period of unemployment was expressed in a memo, dated November 22, 1932, from R. A. Pettingill to Mr. Obenour on behalf of Vail's logging railroad dispatcher:

Big loaders for big logs. The Washington Iron Works tower skidder #3, a state-of-the-art machine for its time was built for Weyerhaeuser's Vail operation in the depths of the Great Depression and was placed into operation in 1932. Here the crew of #3 load logs cut along the 42 Line in June 1938. —Darius Kinsey, Whatcom Museum of History and Art

"Mr. McDonald is in receipt of a letter from our Dispatcher, W. L. 'Dick' Harrington, who has been out of work since our shutdown in June, asking if it would be possible for him to send him $100. He has both life and fire insurance coming due real soon, and would be unable to pay the premiums on same.

In view of the fact that Dick is an old timer, and we are not carrying him in the store, Ronald was wondering if your office could make this advance, otherwise he would send him his personal check. If agreeable, please make the check to W. L. Harrington's order and mail to this office. We will secure a receipt for same.

This amount can be charged to the Vail cash account and we will collect same from future wages due Mr. Harrington, if this meets with your approval."

Despite the Depression, Weyerhaeuser was keen to invest in its logging operations. In the fall of 1931, the company contracted with the Washington Iron Works to build an improved model steam tower skidder, known as the Washington Equalizing Tower Skidder, for the Vail operation. The new and improved tower skidder boasted 46 points of advanced improvements over existing skidders, redesigned specifically to decrease skidding and maintenance costs and increase safety. Some of the improvements included a modi-

Weyerhaeuser moved Camp 3 from Miller Hill to a location on Porcupine Ridge where it joined Camp 4 to create what was known as Spike Camp in the early 1930's. The Cherry Valley camp cars have been given a fresh coat of red paint with white trim at the time this photograph was taken. Two ex-Northern Pacific wood coaches rest at the camp waiting to take the loggers to the woods. To the far left, behind one of the coaches is a small engine maintenance building. Major repairs were made at Vail, but minor repairs and general maintenance of locomotives and donkey engines was conducted at the camps. —Clark Kinsey, Weyerhaeuser Archives

Speeders of different size and design served a variety of functions at Vail. Speeder #25, a Skagit Steel & Iron Works Model 6-60, was one of the larger speeders used at Vail and would carry supplies and mail from Vail to the various camps up in the woods. —Clark Kinsey, Weyerhaeuser Archives

fied boiler with extended firebox, a feed water heater, and roller bearings instead of bronze bearings. The greatest improvement was the equalization of cable drum speeds. This was accomplished using a planetary transmission in the receding drum, which permitted a flexible ratio and eliminating sudden changes in speed that could cause whipping, vibration, and breakage of the slack puller lines and tail rigging. The steel spar, or tower, rose 107 feet from track level, whereas the skidder itself was 60 feet long by 13 feet and four inches wide over the legs. Four hydraulic jacks elevated the machine to its operating position. It was designed for a maximum span of 2,200 feet. The tower skidder required a 24-wheel Pacific Car & Foundry moving car. With a total weight of 425,000 pounds, the 24 wheels distributed the load to approximately 18,000 pounds per wheel. The vehicle cost $75,000 and was put into operation in 1932 as Vail's #3 skidder.

The new Washington Iron Works tower skidder was the largest of its kind at the time it began service at Vail. Initially, it worked along the LD Lines near Porcupine Ridge, serving the recently reactivated Camp 3. On November 7, 1933, at about 1:30 P.M., the rail under the machine gave way while the skidder was being moved to a new side. As the skidder toppled, the engineer and leverman jumped clear, escaping with minor injuries. But unfortunately, Edward Brown, the fireman, failed to escape and was

The Civilian Conservation Corps and Vail

In the midst of the Great Depression, the Civilian Conservation Corps (CCC) first came to Thurston County and the Vail woods in 1933. The CCC was created as part of the Work Projects Administration (WPA) to create jobs for the unemployed at a time when the national unemployment rate exceeded 20 percent. CCC workers improved forest roads and facilities, and in some places were involved in reforestation, working in forest nurseries, and planting trees in logged-off and burned areas. In Thurston County, 225 men were employed to build a forest road from the George Churchill property southeast of Tenino into the Salmon Creek district, across Johnson Creek, up onto the higher land of Bald and Miller Hills north of Skookumchuck, and reaching Mulqueen on Vail's Skookumchuck railroad main line north of LD Camp. The road followed the old logging railroad grade of the Mutual Lumber Company, the Green River Lumber Company, and other old tracks. The forest roads were being built according to Forest Service specifications—the road was 12 feet wide and had a maximum grade of 16 percent. The men were quartered west of Rainier on the old Gruber and Docherty mill site that was known as Camp McKenna. This was the first CCC company to be housed at the camp. The crew made Camp McKenna its winter headquarters, moving to Mount Rainier National Park or to a camp north of Spokane in the summer months. Additional road and trail building in the Vail district in 1934 included a trail from Mulqueen nine miles south to Hunter's Cabin in Lewis County.

The first company was replaced by CCC Company 2929 in April 1936. By 1938, the CCC built a fire road, which initially followed the old Lindstrom Hanforth Lumber Company logging road grade and climbed up toward Porcupine Ridge, where it followed the old Weyerhaeuser Vail LD Line toward Spike Camp. The CCC built a small outpost camp near the top of the ridge, which housed 20 to 30 workers who also manned the 100-foot tall fire lookout tower on top of the ridge. The company was responsible for the planting of 572,000 tree seedlings in Thurston County during 1939 as well. Road building by the Camp McKenna CCC continued in 1939, through Mutual Lumber Company timberlands southeast of Tenino, and on into the early 1940s. In 1941, the CCC crew continued to develop fire protection roads in the Vail district, working to connect the Fall Creek road.

The CCC men were also called into action to battle forest fires in and around the Vail woods. This was especially true during the summer of 1938, when low humidity and a dry east wind increased the fire hazard. By July 22, 20 blazes had broken out, in part due to an arsonist. One of the fires burned over 40 acres around Reichel Lake southeast of Vail.

CCC camps offered more than a day's work. Camp McKenna, like many CCC camps around the country at the time, was equipped with an educational program. The program at Camp McKenna included a teaching staff of 25 housed in a building offering both educational and vocational activities and job training. Credits toward eighth grade and high school diplomas were available at the camp. The CCC created an important bridge for many of the unemployed during the Great Depression, while contributing to the improvement of forest resources.

scalded to death under the 230-ton skidder. The skidder was righted and put back into service shortly after the accident. However, the great weight of tower skidders on light rails in the woods would pose a danger in the future.

On August 25, 1930, the Honorable Sam C. White was appointed postmaster for the Vail Post Office, and on November 10, direct mail service was initiated to Vail. Mail was delivered to Rainier on the Northern Pacific's morning Seattle to Portland Railway post office train #572 (RPO) and dispatched via the Star Route Service (71371) to Vail. The Portland-bound train departed Tacoma at 9:04 A.M., and the mail arrived in Vail by 10:00 A.M. At Vail, it was sorted by camp and loaded onto a speeder departing Vail by 10:30 A.M. to deliver the mail to the camps. In 1933, the Railway Mail Service notified Weyerhaeuser of a change in the mail delivery schedule, whereby the mail would arrive at Rainier on Northern Pacific's Seattle to Portland RPO train #562 at 9:45 A.M. In response to the change in train schedules, the Railway Mail Service planned to amend the Star Route service, delivering the mail to Vail at 4:30 P.M. Weyerhaeuser officials filed a protest to the planned schedule change, citing, "...should the delivery of mail to the post office (Vail) be delayed beyond this time (10:30 A.M.) it would of necessity have to lay over a full day before being delivered to the woods camps." The letter when on to state, "...from the interest of this company the earlier or present service is much more desirable and we trust the present service will not be interrupted."

Spike Camp was the name Vail crews gave to the large joint camp located on the LD 20 line along Porcupine Ridge during the early 1930s. The camp was home to Camps 3, 4 and 6. Camp 4 is in the foreground, its shop located in the center of the wye. Camp 3 composed of Cherry Valley camp cars is directly behind Camp 4 (compare this photo to the previous one). Camp 6 had been moved to its new location on a spur 2G on Branch 2 across the Skookumchuck River. —Clark Kinsey, MSCUA, University of Washington Libraries, UW4841

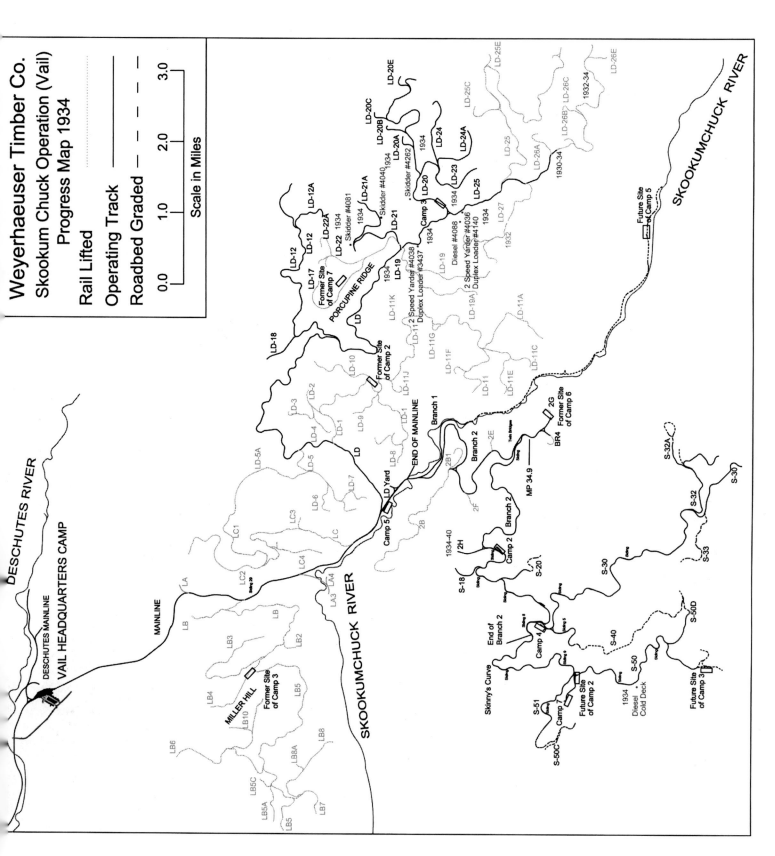

Woods tracks south of Vail representing the general layout between 1934, showing the location of camps and logging spurs. Dates near the tracks indicates when timber was cut in a specific area. —Composite map from various data sources including Weyerhaeuser Archives; Weyerhaeuser Vail section maps located at the Vail office; aerial photographs; Vail Track Mainline and Woods Lines, Barrett Family Collection; Donald Clark Papers, University of Washington Library; drawn by Frank W. Telewski

If a possible change in mail service for Vail was the bad news for 1933, an improving economy and subsequent increased demand for lumber, creating a need for more logs to supply reactivated Everett mills A and B on May 29, 1933, was very good news. Work in the woods resumed in June 1933 with the return of 250 men, including 75 fallers and buckers at Camp 3 located on Porcupine Ridge, the site of Spike Camp. In June, *The Thurston County Independent* reported that prospects for opening other logging camps at Vail was good due to an improving economic outlook. By mid-1933, three sides were opened at Vail, and by the late summer a total of six sides were in operation, producing 900,000 feet of timber per day and regaining its pre-Depression production rate. The effort of laying rails into the Vail woods resumed by July 14, 1933, with the employment of a 20-man track crew installing another side in the timber. By June, 75 men were hired as track crews to replace worn-out ties and reballast the track from Vail south to the camps, while three log trains per day were reportedly departing Vail for South Bay. With increased demand for timber, work repairing existing lines, and the extension of the railroad further beyond the Skookumchuck crossing, operations at Vail were back in full swing. Although the Great Depression would continue through the 1930s and limited camp shutdowns would still occur, at the start of 1934 the future of logging and employment at Vail looked very promising, indeed.

The residents of Camp 4 at Spike Camp pose for a group photograph in front of a former Cherry Valley camp car. Unlike the more commonly recognized Cherry Valley cars which have a clerestory, these cars were built without one. Most of Camp 4 was composed of skid shacks but did have six former Cherry Valley camp cars. —Clark Kinsey, Weyerhaeuser Archives

Settings in the woods were sometimes tucked into tight spaces. Here two steam donkeys power a spar tree rigged in the North Bend system along a curve. In the distance is the trestle of the main logging spur. —Clark Kinsey, Weyerhaeuser Archives

Next page: Woods tracks south of Vail representing the general layout in 1936, showing the location of camps and logging spurs. Dates near the tracks indicates when timber was cut in a specific area. —Composite map from various data sources including Weyerhaeuser Archives, Weyerhaeuser Vail section maps located at the Vail office, aerial photographs and Vail Track Mainline and Woods Lines from the Barrett Family Collection. Drawn by Frank W. Telewski

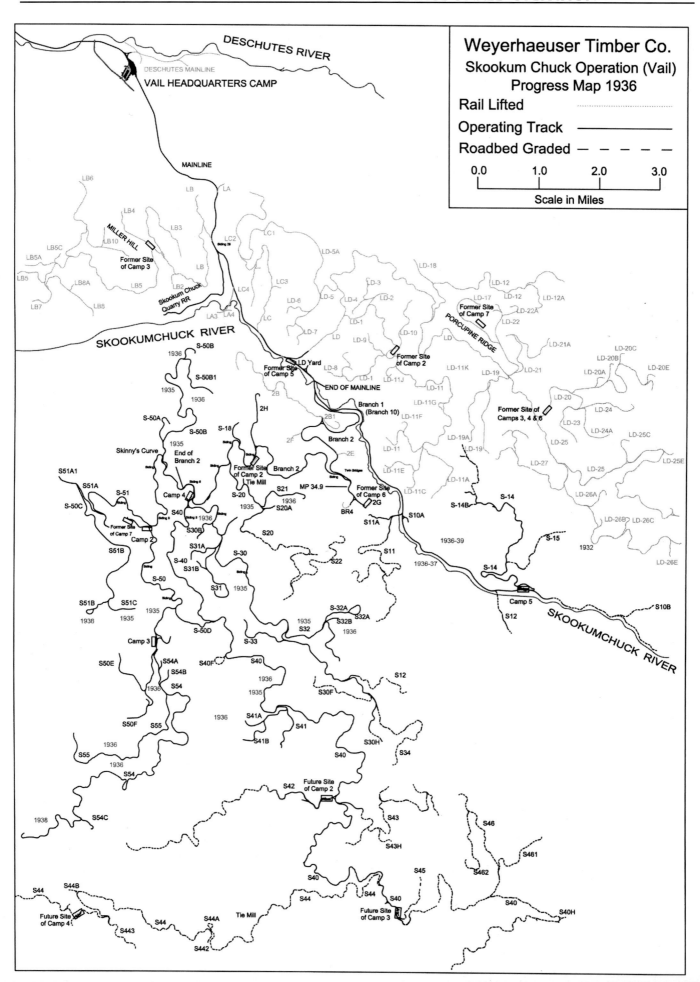

CHAPTER 4
Crossing the Skookumchuck: 1934-1942

In 1927, Weyerhaeuser's rapidly expanding Vail operation had pushed its rail line farther up the Skookumchuck River Valley, to the point that it was about to cross the Skookumchuck River canyon just south of the confluence of the Skookumchuck and Laramie Creek. Here the river carved a steep-walled, narrow canyon through the hard granite rock, which required Lloyd Crosby's crews to construct a 96-foot–high, 420-foot–long combination wood bridge and trestle. At this point, the main line ended and split into two major branches, Branch 1 (later renumbered Branch 10) and Branch 2. Branch 1 continued to follow the Skookumchuck south and would eventually cross the river again about a mile upstream. The second bridge crossing the Skookumchuck was built after 1934, but further expansion of this line was delayed until the late 1930s.

Camp 4 at Siding 8 with the filer's shack to the left and old Cherry Valley camp car to the right. The camp buildings have been repainted from red to a light gray with white trim after their move from Spike Camp.

—Clark Kinsey, Weyerhaeuser Archives

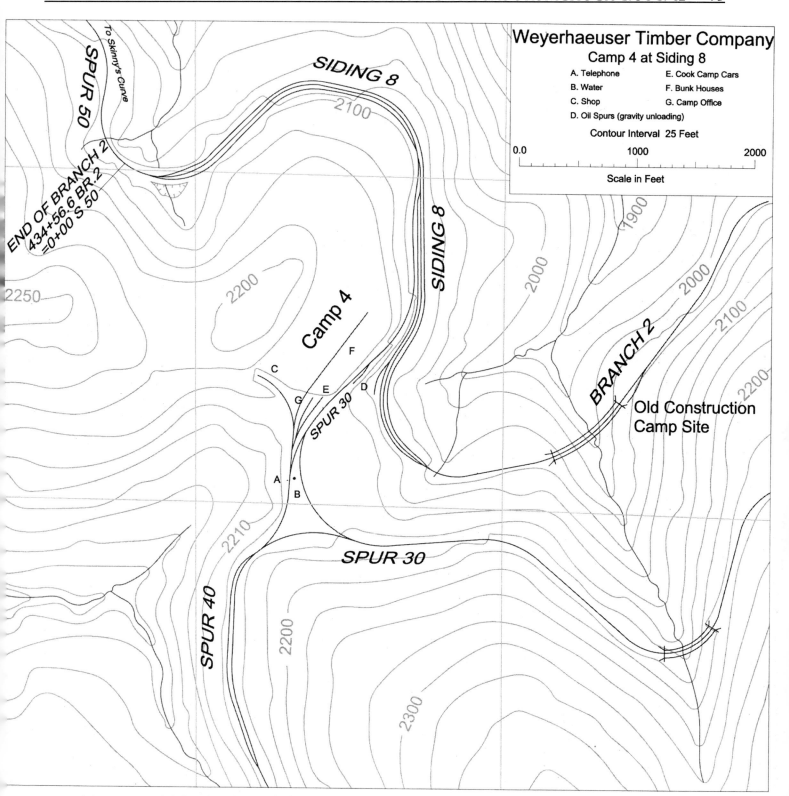

Map of Camp 4 and siding 8 at the end of Branch 2. —Composite map from various data sources including Weyerhaeuser Archives, USGS topographic map and field survey, redrawn by Frank W. Telewski

Opposite page: Camp 4 at Siding 8 was a significant center for woods operations in the mid to late 1930's. Siding 8 is the three sets of tracks to the lower right and represents the end of Branch 2 which climbed up from the Skookumchuck Crossing and LD yard. Beyond the curve and behind the hill the track became the 50 line. Climbing up the hill past the tank cars at the fuel dock is the 40 line then forms a junction with the 30 line as the leg of the wye passing in the lower right foreground. The two legs of the wye which leave the photo on the left unite as the 40 line. —Darius Kinsey, Whatcom Museum of History and Art

Work on Branch 2 continued in 1929 as the rail climbed southwestward into the mountains, gaining 625 feet in four miles with the aid of a switchback. Shortly after beginning its climb, Branch 2 gave rise to the 2B spur, which logged the lower southwest slopes above the Skookumchuck, paralleling the river in a northwestward direction. A wye was located at the junction between the 2B and Branch 2 Line. Three skidder landings, or sides, sat along this spur, and the area was logged over before 1932. The rail and switches of the wye were removed by the steel gang around 1935. A wye was located on the tail track of the switchback at MP 35, 1,342 feet above sea level. One side was located on the B4 leg of the wye. Camp 6 was moved from its Spike Camp location on Porcupine Ridge to the almost circular second leg of the wye, designated 2G. Timber crews logged off this area by 1931, and the track crew extended Branch 2 to siding 8 by the end of 1931. As the Branch 2 Line passed above the switchback, a twin trestle, 301 feet in length and 53 feet high, was built to support the branch line and a 40-car siding just to the west of the switchback tail track and wye. However, the deepening Depression restricted further timber harvesting across the Skookumchuck until after 1934.

Elsewhere in the Vail woods, logging along the LB Lines on Miller Hill was completed by 1933 and along the LC Lines by 1929. The Great Depression had severely curtailed most logging at Vail between 1930 and 1934. What little activity there was had been focused along the LD Line around the combined camps of 3, 4, and 6, also known as Spike Camp. Early in 1934, with a restoration in logging activity in the Vail woods, the majority of logging action continued to take place along the LD Lines that traversed Porcupine Ridge. In 1934, a total of five sides and one cold deck were in operation in the Porcupine Ridge area, whereas only one cold deck was operating across the Skookumchuck on the 50 Line. However, by 1935, logging along the LD Lines was complete, and operations were transferred across the Skookumchuck Bridge. As each rail line shut down, the steel gang lifted the rails and used the iron to extend the logging lines farther to the south and west along Branch 2.

The cooks and dinning hall staff pose outside the kitchen car set out at Camp 4 at Siding 8. —Darius Kinsey, Whatcom Museum of History and Art

With a recovering market and increased demand for lumber, Branch 2 gave rise to several secondary lines, eventually reaching deep into the Newaukum River watershed. Rail Camp 2 was moved early in 1933 from LD 10 to a three-track camp site off Branch 2, about four miles west of the twin trestles at an elevation of 1,750 feet. This campsite was located just above the 2H spur. At this point, the branch line had climbed 1,000 feet above the mainline and Skookumchuck River. Weyerhaeuser woods crews abandoned this site in July 1934 when they moved Camp 2 to the 50 Line. The former site was converted to a smaller camp, which housed the boom-stick crew. The crew supplied long, thin logs that were shipped to South Bay and used to hold large log rafts together, which were then floated to the Everett Mills. The crew would travel by speeder to the sides where boom-stick harvesting took place. Boom-sticks were loaded onto specially designed skeleton log cars equipped with bunks which could rotate or swivel, accommodating the long loads as they moved around curves on their journey to South Bay. Just beyond this camp location, the 2H spur cut off and headed north. Another siding was located at the 2H junction, along with a water tank.

For 12 years, the Branch 2 Line down the mountain would see a majority of rail traffic as secondary spur lines pushed further into the forests of the Vail operation. A final numbering system was initiated for identifying the woods rail lines beyond the 2H junction, beginning with Spur 20, or S20 Line, the first ma-

Rolling down from Siding 8 with a full load of logs, Weyerhaeuser Timber Company #120 handles the load with ease. Purchased in 1936 from the Baldwin Locomotive Works, the #120 was the largest steam engine to work the rails above Vail. —Clark Kinsey, Scott Barrett Collection

Camp 2 was moved to the 50 line at the junction with the 51 line in June 1934. The 51 line runs to the left and the 50 line continues off to the right. The tail track of the wye forms the 50c line which was home to railroad construction Camp 7 less than a half-a-mile away. Two aging ex-Northern Pacific wood coaches rest on one leg of the wye. —Clark Kinsey, MSCUA, University of Washington Libraries, UW4849

jor spur off the Branch 2. The crews referred to these spur lines by their numbers, dropping the "S," or spur designation. Hence, the S20 Line was referred to as the 20 Line. Siding 4 was located at the junction of the 20 Line with Branch 2. The 20 Line was open prior to 1934 and was the site of one of Frank Lamberton's tie mills, which operated on this site from 1934 to 1940. The rail along the 20 was removed by 1940 after the completion of logging activity. Eventually, Branch 2 became the 50 Line at a point designated as siding 8. The 30 and 50 Lines were built in the early 1930s, and the 40 Line was extended during the period from 1934 to 1937.

Camp 4 was relocated from LD 20 to siding 8, which was a major marshalling area for log trains after 1934. Loads from the various woods operations were set out at siding 8, where geared locomotives, saddle-tank engines, and eventually the #120 would carry loads to either the twin bridges on Branch 2, the LD yards, or directly to Vail. From these locations, the loads were hauled by the rod engines #101,

Skidder #3, a Washington Iron Works tower skidder, loads log cars on the 51 Line near Camp 2 in the mid 1930s. —Clark Kinsey, Franncis Newman Collection, Rainier Historical Society

#103, and #105 for the rest of the journey to South Bay. Generally, the #120 would make the entire 39.14-mile trip from siding 8 to South Bay with its trainload of logs. In fact, the #120 could travel as far as the 42 Line but was restricted from proceeding further due to the sharp curves beyond 40F. At siding 8, Branch 2 ended as the railroad split into the 30 Line, the 50 Line, and eventually the 40 Line. This siding consisted of the main line and two siding tracks, a 2,675-foot loads track (62 cars), and a 1,300-foot empties track (30 cars). Locomotives could be turned on the wye located above the camp at the junction of the 30 and 40 Lines and supplied with water, sand, and oil at siding 8. A small locomotive shop and blacksmith shop capable of light repairs met the day-to-day needs of the loggers at Camp 4. Camp 4 would remain in this location until 1940 when it was moved to the southwest at the end of the 44 Line. After the relocation of Camp 4, the old site was turned over to Weyerhaeuser's Reforestation and Land Department (R&L) and became known as R&L Camp. Loggers were trained at the R&L camp to fight fires, burn slash, and remove old ties from the roadbed after logging spurs had been removed.

The east leg of the wye at Camp 4 was the continuation of the 30 Line that originated at siding 8, and the west leg became the 40 Line, which was graded in 1934. The 40 Line would more or less parallel the 50 Line, only at a higher elevation. The 50 Line progressed west and south through a cut and hairpin curve in Blue Ridge, known as Skinny's Curve, to harvest the lower elevations and was in operation before the 40 Line. The 50 Line was the first of the three lines to be logged off during the 1930s. The second location of Camp 7 was at the end of the 50C spur, close to the third location of Camp 2, where the 51 Line originated. Camp 3 was relocated in June 1934 from the LD20 line to the 50 Line at a point between the 52 and 54 lines.

Around 1934, woods crews also moved Camp 5 from its location at the LD Yard, MP 31, to its last location near the end of Branch 1 which had been extended some 12 miles up the Skookumchuck river valley. Frank Lamberton opened a second tie mill on a short spur about a half-mile to three-quarters of a mile north of Camp 5. This placed his new mill closer to the expanding branch lines radiating from Branch 1. While a great deal of activity was taking place along the 20, 30, 40, and 50 Lines in the mid to late 1930s, timber harvesting also continued along Branch 1, later renumbered Branch 10. This branch gave rise to three major spurs: the 11 Line, 12 Line, and 14 Line, which itself gave rise to the 15 Line. There is no evidence a "13 Line" designation was ever used, which may reflect some respect for superstition. The 11 Line crossed the Skookumchuck River and climbed the canyon of Eleven Creek. The 12 Line also crossed the Skookumchuck River, climbing a steep six percent grade up Twelve Creek and eventually joining with the 30 Line. Timber was harvested along the 12 Line and its branches in 1942. Stands of timber were left along the lower slopes of the 12 Line after the rails were lifted in 1946 and would remain for truck logging to remove them in the early 1950's. At Camp 5, the 14 Line climbed northeastward toward Porcupine Ridge. This line was built in 1938 to harvest the lower slopes of the Skookumchuck watershed above Camp 5 but never reached the long-removed D Lines above. Logging on the 14 and 15 Lines began in 1939 and continued into the early 1940s.

Logging crews at Camp 2 finished their work on the 50 Line first and moved the camp to its last location along the 40 Line between 1936 and 1937. Only two of the original Cherry Valley

Tragedy at Skinny's Curve

Just to the west of Camp 4 and siding 8, beyond the end of Branch 2, the 50 Line began to turn north and almost reached the Thurston-Lewis County line. At this point, the line made a sharp hairpin turn to the south through a rock cut in the north end of Blue Ridge and into the watershed of Fall Creek. In 1934, steel and track surfacing crews were hard at work extending the 50 Line south toward the North Fork of the Newaukum River. This work required extensive rail construction traffic to be intermixed with log train traffic.

On the afternoon of June 22, 1934, a misunderstanding of the dispatcher's orders placed a speeder and work train on the 50 Line heading toward each other. The speeder was heading north on the 50 Line, above Fall Creek toward Camp 4, and carried a track-surfacing crew of about 35 men. Their final destination was Vail. A work train carrying the steel crew had just left siding 8 at Camp 4 and was heading back home to Camp 7, which was located off the 50 Line on the 50C spur. The train and speeder first saw each other with less than 40 feet and fewer seconds between them, just as each entered the cut of the sharp curve.

Both train and speeder were estimated to be traveling at 20 mph when they collided. Some of the workers jumped just before impact; the rest were thrown from the demolished speeder. Two workers on the speeder, George McMillan of Tenino and Arthur Bagley of Vail, were reported to be in serious condition. Fourteen other workers, including Ralph Crumley of Yelm; James Taylor; Louis Loftus; John Fairfield; Verne Campbell; Bert Nelson Jr.; William Fuller; Ivar Larsen of Rainier; Fred Neson and F. Blankenship (both from Vail); and William Butler, Lars Larson, Louis Larson, and Ludwig Larson (all from Kent) received hospital treatment for a variety of injuries from broken bones to cuts, bruises, and lacerations.

In an interview with *The Thurston County Independent*, Ronald McDonald stated that the accident resulted from an apparent misunderstanding of a dispatcher's orders. A change in the location of Camp 5 was apparently the cause of the confusion. After the accident, the curve became known as Skinny's Curve, named for the dispatcher on duty at the time.

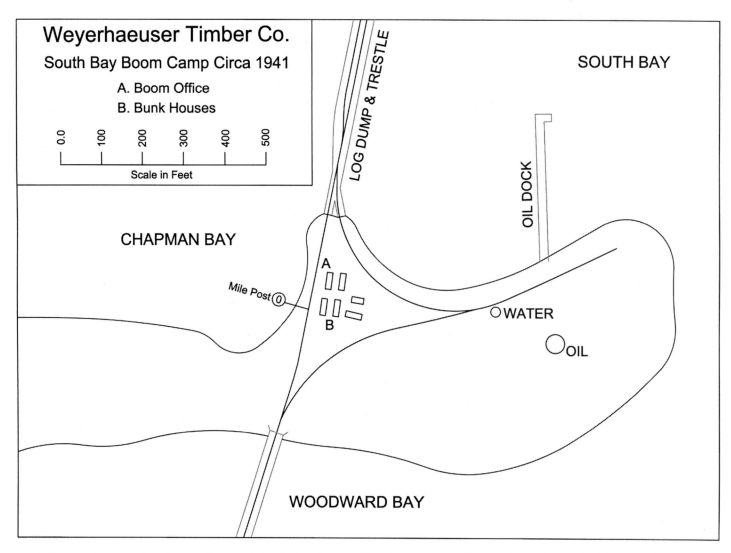

In the early years, the Boom Camp at South Bay housed the boom crew, the workers who sorted logs and arranged them into rafts in the waters of South Bay. The camp was complete with bunk houses, a dinning hall, and office. In later years, as cars became more available, the booming grounds crew would drive to and from South Bay and all the buildings except the office were removed. —Composite map from Weyerhaeuser Arvhives and U.S. Army 1945 photographic mosaic sheet. Drawn by Frank W. Telewski

camp cars would be incorporated into the new Camp 2. When the camp was moved, the remaining rail camp cars, which were now showing their age, were either sent to Vail to serve as warehouses or for storage. One of the old Cherry Valley cars was converted to a fire equipment storage building at Vail. The more worn-out camp cars were abandoned and burned in the woods. A similar fate faced the camp cars of Camp 3 when it was moved from the 50 Line the same year.

    The new and last Camp 2 was located at the junction with the 40 and 42 Lines using new skid shacks and had to be built on the side of a hill rather than on a flat. This required the buildings to be placed on stilts to keep them on the level. The camp was a mix of two remaining rail camp cars and new skid camp buildings, which were not permanently mounted as rail cars. Two 25 car sidings were located at Camp 2, along with two spur tracks for oil, sand, water, and speeder storage. The semi saddle-tank mallet #111 would run loads along the 40 Line to siding 8. With the increased distance between Camp 2 on the 42 Line and Camp 4 at siding 8, the saddle-tanks could no longer hold sufficient water for the long run. As a result, the shop crews removed the semi saddle-tanks and provided the #111 with a tank car tender to increase her range after 1938.

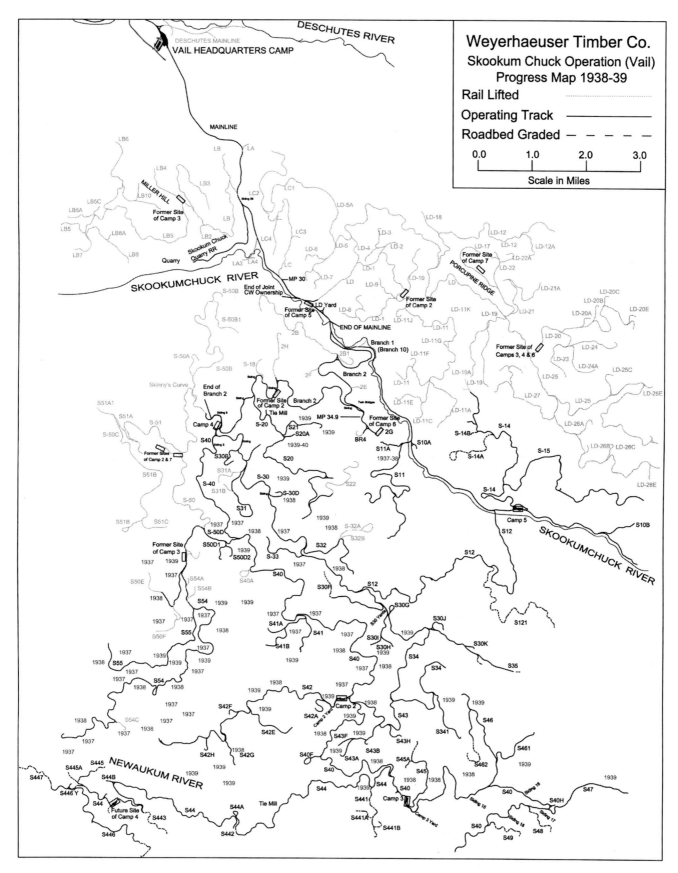

Woods tracks south of Vail representing the general layout between 1938-39, showing the location of camps and logging spurs. Dates near the tracks indicates when timber was cut in a specific area. —Composite map from various data sources including field surveys, Weyerhaeuser Archives, Weyerhaeuser Vail section maps located at the Vail office, aerial photographs and Vail Track Mainline and Woods Lines, Barrett Family Collection, drawn by Frank W. Telewski

Camp 3 on the 50 Line was moved in 1937 to the junction of the 40 and 45 Lines, while harvesting work continued until 1940 on the 54 and 55 Lines. The new Camp 3 was composed of new buildings identical to those used in Camp 2 on the 42 Line. The skid shacks were lifted off flat cars and set on the ground rather than remaining on rails. There was a wye off the 40 Line north of Camp 3 and a two-track siding just below Camp 3 on the 40 Line. Locomotives #110 and #5 would tie up at Camp 3 on a spur located between the junction of the 40 and 45 Lines and the two-track siding for loads and empties. Often a train of logs from Camp 3 would be headed by #110, with the #5 in the rear as a pusher to siding 8.

Camp 3 was moved to the 50 line at the junction with the 52 line in June 1934. —Clark Kinsey, Weyerhaeuser Archives

Both new Camps were modeled after the second Camp 5, located near the end of Branch 1 in the Skookumchuck Valley. The layout was fairly standard, altered slightly as needed to accommodate the site. The camps contained a dominating dining hall and upwards of 30 14×40–foot bunk houses arranged in two rows. A track would run between the two rows of bunk houses, facilitating placement and any future movement of the skid shacks.

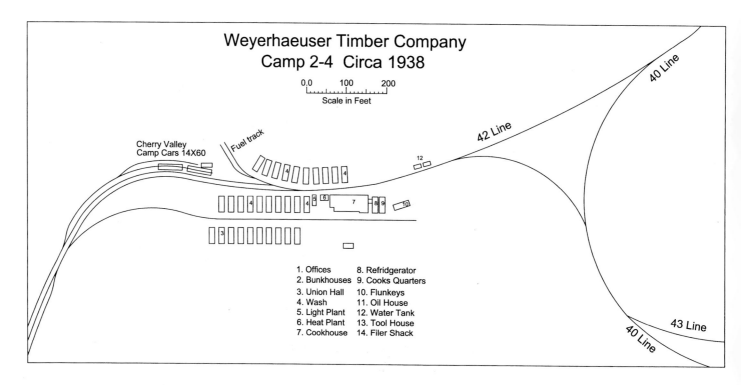

Layout of Camp 2 on the 42 Line. —Drawn by Frank W. Telewski

The new Camp 2 on the 42 line was composed of new bunk houses and a large central dinning hall. Only two of the original Cherry Valley camp cars remain as part of the camp, including the filer's shack. A wood car, a modified flat car for hauling firewood is spotted between two rows of bunk houses. A sand car rests in front of the filer's Cherry Valley car. —Darius Kinsey, Whatcom Museum of History and Art

The expansion of operations during the 1930s required the addition of more rail equipment, including log and tank cars, skidders, and locomotives. In 1935, Vail acquired the 2-6-2 Alco/Cooke (c/n 62965) from the Hetch Hetchy Railroad and numbered it the 100. The Vail steel gang used this locomotive after the 2 spot was transferred to Camp McDonald's steel gang.

In 1936, Weyerhaeuser approved the purchase of several retired locomotives from the Siler Logging Company for Vail. Founded in 1923, the Siler Logging Company was created as a joint operation between Weyerhaeuser and the Port Blakely Mill Company. Siler harvested 10,000 acres of timber in King and Snohomish Counties near the towns of Monroe and Cathcart, supplying logs for both of Port Blakely's mills on Puget Sound and Weyerhaeuser's Everett Mills. Siler completed its

When Weyerhaeuser built a new Camp 2 on the 42 line they equipped it with a large, new dinning hall, kitchen and food storage building. A proud dinning hall staff pose by their new home. —Darius Kinsey, Whatcom Museum of History and Art

Labor Unrest in the Woods

Labor issues have been part of the forest products industry ever since its early days, with laborers seeking improved working and living conditions, job security, and better wages.[1] With the onset of the Great Depression, labor issues once again were brought to the forefront as jobs became scarce and workers lucky enough to have a job were often asked to take pay reductions. In response to the economic conditions of 1931, F. R. Titcomb, then general manager of the Weyerhaeuser Timber Company, cut the workweek to four days, while trying to find employment for those left jobless. By March 15, 1932, wages in the camps and mills were cut 10 percent. The first sign of labor troubles at Vail appeared in April 1934 when the steel gang chose to be laid off rather than accept a 25-cent per day reduction in pay. During the walkout, steel laying on the rail lines was suspended, but section crews were not affected.

After 1935, an improving economy lead to a demand by workers for increased salaries and recognition of a union. A strike by mill and woods workers in early May 1935 began to shut down mills and logging operations across the Pacific Northwest and resulted in the closing of Vail operations on May 12. Vail employees demanded recognition of the union, a 60¢ per hour minimum wage, and a 40-hour workweek. It appeared a settlement had been reached on July 12, with the Vail workers potentially returning to work within a week. On July 22, 120 men returned to work at Camp 4. However, the strike was not settled, and during the last week of July, state police arrested 10 picketers at the picket line near Vail. Shortly thereafter, a 90-foot long trestle near Camp 2 was reportedly dynamited as a result of strike animosity. The strike continued, and by August 2 the company proposed to increase wages by 40¢ per day and set a $4 per day minimum. The strike was finally settled on August 19 when the workers voted to accept the company's offer of a 50¢ per hour minimum wage, a 40-hour week, and recognition of the union. Over 800 workers were affected by the strike, and while it was occurring about 80 men were still working on construction projects in the woods.

On August 25, 1937, a strike by 18 boom men at South Bay threatened a complete shutdown of the Vail operation. The dispute centered on the dismissal of one of the employees at the log dump for "incompetence." The workers wanted the man reinstated. Ronald McDonald met with the boom workers and asked them to reconsider their action. If the strike was to continue, it would result in the closure of four camps. Operations were stalled for 30 days, allowing time for a negotiated settlement between the company and the union on August 27.

In May 1941, a second district-wide strike was declared by the CIO-International Woodworkers of America. The strike closed Vail on May 9, but it ended on June 16 when the Weyerhaeuser employees of Vail and McDonald voted overwhelmingly to resume work, "accepting the defense mediation board's back-to-work proposal." This would not be the last strike or labor issue to affect the Vail-McDonald operation. Labor issues would continue until the last days of railroad operation.

harvest in 1931 and began to shut down. The purchased locomotives included a small 2-6-2T Porter (c/n 5030), a Baldwin built 2-8-2 (c/n 57705), a Baldwin built 2-8-2 (c/n 35781) and renumbered 99, a #102 (third), and a #105 respectively. Using speeders became less practical because of the increasing distances between the woods camps and Vail Headquarters. Hence, the #99 was acquired to replace the #25 speeder, which previously moved supplies between the woods camps and Vail.

A 3-truck shay (c/n 3253), Siler's 2 spot, was renumbered 6 and served for only a year before being sold to the North Bend Timber Company. Additional equipment acquired from the Siler operation for use at Vail included a Lidgerwood spar skidder (Vail's #4), Northwest gas shovel (#1125), several donkey engines, 25 log cars, three 8,000-gallon oil tank cars, one 10,000-gallon water tank car equipped with pump, three PC&F Rogers Ballast cars, three flat cars, one 100,000-pound moving car, and two #40 Sheffield speeders.

Increasing demand prompted Vail to acquire additional locomotives. A Baldwin 2-8-2T (c/n 53146) was purchased from the Simpson Logging Company, originally numbered 2 and then renumbered 102 (second) and finally 3 (second). A Baldwin built 2-6-6-2T (c/n 60343) purchased from Weyerhaeuser's Clemons Logging Company was renumbered from 8 to 114. Weyerhaeuser purchased one new locomotive for Vail in 1936, a Baldwin 2-6-6-2 (c/n 61904). At a weight of 147 tons on 51-inch drivers and an overall length of 69 feet, eight inches, the #120 was the largest locomotive to serve at Vail and would carry log trains on the long run from siding 8 to South Bay. In 1941, the #120 was transferred to the Chehalis West-

---

[1] For an excellent review of labor issues as they related to the Weyerhaeuser Timber Company, read *Timber and Men*, R. W. Hidy, F. E. Hill, and A. Nevins; Macmillan Company, 1963.

ern for main line service to South Bay and was eventually transferred to Weyerhaeuser's Longview operation. Baldwin also built the 120's better-known sister locomotive, #6, to serve Weyerhaeuser's Klamath Falls operation in Oregon. Number 6 became famous as Sierra's #38. Both engines eventually served out their days working for Rayonier in Hoquiam, Washington. In 1937, Vail leased a 3-truck, 80-ton Climax (c/n 1589) from Simpson. It remained lettered for Simpson and wore the number 4. With the installation of the "new" equipment, Weyerhaeuser projected production at Vail to increase from 1,300 to 1,500 board feet per day.

The plans set forth by Minot Davis in his memo of July 19, 1934, to J. P. Weyerhaeuser also led to the buildup of logging equipment at Vail to meet the need for the planned expansion of logging operations west of Chehalis. By 1936, the company had made an arrangement with the Milwaukee for reciprocal running rights. Weyerhaeuser would be able to transport logs over the Milwaukee Line from Chehalis to Western Junction. In return, the Milwaukee Road had access to a rock quarry on the north side of the Skookumchuck River below Miller Hill. This agreement gave rise to the Chehalis Western Railroad in 1936 and the opening of Camp McDonald in 1938. After this time, the entire operation became known as the

Safety in the Woods

Safety in the woods and on the logging railroad cannot be forgotten. Over the years, many workers were injured or killed in the Vail woods. The year 1936 was a particularly difficult one for accidents and deaths at Vail. On May 3, brakeman Wilmer O. Williams was crushed between two cars when he slipped and fell. A second Vail brakeman, C. D. Shelby, was killed on November 23 after being pinned beneath an empty flat car that jumped the track in a train of empty cars returning to the woods from Vail. On June 5, locomotive engineer Joseph Noonan passed away unexpectedly at the age of 41 at his home at Vail. Faller Melbourne Ransey was killed instantly, and his coworker Melvin Kelsey was knocked unconscious, when a vine maple tangled in the canopy of the fir they were felling swung around and hit the men. The accident occurred near the railroad right-of-way about 10 miles south of Vail on June 15. Head loader Frank Milich was killed after being struck by a log on August 19. Antone Schmidt, a logger employed by Frank Lamberton, railroad tie contractor at Vail, was killed while felling tie trees on September 14. Another speeder and log train accident occurred on September 22, 1936, at approximately 3:00 P.M. Nine men, including Deputy Sheriff George Keithahn, were returning on the speeder from making an arrest when a log train came into view around a curve. With only 75 feet between the two, the nine men jumped from the speeder and avoided serious injury. The speeder was damaged in the collision. Another logger, Ed Kinsland, was killed instantly when he was hit by a side-winder[2] on September 21.

Weyerhaeuser Timber Company #111, 10 years after it first arrived at Vail appears to have had a recent paint job in the photograph from May 1938. The more complex timber company logo has been replaced by a lone Weyerhaeuser "W" on the fuel bunker. —Darius Kinsey, Whatcom Museum of History and Art

[2] Falling limb or snag that may fall from above in felling or yarding.

Weyerhaeuser Timber Company #110, 10 years after it first arrived at Vail also appears to have had a recent paint job in the photograph from May 1938. The more complex timber company logo has been replaced by a lone Weyerhaeuser "W" on the fuel bunker and a larger version of the "W" has replaced the wording "Weyerhaeuser Timber Company" on the semi-saddle tank. —Darius Kinsey, Whatcom Museum of History and Art

Post 1938, the #111's semi-saddle tanks were removed and the locomotive was fitted with a tender to increase its range, allowing it to reach Siding 8 from Camp 2 without having to stop multiple times for water. —Al Farrow, Martin E. Hansen Collection

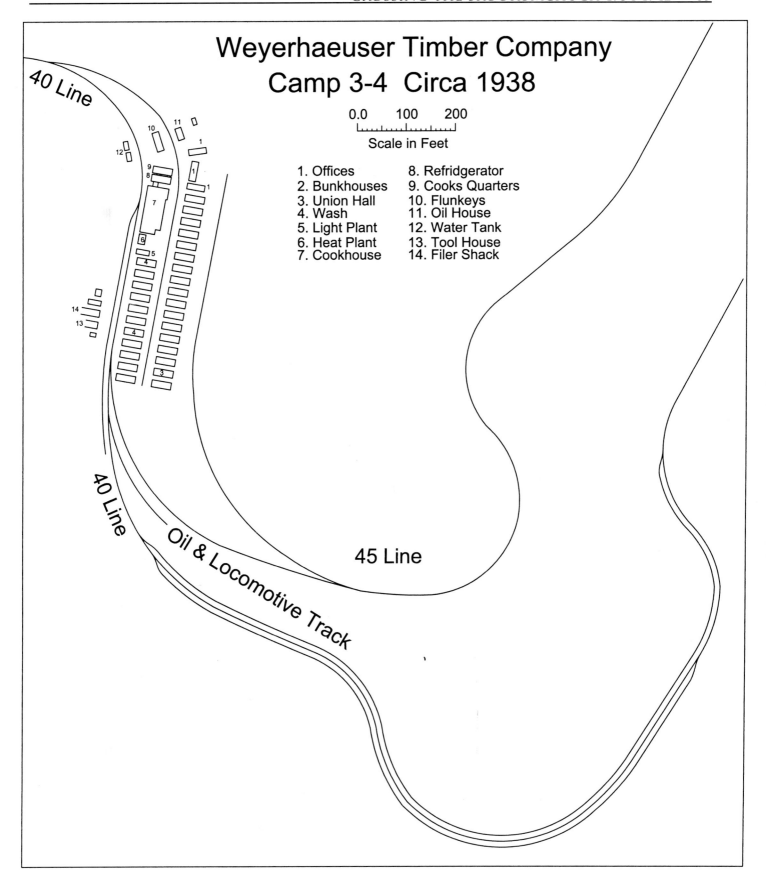

Layout of Camp 3 on the 40 Line. —Drawn by Frank W. Telewski

When Weyerhaeuser moved Camp 3 from the 50 line to the 40 line at the junction with the 45 line, they retired the old Cherry Valley cars and replaced them with all new 40-foot bunk houses. The camp layout and design was very similar to that of Camp 2 on the 42 line. In this view, we are looking south, the 40 line passes camp on the right and disappears behind the hill where it will give rise to the 45 line. The spur on the left side of camp with the wood car branches off from the 45 line. —Darius Kinsey, Whatcom Museum of History and Art

Another look at Camp 3 on the 40 line, this time looking north up through the center of camp. The crew are resting on a speeder on the track between the bunk houses. The camp buildings were painted light gray with white trim.
—Darius Kinsey, Whatcom Museum of History and Art

Vail-McDonald operation, and a significant portion of railroad logging equipment was transferred to the woods operations south of Camp McDonald.

An extended Christmas shutdown of woods operations in 1937 ended with the return of 900 workers during the first week of the following March. A year later, in early 1939, Weyerhaeuser began to experiment with the use of diesel tractors for yarding logs at Vail. This was a joint program between Weyerhaeuser and Smith-Layman, a contract logger who owned the two Allis Chalmers 81 HP Loggers Model (L-O) tractors used in the operation. The tractors were equipped with Carco arches, a hoist, and a bulldozer blade. The tractors would yard timber 2,000 feet from either side of the railroad bringing the logs to within reach of the steam skidder for loading onto rail cars. The idea was to reduce railroad construction costs by increasing the distance between logging spurs from about one mile to two miles apart. The two tractors could reportedly skid up to 70,000 feet of logs per day, but wet conditions would slow production as the machines became bogged down in mud.

By August 1939, the Vail-McDonald operation had grown considerably, and an inventory of equipment at that time included logging equipment amounting to six skidders, 15 yarders, seven duplex loaders, two

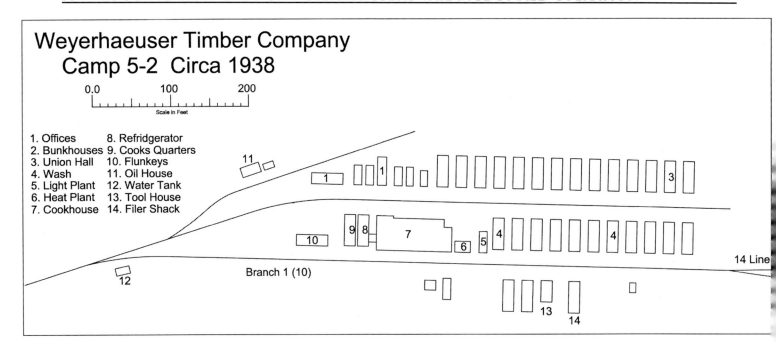

Map of Camp 5 at the end of Branch 1. —Weyerhaeuser Archives, redrawn by Frank W. Telewski

Weyerhaeuser moved Camp 5 from LD yard to the end of Branch 1 sometime around 1934. When the company changed the location, they replaced the original smaller bunk houses with new 40-foot camp buildings. This camp design would serve as a model for future Camps 2 and 3 at Vail and Camps 6 and 7 at Camp McDonald. —Darius Kinsey, Whatcom Museum of History and Art

cranes; railway equipment consisting of two Chehalis Western locomotives, 11 Vail-McDonald woods locomotives, 14 Vail-McDonald speeders, one Chehalis Western speeder, 325 Vail-McDonald log cars, 146 Chehalis Western log cars; and railroad construction equipment amounting to four Vail-McDonald locomotives, four Shovels and Buckets, 55 ballast, flat and gravel cars, one crane, and three speeders.

Vail initiated work on the last major rail line, the 44 Line, in 1937 and by August 1939 the line was extended 3.95 miles, requiring the construction of five trestles. Construction on the 44 Line was in full swing during the summer of 1940. It was particularly dry that year, and fire season struck early and hard. The humidity at Vail had reached dangerously low levels from June 24 to July 4. On June 25, a fire occurred near Camp 3 on the 40 Line. The #110 and 5 spot were dispatched from Camp 3 to battle the fire and had it under control by dark. The source of ignition was assumed to be sparks from a locomotive. The fire consumed 25 acres of standing timber and eight acres of slash but was contained before it could do any more damage.

In the afternoon of June 26, a second fire started near a pump used to supply water to logging donkeys at a logging side on the 42G Line after the crew had quit working for the day. The fire was spotted and reported to Vail by Jack Merritt and Vance Rogers who were patrolling the new 44 Line. Word of the fire was sent to Camp 2 by 4:15 P.M., and the #111 was dispatched with tank cars, pumps, and 150 men supervised by Henry Hansen, logging superintendent, to fight the fire. Hansen reported that the fire was contained in the evening, but by the next morning it had spread outside the fire line. At this time, crews moved logging equipment off the 42 Line to protect it from the advancing flames. The fire spread rapidly in the morning, running across the Newaukum Valley to the south, while logging crews from all three camps and the contractors' crews and equipment were engaged in building fire trails, felling snags, and manning pumps. The fire spread upslope to the 44 Line, where it burned one of the buildings in Charles Larsen's grading camp. Allen Cochran and a small crew quickly extinguished the fire at the camp without further damage.

When it was over, 3,600 acres were burned, including about 300 acres of felled and bucked timber and about 400 acres of standing timber, which was killed. Fortunately, the loss of standing timber was relatively light, and the only loss of equipment was guy lines. Over one million feet of logs in cold decks and 7.5 million feet of felled and bucked timber on the ground burned. The total cost for fighting the two fires at Vail amounted to $63,000. A third fire was spotted on June 27 on Hewitt Land Company land near Onalaska. Weyerhaeuser sent 70 men from Vail under the supervision of Bert Morsen to fight the fire. By

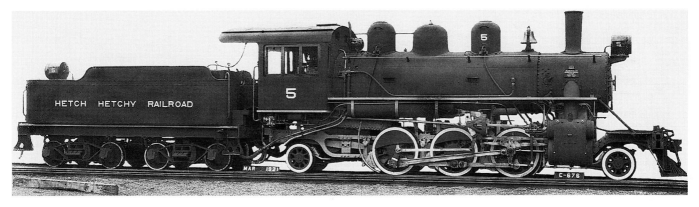

American Locomotive Company Builder's photograph of Hetch Hechy Railroad #5 taken in March 1921. Weyerhaeuser purchased this locomotive in 1935 to become Vail's #100. —American Locomotive Company, Frank W. Telewski Collection

Without running gear, no tires on the drivers and up on blocks, Weyerhaeuser's #100 is receiving some attention from the Vail shop crew in this photograph taken in July 1936. —Al Farrow, Martin E. Hansen Collection

Photographed on June 28, 1937 at the water tank at the south end of Vail yard, Weyerhaeuser's #99 has just finished taking on water in preparation for the climb into the woods. Acquired in 1936 from Weyerhaeuser's Siler Logging Company, the small Porter has yet to be painted and renumbered. The small engine was used to carry supplies to woods camps. Today, the cargo is a clearly marked wood boxcar containing explosives. —Al Farrow, Martin E. Hansen Collection

Another locomotive acquired from Weyerhaeuser's Siler Logging Company in 1936 was Mikado #3. Renumbered 102 by the Vail shops, it was the third locomotive at Vail to wear this road number. Of special interest in this photograph is the rare appearance of an ex-Northern Pacific 36-foot wood radial roof double sheath boxcar with fish belly side sill under frame lettered for W.T.Co. This boxcar was used to ferry supplies from Vail to the woods camps.
—Al Farrow, Martin E. Hansen Collection

The third locomotive acquired from Weyerhaeuser's Siler Logging Company in 1936 was Mikado #5. Renumbered 105 by the Vail shops the locomotive is photographed at Vail in 1938. —Harold Hill, Martin E. Hansen Collection

Lidgerwood spar skidder #4 was acquired by Vail from the Siler Logging Company in 1936. Similar to the Washington Iron Works tower skidder, the Lidgerwood was a completely self-contained yarder and loader with a steel tower or spar instead of a tree. —Darius Kinsey, Whatcom Museum of History and Art

Two Lidgerwood spar skidders operated at Vail in the late 1930s. Vail's #5, a Lidgerwood spar skidder at work loading logs in May 1938. —Darius Kinsey, Whatcom Museum of History and Art

A little locomotive with an identity crisis, Baldwin-built saddle tank Mikado #3 was originally delivered to Simpson Logging Company as their two spot. When it arrived at Vail it was assigned #2, then #102 (the second 102 to serve at Vail) and finally became the three spot. Photographed at Vail on June 28, 1937, the locomotive has no other identifying marks other than its road number on the cab. —Al Farrow, Martin E. Hansen Collection

Left: A view of the left hand side of Lidgerwood spar skidder #5 along with its operating crew. When in operation, the tower skidders were stabilized by taking the weight off the moving cars and jacking up the entire skidder on blocks. Here the moving cars have been left underneath the skidder and cars are loaded off to one side. —Darius Kinsey, Whatcom Museum of History and Art

Below: With the Lidgerwood spar skidder positioned, braced, and lifted off the tracks, empty log cars were pulled under the loader and positioned using cables from the skidder, a design which would save on track laying at landings. When the skidder needed to be moved, the heavy-duty moving cars built specifically for the skidder were placed back under the skidder. —Darius Kinsey, Whatcom Museum of History and Art

July 1, the fire had burned its way north into a stand of Weyerhaeuser timber but was stopped from spreading on the 443 spur.

By 1940, Camp 4 had been moved from siding 8 to its final location near the end of the 44 Line. The camp was located 61.46 miles from South Bay in Section 27, Township 14 North, Range 1 East, close to the North Branch of the Newaukum River in the far southwestern reaches of the Vail land holdings. This would be the fourth and final location for Camp 4. Another tie mill was located near the new Camp 4 location to

Appearing freshly painted and shopped in May 1938, Weyerhaeuser's #100 poses for this portrait at Vail. Both the boiler sheet and steam cylinder sheets appear a lighter color suggesting they may have been painted a color other than black. — Al Farrow, Martin E. Hansen Collection

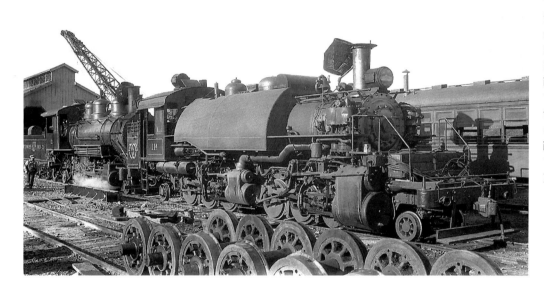

Vail's #114 was a sister to their #110, only it was originally build as Clemmons Logging Company # 8 by Baldwin Locomotive Works in 1928. Arriving at Vail in 1936, the semi-saddle tank Mallet was assigned #114. Here the locomotive is photographed at Vail in 1939. —Harold Hill, Martin Hansen E. Collection

Posed for its 1936 builder's photograph, Baldwin build Mallet #120 was the largest locomotive to ply the rails at Vail. —Baldwin Locomotive Works, Frank W. Telewski Collection

supply ties for the expanding operation.

In the summer of 1941, Skidder #3 had completed its work out of Camp 2 on the 42 Line and was dismantled and moved to the Vail shops for maintenance before being shipped over the Milwaukee Road to Camp McDonald.

Although the majority of activity at the Vail operation from the mid-1930s to the early 1940s centered in the woods south of the Skookumchuck River, routine maintenance work was required to keep the main line and South Bay log dump operational. In 1936, the original lightweight 56-pound rail was replaced with 75-pound rail on the first 16 bents of the log dump. In 1938, a second wye with more gradual curves on the legs was added at South Bay, located above the Woodward Bay trestle. Early in 1939, the Woodward Bay trestle required redecking and replacement of the walkway. In addition, 462.5 feet of the Woodward Bay trestle was filled in with rock hauled from milepost 18. The high bridge across the

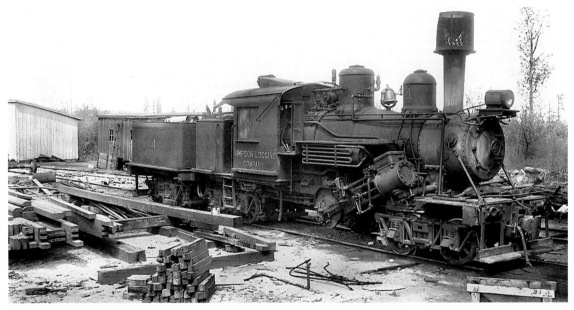

In 1937, Weyerhaeuser leased three truck Climax #4 from Simpson Logging Company. —Harold Hill, Martin E. Hansen Collection

In a display of Vail's motive power at the height of steam operations, seven locomotives are lined up on the south yard ladder track at Vail in this classic Darius Kinsey photograph from February 1938. In the line-up are Mikado #105, semi-saddle tank, simple articulated Mallet #111, three-truck Shay #2, Mallet #120, semi-saddle tank, compound Mallet #110, Mikado #101 and finally Pacific Coast Shay #5. —Darius Kinsey, Whatcom Museum of History and Art

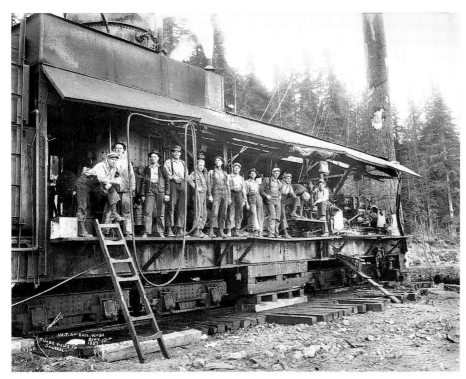

Skookumchuck was rebuilt in 1940, along with a second 234-foot–long bridge on Branch 2 located 0.6 miles southwest of the high bridge. In the summer of 1941, the twin trestle on Branch 2 was rebuilt, and new caps and deck were placed on the wye track and first 16 bents of the log dump. From December 1941 to January 1942, caps, stringers, and ties were placed on bents 17 to 60 on both the load and unloader tracks. A regular maintenance activity at South Bay was the periodic dredging of the log dump, which was on roughly a three-year cycle.

Top: Although Vail had three tower skidders operating in the woods in the late 1930s, the older steam donkeys and Washington Iron Works tree skidders were still in service. Here one of the WIW tree skidders is set up at a landing in September 1937. Notice the extra long and tightly spaced ties placed under the rail supporting the heavy machine.
—Darius Kinsey, Whatcom Museum of History and Art

Center: Caboose #712 and tank car #512 rest at the south end of Vail yard in this photograph taken in 1939.
—Harold A. Hill, Martin Hansen Collection

Bottom: Speeder #35 (1st) was a Gibson cupola type. —Al Farrow, Martin E. Hansen Collection

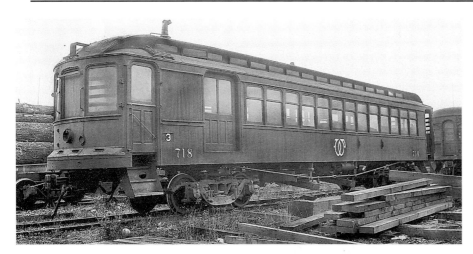

Top: By the late 1930s, the ex-Northern Pacific wood coaches used to ferry crews between camps and the woods were showing signs of aging. To replace them, Weyerhaeuser purchased several retired interurban electric cars from a number of lines. Here Vail crew car #718, ex-Puget Sound Electric Railway combine #504 rests before returning to Camp 3.
—Harold A. Hill, Martin E. Hansen Collection

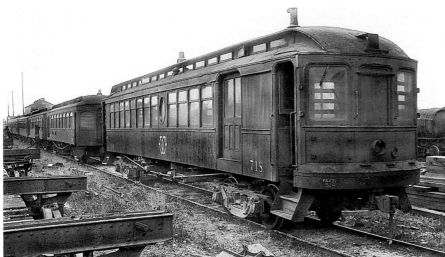

Center: A string of interurban cars acquired by Weyerhaeuser to ferry crews back to their camps wait in the Vail yard on September 19, 1939.
—Harold A. Hill, Martin E. Hansen Collection

Bottom: Caboose #704 was a four-wheel bobber built by Pacific Car & Foundry, and one of at least four to serve at Vail. Looking south #704 is followed by a string of waiting interurban cars ready to ferry crews back to their camps. Car #721 is ex-Northwest Traction #54. —Harold A. Hill, Martin E. Hansen Collection

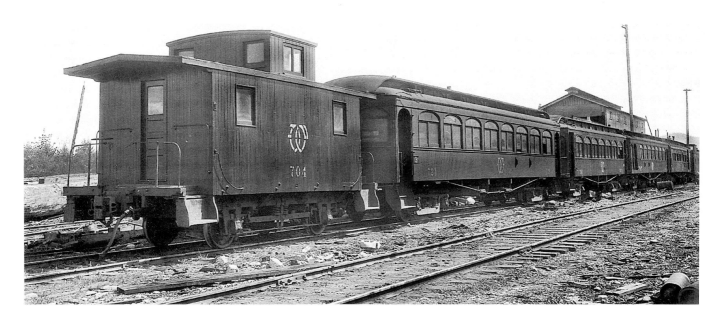

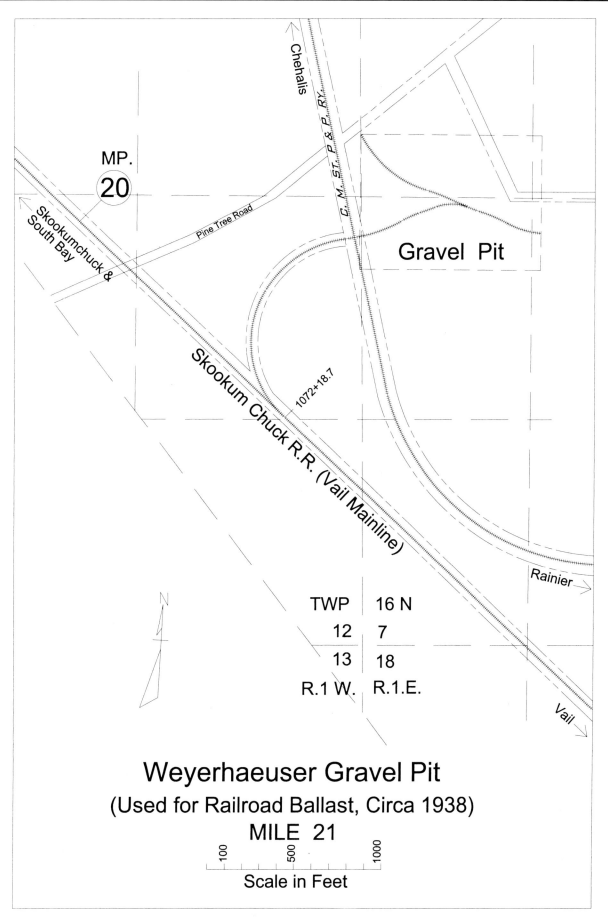

The gravel pit at Mile 21 was still active supplying ballast rock for the expanding rail lines of Vail in 1938. Notice that the track layout inside the pit has changed since 1928. —Drawn by Frank W. Telewski

Top: Ex-Oregon Electric Interurban Railway car #69 now serves as Vail's crew car #741 assigned to Camp 4 and photographed at Vail on March 5, 1939. —Emery J. Roberts, Martin E. Hansen Collection

Center: Pacific Car & Foundry built caboose #703, a four-wheel bobber rests outside the Vail shops. Behind #703 and to the left can be seen part of the sand car, a modified flat car built to carry locomotive sand to woods camps in order to keep an adequate supply of sand for locomotives working the steep grades of the hills. —Al Farrow, Martin E. Hansen Collection

Bottom: Looking south towards the end of the Vail yard in 1939, a string of loaded log cars waits to be carried to South Bay and a speeder departs for the woods as it approaches the Vail water tank. The dispatcher's office which directed traffic over the entire logging railroad is visible as the first building on the right. —T. Lawson, John T. Labbe Collection

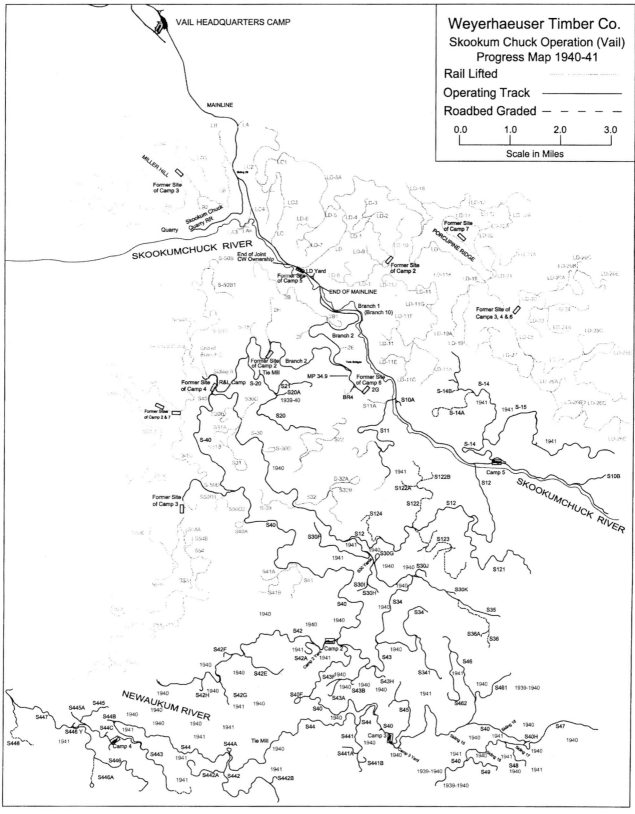

Woods tracks south of Vail representing the general layout between 1940 and 1941, showing the location of camps and logging spurs. Dates near the tracks indicates when timber was cut in a specific area.

—Composite map from various data sources including field surveys, Weyerhaeuser Archives, Weyerhaeuser Vail section maps located at the Vail office, aerial photographs and Vail Track Mainline and Woods Lines, Barrett Family Collection, drawn by Frank W. Telewski

Weyerhaeuser moved Camp 4 one more time in the twilight of logging camp life. By 1940, the camp had been moved from Siding 8 to a position near the end of the 44 line, 48 miles away from Vail and 61.5 miles form South Bay. —Ted Ward

Left: Camp 4 office camp car and Gibson speeder #24 on the 44 line shortly after being moved from Siding 8. Ronald A. McDonald, in suit and tie, rests on the left side of the speeder. —Clark Kinsey, Rainier Historical Society

Below: With paint peeling, Camp 4's office camp car shows its age towards the end of the era of railroad logging spurs at Vail. The Camp's timekeeper (George) stands in the doorway. —Bill Woods Collection, Rainier Historical Society

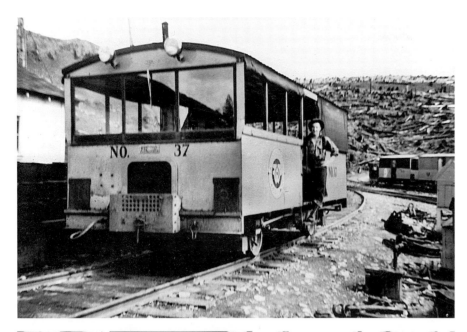

Top: Weyerhaeuser employee Bill Woods stands with Gibson speeder #37 at Camp 4.
—Bill Woods Collection, Rainier Historical Society

Center: Adjusting speeder #37's breaks at Camp 4 on the 44 line in 1940. The speeder was painted yellow and was adorned with the original Weyerhaeuser logo. —Bill Woods Collection, Rainier Historical Society

Bottom: A unique perspective of a tower skidder landing. The dual wood platforms and hose reel tells us these two tank cars are likely firefighting cars, whereas the tank car to the left is probably an oil car servicing the tower skidder.
—Richard Hussey

Right: In the days before radio, communications in the woods was via telephone. Miles of telephone wire had to be run to keep train crews in contact with the dispatcher's office and to connect camps with headquarters. Here a Weyerhaeuser lineman adjusts a telephone line on the 44 line in the early 1940s. —Richard Hussey

Below: Miles and miles of cable were used in the woods for yarding logs to a landing. When the time came to move, cables and donkey engines were loaded up onto flatcars. A sled mounted steam donkey is moved onto its steel donkey moving car as the crew begins to load the pulleys and spar tree rigging from a conventional flatcar at a new setting along the 44 line in the early 1940s. —Richard Hussey

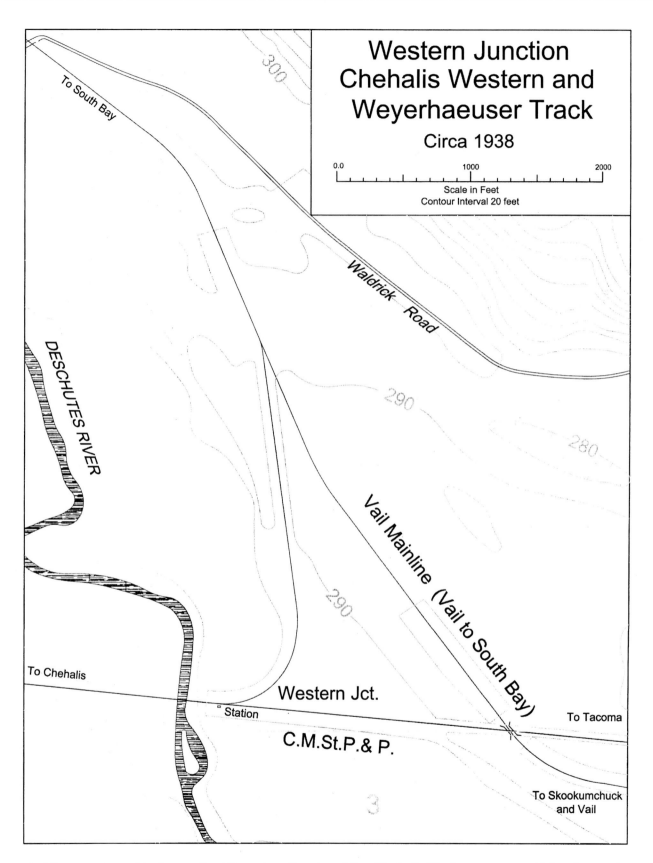

As part of the agreement between the Milwaukee Road and the Chehalis Western, a second interchange between the two railroads was established west of Skookumchuck and was named Western Junction. Weyerhaeuser supplied the small operators shack at the junction which provided Chehalis Western trains clearance to run on the Milwaukee tracks to Chehalis.—Composite map from various data sources including field surveys, Weyerhaeuser Archives, aerial photographs and USGS map, drawn by Frank W. Telewski

CHAPTER 5

The Genesis of the Chehalis Western and Columbia Construction Quarry

The founding of the Chehalis Western Railroad can be traced to a memorandum from Minot Davis to J. P. Weyerhaeuser Jr., dated July 19, 1934. In the memo, Mr. Davis indicates that the existing Everett mills and proposed sulfite pulp mill would require additional timber beyond what Vail was supplying. Three possible sources were noted, including Snoqualmie Falls, Enumclaw, and southwestern Washington holdings in western Lewis County near the towns of Doty and Kalber. Davis also noted that the Chicago, Milwaukee, St. Paul & Pacific was the only railroad capable of supplying transportation of logs from the three timberlands to Everett and that it would be necessary to work out an agreement with the Milwaukee Road for transport of the logs at a cost much lower than standard freight rates.

Construction of the track into the Skookumchuck quarry required blasting a ledge out of the hard granite walls. Here a section crew installs and aligns a switch. The water tank and camp buildings can be seen in the background. —George Hales, George Hales Family Collection

Overview of the Columbia Construction Company's Skookumchuck rock quarry photographed from the other side of the Skookumchuck river canyon. The quarry camp is located to the right and the quarry is on the left. —George Hales, George Hales Family Collection

Given the decision to open up the timberlands in western Lewis County, the Weyerhaeuser Timber Company, represented by Minot Davis, entered into negotiations with the Chicago, Milwaukee, St. Paul & Pacific Railroad on September 14, 1935. The plan was to purchase the abandoned Milwaukee trackage from Chehalis Junction west to a point 1.5 miles west of Station Ruth. The plan also called for the movement of logs over part of the Milwaukee Road's fourth subdivision of the Coast Division from Chehalis Junction to the Skookumchuck interchange, for the "transportation of logs, poles, pulpwood, cordwood, and other timber products (excluding lumber) including the return movement of empty cars and trains." The Skookumchuck interchange was east of the Milwaukee Road and Skookum Chuck Railway crossing, 5.5 miles west of Rainier in Thurston County, Washington. Just west of Skookumchuck, the Skookum Chuck Railway crossed over the Milwaukee Road's tracks.

The Milwaukee, itself in reorganization proceedings during the negotiations, readily recognized the financial advantages of the proposed arrangement. At least three billion feet of logs would move over the leased trackage, producing substantial revenue for the Milwaukee. Without the agreement, the timber company would ship the timber from Doty and Kalber south to the Columbia River and its Longview Mill complex. Weyerhaeuser made it clear that if the agreement was accepted, the Milwaukee would carry the increased traffic from the Everett Mills to eastern markets. Finally, the Milwaukee would secure running rights to the Columbia Construction Company quarry, which was accessible only by the Skookum Chuck Railway via Skookumchuck Junction.

The Weyerhaeuser Timber Company would incorporate the Chehalis Western Railroad as a common carrier subsidiary railroad of the timber company which would operate as a plant facility in the state of Washington for the purpose of executing the agreement. This was necessary because the grant of trackage rights to a shipper—in this case, the Weyerhaeuser Timber Company—was a keystone to the joint agreement, and in and of itself of questionable legality. The incorporation of a common carrier railroad eliminated this concern. A second concern centered on the Railroad Brotherhoods, who had the exclusive right to handle freight over the Milwaukee tracks. Although the agreement was in the best financial interest of both companies and their respective employees, it was not clear whether the Brotherhoods would contest the Chehalis Western's use of their own crews to move freight (logs) over the Milwaukee lines.

On February 28, 1936, following the final agreement with the Milwaukee and securing court approval of the terms of the sale and purchase of the abandoned track, the Weyerhaeuser Timber Company incorporated the Chehalis Western Railroad, with J. P. Weyerhaeuser Jr., president, to transport logs in the Olympia and Vail Districts. The newly incorporated railroad was capitalized with $300,000. By deed, dated February 29, 1936, the Chehalis Western received an undivided 50 percent interest in the Skookum Chuck Railway from milepost 31 (LD Yard) to the South Bay log dump (part of the Vail main line).

The joint ownership of the Skookum Chuck Railroad line to MP 31 provided the Chehalis Western the ability to offer the Milwaukee Road running rights from the Skookumchuck Junction to Mulqueen, where the rock quarry spur branched off the Weyerhaeuser main line. The rights were granted in exchange for Chehalis Western running rights from Chehalis to the newly constructed Western Junction.

With these arrangements made, the deed between the Milwaukee and Weyerhaeuser Timber Company was signed on May 7, 1936. As part of the agreement, the Chicago, Milwaukee, St. Paul & Pacific Railroad transferred ownership to the Chehalis Western via a quit claim deed of its existing Raymond Branch from Chehalis Junction to a point 1.5 miles west of Ruth. The Milwaukee also granted to the Chehalis Western the right to operate as a common carrier using its own power, crews, cars, and trains from Chehalis Junction to Skookumchuck. Commodities could be transported by the Chehalis Western over Milwaukee Road trackage only in less than carload shipments. A provision of the agreement also allowed for the movement of speeders or gas motor cars and the transport of a log jammer or crane on its trains or cars for the purpose of picking up logs that fell from cars along the Milwaukee Road's tracks.

All Chehalis Western trains were required to secure clearance from the Milwaukee Road dispatcher and run in accordance with Milwaukee Road rules and regulations. Chehalis Western trains were not to exceed 40 mph on Milwaukee Road track and were restricted to a minimum of 10 loads. Any trains carrying fewer than 10 loads would be charged the 10-load minimum. The Milwaukee charged the Chehalis Western 16 cents per mile for each loaded log car and did not charge for empty log cars, except when the number of empty log cars exceeded the number of loads during one year. If the number of empty log car movements exceeded the number of loaded car movements, the Milwaukee charged eight cents per mile. There was no charge for cabooses or the movement of Weyerhaeuser motor cars over the Milwaukee track. As for trains, motor car operators had to be approved to run over the Milwaukee Road by the superintendent, and the movement of motor cars had to occur under train order. Motor cars could haul supplies, materials, tools, and equipment. Water for steam engines was provided in the contract, and each company charged 50 cents per tank.

The Chehalis Western agreed to take over the maintenance contract that had been signed between the Northern Pacific Railroad and the Chicago, Milwaukee, St. Paul & Pacific Railroad Company for the automatic interlocking two miles southwest of Chehalis, Washington, on July 21 and August 1, 1914.

Weyerhaeuser agreed to take over this contract and pay 50 percent of the upkeep of the railroad crossing and the automatic interlocker device. This agreement also established Western Junction, a turnout and connecting track just west of the Milwaukee Road and Skookumchuck Railway crossing at a point 6.6 miles west of Rainier and 1.1 miles west of Skookumchuck.

In return, the Milwaukee Road received permission from the Chehalis Western and the Skookum Chuck Railway, joint owners of the railroad from South Bay to MP 31, to operate its own power, crews, cars, and trains between the interchange at Skookumchuck and Mulqueen, located 3.2 miles south of Vail.

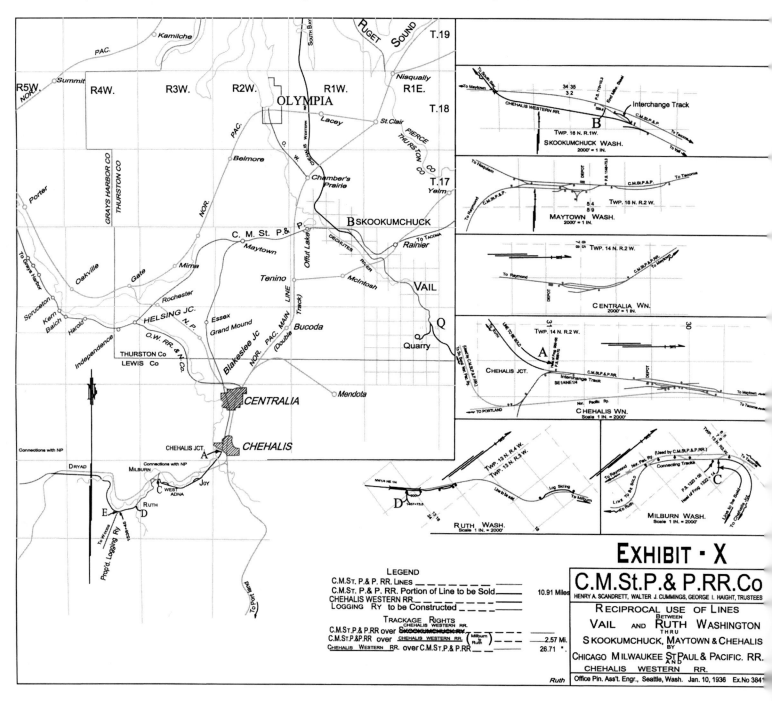

Exhibit X is a Milwaukee Road map from January 10, 1936 of proposed reciprocal use of lines by both the Milwaukee over Weyerhaeuser (Chehalis Western) track and by the Chehalis Western over Milwaukee Road track. This map accompanied the original contract agreement between the two railroads. —Original map Weyerhaeuser Archives, redrawn by Frank W. Telewski

Two 70-ton 3-truck Shays were used in the quarry to switch loaded and empty Milwaukee heavy-duty flatcars. The Shays brought the loads out beyond the quarry to a siding where they were picked up by Milwaukee Road locomotives. —George Hales, George Hales Family Collection

At this location, a spur would be built from the logging railroad main line to a proposed quarry on the northern side of the Skookumchuck River. Shipments by the Milwaukee Road over the joint Chehalis Western and Skookumchuck trackage was restricted to hauling rock from the proposed quarry and any material, supplies, and equipment necessary to construct and maintain the quarry tracks and facilities. Maximum speed was to be restricted to 40 mph, with locomotive weight not to exceed the weight of a Mallet-type Class N-2 locomotive. The Milwaukee Road would also secure permission to operate over the trackage sold to the Chehalis Western from Chehalis Junction to Ruth. Provisions in the agreement covered the eventual sale or abandonment of either parties' trackage. Either party was given first right of refusal to purchase the abandoned trackage from the other party.

Interest in the hard, dense granite in the rock outcrop above the Skookumchuck River south of Vail for jetty construction dates back to 1915, when the Hercules Sandstone Company of Tenino was awarded the contract for furnishing 200,000 tons of hard rock for the north jetty extension at Grays Harbor. The Hercules Company had been founded by Hans Peter Scheel in 1903, and it operated several quarries in and around Tenino. The bid for the jetty project required a harder rock than what Hercules quarried at the time. An outcrop of porphyritic granite, which met the contractual requirements for strength and density, was located on Weyerhaeuser property along the Skookumchuck River about 15 miles up the valley from Tenino. The Hercules Company obtained a 25-year lease and designated the new quarry No. 6.

The operation opened with the construction of a six-mile railroad extension from the Blumauer logging railroad. To accommodate the rock trains, part of the logging railroad was straightened out and

The quarry used a total of five large steam shovels to move and load rock blasted from the quarry's walls. Here two Bucyrus-Erie shovels move and load rocks.
—George Hales, George Hales Family Collection

heavier rails were laid. The Tacoma railroad construction firm of Dibble, Hawthorne & Moor contracted to renovate and build the new rail line. Equipment was transferred from Quarry No. 2 to the new Quarry No. 6. The quarry operated for three months until it was shut down at the start of World War I. The rails were lifted from the roadbed when the contract was cancelled. The idled No. 6 quarry could not pay for the investment made in opening the operation. This, combined with a tight wartime economy and delayed government payments for contract work, led to the failure of the Hercules Company in 1917.

Interest in the Skookumchuck porphyritic granite revived in 1932 when the U.S. government requested bids for supplying 750,000 tons of rock for the construction of a jetty at the mouth of the Columbia River. Kern Contracting Company had secured a majority interest in Quarry No. 6 and was interested in supplying the rock. Moving the rock required the relaying of track into the quarry, joining up this time with the Turvey Logging Company railroad.

The quarry wasn't opened for the Columbia River project, but a second chance arrived in 1935, when the Army Corps of Engineers recommend repair and enlargement of the Grays Harbor jetty. By this time, the Cascade Contracting Company and H. P. Scheel held options on the quarry property. However, when bidding opened, the Columbia Construction Company won the contract. Its anticipated source of rock was the quarry at Fisher's Landing on the Columbia River. The reason the Cascade Contracting Company's bid was beaten was explained in *The Thurston County Independent*: "The difficulty faced by contractors in using the local granite lay in the fact that the first contract was only for a small fraction, 80,000 tons of the total project. The cost of building a railroad connection would be about $50,000, which was too heavy an initial cost for that portion of the contract."

The Columbia Construction Company began to investigate the potential of using harder rock derived from the Tenino area by mid-1935: one consideration was a deposit north of Tenino owned by Graham and Medley Company; a second was a deposit just east of the No. 6 quarry, referred to as East Quarry and reportedly only a mile from Weyerhaeuser's logging railroad at Mulqueen. Weyerhaeuser owned the land. By September 6, Columbia Construction had decided to open up the new quarry east of the old Hercules Company Quarry No. 6, and announced its lease on the Weyerhaeuser Timber Company property.

THE GENESIS OF THE CHEHALIS WESTERN AND COLUMBIA CONSTRUCTION QUARRY   113

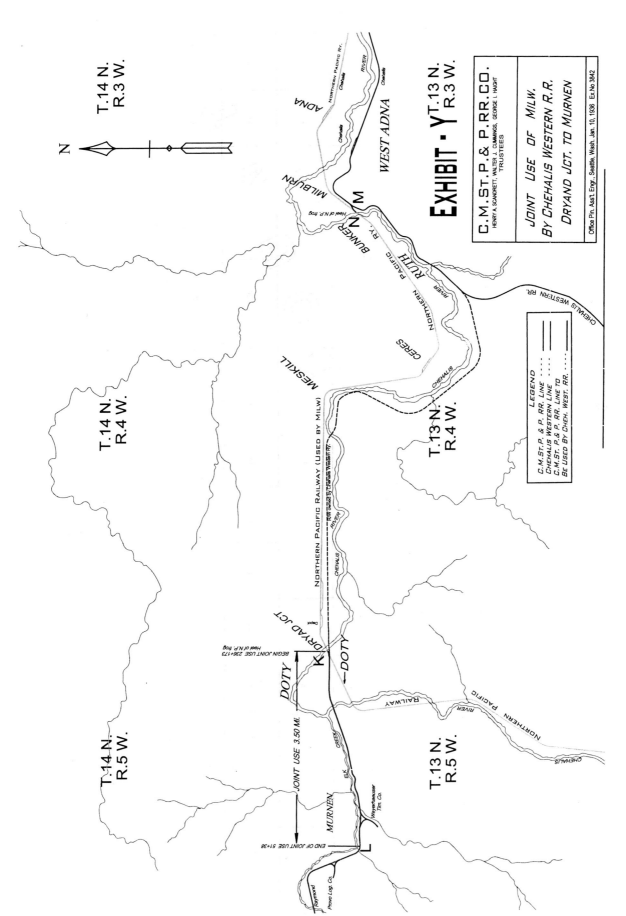

Exhibit Y also a Milwaukee Road map which accompanied the original contract agreement between the two railroads defines the Right-of-Way to be sold to the Chehalis Western and the location of the first Weyerhaeuser reload at Murnen, west of Doty. Access to Murnen also required the Chehalis Western acquired a running rights agreement with the Northern Pacific. —Original map Weyerhaeuser Archives, redrawn by Frank W. Telewski

Despite Columbia's announcement in September that the quarry would be opened in 30 days, poor weather and difficulty in laying out the railroad spur caused delays. Initial work on the railroad was reported to have begun on November 4 with the arrival of a steam shovel, gas donkey, and caterpillar tractor from one of Columbia's construction sites at Bonneville, Oregon. Work was halted a week later when construction was deemed impractical due to a sheer wall of granite between the quarry site and Mulqueen.

The 1.7-mile spur from Mulqueen to the quarry was redesigned on December 13, 1935, and construction was reinitiated on the same day. Workers blasted a ledge from a sloping bench on the cliff 350 feet above the river. They cleared rock using a 2.5-yard diesel shovel, building the grade into the quarry. The track was laid with 65-pound rail beginning on January 6, 1936. This length of track was known as the Skookum Chuck Rock Quarry Railroad.

The rock quarry was named the Columbia Construction Company Quarry and was also referred to as the Skookumchuck Quarry. It was owned and operated by Henry J. Kaiser. Kaiser hired George Hales, a former Weyerhaeuser employee at Vail, to supervise the quarry operation. Since the quarry was isolated with no road access, the only way in or out was via rail. Crews lived in five bunk houses, which had been built at Vail and moved by rail to the quarry campsite. The men were also fed in the cook house at the quarry.

Additional structures included a tool house, water tank, and powder house for storage of the 25-pound cans of explosives used to blast the rock. Equipment at the quarry included two 70-ton 3-truck shays (C/N 3108 and 3304—the 3108 was purchased from Merrill & Ring Lumber Company), which arrived in early January 1936; two 85B Bucyrus steam shovels; two 4141 Marion Steam shovels; one 490 Marion shovel; several tank cars for fuel and water; and flat cars for moving rail and ties within the quarry.

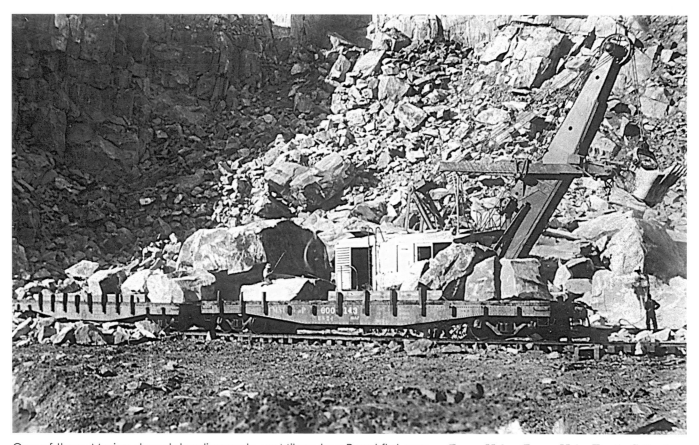

One of three Marion shovels loading rocks on Milwaukee Road flat cars. —George Hales, George Hales Family Collection

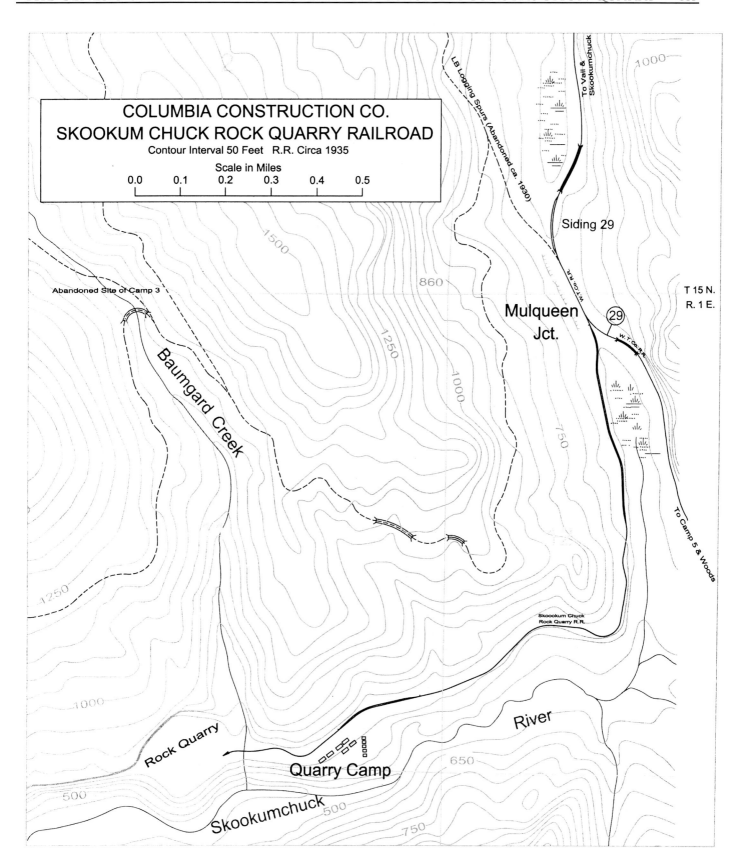

The keystone to the Milwaukee Roads agreement was access to the Skookum Chuck Rock Quarry. The original railroad was designed in 1935. Track layout within the quarry changed continously to meet the needs of the quarry operation. —USGS Topographic map, original blueprint of Skookum Chuck Rock Quarry RR, George Hales Family Collection, redrawn by Frank W. Telewski

In addition to moving rocks, the shovels also were used to move sections of track when a quarry spur needed to be relocated closer to ever receding rock wall. —George Hales, George Hales Family Collection

Heavy loads kept the section crew busy realigning track and repairing the tracks into the quarry. In the background are two tank cars, one Columbia Construction Company #970, near the quarry's office. —George Hales, George Hales Family Collection

THE GENESIS OF THE CHEHALIS WESTERN AND COLUMBIA CONSTRUCTION QUARRY 117

Individual rocks reached a weight of fifty tons each. These great weights quickly wore out the quarry tracks and derailments would occur. Here a flat car with a heavy load is on the ground at the entrance to the quarry.
—George Hales, George Hales Family Collection

The two Columbia Construction Company Shays were serviced at the Vail shops. The water used in the locomotives was extremely hard and rapidly formed scale in the boiler tubes. When the boilers were washed down, the crew would kill the fire, drain the boiler, and then take out the washout plugs and spray cold water on the hot tubes to crack the scale loose.

Rock was quarried by tunneling about 200 feet into the cliff and then setting off heavy explosive charges. The first rock train consisting of 40 cars was shipped from the quarry on the evening of March 17, 1936. Large rocks blasted from the cliffs above the Skookumchuck River were transported by flat car to build the Westport north and south jetties at Grays Harbor and Ilwaco on the Columbia River. Work began on the south jetty at Westport in the spring of 1936. At the peak of construction from 1936 to 1942, between 42 and 54 carloads of rock were shipped daily to Grays Harbor and the Columbia River. The quarry operated 24 hours a day with three crew shifts. Carloads weighed as much as 90 tons early in the operation but were reduced to about 60 tons each to reduce wear and tear on the tracks and ties. The rocks reached a weight of 50 tons each. Flat car traffic from the quarry during the first year (1936) totaled 5,896 loads and increased to 9,758 in 1937, 13,188 in 1938, and a peak of 15,360 in 1939. No traffic was recorded in 1940, but traffic resumed in 1941, with 8,805 loads and 2,690 loads in 1942 shipped to the north jetty project at Grays Harbor.

The wear and tear of transporting heavy loads took its toll on the trackage. Once, near the end of operations at the quarry, the 65-pound rail was so worn that it kept cracking under the weight of a Milwaukee Road N-2 Mallet attempting to leave the quarry with a string of loaded flat cars. The locomotive was only 140 feet from Mulqueen

Perspective! The large rocks used in breakwater construction could weigh up to 50 tons. Here two workers are dwarfed by the large rocks and even larger machinery required to move them. —George Hales, George Hales Family Collection

Milwaukee Road Consolidation #7241 waits at Vail before leaving for the Skookumchuck Quarry spur at Mulqueen in 1936. The largest locomotives to travel to the quarry for rock train service were Milwaukee class N-2 Mallets. —Al Farrow, Martin E. Hansen Collection

The Skookumchuck Quarry was busy supplying stone for the north jetty of the Columbia River when this photo was taken in 1939. Vail's #99 rests behind a Milwaukee wood caboose which is tied on to a Milwaukee locomotive. The appearance of Milwaukee Road locomotives and cabooses at Vail was not uncommon during this period.
—Harold A. Hill, Martin E. Hansen Collection

Milwaukee Road Mallet #52 rests in Tacoma in 1952. —Bob Lorenz

Junction when it derailed. Once on the heavier rail of the logging main, the locomotive was able to return to the Milwaukee Road main line.

In February 1938, Columbia Construction received a contract to build a north jetty on the Columbia River, which ensured work at the quarry. But operations were soon curtailed in May when the wood barge and 18 rock cars carrying about 2 million pounds of rock sank at Hoquiam in 30 feet of water. The rock was unloaded and the barge was raised and shipped to Tacoma for repairs. With repairs completed, the barge was placed back in service. Another contract was awarded for work on the north jetty at Westport in June 1939, while work on the south jetty and on the Columbia River was completed in December 1939. The north jetty contract allowed the quarry to continue operating until 1942, when it shut down for several years.

On August 13, 1942, one Shay (C/N 3304) was transferred from Vail to Declezville, California, and the second Shay (C/N 3108) was left at the quarry with the bell, headlight, and other appliances welded inside the cab. When the quarry started up again in 1948, the cab was cut open and the fixtures put back on the locomotive. On February 17, the remaining Shay was transferred to Consolidated Builders, Inc., of Tenino, an affiliate of Columbia Construction that began to operate the reopened quarry. With the beginning of construction work on the Ilwaco breakwater at the mouth of the Columbia River in 1948, the quarry was once again open for business and shipped a total of 489 loads before closing to rail shipments again for the last time. The rock trains would travel on the Milwaukee Road south to Longview, where the rocks were then loaded on barges for movement to the construction site.

The two Shays would arrange loads and empties at the quarry, while the Milwaukee Road power would travel up the Skookum Chuck Rock Quarry spur, dropping off empties and returning with loaded flat cars. The Milwaukee crews pulled their empty flat cars into the north quarry siding. The mallets could not proceed beyond the north quarry siding due to the sharp curves of the quarry track. After setting out the empties, the Milwaukee crew would run back to Vail where they turned the locomotive on the wye and tied up for the night. The appearance of a Milwaukee Road caboose and engine in the Vail yards was not uncommon when the quarry was open.

A board system was used to dispatch trains at Mulqueen. When the train left the yards at the quarry, the crew would line the board back behind the train and no one else could go by it until it was lined back. Milwaukee Road rock trains were required to secure clearance from the Vail dispatcher before proceeding on the logging main line and could not use siding 29.

The original contractual agreement between the Chehalis Western and the Milwaukee Road was specified to last 50 years, until May 7, 1986. In fulfillment of this contract, the rail from Mulqueen Junction to the Skookumchuck quarry remained on the ground until the late 1970s, even though the Vail logging main line was removed in the early 1950s. If rail access was required to the quarry, the relaying of a short length of track would have been necessary to rejoin the Skookum Chuck Quarry Railroad with the Weyerhaeuser reload spur (Branch 6), located a mile north of the old Mulqueen Junction. However, the contract would never see the expiration date, because the Milwaukee Road abandoned its western lines, including the fourth subdivision of the Pacific Division, from Chehalis to Tacoma, in 1980. This led to a rebirth of the Chehalis Western the same year. Previously, the Chehalis Western had been relegated to a paper railroad in the late 1970s when Weyerhaeuser incorporated the Curtis, Milburn & Eastern Railway in the summer of 1975.

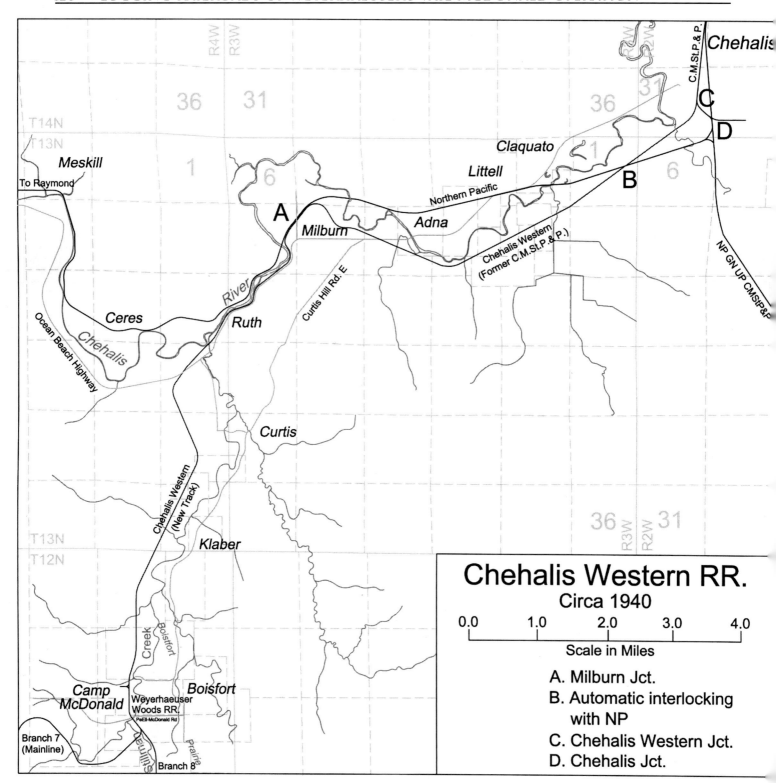

Map of Chehalis Western RR, Chehalis to Camp McDonald. The track from Chehalis to a point just beyond Ruth was originally part of the Milwaukee Road. Beyond Ruth to Camp McDonald, the Chehalis Western built a new rail line. —USGS Aerial Photo, USGS Topographic Map, Weyerhaeuser Archives, Drawn by Frank W. Telewski

CHAPTER 6

The Chehalis Western and Camp McDonald: 1937-1945

Shortly after its founding on February 28, 1936, the fledgling Chehalis Western Railroad began to replace ballast and ties on the 10 miles of acquired Milwaukee Road track, from Chehalis Junction to Ruth, Washington (which is near Curtis, Washington). The Chehalis Western also commenced building 0.61 miles of connecting track, linking the Milwaukee Road to the Vail main line (Western Junction), and secured the right-of-way for an additional five miles of track heading south-southwest of Ruth up Boisfort Valley to the site of its new headquarters, Camp McDonald, located south of Klaber. In early 1937, construction of the new line south of Ruth was initiated, and the railroad was granted the right to cross four Lewis County roads on its way toward the woods. By the fall of 1938, the five miles of track from Ruth to Camp McDonald was laid, and an additional 20 miles of logging railroad south of Camp McDonald had been graded.

Chehalis Western #211, ex-Atlanta, Birmingham & Coast #211 poses for a portrait in the Vail yard after being painted and lettered for its new owner in Vail's shops. —Weyerhaeuser Archives

Chehalis Western #211, ex-Atlanta, Birmingham & Coast #211 poses for a portrait in the Vail yard after being painted and lettered for its new owner in Vail's shops. —Weyerhaeuser Archives

Construction of the rail lines was similar to that at Vail. Strong & McDonald of Tacoma graded the right-of-way using Northwest shovels with fast Dumptor trucks, Caterpillar tractors, and Le Tourneau bulldozers. Most of the grade work was in dirt, but there were a number of rock cuts and some deep earth cuts that meant moving large volumes of soil. The final step was laying a sub-surface of rock for each line of track. This was spread by means of a log frame similar to a loading boom, in which plank fins were inserted to evenly spread the rock. Dumptors poured rock into the front section, as a tractor pulled the rig along.

Weyerhaeuser laid the steel under the direction of William Ehrengart, who had come down from Vail to supervise the work. Ties for the new line were cut at Frank Lambertson's tie mill located at Vail and were hauled over the Milwaukee tracks to Ruth for railroad construction. Later, when the McDonald woods track was constructed far enough into the timber, Mr. Lambertson established a tie mill off one of the woods lines. There were 60-, 68- and 72- pound rails was used in various parts of the system. Construction crews used a Shay on loan from Weyerhaeuser's Willapa Harbor Lumber Mills in September and October 1938 to build Camp McDonald.

Before any loads could be shipped over the new railroad, the Chehalis Western needed to secure equipment to operate. To this end, the first order of business in early 1938 was the acquisition of locomotives. At first, Weyerhaeuser weighed the cost benefit of purchasing new versus used locomotives and contacted Baldwin Locomotive Works to address the needs of the Chehalis Western. By February, the company decided on used locomotives and entered into negotiations with the Union Pacific to purchase two older Mikado locomotives, #2106 and #2110, stored in Oregon, from their subsidiary, Oregon-Washington Railway and Navigation Company.

After an initial inspection of both locomotives, Weyerhaeuser's civil engineer Walter Ryan decided only the #2110 was in good enough condition to restore to operation under Interstate Commerce Commission (ICC) rules and offered the Union Pacific $5,000 for the locomotive delivered to Chehalis or Tenino, Washington. By May 10, in a memo to Minot Davis, Ryan presented a formal offer from the Union Pacific to deliver the locomotive in "operating condition" around October 1, for the sum of $10,000. Ronald McDonald approved the memo.

Chehalis Western #215, ex-Atlanta, Birmingham & Coast #215 rests in the Vail yard after being painted and lettered for its new owner in Vail's shops. —Harold A. Hill, Martin E. Hansen Collection

THE CHEHALIS WESTERN AND CAMP MCDONALD: 1937-1945

Left: Train dispatcher at his board at Camp McDonald.
—Weyerhaeuser Archives

Below: Dispatcher's Chart—by which all movement of trains is controlled at Camp McDonald. Represented on this 28x72-inch chart is the completed railroad system of 35 miles of mainline and spurs. This map shows the original track plan; Camp 7 and its additional trackage are not depicted here.
—Scott Barrett Collection

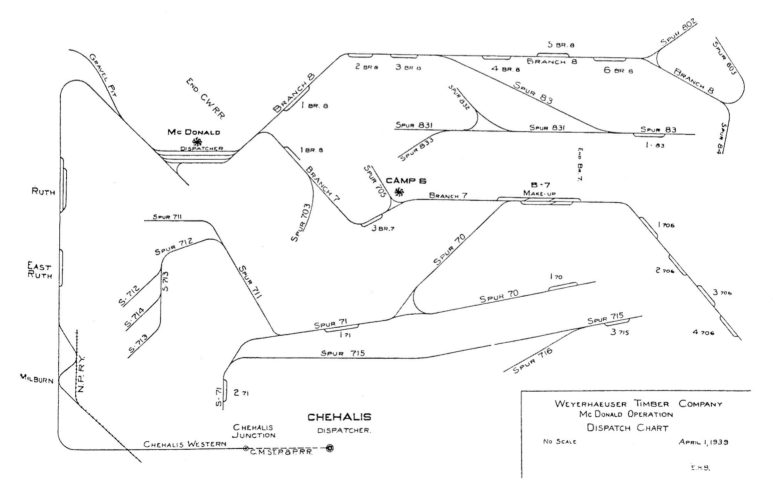

Weyerhaeuser had hired H. A. Gibson of Gibson Manufacturing in Seattle to conduct a complete inspection of the locomotive. His report was filed on October 27: "My conclusion is that this equipment was in good mechanical condition when it was taken out of service in 1931. All inspection dates have of course been outlawed. This means that it would be necessary to put in new flues, inspect all stay bolts (and install a lot of new ones), remove the jacket and inspect wrapper sheets. The present jacket probably should be replaced by a new one. Tires are now less than 2 inches thick, and need turning. I do not think this would be justified, as they are too close to the limit. The present cab is in very bad shape, and would have to be replaced." This is the last correspondence on record regarding this locomotive, and it is not known if the Chehalis Western ever took delivery of the engine.

Because the Chehalis Western needed two locomotives, and the Union Pacific's second Mikado was ruled out early in 1938, Walter Ryan asked Ronald McDonald if he would consider a Northern Pacific compound mallet being offered by Johnson Ropes, Inc., as a substitute or addition for the sum of $12,500. It appears that both the Union Pacific and Northern Pacific locomotives were rejected, given that the Chehalis Western purchased two ex-Atlanta, Birmingham & Coast Railroad Mikados, #211 (c/n 41739) and #215 (c/n 41743), from the Georgia Car & Locomotive Company in Atlanta, Georgia, in November 1938. The engines were converted to oil and shipped to Vail,

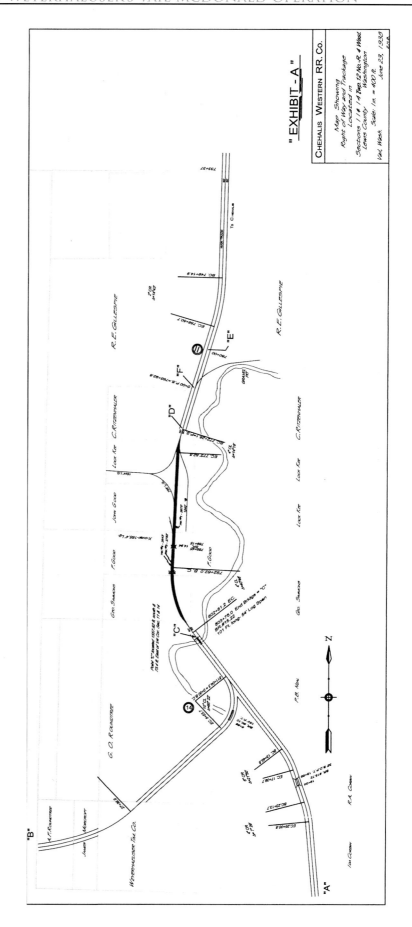

Exhibit A shows the initial track layout for Camp McDonald. This map only shows the mainline and three yard tracks, the wye and the two branches, Branch 7 (B) and 8 (A) which ran into the woods. The ballast gravel pit was located just north of Camp McDonald along the bank of Stillman Creek. Half of the track at Camp McDonald was owned by the Weyerhaeuser woods railroad and all of the track south of the yard switch was the property of the woods railroad. —Weyerhaeuser Archives, redrawn by Frank W. Telewski

where they were painted and lettered for the Chehalis Western, tested, and ICC-certified. "Dog houses" and steam-driven water pumps and hoses were also added to the tenders. ICC certification approved the engines to run over the Milwaukee trackage from Western Junction to Chehalis Junction to begin service on the Chehalis Western.

In November 1938, just as the operation was about to start up, the entire future of the Chehalis Western and the plan to supply logs to Everett from Camp McDonald was put on hold. The Railroad Brotherhoods had challenged the agreement between the Milwaukee and Chehalis Western to allow Chehalis Western crews to operate trains over Milwaukee trackage. The chairmen of all four Brotherhoods had joined in a written protest to the Milwaukee's general manager, calling attention to three awards of the National Railroad Adjustment Board, "which sustain the position of the employees to protests of bona fide railroads entering into trackage agreements with logging companies." After numerous conferences with the Brotherhoods and a letter from J. P. Weyerhaeuser Jr., explaining the numerous advantages of the agreement to the Milwaukee and its employees, the Milwaukee was finally able to obtain the Brotherhoods' acceptance in the implementation of the joint trackage agreement.

With the joint agreement intact and the acquisition of the two locomotives in November, the Chehalis Western moved forward in January 1939 with the purchase of 50 44-foot skeleton log cars (#801-850) with 41-inch wide sills and safety appliances (including steps), plus a 30-foot combination baggage car and caboose (Skagit type, #800) from Pacific Car & Foundry in April. A second caboose (#711) was also purchased. An additional order of 96 rebuilt 44-foot skeleton cars (#851-946) was placed with Pacific Car & Foundry on May 11, 1939. ICC regulation required that Chehalis Western log cars be equipped with steps and other safety appliances, unlike the Vail log cars, which did not run over any common carrier track.

This is a later photo of #211, taken in June 1948. Shortly after being repainted, both Chehalis Western engines were fitted with dog houses on the tender. The dog house protected the brakeman from inclement weather on the long runs from Camp McDonald to South Bay. Notice the headlight has been moved from the top of the smoke box to the front of the smoke box to conform with Milwaukee Road standard practices. —Al Farrow, John T. Labbe Collection

With new equipment on hand and ICC certification intact, the Chehalis Western shipped its first trainload of logs from Camp McDonald to South Bay on April 27, 1939.

The arrival of new motive power for the Chehalis Western meant modifications were required at the South Bay log dump. The original (lower) wye was too tight to turn the larger Chehalis Western Mikados. This required the construction of a second (upper) wye in 1938, which was located above the Woodward Bay bridge with a larger radius curve. Since there wasn't sufficient space for the tail track of the upper wye, a small trestle was built into Woodward Bay to support the rail. Chehalis Western main line locomotives, the #211, #215, and the #120 after 1940, would dump a train of logs into Puget Sound near Olympia, Washington, and return to headquarters camp with the same string of empty cars. The ICC inspected all of the Chehalis Western main line locomotives before they could run over the Milwaukee and Northern Pacific track, and they had to be maintained to ICC standards. Even though the three main line locomotives were dedicated to long haul runs, the #120 would occasionally be sent into the woods

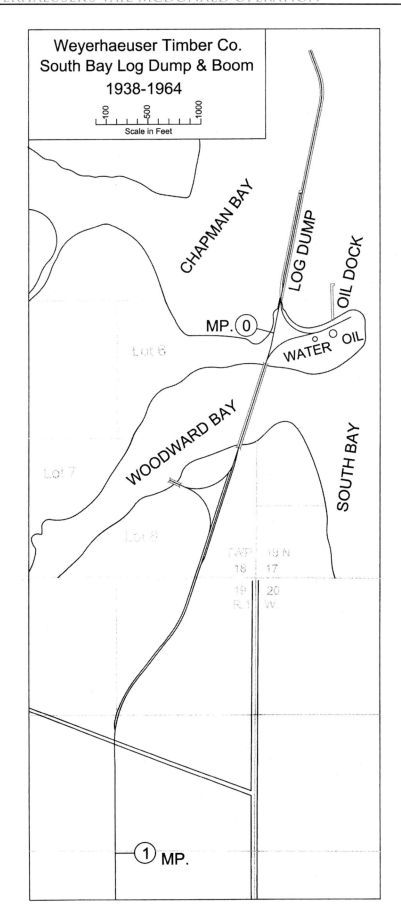

Right: The acquisition of Weyerhaeuser #120 and Chehalis Western #211 and #215 in 1938, larger locomotives than those previously operated to South Bay, required the construction of a larger wye for turning the locomotives. This resulted in the construction of the upper wye and an alteration of the track layout at the bay. — Weyerhaeuser Archives, redrawn by Frank W. Telewski

Pacific Car & Foundry delivered thirty foot combination baggage car and caboose (Skagit type) # 800 to the Chehalis Western in April 1939. —PC&F Builders Photo, PACCAR Inc. John Henderson Collection

This end view of PC&F Chehalis Western #877 provides an excellent look at the details of the Seattle bunk, end steps and brake. The wood sill between the bunks was painted yellow with black safety stripes. —PC&F Builders Photo, PACCAR Inc. John Henderson Collection

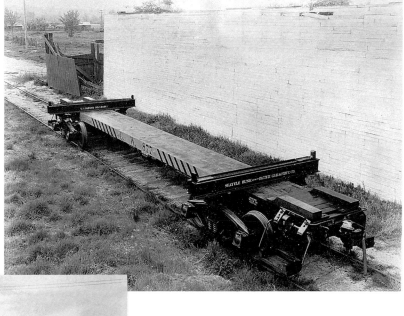

Pacific Car & Foundry also supplied the Chehalis Western with heavy duty wood skeleton cars equipped with safety appliances which permitted the cars to be run on interstate common carrier railroads, the Milwaukee and the Northern Pacific.

—PC&F Builders Photo, PACCAR Inc. John Henderson Collection

Chehalis Western caboose #711 is similar to Weyerhaeuser's #712. Here the #711 brings up the rear of a loaded train heading north out of Camp McDonald on July 22, 1954. Weyerhaeuser and Chehalis Western cabooses were painted yellow rather than red after the late 1940's. An aging Weyerhaeuser four-wheel bobber caboose rests on a siding just beyond #711. —John T. Labbe

with empty log flats if the woods were running short on log cars.

The Chehalis Western Railroad officially terminated at Camp McDonald, and the Weyerhaeuser woods railroad, owner and operator of the tracks south of Vail, ran the logging lines south of Camp McDonald. The tracks at Camp McDonald were jointly owned by the Chehalis Western and Weyerhaeuser woods railroad. Loads would be brought down from the woods to a jointly owned yard at Camp McDonald, where the Chehalis Western would make up the trains for movement to South Bay. The yard had four tracks, some 3,000 feet long to handle the exchange of loads and empty log flats. The number of loads arriving from the woods operations varied. A woods locomotive might bring in 10, 18, 25, or as many as 47 loads to headquarters. The only constant operational maxim for logging trains practiced at Camp McDonald, as well as at Vail, was to keep the cars moving. Weyerhaeuser also had a car shop to maintain the Chehalis Western log cars and other railroad and woods equipment. Although there was a locomotive shop at Camp McDonald, major locomotive overhauls were done at the Vail shops.

Headquarters Camp was built on an old farm site, and was designed to accommodate the approximately 80 men required to run the camp. By spring 1939, the construction of Camp McDonald was nearing completion. Shop and maintenance men, office staff, plus cooks, flunkies, and so on lived and worked at this camp. The original farmhouse was remodeled and used by the timekeeper as living quarters. The camp was composed of nine major buildings: round house (140×40 feet), shop building (unknown), office (32×68 feet), cook house (26×60 feet, with a 24×30-foot wing), recreation room (30×30 feet), warehouse (unknown), three garages of 20 autos each (18×200 feet), bunk houses (18 housing eight men each), and a hotel (unknown).

The camp also included various smaller support buildings, such as the sand house, gas shop, fire equipment storage, and filing house. Although contractors constructed the camp buildings, the lumber was purchased from Weyerhaeuser's mill at Everett. Bunk houses and cook houses were built along the same lines as those at Vail.

THE CHEHALIS WESTERN AND CAMP MCDONALD: 1937-1945 129

The camp had a commissary, similar to the one at Vail, where workers could buy gloves, shirts, and pants and order work shoes, including caulk boots. The largest town near camp was Chehalis, Washington, and several smaller communities like Boisfort, Pe Ell, and Adna were located nearby. All of the smaller towns had schools, post offices, and small shops, and Weyerhaeuser played a big role in community life by providing many sustainable local jobs.

Workers could commute to Camp McDonald, unless they were assigned to one of the outlying camps. McDonald was connected to the outside world by telephone and, of course, the railroad right-of-way was connected to the train dispatcher by telephone, where trains could receive their clearance at telephone booths located at strategic spots.

The initial plan called for some 25 miles of track to be laid in the woods, plus the construction of Camp 6, the first of two logging camps at McDonald. The Vail operation, a physically separate yet co-managed venture, already had five logging camps, hence the number 6 designation. The manager for the entire Vail-McDonald operation was Ronald McDonald. Camp 6 had 25 eight-man bunk houses, a cook house, a warehouse, and a filing shack, plus water and oil for locomotives. The camp was located approximately seven miles southwest of Headquarters Camp on the woods mainline (also known as Branch 7 or 70 Line) and was built roughly at the same time (1938–39) as Headquarters Camp so that logging could commence immediately. To accomplish this, rail had been laid to the campsite at the same time the Chehalis Western was built. The woods main line headed west across Stillman Creek and up toward Baw Faw Peak. As the McDonald operation grew, grades for the logging railroad were constructed by Strong & MacDonald, con-

Chehalis Western #215 delivers a load of logs from Camp McDonald at South Bay. At the time this photo was taken, a doghouse had been added to #215's tender. —Weyerhaeuser Archives

Weyerhaeuser Timber Company #120 from Vail was relettered for the Chehalis Western and transferred to Camp McDonald in the early 1940s. Here the locomotive hauls a string of loads through Chehalis, Washington on June 30, 1948. —Al Farrow, Martin E. Hansen Collection

tractors from Tacoma who worked with Hart Construction and another contractor by the name of McClean to build new trestles and repair the former Milwaukee trestles. Weyerhaeuser crews laid rail and ballast using rock from a gravel pit just north of Camp McDonald. This pit was abandoned in 1942.

At Camp 6, the rail line was designated the 70 Line and split into a series of logging spurs. Spurs off the 70 Line were identified as 703, 705, and 706. The 70 Line also gave rise to the 71 Line and its series of logging spurs. These spurs and lines logged the western slopes of the Stillman Creek watershed.

The first woods locomotive used at Camp McDonald was the 1 spot (transferred from Vail) and a small 2-truck Shay used for hauling construction materials and later used for the steel gang at Camp McDonald. The steel gang worked at both Vail and McDonald. As steel was pulled from the Vail Line, the company kept some of the better heavier steel such as the 68- and 70-pound rail for use at McDonald and scrapped the worn-out steel. Steel lifted from the spurs at McDonald, which had completed logging, was relaid on new lines or scrapped if the rail was worn out. In 1941, spur 703 became one of the first to be removed once logging along the line was completed. In 1943, the steel was lifted on the 706, 832, 831, 843, and 842 spurs and laid on the 85, 88, and 71 Lines and on spurs 852 and 833. The 71 Line was the last track laid at Camp McDonald. Not all of the railroad grades constructed at McDonald had rails laid on them for use by the railroad operation. Most of the unused grades were turned into logging truck roads in later years.

The next locomotives to arrive from Vail were the #100 and #105. These were later joined by the 2-spot, a 2-truck Shay used to switch sides, along with the mallets, the #112, and the #114. The #110 came down later when Vail ended its woods railroad operation after World War II. Crews working on woods trains were called early in the morning and often worked long hours. Locomotives would be kept out in the woods at both camps, and each camp had a place for sand and a place to take oil. It was not uncommon, however, to have the mallets tie up at Camp McDonald every night. On the weekends during fire season, each camp had a steam locomotive coupled to a water car ready to roll in case of alarm.

Photographed at Camp McDonald in the mid 1940s Chehalis Western #215 has had its headlight moved from the top of the smoke box to the front of the smoke box. —Weyerhaeuser Archives

The older Pacific Car & Foundry 42-foot skeleton cars used at Vail needed to be rebuilt to 44-foot with the addition of safety appliances before being transferred to Camp McDonald, so they could operate over Milwaukee Road and Northern Pacific track in Chehalis Western trains. This included the addition of end steps and hand grabs. The Vail shops made the modifications beginning in 1939 using sill timbers from Everett. With the expansion at Camp McDonald, Weyerhaeuser also purchased five interurban cars, one from the Puget Sound Electric Railway and four from Pacific Northwest Traction Company, for moving crews back and forth between the camps and sides.

In 1942, Weyerhaeuser decided to relieve train crews of hauling loggers to and from the woods in the old wood and steel interurban cars and purchased heavy-duty Gibson speeders coupled with a trailer. These speeders were equipped with air brakes and sanders and even had their own frogs for speeder derailments, and were capable of handling grades up to four and six percent. During World War II, a Gibson speeder even ran workers from Chehalis to Camp McDonald to help relieve the labor shortage. Speeder operators also hauled supplies and mail after carrying the crew in the morning.

In the early summer of 1940, the fire season struck early and hard just as it did at the Vail side of operations. The humidity at Vail was recorded at dangerously low levels from June 24 to July 4, and fires began to appear throughout the woods. Fortunately for Vail, most of the fires were relatively small and losses were minimum. This would not be true for Camp McDonald.

On June 11 at 2 P.M., a fire started in the NW¼ of Section 5, Township 11N, Range 4W, apparently caused by friction of a line in the tail block of skidder #2. The fire started shortly after the crew had left the landing for the day, but was discovered immediately by Mr. Murphy, the watchman at the landing. After emptying his portable pump and water can without being able to extinguish the fire, Murphy returned to the landing for more water. Upon his return, the fire was beyond his control. After a call for assistance, the crew returned immediately from the next landing and built a trail around the fire. By the next morning, Strong and MacDonald had committed three bulldozers to building firebreaks. Crews controlled the fire by June 13, and logging resumed on June 14 with a high lead side and skidder #6. Skidder #2 resumed logging on June 27 on the side where the fire occurred. The fire had burned over 65 acres of felled and bucked timber, 13½ acres of standing timber, and nine acres of slash. Two cold decks containing 1½ million feet of

Looking north into Camp McDonald. Buildings from left to right include: two residences, cook house, storage building, machine shop, warehouse, office, the end of a garage.

—Ted Ward

logs were entirely consumed. The cold deck yarders, one steam and one diesel, at these landings were both damaged by the fire and sent to the shop for repairs. But the worst was yet to come.

On June 29, the Camp McDonald Branch experienced a devastating fire in the Stillman Creek drainage. It all started shortly after the logging crews had finished work on Friday, June 28, and the camps were closed for the July 4 holiday. The fire broke out near the center of Section 4, Township 11N, Range 4W late on the night of Saturday, June 29. Bob Roland of the Washington Forest Fire Association and Davis Morgan, a Weyerhaeuser patrolman, discovered the fire. Both men were watching the fire lines of the June 11 fire, which had been completely extinguished and showed no signs of activity for several days. They reported the fire to Jack Collins at Camp 6, who in turn called Ed Amundsen at headquarters at 12:30 A.M. on June 30. In response, Mr. Amundsen dispatched a locomotive with three tank cars and a crew of 20 men to the fire a little after 1:00 A.M. The foreman for Strong and MacDonald, Neal Miller, heard the alarm and took some of his crew to their camp in Section 8. The lookout on Baw Faw Peak reported the fire to Mr. Panush in the Chehalis office of the Washington Forest Fire Association. He ordered two portable pumps and auxiliary equipment to fight the fire. By dawn, over 50 men were fighting the blaze.

Later when the fire threatened the ranches in the valley, the state furnished 25 CCC boys from Camp Doty, and the Association dispatched its special fire truck from Seattle to patrol the roads and extinguish any spot fires that developed from sparks. Early Sunday morning, both Ronald McDonald and A. S.

A loaded train of logs from the woods has just arrived at Camp McDonald. Looking at Camp McDonald from the Southeast, beyond the string of log cars one can see, from left to right, roof of the car garage, old farmhouse residence, cook house, office building and machine shops. The photographer was standing on top of a caboose (notice the cupola in the lower right hand corner). —Weyerhaeuser Archives

The south end of the three-stall machine shop at Camp McDonald. —Ted Ward

MacDonald were at the fire, along with a crew from Long-Bell. The pile driver being used in construction of a rail line in the path of the fire was loaded onto a moving car, and the contractor moved his powder out of what he thought was the danger zone. However, on Monday, the fire had spread rapidly and caught the pile driver and powder. Late on July 1, the fire was almost completely surrounded by a fire break, but the winds shifted from the southwest to the northwest and pushed the fire into the crowns of the trees, where it spread very rapidly during the afternoon and evening. The humidity at that time was reported at 22 percent with a strong wind.

The fire crew from the Strong and MacDonald camp on the 84 Line to the south of the fire were practically cut off from help and were forced to retreat to the Long-Bell's operation in Section 20, where they secured assistance in the form of 13 men and two additional pumps. Three Strong and MacDonald bulldozers were used in continuous operation until wide trails were built around the entire fire.

The fire blew up a second time on the 3rd of July when a strong wind from the northwest drove it into the Long-Bell operations in Section 12, Township 11N, Range 4W. Mr. Cowan of the Washington Forest Fire Association established a fire camp with a crew of 60 men in Section 12 in the Long-Bell timber near spur 540. The fire was finally contained but wasn't completely extinguished until August. The cause of this fire has remained a mystery.

A total of 10,000-plus acres were contained within the fire lines. About 200 acres were felled and bucked timber, and 2,500 acres of green timber were killed by the crown fire. The remaining acreage contained slashings, or green timber, in which the fire remained on the ground and caused relatively little damage. Company officials estimated a total of 15 million feet of felled and bucked timber was lost in the fire. Damaged equipment included 20 rail cars (including skeleton log cars and a moving car), two yarders and two loaders, one pile driver, $10,000 worth of wire rope, $10,000 in damage to the railroad (including culverts, rail, and ties), and $10,500 in damage to bridges and trestles.

In the aftermath of the 1940 fires, the company determined that a new camp was needed to bring the crews closer to the burned timber. To access the burned timber, McDonald ordered the construction of railroad Branch 8 (or the 80 Line), which extended up the east side of Stillman Creek and gave rise to several logging branches (81, 82, 83, etc.) and their respective logging spurs (812, 813, 821, 822, etc.). Camp 7, nearly a carbon copy of Camp 6 except for some differences in layout, was built in late 1940 and early 1941 on the 84 Line. Logging of fire-killed timber began in the spring of 1941. As the lines along Branch 8 developed, eventually two of the spurs would link up with Branch 7, creating a large loop in the woods. Spur 837 off the 83 Line linked up with Branch 7 at Camp 6 via a series of switchbacks, and the 84 Line merged with the 715 spur south of Baw Faw Peak. The connection via spur 837 was lost in 1943 when rails were lifted from spur 831, which linked the 83 Line to spur 837.

Both camps were used simultaneously for logging operations. Camps 6 and 7 both had a skidder and highlead sides, and sometimes both camps had two skidders and a highlead, for a total of six sides working in the McDonald woods at the height of logging railroad production. A good crew and a good show could get out 20 loads a day, and if you had a really good show, a crew would load out 30 loads a day.

Camp McDonald's cookhouse looking to the southwest. —Ted Ward

The hotel at Camp McDonald provided rooming for workers and guests. In the foreground to the right is the end of a 10' x 20' eight-man bunkhouse, one of eighteen at Camp McDonald. —Ted Ward

Newly constructed camp bunk houses at Camp McDonald. —*The Timberman*

An interesting piece of railroad track located just south of Camp 7 was a loop track rather than a regular siding layout, situated on a mountaintop directly above the camp. This short section of track was called the 873 Line. Jim Barrett, retired Chehalis Western locomotive engineer, remembers switching this loop with the 2 spot and hauling the crew to and from the logging site. The train crew would shove 10 empties into one end of the loop, go back and get 10 loads off the other end of the loop, and then head to a small make-up yard down at the bottom of the hill. The yarding machine that logged this mountain had a spot line to move the empty cars into position for loading.

In 1941, the United States entered World War II, which had as much impact on Weyerhaeuser as it did on the rest of the country. Like every place in the country, Vail and Camp McDonald were short-handed, and a person could end up working in a variety of jobs. It was not uncommon to work on a skidder one day, on a highlead the next day, on second loading the next, or on the locomotive crane, which often loaded logs in the woods. McDonald had two locomotive cranes: one was a gas-powered machine, and the other was a steam-powered machine that came from Weyerhaeuser's Clemons operation.

A view of Camp McDonald looking south toward BawFaw Peak. The track in the foreground will continue north to the three-stall machine shop. On the right of the track are a warehouse and the office, to the left are two storage buildings, probably former camp buildings. The track continues south until it joins the yard tracks at Camp McDonald. A string of Rogers ballast cars and a string of loaded Chehalis Western skeleton log cars are spotted in the yard.

—Ted Ward

Camp McDonald's office was also the home for the dispatcher who controlled the traffic along both the woods railroad lines above Camp McDonald and on the Chehalis Western. —Weyerhaeuser Archives

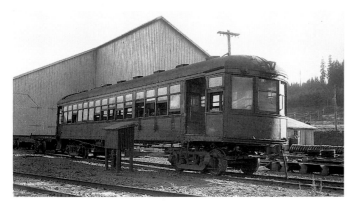

Unlike crew cars #1 and #2 which were made of wood, crew car # 76 had a steel body. Here the car rests just north of the three-stall machine shop in 1939. All three crew cars were owned by Weyerhaeuser Timber Company and not the Chehalis Western. This was true of half the track at Camp McDonald and all of the woods trackage.
—Harold A. Hill, Martin E. Hansen Collection

Just like at the operation at Vail, Weyerhaeuser used ex-interurban railway cars to ferry crews from Camp McDonald Headquarters camp to Camps 6 and 7 in the woods. Weyerhaeuser #1 and #2, ex-NCL wait outside the engine house at Camp McDonald in 1939. —Harold A. Hill, Martin E. Hansen Collection

When a locomotive crane was assigned to load logs out in the woods, the crew did not always have siding tracks to move cars around into position for loading. The crane would just move cars around them by placing a strap through the arch bars of the logging car truck, setting one end of the log car out in the brush, and then repeating the same motion on the other end of the car. The crane would motor past the empty, which would then be sitting in the weeds, and place it back on the track. After re-railing the empty log car, the crew would carefully check the brass and wedge on each wheel to make sure the car didn't have a hot box on its trip to South Bay. After the crane loaded the log car, the load would be pushed down to a derail since the crane was usually working on a steep grade and was tied down with a hand brake. The crane crew would repeat the process all over again with the next car. A woods locomotive would keep the crane supplied with empties and swing the loads to a marshaling point for the trip into Camp McDonald.

Beginning as early as 1940, the Weyerhaeuser Timber Company and Chehalis Western Railroad began negotiations with both the Northern Pacific Railway Company and Milwaukee to gain access to their holdings near Doty in western Lewis County. On December 9, 1943, the Chehalis Western and Northern Pacific entered into an agreement granting the Chehalis Western running rights as a common carrier with its own power and crews, cars, and trains, on the 21st subdivision (Willapa Harbor Line) between Milburn and Dryad Junction, a dis-

The Weyerhaeuser Sales Company featured McDonald operation's Camp 6 in their ad which appeared in *Weyerhaeuser News*.

This montague of images provides a good overview of railroad construction activities at Camp McDonald. 1. Mess hall (left) and Hotel (right), 2. Office and dispatcher's office, 3. A new filer's shack with filing rooms on either end and living quarters in the middle, 4. New trestle construction in the woods, 5. Bulldozer grading a new roadbed, 6. Building the railroad grade with dumptor trucks, 7. Finished grade with ballast ready for ties and rails, 8 & 9 Laying the subsurface with rock using a log boom and wood plank fins for ditching.
—*The West Coast Timberman*

tance of 10.3 miles. The terms of the agreement were similar to those outlined in the May 6, 1936, agreement with the Milwaukee. This agreement was more restrictive, limiting traffic to "the transportation, as a common carrier, of logs, log empties, supplies and equipment of the Weyerhaeuser Timber Company that are usually handled on logging trains." The agreement was not long-term, and either party could cancel or terminate it with six months' notice.

At the same time the Northern Pacific agreement was established, the Chehalis Western also entered into a supplemental agreement with the Milwaukee, broadening the original 1936 document. Also dated December 9, 1943, the Chehalis Western gained additional running rights over the Milwaukee from Dryad Junction to Station Murnen and use of the interchange track at Milburn. These agreements gave the company access to the Cox Brothers' operation at Murnen where three loads per day were picked up. A wye was located at Murnen. It also provided access to the company's own timber in the far western region of

Camp 6 located above Camp McDonald on Branch 7, also known as the 70 line. —Weyerhaeuser Archives

The crew of this duplex operation loads a string of Chehalis Western log cars in the woods above Camp McDonald. These cars will be carried to Camp McDonald by a Weyerhaeuser woods locomotive. At the McDonald yard, the loaded cars will be handed off to a Chehalis Western locomotive for the tip to South Bay. —Francis Neuman Collection, Rainier Historical Society

Lewis County, where it would pick up logs from the Weyerhaeuser transfer at Doty (Station Hilda). The Weyerhaeuser transfer siding off the Milwaukee's Tenth Subdivision track at Hilda was 3,236 feet in length and was the location of Weyerhaeuser's Camp Doty. The track had two switches off the Milwaukee's main line; the eastern switch was located at milepost 42.1. Approximately 85 men worked at Camp Doty, but most commuted to the campsite from their homes in Doty, Pe Ell, and Dryad, reducing the need for a large camp of bunk houses. A second supplemental agreement was reached with the Milwaukee on January 26, 1945, which incorporated and superseded the first supplement extending the Chehalis Western's right to operate from Dryad Junction to Hilda and Swem in Pacific County. The reload at Swem was located at milepost 45.3 on the Milwaukee's Tenth Subdivision.

Late in 1943, the Vail-McDonald Branch purchased 30 log cars from the Willapa Harbor Lumber Mills of Raymond, Washington, a Weyerhaeuser subsidiary, in anticipation of an increased demand for timber. The cars were shipped to Camp McDonald after Willapa Harbor put the cars into ICC condition, a prerequisite of the sale. The plans were to use the cars on Chehalis Western trains running over Milwaukee Road tracks. However, by November 1, the cars were lying idle at McDonald, and John Wahl, who replaced Ronald McDonald when he retired, recommended renting the cars to the Milwaukee. The Milwaukee rejected the offer on November 15, citing that the cars didn't meet ICC standards for main line use. This resulted in a debate between Willapa Harbor and Vail-McDonald over the conditions of delivery of the cars at Camp McDonald. By February 15, 1944, A. L. Raught, assistant manager, wrote John Wahl at Vail that about half the cars were capable of being placed in usable condition and recommended keeping the high bunks for use in truck-to-rail transfer loading.

By the end of 1943, the steel gang had picked up the rail on the 706, 813, 831, 832, 842, and 843 spurs and laid rails on the 71, 85, and 88 Lines and on the 833 and 852 spurs. Although logging-spur railroading at Vail was rapidly declining, woods railroading would remain an active part of the Camp McDonald side of the operation for another four years.

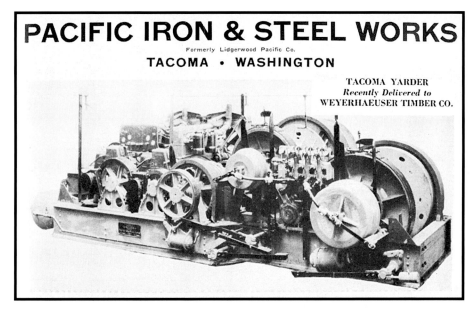

Like the Vail Operation, Camp McDonald used a mix of steam and diesel technologies. Weyerhaeuser purchased Pacific "Tacoma" tandem Diesel variable torque converter yarder from Pacific Iron and Steel Works, formerly known as Lidgerwood Pacific. Pacific Iron and Steel featured the McDonald yarder in their ads placed in *The Timberman* and *West Coast Lumberman*.

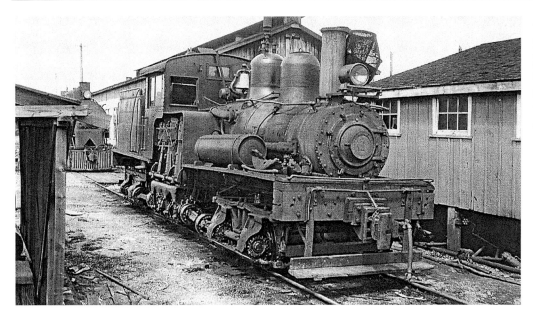

Weyerhaeuser's one spot Shay rests at Vail in 1939, just before being transferred to the Camp McDonald woods operation. —Harold A. Hill, Martin E. Hansen Collection

Another Vail transfer was the #100, seen here at Camp McDonald on April 27, 1948. —Bob Huff, Martin E. Hansen Collection

Vail's #105 was the third Weyerhaeuser Timber Company locomotive to serve the woods lines above Camp McDonald. Resting in the weeds in July 1947, the old Mikado shows signs of its age on the spur track in the south end of Camp McDonald yard. —Gurnsey Photo, Martin E. Hansen Collection

Weyerhaeuser Timber Company #112 was given a tank car tender to increase its range, but kept its saddle tanks, unlike the fate of #111. Here it heads up a work train with a wooden Rogers ballast car tied on to its front end. —Al Farrow Photograph, Martin E. Hansen

Located in the woods above Camp McDonald, Camp 7 was built along the 84 line to house loggers involved in the salvage of timber after the fires of 1940. Similar to Camp 6 in its layout, the significant difference between the two camps is the location of the large dinning hall, in the center of the wye of Camp 6 and along one of the trail tracks of the wye of Camp 7. —Peter J. Replinger

In 1942, Weyerhaeuser purchased a small fleet of Gibson heavy duty Model L4 speeders and trailers to ferry crews from headquarters to the woods. These replaced the aging interurban cars which were scrapped shortly after the new Gibson speeders arrived.

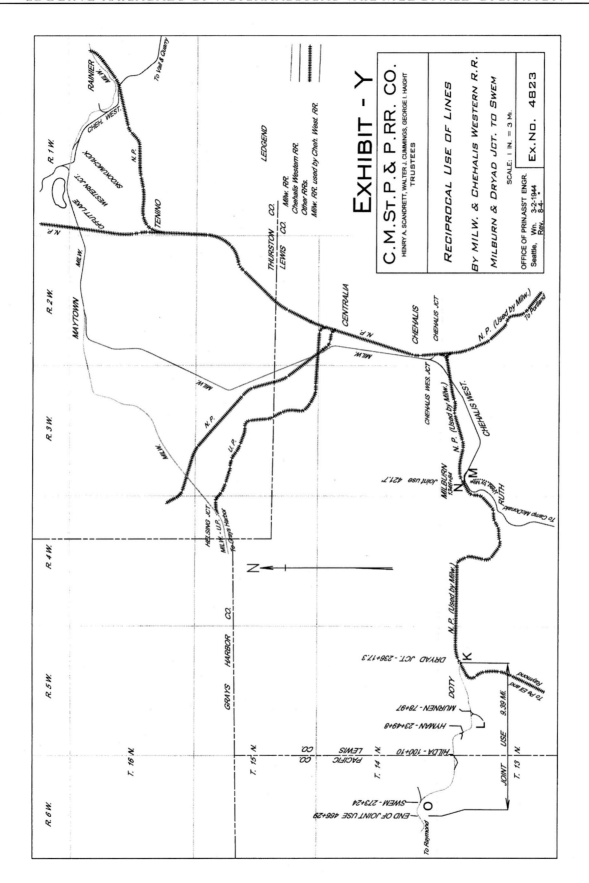

Exhibit Y was part of the second reciprocal use of lines agreement between the Milwaukee Road and Chehalis Western which extended the joint use of the Milwaukee tracks west of Dryad Junction to 9.39 miles in 1944, providing access to Weyerhaeuser timber at Hilda and Swem. —Weyerhaeuser Archives, redrawn by Frank W. Telewski

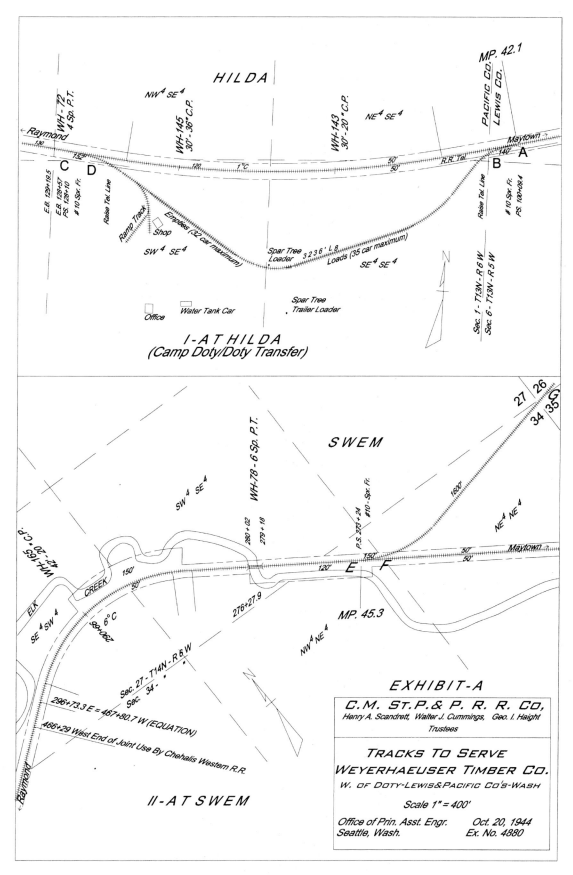

Although Weyerhaeuser's large reload west of Camp McDonald was located at the Milwaukee Road's Station Hilda, the company named it Camp Doty, for the town located just to the east of this woods operation. A second reload was located further west of Hilda at Swem. —*Weyerhaeuser Archives, redrawn and modified by Frank W. Telewski*

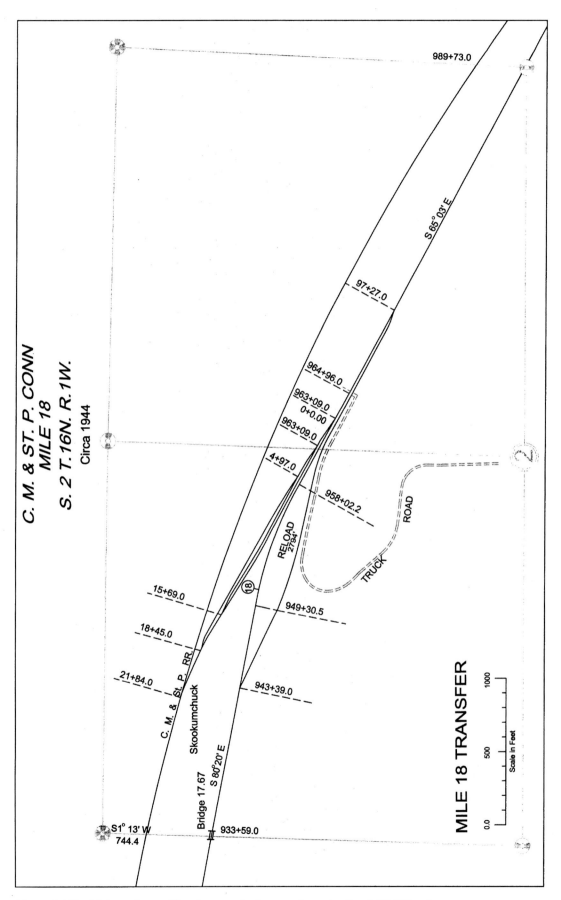

Map of Mile 18 transfer. —Weyerhaeuser Archives, redrawn by Frank W. Telewski

CHAPTER 7

The Transition Years at Vail-McDonald: 1943-1953

The truck and internal combustion engine were introduced to West Coast logging early in the 20th century. By the mid-1930s, developments in metal strength, axle, wheel, transmission, and engine design began to prove the truck to be a viable means of moving logs from the woods to a railroad or directly to the mill. The introduction of the diesel engine and its incorporation into truck design also increased the power and size of individual trucks by the late 1930s.

Diesel tractors began to replace spar trees and tower skidders in the Vail woods during the 1940s. Gunner Swanson (top right), John P. Ward (sitting on the tread) and the rest of the logging crew pose with their Allis-Chalmers HD-19 Diesel tractor equipped with a Carco arch in 1943.
—Weyerhaeuser Archives

The trend toward using trucks, tractors, and internal combustion donkeys to replace railroads, steam locomotives, steam skidders, and steam donkeys became evident during the 1935 logging congress in a session called "Logmania." The "Logmania Problem" was created by Robert J. Filberg. His idea was to present loggers with a theoretical virgin tract of a million feet of timber, at a stumpage cost of $4, and liquidate this stumpage at a rate of 10 percent of the total volume of timber per year, completing the logging at the end of 10 years. The detailed outline of the problem was prepared by E. T. Clark, from the Sauk River Lumber Company operating out of Everett, Washington. Robert P. Conklin (Weyerhaeuser Timber Company, Longview, Washington) was charged with preparing an outline for the engineering work and the basic map. The physical location of this hypothetical timber was supposed to be adjacent to Puget Sound, at an elevation of from 800 to 3,000 feet, with a mixed stand of 60 percent Douglas fir, 15 percent cedar, 20 percent hemlock, and five percent balsam, pine, and spruce—practically all old growth.

Weather conditions were set to represent a normal rainfall of 60 inches, concentrated during six months, snow four to six feet deep for four months at higher elevations, and two feet of snow for two months at lower elevations. The problem involved a solution for the engineering, construction, transportation, yarding and loading, investment, and general organization of a logging operation. The objective was to

D-8 Caterpillar tractor equipped with a Carco arch bringing in logs through the mud to the truck landing at Mile 18. —*Ralph Vincent, Weyerhaeuser Archives*

The first transfer operation took place at Mile 18, close to the Skookumchuck interchange with the Milwaukee Road. Logs skidded to the truck landing were assembled into loads and lifted onto trailer trucks equipped with 10-foot bunks using a spar tree. —Ralph Vincent, Weyerhaeuser Archives

The entire load was lifted from the truck at the rail transfer and placed on waiting log cars. —Weyerhaeuser Archives

present the participants with a virgin problem, which was to be planned and developed using the most modern and efficient methods. This problem presented several loggers the opportunity to describe how they would harvest the tract of land using the changing methods and equipment of the day. At the Mr. Filberg's insistence, a number of loggers prepared logging plans for "Logmania" in writing, and these plans were presented in bound form to the congress.

A total of nine solutions were presented, including two by Weyerhaeuser Timber Company employees Walter J. Ryan (Tacoma [Vail], Washington), Robert P. Conklin (Longview, Washington), and former Vail railroad designer Lloyd R. Crosby (who was at the time with the Consolidated Timber Company in Glenwood, Oregon). Both Crosby and Ryan recommended using a logging railroad; Ryan proposed the use of tractors to bring logs in from some of the steeper regions. Conklin's solution, along with that of three other participants, proposed 100 percent truck logging. Those who proposed truck logging also recom-

Above: Both the spar tree and the tail tree of the Mile 18 reload are visible along with a tank car and steam loader which is in the process of loading a log car. —*Weyerhaeuser Archives*

Left: Willamette Diesel loader set on old railroad car wheels was used at the truck landing to set log loads assembled on false bunks onto trucks. —*Lee Merrill Photograph Weyerhaeuser Archives*

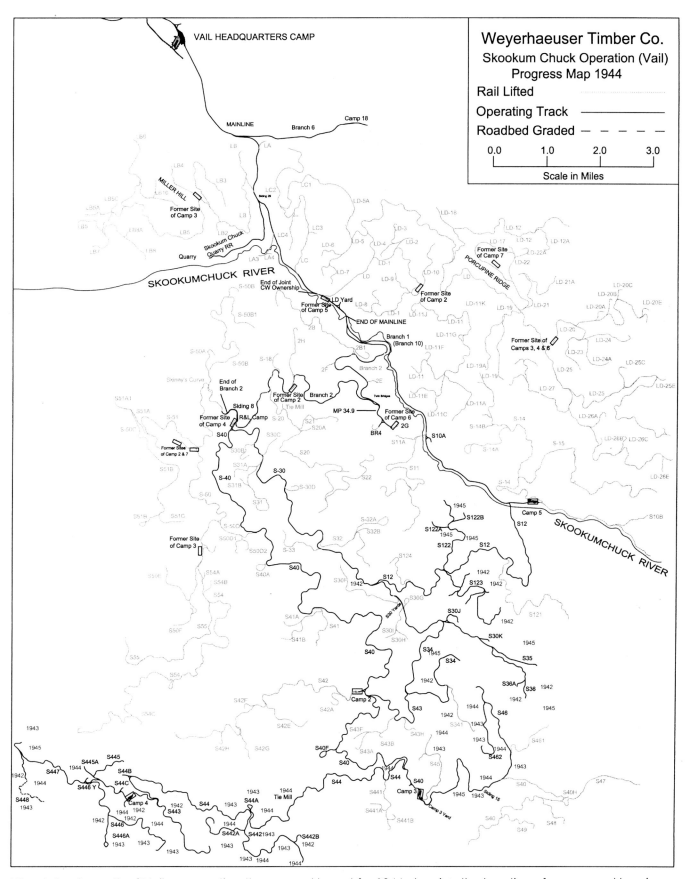

Woods tracks south of Vail representing the general layout for 1944, showing the location of camps and logging spurs. Dates near the tracks indicates when timber was cut in a specific area. —Composite map from various data sources including field surveys, Weyerhaeuser Archives, Weyerhaeuser Vail section maps located at the Vail office, aerial photographs and Vail Track Mainline and Woods Lines, Barrett Family Collection, drawn by Frank W. Telewski

mended 100 percent private roads to ensure that heavy trucks that were not permitted on public highways could be used. Axel J. F. Brandstrom of the Pacific Northwest Forest Experiment Station in Portland proposed 100 percent truck logging and calculated a cost of $1 per thousand feet of timber for the entire hypothetical operation. He stated that diesel trucks would undoubtedly soon be in operation and that the cost estimate would be lowered.

With the mounting evidence of potential cost savings resulting from use of the internal combustion engine and truck logging, it was becoming clearer to all loggers in the Pacific Northwest that the day of logging railroad spurs and steam operations were numbered. It was just a matter of time until the large steam and rail show at Vail and McDonald would be transformed by the wave of new technology descending upon the region.

One of the first Weyerhaeuser operations to quickly adopt the new technologies was Snoqualmie Falls, under the watchful eye of logging superintendent John Wahl. The first phase of the transition at Snoqualmie was to move from railroad logging spurs to truck reloads. Truck roads replaced the logging railroad spur lines in the woods. Trucks loaded logs at the skidder sides and moved them to a reload, where they were directly transferred from the trucks to railroad log cars. Eventually, Snoqualmie Falls converted entirely to a truck logging operation, and the railroad equipment was offered for sale by the Weyerhaeuser subsidiary.

Chehalis Western #120 steams up at Camp McDonald in 1948, the twilight of the steam age. —Martin E. Hansen Collection

The entry of the United States into the Second World War reduced the labor force in the woods while increasing demands on production. Wood was used in numerous wartime applications, from the construction of war emergency freight cars for railroads, to wood for munitions boxes, airplanes, and even plywood landing craft used in the D-Day invasion of France. Wood was also required for small and large prefabricated buildings, for structures that included aircraft hangers and warehouses, and to supply pulp needed in paper manufacturing. Because steel was required for a number of wartime applications, a steel shortage soon developed. Wherever wood could be substituted for steel, it was used.

In the woods, steam technology demanded labor to operate and maintain, whereas diesel technology required less staffing and maintenance. The war had caused both a rapid maturation of diesel technology, plus the manufacturing capacity to produce it reliably and cost-effectively. The war also increased the efficiency of diesel engines and improved the construction of larger, more durable trucks. The introduction of the pneumatic tire also revolutionized truck technology. Although engines and trucks were in short supply during the war years, the demand for forest products in the wartime economy placed a priority on their use in logging. In addition, trucking reduced labor requirements in a restricted labor market and eliminated the cost of railroad construction, especially the volume of timber used for ties

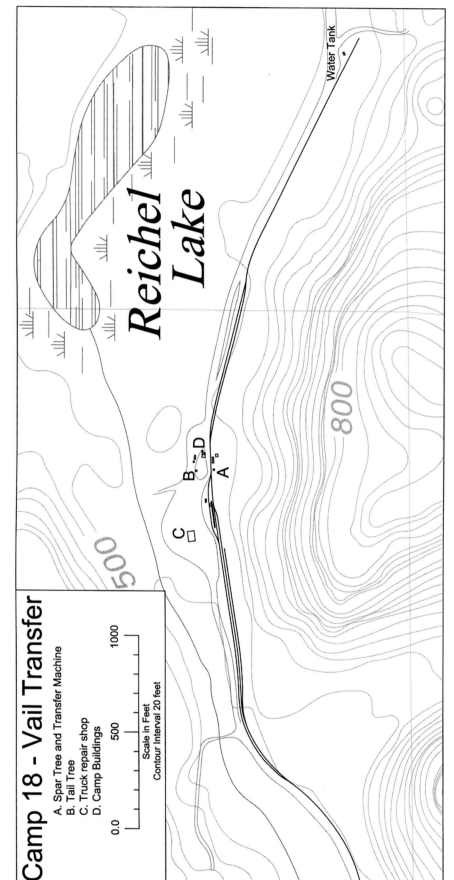

Camp 18-Vail transfer located at the east end of Branch 6. Track construction began in 1944 and the transfer was in operation by 1946. —USGS Topographic Map, Washington DNR Aerial Photograph, Drawn by Frank W. Telewski

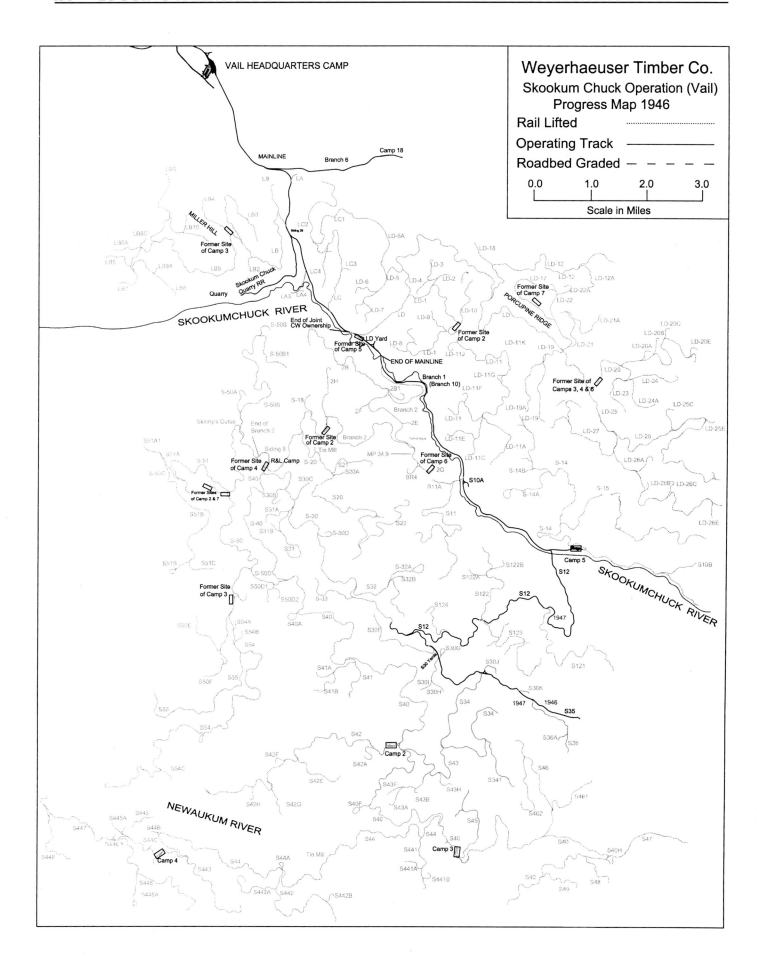

and trestles. All of this favored the use of trucks in the woods and made rail logging less attractive.

Nowhere was the concern for tie costs more clearly illustrated than in a 1948 memo from John Wahl (who was reassigned from Snoqualmie Falls to Vail) to A. L Raught Jr. in the Tacoma office. The memo provides perspective on the cost and demand for ties by a railroad. In 1948, 20 carloads of creosoted ties were required as replacements on the Vail and McDonald main line, and the ties were ordered from the Everett Mill. The price per thousand came to $123, plus $113 per car for shipping. Mr. Wahl was astonished when he was quoted the price, and in response he tried to cancel the order. However, the mill had already cut most of them and could not dispose of them at the price offered Vail-McDonald. In his memo, Wahl stated, "What we will do about the rest of the requirements for ties I do not know at the present time. If you have something to suggest I would appreciate it. I just cannot see putting these gold pieces in a railroad track."

Not only would truck logging eliminate the need for ties, but the ability of trucks with improved transmissions to climb steeper grades and make sharper turns than a railroad allowed bypassing many trestle sites by using a "shoo-fly" built across mountain streams with the use of fill and a culvert. After the war, many of the machines and technology used on the battlefield would find their way into a peacetime economy, further reducing production costs during a period of increased demands for lumber due to a growing post-war demand for new home construction.

When John Wahl transferred to Vail in 1943, he was already well versed in the savings the new technology offered. By mid-1944, he had begun to experiment with truck-to-rail transfers at a new side located at milepost 18, just north of Vail on the Vail to South Bay main line. A transfer was different from a reload.

Abandoned initially as a railroad bridge in 1948 and converted for log truck use, the high bridge (bridge # 31.42) over the Skookumchuck was completely abandoned in May of 1954. Shortly there after, Weyerhaeuser dynamited the bridge so it would not be a safety concern. —Weyerhaeuser Archives

Previous page: The last of the Vail's woods railroad logging took place along the 35 line in 1946. The remaining woods rail lines were removed after that date with only Branch 10 to Camp 5 remaining active for a few more years. Dates near the tracks indicates when timber was cut in a specific area. —Composite map from various data sources including field surveys, Weyerhaeuser Archives, Weyerhaeuser Vail section maps located at the Vail office, aerial photographs and Vail Track Mainline and Woods Lines, Barrett Family Collection, drawn by Frank W. Telewski

The end of the line. Retired from service, a string of old steam locomotives including #101 and #215 await the scrapper's torch. —Paul LeRoy

With their tenders removed locomotives 215 and 101 rest back to back at the deadline at Vail. The tenders would continue to serve the railroad as water cars, with the tender of 215 surviving to the closing days of the Chehalis Western in 1992. —Paul LeRoy

At a reload, logs were loaded off the log trucks, stacked, and then reloaded onto railroad cars. At a transfer, an entire load of logs was removed as a unit from the truck and placed on the waiting log car. This took place in a single motion, saving time and increasing efficiency. John Wahl opened a stand of timber for harvesting at milepost 18 via a two-mile private truck logging road.

Thus the technology of the truck-to-train transfer was established. Crews skidded logs to the truck landing using D-8 caterpillar tractors equipped with Carco arches. There the logs were assembled into pre-formed loads on false bunks constructed at the Vail shops from double-length rail car axles. The loads were lifted using a single spar tree rigged with a 70-foot heel boom and placed on a truck. A Skagit model BU-65-W, Type 2D-2SD, powered with a Waukesha 145GK 165-hp gasoline engine was used for loading. The trucks traveled to the reload rail siding where two raised spar trees were used in the transfer process. The head tree was located alongside the railroad track, and power was supplied by a Washington Iron Works duplex 9×10.25.

The truck road ran parallel to the track, and both were located between the head spar and the tail spar tree. A log was used as a spreader bar for the false bunks, which were suspended from the ends. The loaded truck would drive up alongside the train car to be loaded, the false bunk axle lifts were positioned

Shortly after arriving from Fairbanks-Morse, Vail's first diesel-electric locomotive #481 crosses the Woodward Bay trestle at high tide with caboose #712 and an empty log car. This could well be the first run of the new engine to South Bay since it does not have its signature steam bell from the two spot Shay on the front of its hood. Caboose 712 has been repainted yellow when this photograph was taken in 1948. —Weyerhaeuser Archives

under the load, and the entire load was secured with the short length of cable thrown over the load and fastened to the other end of the axle through a slot and secured using a steel pin. Once secured, the entire load was lifted off the truck trailer and placed on the log car, as the truck headed back to the woods for another load. Two Mack trucks (model LM SWM, fitted with 10-foot bunks) and two Sterling trucks with Fruehauf and Gunderson trailers were used at the milepost 18 transfer.

The transfer concept employed at milepost 18 revolutionized logging at Vail and resulted in the removal of the majority of the woods railroad. After a little over four years in service, the 44 Line was targeted for removal in 1945, as trucks assumed a greater role in log transport. John Wahl proposed selling the 60-pound and lighter rail used on the line for scrap iron, whereas the more than eight miles of 70-pound rail was to be stockpiled at Vail after being lifted. The rails were finally removed in 1946, and the lighter rail was shipped to India for use as telephone poles.

Following the end of World War II, the Vail-McDonald operation returned to its pre-war levels of employment and output. In 1947, for example, combined Vail-McDonald employment averaged 650 employ-

#481 is flanked on either side by Chehalis Western #492 and #493, photographed at Vail shortly after their arrival. The #481 now has the bell from the 2 spot Shay installed on its hood. —Lee Merrill, Weyerhaeuser Archives

ees and had an annual payroll of $2.6 million. Many jobs were transformed during this timeframe as truck logging replaced the woods railroads and power saws were introduced. Keeping skilled loggers at Vail and Camp McDonald was important to Weyerhaeuser, and their retention was made a priority. By mid-1950, Weyerhaeuser employed 700 people at the Vail-McDonald operation.

Camp 3 on the 40 Line remained in operation until 1945 and was the last woods railroad show. "The show at Camp 3 was a big one," recalled Al Olsen, camp foreman. "At one time, two skidders, two high leads and a couple of cold decks were running." The last logging spur to see active duty at Vail was the 30F Line in 1946. Loads were pushed down the 30F to the 30 Line and then down the five to six percent grade of the 12 Line through standing timber to the flat at Camp 5 on the 10 Line. At the end of rail logging, the 12 Line was briefly used by gravel trains to haul gravel for truck road construction. The majority of the logging spurs were converted to truck/fire roads. The 12 Line was removed when gravel delivery was complete and a transfer was established at the end of the 10 Line near Camp 5. The transfer concept was widely accepted at Vail, and by 1947 the entire Vail operation had converted to a 100 percent truck-to-rail transfer operation.

With the elimination of the woods rail lines, resulting in shorter train runs to South Bay, both Vail and McDonald were faced with a surplus of skeleton log cars. In October 1946, A. L. Raught recommended John Wahl consider rebuilding and transferring 100 of the idle cars to Weyerhaeuser's proposed operation at Sutherlin, Oregon. The cars would need to be placed into Interstate Commerce Commission (ICC) condition for transport over the Southern Pacific to Sutherlin. Many of the Vail skeleton cars had been converted to ICC standards years earlier by the Vail shops before transfer to Camp McDonald. The 42-foot sills on the cars had been replaced with 44-foot sills, and safety appliances such as hand rigging and end steps had been added. (The replacement sills were fabricated at the Everett Mills and shipped to Vail.) For this reason, the 44-foot cars idled at Camp McDonald were given first consideration because they would require minimal renovation for use on the Southern Pacific from Sutherlin to the Weyerhaeuser Mill in Springfield, Oregon. In addition to the log cars, the Cooke 2-6-2 #100 and a four-wheel caboose were also shipped south to the Sutherland operation.

THE TRANSITION YEARS AT VAIL-MCDONALD: 1943-1953

A second log transfer, named Camp 18, was established at the end of Branch 6 near Reichel Lake after the milepost 18 transfer was closed. Camp 18 also had a sorting yard, some camp buildings moved from Camp 5, and a truck shop. In 1947, the average truck haul to Camp 5 was seven miles, and nine miles for Camp 18. Seventy-five percent of the timber harvested at Vail in 1947 was logged on state land. In 1948, Camp 5 and the transfer were abandoned, the camp buildings were removed, the steel from the 10 Line to Mulqueen was lifted, and the roadbed was converted into a truck-logging road. With the steel removed from Bridge No. 31.42, trucks were able to use the high trestle over the Skookumchuck, making it the last trestle in use at Vail. However, the bridge was abandoned in May 1954 after a new 1.5-mile road was cut from the Skookumchuck canyon's slope, eliminating the need for the double crossing of the river to reach the location of the former Camp 5. The removal of steel from the roadbed from Mulqueen to LD siding, the first location of Camp 5, resulted in the need to modify the Chehalis Western's deed of 1938. On December 9, 1949, the Chehalis Western reconvened to Weyerhaeuser Timber Company its undivided one-half interest in approximately 2.35 miles of Skookum Chuck line.

The main rail line that crossed from the Deschutes River watershed into the Skookumchuck watershed to Mulqueen Junction was left intact per the contract Weyerhaeuser had signed with the Milwaukee Road. This would maintain access to the Skookum Chuck Quarry Railroad, which would see more activity in the late 1940s. The great reduction in trackage also reduced the need for an extensive fleet of locomotives, and many of the steam engines were either transferred to Camp McDonald or retired in the mid to late 1940s. The 2 spot Shay was sold for scrap in support of the war effort on August 17, 1943; the #99 was also scrapped during the war years; the #111 was sold to Canadian Forest Products, Ltd.; and the 5 spot Pacific Coast Shay was sold to B.C. Forest Products in 1946. The Clemmons operation 6 spot, a 2-6-6-2T, was transferred to Vail early in 1946 and was shipped to the Longview operation in November of that year.

However, steam locomotives still moved the log trains from the transfers to South Bay up until 1950 and from Western Junction to South Bay until 1952. The #101 serviced the milepost 18 transfer and

Chehalis Western #211 showing signs of age in 1951. —Al Farrow, Martin E. Hansen Collection

Tenders from Chehalis Western's #211 and #215 were converted to water cars after the engines were sold for scrap. The original lettering and striping shows through the yellow paint on #211. Resting at Western Junction when they were photographed in October 1992, these reminders of the age of steam railroading served the Vail-McDonald railroads until it's final days. —Frank W. Telewski

moved trains 10 cars in length to the log dump. The last steam locomotive to make the main line run with a load of logs was the #112. In 1948, Weyerhaeuser purchased three diesel electric locomotives for the Vail-McDonald operation from Fairbanks-Morse (FM). The first FM 10-44 arrived at Vail lettered for the Weyerhaeuser Timber Company late in 1948 and was numbered 481. This established a unique numbering system for all future diesel locomotives working the Vail-McDonald operation. The first two digits represented the year the engine was purchased, and the last digit represented the locomotive's number. The #481 was the first diesel engine and was delivered to Vail in 1948. In honor of a proud era of steam locomotive service, the #481 was equipped with the bell from the 2 spot Shay, which was mounted on the front top of the diesel locomotive's hood. The two sister engines arrived in 1949, lettered for the Chehalis Western, and bore the numbers 492 and 493. However, the #492 arrived from the manufacturer with flat wheels. This required sending the engine to Tacoma for refitting, which prolonged the life of the #112 on its runs to South Bay with log trains. All three diesel engines received ICC certification and were equipped with marker lamps for operation over the Milwaukee Road and Northern Pacific, a task usually reserved for #492 and #493.

Even after the arrival of the diesel locomotives, Vail retained a few steam engines in reserve. The steam engines were used during the few days when the diesel locomotives were undergoing their annual inspections. One such operation occurred on October 18, 1950. The #101 and #112 remained until 1950; the #105 remained at Vail until 1952; and both the #102 (2nd) and #110 remained on the roster until 1953. Even after the last steam engine left Vail-McDonald, the engines' presence was still felt because the tenders from Chehalis Western locomotives #211 and #215 and the tender of the #102 (2nd) were converted into water cars for fire suppression. The Chehalis Western tenders retained their numbers as road numbers; the #102's tender was renumbered 150.

Another advance during this period of transition was the introduction of FM ultra-high frequency radio communications. This technology supplied two-way radio communications between different locations of the operation and began to replace the extensive telephone network once used for dispatching. Early radios were installed in some of the steam locomotives and eventually in the #481, but the greatest advantage of the two-way radio was in dispatching fire trucks to the location of fire outbreaks.

With the removal of the extensive network of rails through the woods, the service once supplied by spotting tank cars with fire-fighting equipment needed to be replaced. This need was met with the addition of four small tank trucks equipped with fire-fighting equipment. With the end of World War II, there was an increase in surplus military equipment, and in 1946 John Wahl purchased three surplus International

Navy six-wheel drive refueling tank trucks. Two of the three trucks had 800-gallon tanks, and the third was equipped with a 1,500-gallon–capacity tank. Two truck trailers were equipped with old rail tank car tanks, one with 6,000-gallon capacity and the other with an 8,000-gallon tank. The trucks were converted from fuel to fire trucks in the Vail shops where the flue piping, meters, fuel hoses, and pumps were removed and the fire pumps, water hoses, and live hose reel were installed. The tank trailers and tank trucks were filled with water and placed at strategic points throughout the woods operation.

At Camp McDonald, steam and the woods railroad had survived a few years longer, but were definitely on the way out by 1947. The company abandoned several miles of developed railroad grade before track laying could take place, and the railroad right-of-ways were converted to truck roads. Bulldozers and other road building equipment, as well as the availability of powerful and capable diesel trucks, spelled the end of the railroad in the McDonald woods. In 1947, the steel gang removed 29 miles of rail on the McDonald operation. Much of the rail picked up at McDonald was shipped to Weyerhaeuser's operations in Sutherlin and Springfield, Oregon. By 1948, Weyerhaeuser had closed down its woods railroad operation at Camp McDonald, choosing instead to build logging roads and use diesel-powered logging equipment and trucks to harvest and haul the timber to the transfers. The woods tracks were torn up except for a few miles of track southwest of headquarters camp where the company constructed a transfer directly to the Chehalis Western railroad cars. This development led the Weyerhaeuser Timber Company to convey the right-of-way of the railroad south of Camp McDonald to the truck reload, once exclusively Timber Company trackage, to the Chehalis Western on November 27, 1950. The woods railroad was once again operational only out of Vail.

Harold L. "Buck" Reichel took over the management of the Vail-McDonald operation from John Wahl in 1949. Buck was a longtime Vail employee. He had started in the summer of 1926 working on railroad construction and was bucking windfalls by 1928. Having worked most jobs on the roster, he was well versed in the needs of the logging operation.

Radio communications require antenna to broadcast their signals and in 1949 this tall Douglas fir pole was erected to support the FM dipole antenna. The pole was located just north of the dispatcher's office in Vail.

—Merle Junk, Francis Neuman Collection, Rainier Historical Society

On January 7, 1949, the Chehalis Western and Weyerhaeuser Timber Company came to an agreement allowing for the loaning of railroad equipment from one to the other. The Chehalis Western owned all of the rolling stock needed to operate its log trains and only occasionally needed to borrow timber company equipment. Older skeleton cars used by the woods road at Vail could not be interchanged for use by the Chehalis Western until they were rebuilt, extending them from 42-foot to 44-foot and adding safety appliances—specifically end steps and hand rigging.

Old railroad tank car tanks were fitted to truck trailers to provide water for fire fighting. —*Weyerhaeuser Archives*

In the fall of 1949, shortly after the arrival of the Chehalis Western's new diesel locomotives, the company decided to shorten the haul of many Chehalis Western trains by having them set out their log cars at Western Junction. From Western Junction, the timber company's steam locomotives would move the cars the final 16½ miles to South Bay. The decision apparently was centered on the fact that surplus steam locomotives at Vail were more economical to use on the run from Western Junction to South Bay than the Chehalis Western diesels, which had a longer return run to Camp McDonald (47.31 miles) and Doty (43.7 miles) than the run to Vail (29 miles). Because of the long run, the first train from Camp McDonald departed for Western Junction at 4:30 A.M. To accommodate this change in operations, two sidings were built to house loaded cars and empty cars at Western Junction. The large-scale switching of Chehalis Western log cars at Western Junction ended in 1952, but occasional switching of Chehalis Western trains at Western Junction was continued into the 1960s to comply with the 16-hour legal limit on continuous service by a train crew or to avoid unfavorable tides at the South Bay log dump.

In 1948, a truck-to-rail reload was established at Vail to receive timber harvested from company lands in the Eatonville area. The Vail reload required the construction of a balloon track, which joined the tail track of the wye on the north end of the Vail yards with the south end ladder track. A short siding was built off the loop and used for loading. The timber was transported by truck over a new road designated the Branch 7 Truck Road. Log cars were then loaded at Vail for the run to South Bay.

The average length of a truck haul at Vail in 1951 was 15 miles and eight and five miles, respectively, at McDonald and Doty. The log truck fleet stood at 40, including three "new" highway type vehicles assigned to the Morton operation. The Morton operation was developed as an emergency salvage measure after the Huffaker Mountain fire in July 1951, which burned 5,000 acres, of which 1,165 acres were company-owned timber lands. Weyerhaeuser purchased an eight-acre parcel for the development of a reload facility on the Milwaukee Road-Kosmos Timber Company railroad two miles southeast of Morton near Davis Lake, with truck road access via State Highway 12 (White Pass Highway) and Davis Lake Road.

The Morton operation was a reload but not a transfer, since the logs needed to be loaded individually onto the Milwaukee log cars. At the reload, the logs were parbuckled off the trucks with a line and fall block and then reloaded onto the cars using a shovel loader, which handled logs faster than a conventional tree rig, which was installed at the start of operations. John Clark, head loader at Morton, explained that "every load had to be lined up to the inch" and "every car was inspected by the Milwaukee" before being shipped to Western Junction. A camp housing the salvage crews was established in the burned timber and

THE TRANSITION YEARS AT VAIL-MCDONALD: 1943-1953

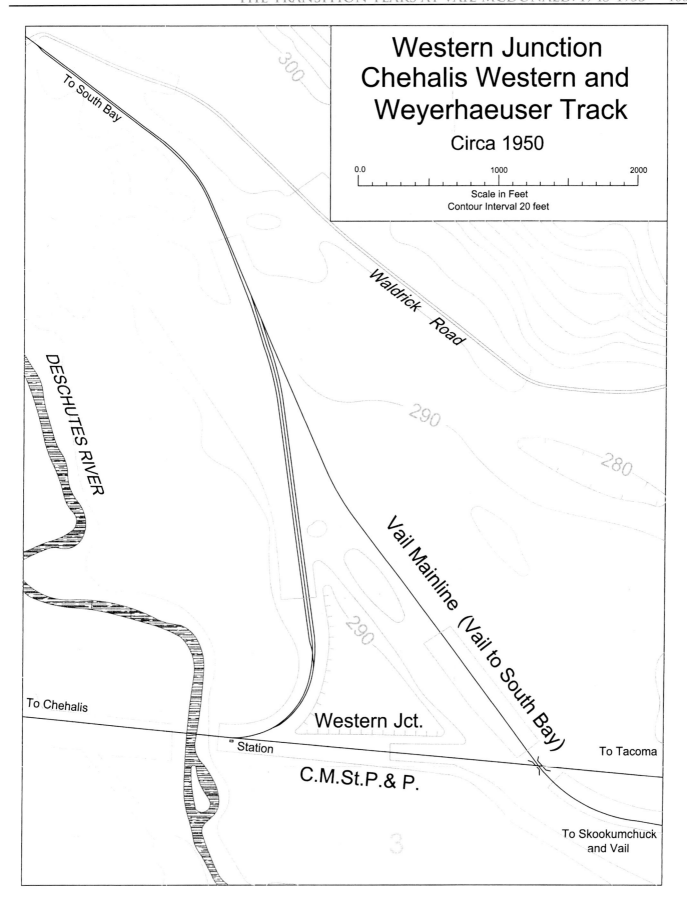

Western Junction after the autumn of 1949 was modified to include two sidings which would accomodate set-outs of log cars by Chehalis Western crews for the Vail railroad crews to take to South Bay. —USGS Topographic Map, Washington DNR Aerial Photograph, Redrawn by Frank W. Telewski

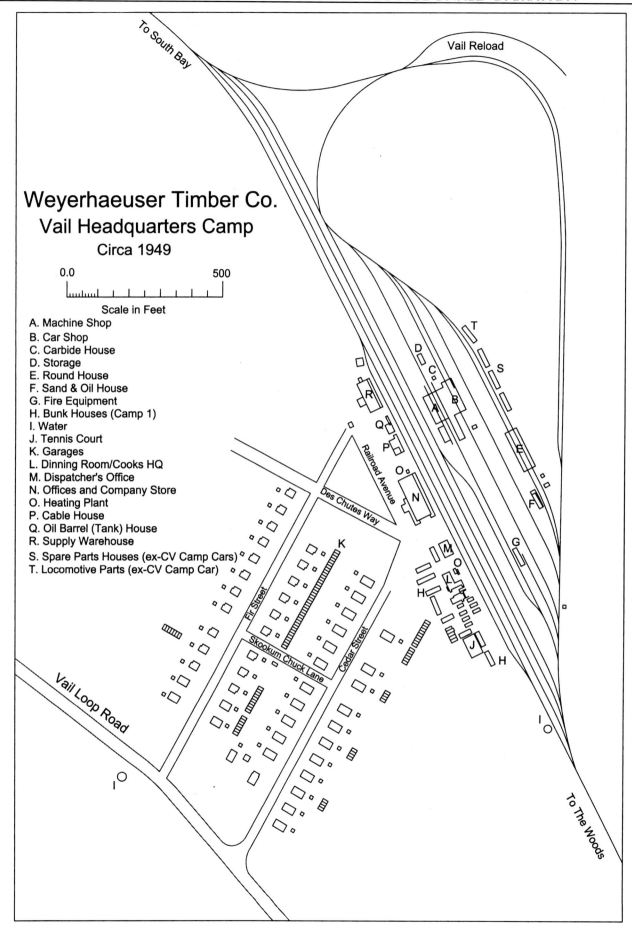

In this photo from November 1944, the logging engineer's crew at Vail-McDonald study one of the many maps to best determine how best to log a region. From left to right are: H. Reichel, C.A. Clark, G. R. Bucklin and R. E. Manning. Harold (Buck) Reichel would replace John Wahl as manager of the Vail-McDonald Tree Farm in 1949. —Ralph Vincent, Francis Neuman Collection, Rainier Historical Society

named Camp Randle, after a town the log trucks passed through on their way to and from the Morton reload. Several skid shack bunk houses originally from the Vail camps were moved to Camp Randle via lowboy trailer truck.

By 1952, production at the Morton reload had reached 15 cars per day. Much of the timber killed by the fire was relatively small. Randle foreman Gunnar Swanson noted one day that only 13 cars were required to carry 462 logs from the reload. A total of five trucks were used on this side, including two reconditioned Sterlings. The timberlands were 23 miles from the reload. The logs salvaged from the Huffaker burn were hauled by trucks over the White Pass Highway (State Highway 12) to the reload. There they were loaded onto Milwaukee cars for the 82-mile run to Skookumchuck junction, where Weyerhaeuser trains picked them up for delivery to South Bay.

A second salvage operation was also taking place at Doty, which had originally opened in 1943. A blow-down of timber had occurred during a blizzard on January 13, 1950. The storm's heavy snow and high winds closed Camp McDonald and Doty for nearly a month, and Vail for two weeks. In the woods west of Doty, 75 million feet of hemlock and old-growth fir were in a broken tangle on the ground in 100- to 500-acre patches. A total of 1,500 acres of timber had been downed by the storm. Salvage required rapid action before insects, fungi, and fire could consume the downed timber. Weyerhaeuser built 14 miles of logging roads from Doty that linked with the Clemons Tree Farm, and logging and road construction at McDonald were curtailed in 1951 so that work could focus on the salvage operation at Doty. While salvage crews were busy loading log cars at the Doty reload, activity a few miles to the east at the Murnen reload focused on removal of rails and ties. Originally established in 1943, Weyerhaeuser abandoned the Murnen reload in 1951. On December 27, 1951, George S. Long and J.P. Weyerhaeuser signed a termination agreement with the Milwaukee Road officially ending logging activity at Murnen.

After the Murnen reload closed, the company secured a new reload facility near Centralia for future harvesting of timber in the Centralia-Chehalis area. Road construction into Section 31, T15N, R1W, four miles east of Centralia, proceeded in 1952, and the logs were shipped to the Centralia reload shortly thereafter. Also in 1952, Weyerhaeuser civil engineers designed and built a five-mile–long logging road to open up stands of timber between Mountain Highway (SR) 7 and the Nisqually River, including the Hart's Lake area and on toward McKenna. They designated the new road 81, and their design required two new bridges, one spanning Ohop Creek and a larger structure crossing Mashel River. Similar to the Eatonville Road, trucks delivered logs to the reload at Vail. The first carload of eight-foot pulpwood was shipped from the Vail reload directly to the pulp mill at Everett in early 1953. Consisting mostly of wood chunks and treetops salvaged from recently logged areas, it was the latest experiment in the campaign for complete utilization of harvested timber. Typically, the pulpwood was loaded into gondola cars for the trip to Everett.

During the fall of 1953, Weyerhaeuser established another reload, this time in Chehalis. Logs hauled from Randle and Bunker Creeks near Adna were reloaded onto log cars. Eventually, the reload handled logs from other patches of company timber. The first load was shipped on October 26, 1953, and averaged

A reload was established off the end of the Milwaukee Road's tracks at Morton to receive timber salvaged from the Huffaker burn of 1951. Milwaukee Road steel drop stake skeleton cars were loaded at the Morton reload and set out at Skookumchuck where the logs were hauled by Weyerhaeuser trains to South Bay. —Weyerhaeuser Archives

15 car loads per day. Saw logs were shipped north to South Bay while pulpwood was loaded into gondola cars and shipped south to the paper mill at Longview. The pulpwood consisted mostly of hardwoods such as alder, cottonwood, ash, and maple, which were bought on the open market at the Chehalis reload. The new reload consisted of a double-track spur off the Chehalis Western and was located next to Highway 99 to the southwest of the Chehalis city limits, near Alexander Park. This was close to the confluence of the Chehalis and Newaukum Rivers. Trucks reached the reload from Ocean Beach Highway (Highway 12) via Riverside Road. Flooding forced the closure of the reload in December when high water from the two rivers inundated the site by as much as four feet in places.

The Vail shops continued to experiment with and develop their own equipment, as evident in the construction of fire equipment using old tenders and tank cars. In 1950, the shops built five 30-passenger busses, two for Springfield, and one each for Coos Bay, Snoqualmie Falls, and Vail. The most notable pieces of rail equipment built by the Vail shops were two cars used for maintenance-of-way work. In 1949, the Vail shop crew built a 35-yard, center dump, all-steel gravel car (#587). In 1951, the shop crew built a 33-yard, center dump all-steel combination ballast car and spreader (#581), also referred to as the brush car, and used it for roadbed work and plowing snow. The steel plow blade could be raised and lowered using compressed air. Both cars replaced aging wooden cars.

Section crews did a significant amount of track maintenance during 1950–51, putting the new cars through their paces. The bridges over Highway 99 and spanning the Deschutes River were completely rebuilt during the Christmas shutdown in 1950. Hart Construction Company rebuilt the 356-foot Woodward Bay Bridge at South Bay in 1951 during the July 4 shutdown. Vail section crews removed the steel and decking down to the bent caps, while Vail and McDonald engineering crews laid out the grades and elevations for cutting the pilings. The construction company completed the job. Prior to construction, fir logs 30 to 70 feet in length were cut in the Vail woods and shipped to South Bay, where they were towed to Eagle Harbor for creosoting by the West Coast Preserving Company. The pile driver drove 24 bents containing five to eight piles each, for a total of 160 new piles, into the floor of Woodward Bay. The section crew cut off the old piles, decked the new bents, and relayed rails before rail operations resumed on July 9.

Crews also re-tied and ballasted eight miles of railroad in 1951. The old ballast pit at milepost 21 was beginning to play out, and by 1959 the pit was abandoned and the tracks removed. Vail crews opened a new ballast-loading spur at milepost 13 to supply gravel for the mainline track work in the early 1950s. Two loading ramps were constructed alongside the milepost 13 ballast siding and a smaller ramp for unloading D-8 cats, and the main ramp was constructed of logs and gravel for dump truck unloading. Approximately 800 feet to the south of the ballast track, a spur housed the section crew's #30 speeder. Workers built a speeder shed and a tool shed out of an old filing shack from Vail. The Vail shops cut the shack in two and moved the halves to milepost 13 on a bull car, where they were set in place by the locomotive crane.

The section crew used the speeder shed and tool shed for various purposes. The tool shed stored track supplies, track jacks, barrels of gasoline, fencing supplies, track bolts, angle bars, and spikes. Several crosscut handsaws were also left hanging in the shed up until the 1970s. The

Old camp buildings salvaged from Vail were brought to Camp Randle for use by the salvage logging crews. —*Weyerhaeuser Archives*

speeder shed was used to keep the speeder locked up and safe from vandals.

Milepost 13 represented the halfway point between South Bay and Vail. The gravel spur and speeder spur would remain operational until the end of the railroad to South Bay in 1984. Since 1948, 63,364 ties had been purchased, enough to re-tie 21 miles of track. Additional maintenance conducted in 1951 included the reroofing of the shop buildings at Vail and Camp McDonald, and the houses at South Bay and Vail were insulated.

Innovation in developing equipment was not limited to the Vail shops. In 1950, the Camp McDonald shops built a 70-foot portable spar tree. The spar tree, complete with blocks and shackles, was mounted on a heavy, movable base with hinges so that it could be raised and lowered. The base was made up of 28 railroad car wheels with the flanges removed, fastened to four axles in the frame. The front axle could be turned for steering. The multiple wheels added a counter balance to the spar and provided greater surface

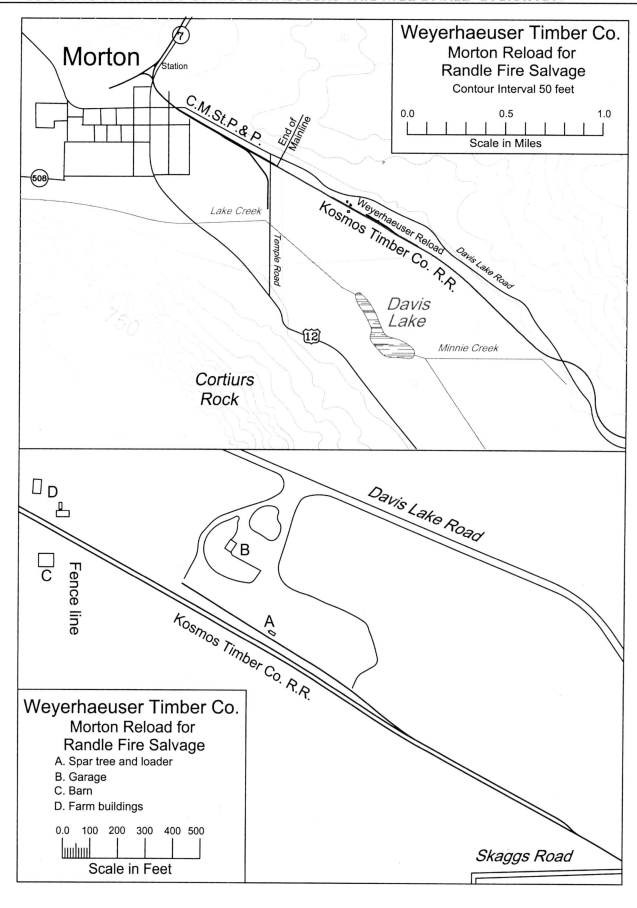

Previous page: The Morton Reload was located east of the town of Morton. The track which served the reload extended off of a siding track owned by the Kosmos Timber Company and joined with the Milwaukee Road near Temple road. —USGS Topographic Map, Washington DNR Aerial Photograph, Redrawn by Frank W. Telewski

for the 25-ton weight of the unit. The portable spar tree was placed in service on the 52 Road at Doty in the fall of 1951. In 1952, the Chehalis Western redecked its bridges between Camp McDonald and Milburn using treated timbers, while Hart Construction Company completely rebuilt bridge 6.70 near old Highway 99 on the rail line to South Bay, which required 80 new pilings. The pilings were driven using a steam hammer, one of the last pieces of steam-driven equipment at Vail-McDonald.

By 1953, the last vestige of steam at the Vail-McDonald operation was eliminated when the South Bay log unloader was converted from steam to a gasoline engine. The transition was now complete. Once almost exclusively a steam rail logging show, the Vail-McDonald operation had completed its modernization to diesel and gas.

Home-made at Vail, a new steel thirty-three yard ballast car #587 poses for a builder's photograph. Painted yellow, and lettered in black, the car was built in 1949. —Weyerhaeuser Archives

"The Tree Growing Company"

Less than a decade after Weyerhaeuser Timber Company's founding, General Manager George S. Long began to champion conservation and reforestation, not only on company lands but also across the Northwest. In 1909, such an idea was almost radical. To attain a sustainable forestry program, changes had to occur in the way property owners addressed forest fires and how local government set property taxes. Fire not only destroyed mature timber, it also threatened regeneration. High property taxes discouraged land owners from retaining productive forestlands for regeneration once they were logged off.

A change in how people would deal with fires and taxes set the stage for sustainable forestry. The next step was to experiment and see how people could help nurture and accelerate the regeneration process. In 1924, the Weyerhaeuser Timber Company hired its first professional forester, Charles S. Chapman. In 1941, the Clemons Tree Farm was formally dedicated and was the first certified American Tree Farm. The tree farm concept was applied to other company operations, and Vail (September 28, 1943) and McDonald (October 22, 1943) were included in the tree farm model shortly thereafter.

Conservation, reforestation, and sustained-yield efforts at Vail began as early as 1939 when Weyerhaeuser employees collected 500 pounds of Douglas fir cones for seed extraction. W. H. Price, manager of the reforestation and land development department, shipped the cones to Weyerhaeuser's seed extraction plant at Melbourne. The extracted seeds were returned to Vail, where foresters broadcast them over burned and cut-over lands. The reforestation program came into full swing during the late 1940s and early 1950s as the Vail-McDonald operation lived up to its new designation as a tree farm. Fire suppression was the first phase, followed by seeding and replanting cut-over areas, but Weyerhaeuser began to experiment with and apply several methods of reforestation.

Initially, natural seeding methods, hand seeding, and hand planting were used. For manual planting, cones were collected from trees on the company land and dried, and the seeds were extracted. The seeds were the either spread directly over logged-off lands or planted at the West Coast Lumbermen's Association Nisqually Nursery. A new method used helicopter reseeding of more than 1,000 acres of Vail-McDonald logged-off lands in December 1949. The helicopter sowed the 1,000 acres with Douglas fir seeds from 50 to 200 feet above the rugged terrain in a single day. The aerial method was successfully used in reforestation of company lands in Clarke County's Yacolt burn and in Pacific County.

Aerial methods worked well for seeding, but handwork was still required to plant the seedlings. In 1951, Camp McDonald employed a full-time planting crew of 15 from January to April, plus 13 high school students from Boisford and Pe Ell, who worked on Saturdays. Vail's planting crew was 12 strong, with as many as 70 Saturday planters from the Rainier, Yelm, Tenino, and Centralia High Schools, as well as from St. Martin's College. Over 456,000 one-year-old Douglas fir seedlings, up to six inches in height, were planted at Camp McDonald, and 597,000 were planted at Vail in the spring of 1951. The program would resume during the cooler, wet months, giving the seedlings the best chance for establishment. From December 1951 through April 1952 an additional 1.8 million seedlings were planted at Vail-McDonald. During the planting season of 1953, full-time employees and students planted 435,000 Douglas fir seedlings on 540 acres at McDonald. Two different areas were restocked at Vail, one crew working out of Mineral to replant some of the old Pacific National logging area, and the second crew planting in the area of Camp 4 at siding 8 on the 50 Line, also known as the old Reforestation & Land Camp. A total of 800,000 two-year-old seedlings were planted by the Vail crews.

Weyerhaeuser also experimented with transplanting 5,000 hemlock seedlings at Doty, where it was too shady for Douglas fir regeneration. After the first year, the hemlocks had about a 50 percent rate of survival. Between 1945 and 1953, more than 3 million trees were planted on the McDonald tree farm alone, covering 4,435 acres, most in the area burned by the 1940 fire. Although the rails were lifted over eight years earlier, some of the building at Camp 3 on the 40 Line were still maintained. In the fall of 1953, the tree planting crew took up housekeeping at the old Camp 3, replanting 500 to 600 acres burned in the 1940 fire between the 42 and 44 Lines. Located approximately 20 miles from Vail, Camp 3 also served as base camp during this period for road repair work along the 40 Line in support of salvage logging.

The Vail-McDonald Depreciation Schedule reported for 1953 provides an interesting insight into the size of the post-steam logging operation and the variety of equipment in use—new, old, and used—at the time. Logging equipment included the following:

* Washington Iron Works skidders (WIW) #3 and #6
* One Clyde Iron Works yarder (#23)

- Three Pacific diesel yarders (#28-D, #30, and #32)
- Three WIW diesel yarders (#33, #34, and #35)
- Two Berger yarders (#36-D and #37-D)
- Two Willamette diesel yarders (#3 and #39)
- One Clyde pre-log yarder
- Two Skagit loaders (#2-D and #3-D)
- One WIW loader (#4-D)
- One Willamette loader (#5-D)
- One Lidgerwood loader (#10-D)
- One Koehring shovel (#3-D)
- One Thew-Lorain shovel (#8-D)
- Four Bucyrus-Erie shovels (#8-D, #10-D, #11-D, #15-D, and #16-D)
- One Northwest shovel (#18-G)
- Three Lima-Mack auto cranes (#5-G, #12-G, and #13-G)
- Two Clyde locomotive cranes (#8 and #9-G)
- One Brownhoist locomotive crane (#11)
- Three Cletrac dozers
- One #D-7 Caterpillar dozer
- 12 #D-8 Caterpillar dozers
- Nine Allis-Chalmers tractors
- Eight International tractors
- 16 Carco arches
- One Isaacson arch
- Four Trackson Crawler wheels
- 28 Carco hoists
- Three Hyster hoists

Railroad equipment, not including the Chehalis Western equipment, consisted of the following:
- One Baldwin (#102)
- One FM diesel (#481)
- 181 skeleton log cars
- Four speeders (#19, #28, #29, and #32)
- One tender (#101)
- One gas trailer (#67)
- One combination steel gravel car–snow plow (#581)
- Five moving cars
- One wood sand car
- One gondola car
- One wood car
- 32 flat cars
- 10 tank cars
- five cabooses (#701, #703, #709, #712, and #002 from White River)
- One crew car (#744)
- Two snow plows (#700)
- One Browning ditcher-gas
- 10 gravel cars (one steel #587)
- 18 Rogers ballast cars
- One pile driver

Built on the frame of a PC & F moving car, Vail's combination ballast spreading and ballast car was built in the Vail shops in 1951. Known as the brush car, it would also double as a snow plow during winter. —Ken Schmelzer Collection

Both steel ballast cars #587 and #581 await loading at the Mile 13 ballast pit. —Ken Schmelzer Collection

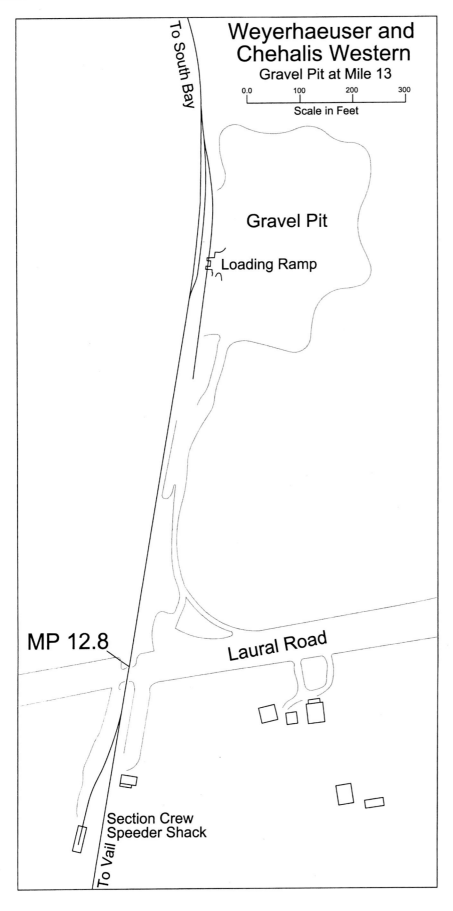

The Mile 13 ballast pit was served by a siding and a spur loading track. Just south of Laural Road was the section crew's speeder shack, a converted old filer's shack from Vail.
—USGS Topographic Map, Washington DNR Aerial Photograph, Redrawn by Frank W. Telewski

Top: The #30 speeder was used by the section crew. —John Henderson Photograph

Center: Caboose #002 was transferred from Weyerhaeuser's White River Lumber Company at Enumclaw to Vail in the early 1950s. It was apparently never lettered or renumbered and is seen here in White River (W.R.L.Co.) lettering outside the Vail machine shop. —Ken Schmelzer Collection

Bottom: The last steam engine listed at Vail was the second #102 in 1953, seen here resting on a shop track at Vail. —Frank W. Telewski Collection

Both photos: In 1953, Weyerhaeuser replaced the old steam unloader at South Bay with a gasoline powered unloader. —John R. Cummings

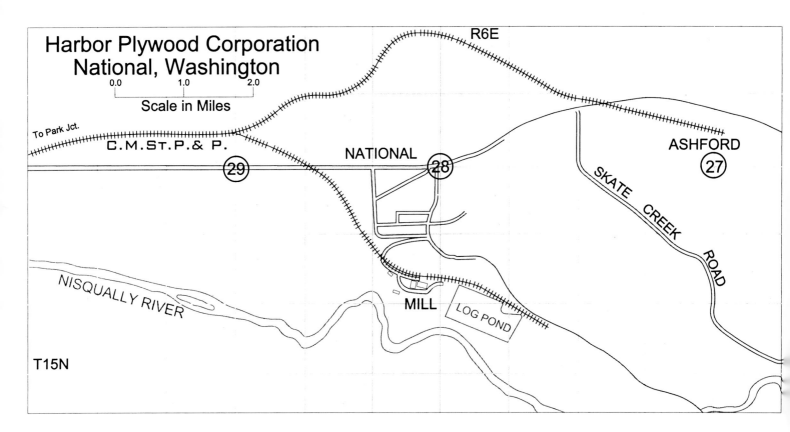

In April, 1957, Weyerhaeuser purchased 1,400 acres of timberland and the town of National from Harbor Plywood. The purchase included the railroad spur which once served the Harbor Plywood mill. Weyerhaeuser would use this track as a reload, shipping the cars over the Milwaukee Road's Ashford branch to Park Junction and then on to Skookumchuck. —*Weyerhaeuser Archives, redrawn by Frank W. Telewski*

CHAPTER 8
Vail-McDonald: 1954-1961

With the total conversion to truck transfer and reload by 1948 and the departure of the last of the steam locomotives in 1953, the railroads of the Vail-McDonald operation settled into a steady routine of moving loads from transfers and reloads and supplying empty cars on the return trip from the South Bay log dump. On average, two daily trains pulled by the #481 moved logs from the Camp 18 transfer south of Vail, picked up cars at the Vail reload, and headed north to South Bay to unload them. The short distance of 29 miles each way permitted the #481 to make two daily round-trip runs.

A wire-strapped load of pre-logging hemlock is about to be shoved into the waters of South Bay by the gasoline powered kicker boom of the unloader. The loads will be combined into a raft for the trip to the pulp mill at Everett. —Weyerhaeuser Archives

Left: An old tank car supported on log cribbing serves as a stationary water tank at the Doty transfer.
—*Lyle Spears*

Right: Weyerhaeuser's Doty transfer was located west of the town of Doty at Station Hilda (MP 42.1) along the Milwaukee Road's Tenth Subdivision track to Raymond. Photographed here in August 1971, the Doty transfer still used a spar tree for transferring logs from trucks to skeleton log cars. Diesel equipped skidder #5 provides the power to the spar tree for loading. —*Lyle Spears*

Left: The transfer crew at Doty is busy loading cars for the trip to South Bay. —*Lyle Spears*

The Chehalis Western continued to operate two daily trains, one made up at Camp McDonald and running directly to South Bay, and one from the Hilda reload, where logs from the Camp Doty logging operation were loaded. This second train would also pick up some cars from the Chehalis reload and sometimes from Camp McDonald. These trains were pulled by the #492 and #493. The Chehalis reload was established in 1953 and shipped its first load of logs to South Bay on October 26 of that year. The Chehalis reload also began shipping alder, maple, ash, and cottonwood logs in gondola cars to Weyerhaeuser's Longview pulp mills. The Chehalis reload remained active until the late 1950s, when it was shut down for want of harvestable timber in the area. Salvage logging in the National area near Elbe produced 1,900 cords of pulpwood in 1954, mostly from a blow down.

Some days on the Chehalis Western were anything but routine, however. One day in February 1954, the crew of #493, including Milt Forner, Don McClure, and Ed Haunreiter, spotted a lost boy, 2½ year-old Scott McNiven, wading in the Skookumchuck River. The crew, noticing searchers scouring the countryside, stopped the train and pointed out the lost boy to them. It was a happy reunion with family and a happy ending for the searchers, thanks to a watchful train crew.

In 1954, the Chehalis Western reported a railroad inventory of two diesel electric locomotives, 256 skeleton log cars, and two cabooses. Vail's Weyerhaeuser Timber Company railroad reported one diesel electric locomotive, 148 log cars, two tender-water tanks, three cabooses, two speeders, three donkey moving cars, one tank car, one snow plow, and one gravel-car snow plow. These figures represented a significant reduction in the fleet of railroad equipment, which had been reported in inventory only a year earlier.

By the mid-1950s, the combined Vail-McDonald operation had over 500 miles of truck roads in the woods, 150 log trucks, and 75 miles of railroad (down from some 200 miles of track a decade earlier). A third of the land holdings were still cloaked in old growth forests, however the old ways of logging continued to fade. The company no longer housed timber crews in woods camps. Even the company town of Vail began to see fewer residents, because workers preferred to live in local towns and commute to and from

The Chehalis reload was flooded by the Chehalis River in December 1955. —*Lyle Spears*

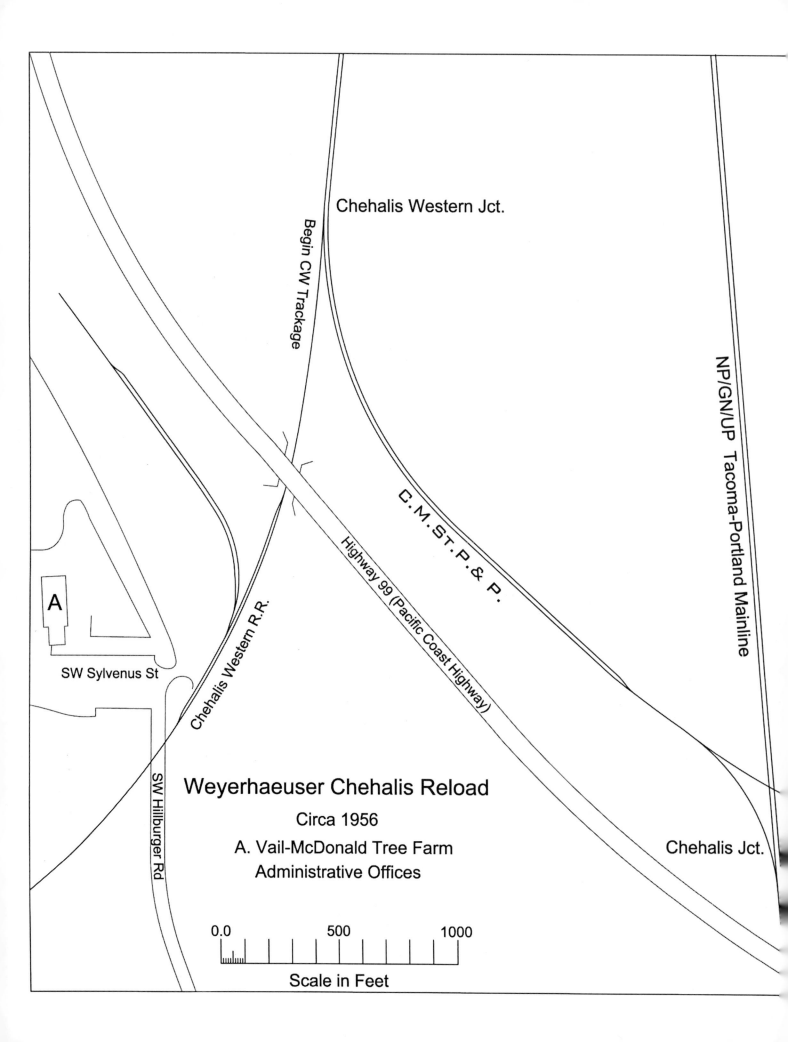

Wire-strapped loads of pre-log under story hemlock, harvested prior to yarding heavy old growth trees, rests in the Vail yard before being transported to South Bay and finally to the Everett pulp mill. —*Weyerhaeuser Archives*

the woods for work. One casualty of the changing lifestyle of the logger was the Vail cook house. After 27 years of faithful service, the staff served their last meal on December 22, 1954. After the meal, the dining facility was retired. The importance of Vail as the headquarters for the tree farm also diminished in August 1955 when Weyerhaeuser moved the administrative offices of the Vail-McDonald operation from Vail to Chehalis, where the company built a new 4,200–square foot headquarters building at the Chehalis reload. The new office building housed 21 employees, including forestry, accounting, engineering, and other personnel. Although the administrative unit was removed from Vail, the single-family houses of the company town remained home to many field employees. In addition, the railroad and truck shops at Vail stayed active for many years.

The Vail shops continued to maintain logging equipment, the focus shifting from almost exclusively rail cars and equipment to include servicing the fleet of logging trucks. Old skidders, yarders, and loaders also received upgrades and modifications in addition to routine maintenance. One of the modifications conducted by the Vail shops in 1956 was the rebuilding of the #34 yarder. Originally purchased in 1928 as a Washington Iron Works steam two-speed yarder #14, it was rebuilt in September 1948 with a 250-horsepower diesel engine; equipped with a three-speed, air-controlled transmission; and renumbered 34. In 1949, the log sled was replaced by 54 railroad-car wheels, which provided greater mobility. The modifications made in 1956 included an upgrade to a V-12 400-horsepower diesel motor with torque converter and a two-speed transmission. The yarder, named King George by the Vail crews, was equipped with three drums, a 1-3/8-inch main line of 1,500 feet, a 7/8-inch haul-back of 3,500 feet, and a 7/16-inch straw line of 2,200 feet. The Vail shop crew added a small wood burner to keep the operator's feet warm during winter operations.

Weyerhaeuser expanded Camp McDonald by constructing a large seed cone extractor in 1954 as part of the company's progressive reforestation and tree farm concept. During September and October of the first year, more than 6,000 bushels of Douglas fir, hemlock, Western red cedar, silver fir, noble fir, and grand fir cones were collected by the various operating branches of the company. In the autumn of each year, the company paid workers and their families extra to collect closed, green cones. The closed cones were shipped to the Camp McDonald facility, where they were dried and opened, and the seeds were extracted. The seeds were either stored or sent directly to the forest nursery in Olympia, where they were sown in nursery beds and grown into seedlings. The seedlings were then replanted at the various Weyerhaeuser tree farms, including Vail-McDonald. During the 1953–54 planting season, 2.05 million seedlings were planted on 2,832 acres. In 1955, a million seedlings were hand-planted on 1,400 acres of land. In the mid-1950s, the Vail-McDonald operation employed 125 laborers for tree planting during the summer months, in addition to 700 full-time workers.

Weyerhaeuser increased the land holdings on the Vail side of the operation in April 1957 when it purchased 1,400 acres of timberland and the town of National from Harbor Plywood Corporation. This parcel of land and the company town were located just to the south of Elbe and were connected to the Morton branch of the Milwaukee Road via a short railroad line. The rail line, once used by the previous owner, would serve as a reload for Weyerhaeuser in the late 1950s and early 1960s. Most of the purchased land had been logged off by Harbor Plywood and was replanted with seedlings shortly after it was acquired. The Eatonville operation was still active in 1955 as "gyppo," or independent contract loggers, worked to move salvage logs over the 30-mile road to the Vail reload.

Engineer Ray Essena watches his brakeman for signals from the cab of Vail's #481. Photographed in 1957, the old Weyerhaeuser "W" had been replaced by a newer Weyerhaeuser Timber Company logo which was introduced in the early 1950s. —*Weyerhaeuser Archives*

A severe windstorm in 1958 created a large blow down, with a significant volume of wind-thrown timber. As with previous blow downs, Weyerhaeuser gave priority to salvage operations before insects, fungi, and fire could consume the timber. A large volume of timber was wind thrown at McDonald. The great majority of the blow down occurred in inaccessible regions of the tree farm, requiring extensive road building to reach the downed timber. Salvage of the 1958 blow down would last for five years. In 1961, a total volume of 26 million board feet of timber was salvaged from 994 acres.

The South Bay log dump saw additional renovation during the 1950s. One change in woods operations was the harvesting of "pre-logging" hemlock, which was cut in thinning operations in the regenerating second-growth forests at Vail-McDonald. The smaller logs needed to be bundled by fastening straps around the loads, either on the log cars or shortly after being dumped into the bay. At the bay, two bundling machines, one made from an old Ford truck motor and the second from a small Skagit donkey, were

The Morton turn, headed by Milwaukee Road SD7 #2223, crosses the Nisqually River covered bridge with a train load of logs in 1958. Weyerhaeuser logs headed for South Bay will be set out at Skookumchuck. —*Weyerhaeuser Archives*

Vail's #481 passes under the Woodward Bay Road on its way down to South Bay. Photographed in 1960, the cab of #481 no longer has a logo. Weyerhaeuser changed the name of the company by dropping "Timber" and created the modern logo of a tree inside of a green triangle. This logo was never applied to the #481 despite the fact it would operate for at least 15 more years. —*Jim Shaw, Frank W. Telewski Collection*

installed. Bundling was necessary to save the smaller, dense hemlock logs, which frequently sank, or due to their small size, escaped when dumped. These smaller logs were sent to the pulp mill at Everett. One machine operated at high tide, while the other was used during low tide. The South Bay trestles also required additional maintenance.

In October 1954, two stringers and a few ties were replaced on the wye leg. New treated ties were installed on the unloader track in June 1955 and summer 1956, when 16 bents on the approach to the dump were redecked. A report filed on September 14, 1956, recommended the caps and stringers be replaced on the dump and tail track. Facing an estimated expenditure of $80,000 for redecking over the next two years, company engineers proposed to redesign the South Bay dump. They recommended building a new track in the form of a 1,200-foot loop, with 400 feet extending out over the water and a one-car spot where an unloader would lift the load off the log car and set it into the water. The engineers cited six advantages to this new design, including less annual maintenance, reduced breakage due to the dumping of logs in the current design, no need to unstrap loads for unloading, and a reduced dredging area.

Chehalis Western #493 and caboose #712 at South Bay's upper wye. Originally a Weyerhaeuser caboose, the #712 was transferred to the Chehalis Western in exchange for #800 in the 1950s. Milt Fournier, Engineer and Don McClure, Fireman. —*Jim Shaw, Frank W. Telewski Collection*

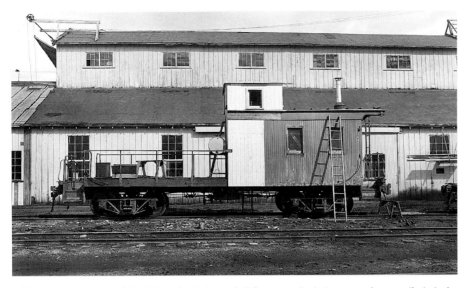

After a severe accident in which logs fell from a skeleton car immediately in front of caboose #800, the car was rebuilt by the Vail shop crews in March 1959. —*John R. Cummings*

The new design was never implemented. Instead, the company went ahead with the original plans to restore the old log dump trestle and in 1959 redecked the unloader track from bent 15 to 39 with untreated stringers and ties. The tail track from bent 61 to the end was redecked with one 14x20–inch treated stringer under each rail and treated ties. In December, construction crews reinforced the unloader track from bent 15 to 24 with two additional stringers per span. In May 1961, Weyerhaeuser hired a pile inspector to core all piles in bents 7, 11, 12, 16, and 19. All of the piles were treated with creosote before being installed in 1927 and 1928. Of 31 piles tested, only one pile was found to be unsound because it was split vertically in two. However, the two halves were solid and showed no signs of deterioration, a testimony to the quality of pole treatment during the creosoting process some 30 years earlier.

Bridge maintenance on the railroad also continued to require attention during this period. The most notable upgrade was the addition of a new steel log-catcher apron on the bridge spanning Highway 99 one

With a long string of loaded log cars in tow, Chehalis Western #493 passes Lacey on its way to South Bay in 1960. Notice the two wire telephone poles to the left, providing contact between South Bay and the dispatcher's office at Vail. —*Jim Shaw, Frank W. Telewski Collection*

Weyerhaeuser Vail's #10 was a Clyde Ironworks locomotive crane (ex-White River Lumber Company #946) seen here with Chehalis Western log car #207. The #207 was originally a Vail car modified by the Vail shop crews. Two bunks were added to the car along with safety appliances (including end steps) which permitted use on both the Milwaukee and Northern Pacific. The car was built specifically to hold logs retrieved from along the tracks. Photographed at Vail on March 15, 1959. —*John R. Cummings*

New log-catcher apron on old PC&F moving cars at Vail. The bridge guards were taken by rail to the Highway 99 overpass where they were installed to protect traffic from the danger of falling logs.

—*Weyerhaeuser Archives*

mile east of Olympia. The old wooden log-catcher, designed to prevent the possibility of a loose log from falling on passing traffic, required replacement in May 1955. The new steel aprons were fabricated in Seattle and shipped to Vail in six sections. At Vail, the shop crews assembled each group of three sections into one half of the bridge and loaded each half section onto two old Pacific Car & Foundry moving cars once used for moving donkey engines in the woods. The railroad crew then hauled the two sections to the bridge site. Once at the site, the sections were set in place by two railroad cranes, one on each end of a span. During the late 1950s, the Vail shops undertook the job of replacing the untreated wood sills of the Pacific Car & Foundry skeleton cars with treated wood sills. This significantly reduced the cost of rail transportation by lowering log car maintenance and repair. The job of replacing the sills was completed in 1960.

Grade-crossing accidents involving Chehalis Western or Weyerhaeuser trains occurred from time to time. One such accident involving the #493 with 30 loads of logs occurred on June 9, 1959, at 8:05 A.M. The locomotive struck a loaded log truck when it approached the West 1st Street crossing in Centralia. Engineer Milton Forner received injuries to his back and leg and was taken to the hospital. Conductor

A Clyde crane rests in the Vail yard across from the machine shop on March 15, 1959. —*John R. Cummings*

Once part of a much larger fleet of tank cars, #538 was one of only a handful of remaining water cars used at Vail in March 1959. Equipped with two water hose reels which are protected from the elements, the car set ready for the dry season. —*John R. Cummings*

Harry Kell, Fireman Ora Quinill, and the driver of the truck, Clarence Wolff, were not injured. Apparently, the truck driver did not see the approaching train. The locomotive railing, pilot, and the front of the hood were severely damaged, and the crew had to wait for locomotive #492 to arrive to move the train. A few years later, the #493 was involved in another grade-crossing accident with a loaded log truck, which required extensive repairs to the locomotive's hood and completely changed its appearance.

In early 1959, another accident occurred on the Chehalis Western, which would alter forever the look of caboose #800. The caboose was assigned to the Vail side of operations, working the run from the Camp 18 transfer south of Vail to South Bay. Just north of Western Junction, three large logs came off the log car in front of the caboose, destroying about half of the cabin. Head Brakeman James F. Barrett was the only one riding in the caboose at the time and was fortunately not injured. The crew inspected the car at the time of the accident and determined it could not pass the log catcher apron of the Lacey overpass. The caboose was set out at the siding at milepost 10 and was picked up when the train returned to Vail. Weyerhaeuser shop crews rebuilt the caboose at the Vail shops in March and returned to service with half the cabin. Since the cupola was on the damaged half, a new cupola had to be built on the intact portion of the caboose. The stove also was moved to the end of the caboose as part of the reconstruction work. The remaining deck was left uncovered and was used for a variety of functions, including holding a water tank to help put out any fires that might have started as the train passed during dry weather.

In the late 1950s the concept of tree farming began to produce smaller diameter logs that needed to be hauled on skeleton log cars designed to carry large, old-growth logs using cheese blocks. Cheese blocks were small angles of steel at the end of the log bunk and the shear weight of the huge logs against these blocks usually held them in place on the car. The smaller logs did not weigh enough to remain pressed against the blocks and would fall off the cars along the railroad right-of-way. To address this problem, Weyerhaeuser experimented with an interchangeable high-stake bunk which could be slipped over the sill of older wood skeleton cars when they needed to transport the smaller logs. Here we see the metal frame and bunks resting on the ground and installed on a car ready for service. —*Lyle Spears*

In 1959, the Chehalis Western secured running rights from Dryad to Pe Ell on the Northern Pacific, where it established a transfer. The Chehalis Western continued to operate out of Camp McDonald until 1961, when the headquarters camp and truck-to-train transfer were moved to Pe Ell, Washington. Weyerhaeuser had cut over the great majority of timber from its holdings south of Camp McDonald, and the land, replanted with hundreds of thousands of seedlings, would be left to regenerate a future crop of trees. As logging operations at Camp McDonald closed down and the focus of activity shifted to the west, the shop and support buildings were abandoned and eventually torn down after a period of several years. Eventually, even the seed extraction facilities and forestry program were removed from McDonald, leaving little more than a few concrete foundations hidden by a rapidly growing forest.

Above: The solemn remains of a once productive Washington Iron Works tower skidder rests in the weeds at Camp McDonald on an August day in 1960. —Lyle Spears

Left: Burro crane resting on W.T.Co. flat car #605 photographed at Camp McDonald in August 1960. —Lyle Spears

By the time this photograph was taken in August 1960, Camp McDonald was showing signs of reduced maintenance and an accumulation of scrapped steam era logging equipment. The building to the left was referred to as the round house and the machine shop is in the distance in this view of Camp McDonald looking south. One leg of the wye is in the foreground. In less than three years, Camp McDonald would be abandoned and the buildings razed as the focus of operations moved to Pe Ell. —Lyle Spears

Speeders #28 and #32 on a weedy siding at Camp McDonald. —Lyle Spears

Weyerhaeuser purchased Clyde Ironworks locomotive crane #8 from Simpson Timber for the Vail operation in 1942. In August 1960, it was on a siding at Camp McDonald just beyond the roundhouse. —Lyle Spears

Shortly after rebuilding in March 1959, caboose #800 was lettered for Weyerhaeuser Timber Company, W.T.Co. Later in the year, Weyerhaeuser dropped the word "Timber" from the company name and introduced its green, triangle tree logo. —Ken Schmelzer

After Weyerhaeuser changed its name from Weyerhaeuser Timber Company to Weyerhaeuser Company, equipment at Vail was relettered from W.T.Co. to W.Co. as seen here on caboose #800. This practice was also applied to the fleet of wood skeleton log cars. —Ken Schmelzer

Pacific Car & Foundary wood skeleton car #301 lettered W. T. Co. is a swivel bunk car used to carry more-than-car-length poles and boom sticks rests at Vail yards. —Ken Schmelzer

Pacific Car & Foundary wood skeleton car #142 relettered W. Co. rests next to the Vail shop building. —Ken Schmelzer

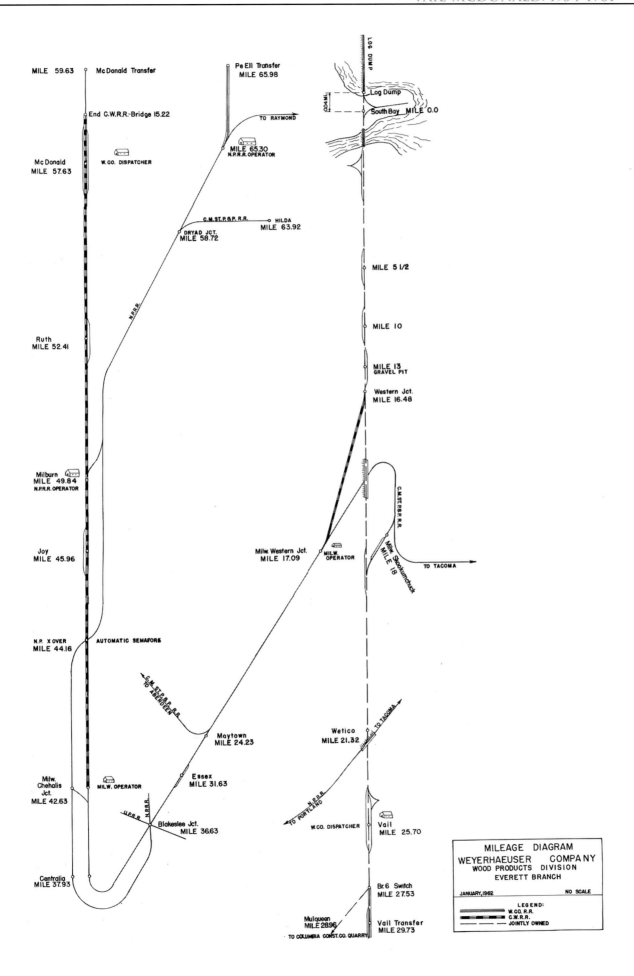

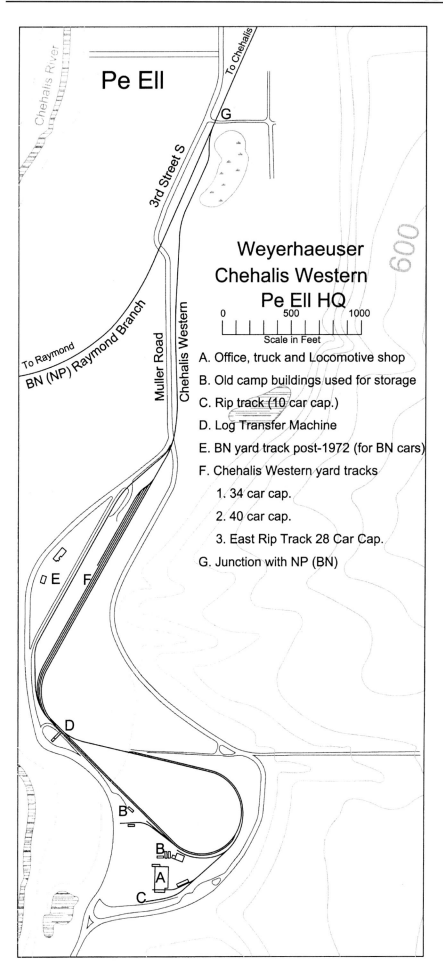

Weyerhaeuser's and the Chehalis Western's headquarters were moved from Camp McDonald to Pe Ell with a balloon track and yards just off the Northern Pacific's Raymond Branch. —USGS Topographic Map, Washington DNR Aerial Photograph, Weyerhaeuser Archives Aerial Photographs, redrawn by Frank W. Telewski

CHAPTER 9

The Pe Ell Years: 1961-1975

Shortly after the Chehalis Western secured running rights over Northern Pacific's 21st Subdivision (Willapa Harbor Line) from Dryad to Pe Ell, Weyerhaeuser began building a new headquarters camp, complete with locomotive shop and a balloon track with a log-load transfer machine. The transfer machine was built to lift the entire load off a log truck and transfer it directly to a log car. The company built the behemoth to move back and forth on two tracks supported on a set of recycled Pacific Car & Foundry trucks salvaged from tower skidder #3 once used in the woods.

Aerial photograph of Weyerhaeuser's Pe Ell headquarters and Chehalis Western shops and transfer looking north. One of the CW's FM 10-44 locomotives can be seen in the foreground. The tight radius curve of the loop track, while providing the ability to turn the locomotives without a wye or turntable, required very slow movement to prevent derailment of locomotives and cars. —*Weyerhaeuser Archives*

The Chehalis Western continued to operate out of Camp McDonald into 1962, by 1963 construction work on the Pe Ell maintenance shops was complete, and the McDonald shops were abandoned. As a result, 10 miles of railroad from Milburn to the McDonald transfer were abandoned; the steel and 31,000 treated ties, plus 214 million feet of treated bridge materials, were salvaged.

The Vail shops upgraded both Fairbanks-Morse 10-44 locomotives #492 and #493 from 1,000 horsepower to 1,200 horsepower diesel-electric engines prior to their transfer to Pe Ell. This change effectively made the two engines 12-44–class locomotives. The shop crew at Pe Ell maintained the engines in the new locomotive shop, which opened in 1963. The #493 hit a logging truck at Centralia in 1966, severely damaging the locomotive's hood. Repair work was completed at the Pe Ell shops, giving the #493 more the appearance of a Fairbanks-Morse 12-44 from the front. By the mid-1960s, both Fairbanks-Morse locomotives were beginning to show their age, and the Chehalis Western purchased a new Alco Century 415 in 1968. Using the numbering scheme applied to the first three diesels at Vail-McDonald, this engine was assigned 684 for its road number (fourth diesel purchased in 1968). When the #684 arrived, the Chehalis Western placed the #492 in standby service at Vail. Eventually, the #492 was rehabilitated, and the #493 was placed in storage at Vail as a source of spare parts to repair the #481 and #492. By 1974, what was left of a gutted #493 was cut up for scrap behind the Vail locomotive shops.

Weyerhaeuser made preliminary plans to begin logging in the Mineral Creek area, south of the town of Mineral, in 1961. Road construction, construction of the Mineral reload off the Milwaukee's Morton Branch, and timber harvesting began in 1962. Weyerhaeuser log trucks brought the logs to the Mineral Reload where they were scaled, sorted, and loaded onto Milwaukee Road steel log cars. The Milwaukee Road then shipped the logs from the Mineral reload, through the covered bridge crossing the Nisqually River, and on to the Skookumchuck interchange with the Weyerhaeuser line to South Bay. The National reload, only a few miles to the north, was also active in 1962.

A shortage of peeler logs for plywood production at Weyerhaeuser's Snoqualmie Falls Mill added a complication to Vail-McDonald logging railroad operations early in 1962. Approximately six million feet of peeler logs were shipped via rail to the Snoqualmie Mill in the

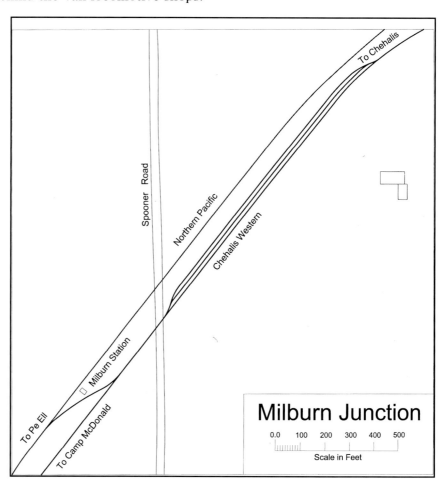

Chehalis Western trains had running rights over the Northern Pacific from Pe Ell to Milburn where they entered onto their own trackage. The track to Camp McDonald was abandoned in the early 1960s after the closure of the Camp McDonald transfer. —USGS Topographic Map, Washington DNR Aerial Photograph, Drawn by Frank W. Telewski

Another aerial view of Pe Ell, looking south, clearly showing the transfer machine and loading track. —Weyerhaeuser Archives

first four months of the year. Normally, the logs would have been cut to 40-foot lengths and transported to the Everett Mills via South Bay. However, the shortage at Snoqualmie required the logs to be cut as peelers to a length of 35 feet. Because wood sill log cars had been outlawed years earlier in common-carrier service, log shipments to Snoqualmie Falls required steel log cars. The logs were shipped over the Milwaukee Road, which required the use of Milwaukee Road steel log cars.

The introduction of Milwaukee cars into the log train delayed the transferring process, resulting in lost time and increased shipping costs. To handle the mixed shipments, the Vail train crew would go to work at 7:00 A.M. and head for the transfer. The empty Milwaukee and Weyerhaeuser cars would already be at siding 1 from the day before. The Vail crew would pull the loads out from the transfer and then spot the empty cars. Crews would place 15 Milwaukee Road cars in the 15-car pocket and 52 wood cars on the long spot track. When a Snoqualmie Falls peeler log load arrived at the transfer by truck, the transfer crew had to cut away from the wood cars used to haul logs to the South Bay boom grounds. Using their spot line, they pulled the loads ahead and then used the cut of loads to back into the pocket and tie on to one Milwaukee car. The transfer machine crew then used the spot line to pull the string of loads and empty Milwaukee car ahead, inserting the single Milwaukee car into the string of Weyerhaeuser wood cars. The Milwaukee car would then be positioned at the transfer to load Snoqualmie Falls peeler logs.

After spotting the empty cars for the transfer crew, the Vail train crew attached their caboose to their loads at siding 1 and shoved their train back to make room to organize the cars by destination. The peeler

Pe Ell yards photographed in the early 1970s clearly shows the track for Burlington Northern steel log cars to the right and the original yard tracks for Chehalis Western wood cars on the left. Logs loaded on the BN steel cars were hauled by the BN to Weyerhaeuser's Tacoma sort yard for export. —Weyerhaeuser Archives

loads were spaced throughout the log train, which required the crew to switch each Milwaukee log car out of the train and into a block of cars. The Milwaukee cars were blocked by destination and set at the head end of the train. After switching their train, the Vail crew would head toward South Bay with the entire train of loads. The Vail crew set out the Milwaukee loads at Skookumchuck (milepost 18) and then proceeded to South Bay.

Wind storms, blow downs, and wind-thrown timber were not uncommon in the Pacific Northwest. Notable storms resulting in significant blow downs hit the Pacific Northwest in 1880, 1921, 1931, 1951 (two storms), 1955, and 1958. Salvage operations to clean up blow downs were not uncommon at Vail-McDonald. The blow down of 1958 was large, with approximately half a billion feet of timber thrown to the ground at the tree farm. By 1962, Weyerhaeuser was still in the process of salvaging the timber from the 1958 blow down, and had cleared 30 million feet from 400 acres at McDonald that year.

By early autumn 1962, the salvage of the remnants of the 1958 storm was within sight. Meanwhile, early in October, Typhoon Frieda was spinning its way from the coastal waters off Japan toward the West Coast of North America. The warm, wet remnants of the typhoon collided with a mass of cold air descending from the Gulf of Alaska some 400 miles off the Northern California Coast and spawned two storms. The first raced up the coast on October 11, with rain and gale-force winds of 40 mph and gusts of up to 90 mph. However, with the arrival of Columbus Day, a second, more violent storm was reported off the coast by a Navy picket ship 340 miles west of Fort Bragg, California. This storm was reported with 92 mph winds and a low barometric reading of 28.42 inches, prompting the National Weather Bureau to issue high wind warnings for Northern California, Oregon, and Washington by 10 A.M. of the 12th. The storm, packing high winds, raged toward the Northwest coastline, approaching from the west-southwest heading toward southwestern Oregon, and began tracking north by northeast along the coastline. Winds picked up as the day progressed, and by evening the full force of the storm had struck.

Weyerhaeuser's 25 Ton American crane w/log boom (ex-Port of Olympia) was not assigned a road number. —John Henderson

At Fort Lewis, just northeast of Vail, wind gusts were reported at 120 mph. Wind gusts in Vancouver, Washington, were recorded in excess of 90 mph, while in downtown Portland, Oregon, the wind gusts were clocked at 93 mph. Gusts of 116 mph were recorded at Portland's Morrison Bridge. People who witnessed the storm said trees were blown over like matchsticks. By daybreak on October 13, a total of 48 people had been killed, including 11 in Washington. The storm left streets and highways littered with downed trees and power lines. Many roads were impassable, and homes, businesses, and cars were damaged or destroyed by falling trees. Damage to utilities was extensive, and many residents of the Pacific Northwest went without power for weeks. The Columbus Day Storm of 1962 became the standard against which all other statewide disasters would be measured.

By the end of 1962, Weyerhaeuser made initial estimates of wind-thrown timber at Vail-McDonald at about 500 million feet. Three years later, after an aggressive salvage logging program, the actual volume of

These four photographs show how the log load transfer machine at Pe Ell picked up an entire load from a log truck and placed it directly onto the rail log cars. Former tower skidder Pacific Car & Foundry trucks support the unloader. —Lyle Spears

timber blown down by the Columbus Day Storm was 40 percent lower than original estimates to 297 million feet, although the company sustained over 83,000 acres of downed timber over its entire timberland holdings in Washington and Oregon. Unlike the 1958 blow down, the damage done by the Columbus Day Storm was close to existing roads, facilitating relatively rapid access to the downed timber. The largest of the blow downs was 75 million feet of timber in a 125 year-old stand in the Harmony-Cinnabar area at the southernmost edge of the Vail land holdings. Downed timber from this area was trucked to the reactivated Chehalis reload for delivery to South Bay. The Chehalis reload remained active up until 1965, when the last of the concentrated areas of the blow down were logged.

Although Weyerhaeuser had engaged in timber and lumber export as early as 1951, and Vail-McDonald logs had been exported to Asia via the Port of Tacoma in 1961, the export log market was not a significant part of Vail-McDonald production until after the Columbus Day Storm. The windfall of hemlock and a weak domestic market for the wood led Weyerhaeuser to explore marketing options in Asia. The company found a ready market in Japan, and the export of hemlock logs greatly increased from the Columbus Day blow down. The export of logs via Tacoma would play a significant role in the future operations of the Chehalis Western. As a result of the Columbus Day Storm, Weyerhaeuser curtailed harvesting activity at the National and Mineral reloads, focusing more attention on salvage logging and road construction in downed timber. The reduced movement of logs from the National reload to South Bay was also affected by the construction of a new log dump at Everett's Mill B in November 1962. The new dump's design enabled Weyerhaeuser to unload loose or bundled logs from railroad cars directly into the mill pond. With

Resting in the Vail yard is a string of skeleton log cars with platform ends. In the background is a stack of new wood sills which will be used to rebuild older PC&F wood skeleton cars. The sills were manufactured at the Everett mills and shipped by rail to Vail. Originally, the sills were made from three solid wood beams. In later years, Weyerhaeuser experimented with laminated wood beams in the sills to replace the solid timbers. —Peter J. Replinger

Chehalis Western's #493 required extensive sheet metal work to the front of its hood after hitting a logging truck in Centralia in 1966. With a new physical appearance and a new 1,200-hp power plant, the old FM 10-44 was now a FM 12-44 class locomotive. —Jim Shaw, Frank W. Telewski Collection

The Chehalis Western purchased a new Alco Century 415 in 1968. It was the fourth diesel locomotive on the Vail-McDonald roster and was assigned #684. Notice in this builder's photograph, the exhaust stack is diverted up against the high cab of the locomotive. Shortly after arriving at Pe Ell, the exhaust stack was redesigned and went straight up from the top of the hood where the diesel vented. . —American Locomotive Company, Bob's Photo

Chehalis Western #492 rests on the loop track at Pe Ell as the recently acquired #684 and a caboose are on the shop track. —Bob's Photo

the completion of the new log dump, the Milwaukee shipped logs directly from the National reload to Everett rather than delivering them to Weyerhaeuser at Skookumchuck for rail transport to South Bay.

Weyerhaeuser rebuilt the entire log catcher apron on its railroad bridge at Lacey in 1963. That same year, the company also began the modernization program at South Bay by extending the tail track trestle in preparation for the installation of a new type of log unloader. Similar in construction and function to the machine at Pe Ell, the new log unloader required the new trestle to support the two tracks, which allowed for its back and forth movement. Weyerhaeuser installed the new electric log unloader in July 1964, and it was

Chehalis Western's #684 at Pe Ell with its modified exhaust stack which now goes straight up from the locomotives hood rather than being diverted past the cab as originally built. —Lyle Spears

operational by March 1965. The company designed the new unloader, referred to as a bundle dump, in order to reduce log breakage and loss during the dumping process. Logs, which were now bundled together on the rail cars, were lifted vertically by the machine and gently placed into the waters of South Bay.

Prior to the installation of the bundle dump, only a portion of the logs arriving at South Bay were bound together with steel straps. After the new loader was placed into operation, all log loads were bound at the reloads and transfers prior to shipping. Stringers used in the trestle to support the unloader were recycled from the now abandoned Chehalis Western main line bridges between the McDonald transfer and Milburn. The bridges on this portion of the railroad had been rebuilt only 12 years earlier. Additional maintenance work in 1964 at the log dump included the replacement of the load track stringers, wedge caps, and ties from bent 16 to 33, and from bent 39 to 47.

A second addition to South Bay also altered how log trains were unloaded at the dump. In 1964, Vail civil engineers modified the track plan south of the Woodward Bay trestle to accommodate an electric "snub," or incline cable car. The snub car lowered the log cars by gravity out onto the dump trestle rather than crews using a locomotive to push the cars out onto the trestle. This allowed the locomotive to leave the bay with a string of empty log cars without having to wait for the cars it just brought to the bay to be unloaded.

In 1965, a truck road trestle was constructed from the shore to the unloader trestle using new treated pilings and braces with a planked surface to cover the old log jammer track, which was no longer needed after the installation of the new log unloader. This trestle paralleled the existing dump track trestle, so trucks could approach the unloader and have their loads placed into South Bay. The truck road trestle to the unloader was built to accommodate the large volume of salvage timber from the Columbus Day Storm blow down that was being collected from various scattered land holdings too remote from easy rail access.

A light coating of snow covers PC&F moving car #414 at Pe Ell. The large office and shop building, painted Weyerhaeuser olive green, is in the background. This building served as the headquarters office for the McDonald tree farm as well as the truck and locomotive maintenance facility. The locomotive shop would be just beyond this photograph to the left. —John Henderson

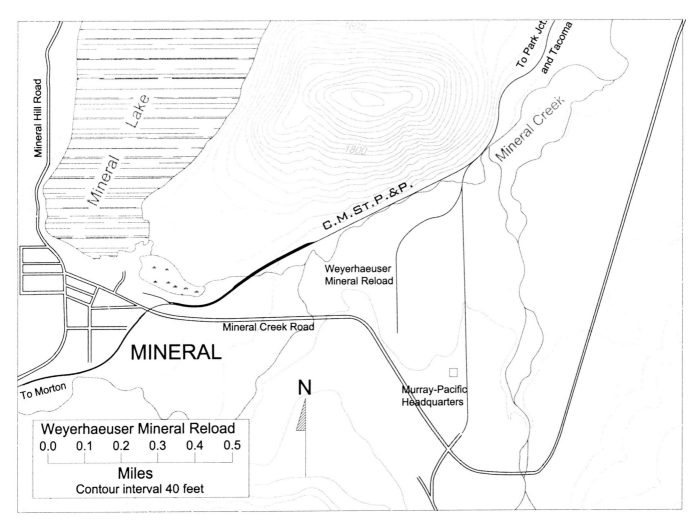

Weyerhaeuser's Mineral reload was located off of Milwaukee tracks east of Mineral and off of the Murray Pacific spur. —USGS aerial photo, USGS topographic map, redrawn by Frank W. Telewski

Weyerhaeuser Timber Company #481 moves a gondola for pulpwood loading at the Chehalis Reload in June 1963. —Lyle Spears

Weyerhaeuser Timber Company #481 spotting cars at the Chehalis Reload in November 1963. Equipped with marker lights, the #481 was also certified to run over the Milwaukee tracks between the Chehalis reload and Western Junction as did her sister engines from the Chehalis Western, #492 and #493. The overpass in the distance is Interstate 5. —Lyle Spears

Weyerhaeuser's #8 Clyde Ironworks locomotive crane rests at the Chehalis Reload in March 1966. Equipped with log tongs, it was used to load cars with timber from the Columbus Day storm salvage operation. —Lyle Spears

A truck scale ramp was also built just west of the track, which received the loads. At this location, scalers weighed and recorded the amount and species of logs prior to dumping.

In the mid-1960s, the supply of logs to the Everett Mills began to reflect the changing silvicultural practices set in motion decades earlier at the Vail-McDonald tree farm. Acres of prime timberland cut over in the 1920s and 1930s were beginning to yield the first logs from stand-thinning treatments and harvests of second-growth timber. Compared to the giant Douglas fir, hemlock, and cedar logs that preceded them, these new logs were relatively small in diameter. The mills originally designed to cut the large-diameter logs, such as Everett Mills A, B, and C, were not efficient at handling this new generation of timber. As a result, Weyerhaeuser designed and built a new sawmill at Everett specifically to cut the smaller second-growth logs. During the Golden Anniversary observance of Everett's Mill B in August 1965, Weyerhaeuser Company officers and shareholders participated in the dedication of the new Mill D.

With the change in unloading operations at South Bay, reduced log size, and a focus on safety, the old Pacific Car & Foundry bunks on the wood skeleton log cars were modified by removing the cheese blocks and replacing them with permanent three-foot–high stakes. All of the skeleton log cars were fitted with the new stakes in 1965. The addition of the stakes increased the average load carried by an individual car, reducing both truck and rail transportation costs for the company. Later in the 1960s, these stakes were extended another two feet to bring their total height to five feet. Because of a serious fatal accident in October 1974, in which two people were killed at a grade crossing, the Chehalis Western volunteered to paint the bunk stakes a bright orange color to increase the visibility of the log cars. Prior to the use of the bundle unloader, log loads were held in place by the cheese blocks and gravity, or bunk stakes. Occasionally, the logs were tied together with steel straps to prevent loose logs, which were shorter than the bunk stakes,

James F. Barrett carefully watches as the gasoline unloader pushes a load of boom sticks into the waters of South Bay. Boom sticks were long poles that could be longer than 120 feet. They were used to create the pens that separated the different grades and species of logs floating in the booming grounds. Since these "sticks" were longer than the standard 44-foot log car, a special bunk known as a swivel bunk was required. The swivel bunk permitted the load to move when the train went around curves without derailing the train. Cars #52 and #864 are equipped with swivel bunks in this photograph. The long load extends over three and a half car lengths. —John R. Cummings

from falling off the train while it was in transit from the transfer to South Bay. With the regular use of straps after 1965, a 12x32–foot strap storage dock was built at South Bay 100 feet south of the unloader trestle and next to the truck trestle.

Sometime in mid to late 1966 or 1967, the Chehalis Western purchased 22 44-foot steel frame skeleton log cars from Canada, which were relettered and renumbered for the Chehalis Western in the 800 series. These cars were converted tank car frames with wood sides. The sides had to be removed because they interfered with the unloader at South Bay.

In November 1970, Weyerhaeuser began to investigate the possibility of shipping logs from the Vail-McDonald Tree Farm directly to the Port of Tacoma for the export market. To facilitate shipping export quality logs from Pe Ell, the Chehalis Western expressed interest in acquiring running rights on the Milwaukee Road from Skookumchuck to Tacoma. In Tacoma, the trains would interchange with the Tacoma Municipal Belt Line Railway for the purpose of delivering the export logs to the proposed Weyerhaeuser

Vail PC&F skeleton log car #142 is a swivel bunk car. The bunk rested on a small circle of light weight rail which provided support to the bunk as well as guided its circular swivel motion. Photographed long after Weyerhaeuser dropped "Timber" from its name, the car is now lettered W. CO. rather than the earlier W. T. Co. —John Henderson

Used in both pole and boom stick service for more-than-car-length loads, Weyerhaeuser's skeleton log car #52 is equipped with a circular swivel bunk. —Ken Schmelzer Collection

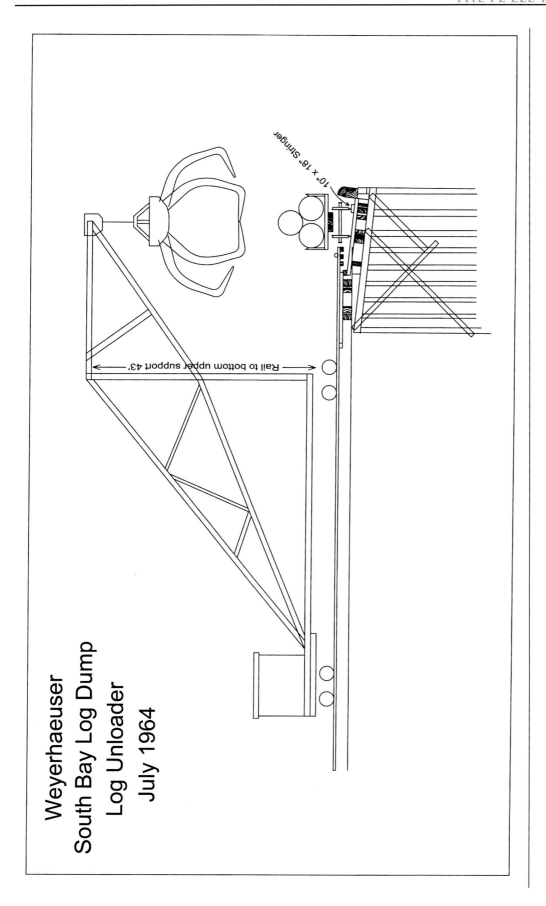

Sketch of the South Bay electric unloader and revised unloading trestle design. The original trestle built in 1927-28 was retained, but there was no longer a need for the parallel unloader track. The log track, once tilted towards the water, needed to be leveled to accomodate the new unloader. This was accomplished by raising the eastern rail with a 10" x 18" stringer. —Weyerhaeuser Archives. Redrawn by Frank W. Telewski

Tacoma sort yard. In a letter to William L. Bush, director of transportation and distribution for Weyerhaeuser, Mr. F. Gregg McGinn, vice president for operations for the Milwaukee, acknowledged the request and reported that he would refer it to the appropriate people within the railroad, "...in order to determine precisely what might be involved with regard to possible economics and its practicability."

The two companies began to explore a possible agreement. The Milwaukee Road expressed some concern about the Chehalis Western's equipment, specifically the type of brakes used on Chehalis Western log cars. "C.W. cars currently operating on our line have special exemption for their 'K' type brakes but almost certainly would need to be equipped with 'AB' brakes, both to allow operation into Tacoma and interchange with Tacoma Belt," wrote Gregg McGinn. "Size of trains and motive power would also be of importance up the hill." The "hill" was Tacoma Hill, the steep three miles of track that led out of Tacoma toward Frederickson, with a maximum grade of 3.3 percent. In August 1971, William Bush requested clarification from the Tacoma Belt Railway about the possible operation of Chehalis Western trains to Tacoma. Specifically, would the Tacoma Belt grant trackage rights to the Chehalis Western from the Milwaukee to the Tacoma sort yard, or would the Tacoma Belt handle the cars to and from the sort yard at the same cost per car offered other trunk lines.

By February 1972, Gregg McGinn responded to the Chehalis Western's request for running rights. The major point preventing the two companies from reaching an agreement centered on labor. Mr. McGinn pointed out that the operating labor organizations, or crafts, had been opposed to the 1936 agreement but did agree to accept the exchange of running rights between the Chehalis Western and Milwaukee. However, the crafts had opposed any extension of Chehalis Western rights on the Milwaukee over the years since the original agreement. Citing these concerns, Mr. McGinn wrote, "I regret the MILW cannot give favorable consideration to the granting of additional trackage rights in this territory."

With the inability to secure running rights over the Milwaukee to Tacoma, the Chehalis Western arranged for the logs to be shipped via the Burlington Northern from the Pe Ell reload to the export sort yard in Tacoma. As a result, Weyerhaeuser shipped the majority of its export traffic over the Burlington Northern using Burlington Northern steel log cars. Cars were shipped directly from Pe Ell or picked up from Vail's 10-car interchange track with the Burlington Northern at Wetico. At Pe Ell, the Burlington Northern crews and power pulled loaded Burlington Northern cars and set out empties from the siding to the transfer track. Chehalis Western crews would spot the cars for loading.

During this time, Chehalis Western crews still hauled domestic logs over the Burlington Northern to Milburn, from Milburn to Chehalis Junction over the home track, and from Chehalis Junction to Western Junction on Milwaukee Road trackage using Chehalis Western wood skeleton cars. Although Burlington Northern never granted running rights for Chehalis Western trains to run beyond Milburn, the Chehalis Western crews would from time to time operate a train between Pe Ell and Tacoma for the sole purpose of picking up Weyerhaeuser logs that fell off the log cars and onto the Burlington Northern's right-of-way. Burlington Northern required the Chehalis Western to lease a Burlington Northern locomotive for the special train, which included a crane for picking up the logs. Burlington Northern locomotives used in this service included #1630, #1637, and #1846.

Late in 1972, the Chehalis Western entered into negotiations with the Burlington Northern for trackage rights from Milburn to Chehalis Junction and for interchanging Chehalis Western cars loaded at the Chehalis reload through the Milwaukee Road–Chehalis interchange to the Burlington Northern. The Chehalis Western also considered purchasing a new steel caboose from the International Car Company. Eventually, the Chehalis Western and Weyerhaeuser would acquire three former Southern Pacific steel cabooses for use on both railroads. In addition to acquiring steel cabooses, the Chehalis Western began to express interest in acquiring steel log cars and contacted the Burlington Northern to inquire if any were for sale in November 1974.

Rail Access and the Atlas Powder Company Site

In 1967, the Northwest Aluminum Company was considering the purchase of 900 acres on the Nisqually flats for the purpose of building a new manufacturing plant that would require rail access. The land was owned by the Atlas Powder Company. On May 5, William L. Bush wrote George H. Weyerhaeuser and Rowland C. Vincent regarding this possibility: "This situation presents several interesting aspects for study on the part of the Chehalis Western." Mr. Bush continued, "that portion of the Chehalis Western north of the freeway and approaching the South Bay log dump is within three miles of the plant site. The nearest Northern Pacific rail availability is south of the freeway and any connection with Great Northern, Union Pacific or Milwaukee rail service would be a considerable distance south."

The Chehalis Western was possibly in a position to provide the rail access sought by Northwest Aluminum, providing an estimated movement of 10,000 cars annually. For this to become reality, the Chehalis Western would have to operate as a common carrier, providing inbound and outbound freight revenue on traffic to and from the proposed aluminum plant and the establishment of an interchange with the Northern Pacific track at Lacey. Weyerhaeuser officials weighed several options regarding Northwest Aluminum's request. One operational possibility would make the Chehalis Western a northern extension of the Columbia and Cowlitz Railway, Weyerhaeuser's Southwest Washington common carrier. Another option was for the Chehalis Western to provide trackage rights to enable several common carriers to reach the plant. During this period, the new north-south interstate highway, Interstate 5, was being built, requiring the construction of a new bridge on the joint Weyerhaeuser and Chehalis Western rail line from Western Junction to South Bay.

By June 27, Chehalis Western's hopes of providing access to the old Atlas Powder Company site dimmed as the Northwest Aluminum Company received an incentive from the Oregon legislature and governor to locate its proposed plant on a site near Astoria, Oregon. William L. Bush realized the potential of the Nisqually flats site and wrote George H. Weyerhaeuser and Roland Vincent with regard to the access question: "However, for long-range planning, we would like to continue our review insofar as it relates to the possibility of common carrier operations by the Chehalis Western." Mr. Bush's hopes for the Chehalis Western's role in providing common carrier or trackage right access to the flats were realized two years later, in September 1969, when the Great Northern approached the timber company about trackage rights. The Great Northern was interested in purchasing from or exchanging properties with Atlas to secure the Nisqually flats industrial area for the purpose of developing the site to generate rail traffic and provide rail access.

Weyerhaeuser and Weyerhaeuser Properties Inc. also owned land in the Nisqually flats area, and the Great Northern wanted to include the company properties in its marketing efforts to attract industries to the site. In December, the Great Northern entered into discussions with Weyerhaeuser to secure a trackage agreement for use of the jointly owned Weyerhaeuser and Chehalis Western Line. Two years passed with no agreement between the two parties. During this period, the Great Northern merged with the Northern Pacific and the Chicago, Burlington & Quincy to form the Burlington Northern before a draft of the proposed agreement was reviewed by Weyerhaeuser in March 1972. On July 9, 1973, Richard Beulke, vice president for the Seattle region of the Burlington Northern, requested a response to the proposed contract presented in 1972. The Burlington Northern was also interested in proceeding with the acquisition of a right-of-way from the Chehalis Western to the Atlas site, hoping to have approval by October 1.

Negotiations continued, and revisions were made to the proposed agreement. On January 27, 1975, Beulke sent a revised agreement to Weyerhaeuser: "We have revised the proposed agreement formalizing these 'bridge rights' over the Chehalis Western Railroad trackage to include the additional provisions suggested by you in our discussions, such as the future sale or lease of the Chehalis Western Railroad right-of-way, and now feel that the agreement as revised should be mutually acceptable to both Weyerhaeuser and the Burlington Northern." The industrial site was never developed, and the spur was never built off the Weyerhaeuser and Chehalis Western track. Instead the area was developed as residential with some light industry.

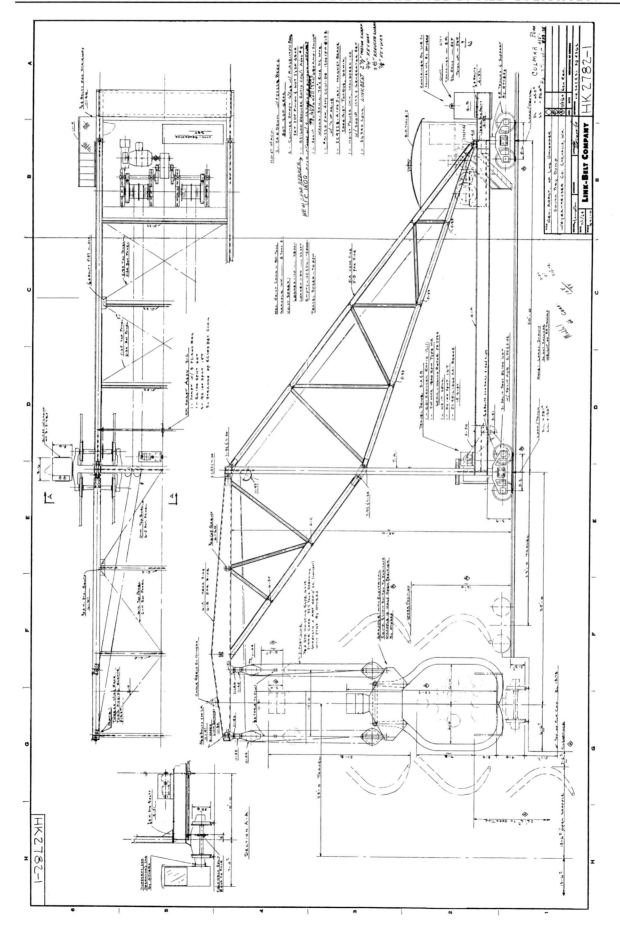

Copy of the original Link-Belt Company drawings for the South Bay electric unloader. —Weyerhaeuser Archives

Beginning in the mid-1970s, export logs were also shipped from a reload at Mineral, referred to as Mineral Yard, just off the Morton Branch. Weyerhaeuser crews loaded the logs onto Milwaukee steel frame log cars. The Milwaukee transported the logs to the Tacoma sort yard, or some were shipped directly to the Everett Mills. This reload remained active until February 26, 1980, and later became part of the shop storage tracks used by the Mount Rainier Scenic Railroad in the mid-1980s.

Logging railroads were well known for their innovations and ability to improvise with whatever materials were at hand. Weyerhaeuser and the Chehalis Western were also known to have built several pieces of their own equipment. In 1971, the tradition continued as the Chehalis Western experimented with converting old baggage cars to log cars. The idea was to increase the capacity for hauling logs using the surplus longer cars. The Chehalis Western purchased two ex-Spokane, Portland & Seattle baggage cars, one 72-foot and one 80-foot from the Burlington Northern, and stripped them down to their frames. The Vail shops added log bunks and truss rods to increase the strength of the cars. They were numbered CW 299 and CW 300, respectively, and were put into service. Unfortunately, the frames of the old baggage cars weren't sturdy enough under the loads of logs, and the frames began to sag. The addition of truss rods failed to correct the problem, and after only about six months of service the cars were retired and scrapped. Weyerhaeuser made no further attempts to convert old passenger equipment into logging equipment.

This view clearly shows the circular track supporting the swivel bunk on car #5. —Ken Schmelzer

Many of the swivel bunk cars had octagonal rails supporting the movable bunk. This view clearly shows the octagonal track supporting the swivel bunk on car 301. —Ken Schmelzer

At South Bay, construction crews incorporated an old steel skidder frame into the tail track trestle between bents 78 and 81 in 1971. This required the addition of two four-pile bents placed at equal distances on 20-foot centers between the bents to support the weight of the frame. At Vail, what remained of the old high bridge over the Skookumchuck River was blown up using explosive charges set at the base of the trestle bents.

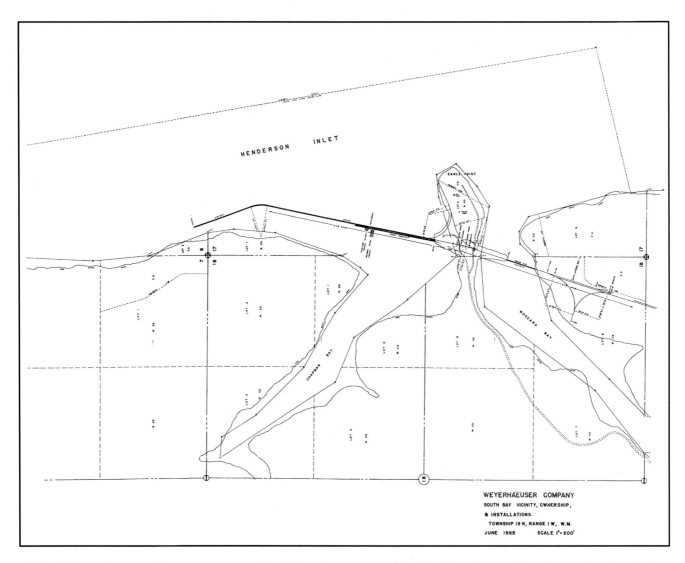

Original Weyerhaeuser Company map of South Bay from June 1965 showing the modification to the tracks to accomodate the spotting car (incline machine), new unloader trestle, truck trestle and truck turn trestle.
—Weyerhaeuser Archives

Opposite page, top: Weyerhaeuser #481 delivers a train load of to the South Bay unloader in June 1969. —Lyle Spears

Opposite page, bottom: In July 1964, Weyerhaeuser began to install a new unloader at South Bay which would be similar to the loader installed at Pe Ell. The innovation was the use of the grapple hooks which would grab a load of logs, lift them from a car and then gently set them down into the water of South Bay. The electric unloader began operation in March 1965. Notice that the log cars have permanent three foot stakes welded to the ends of the bunks. The new unloader made the use of safer fixed stakes feasible. Another addition to the South Bay pier was the construction of a truck unloading facility. Since the old unloader track was no longer needed, it was filled in with boards which permitted trucks to drive out to the unloader. The smaller crane in the foreground was used to lift the empty log trailer onto the rear of an empty truck for the trip back to the woods.
—Weyerhaeuser Archives

Weyerhaeuser opened its fifth and final saw mill at Everett in 1972. Designated Mill E, it was designed specifically to mill smaller second-growth logs using improved technologies not available when Mill D had been built 10 years earlier. With a decline in larger, old-growth timber destined for Mills B and C, the majority of Vail-McDonald logs were marked for the new mill, while the older mills were taken out of service.

By 1972, Weyerhaeuser's #481 was showing serious signs of aging, so the company leased Burlington Northern GP9 #1888, which was delivered to Wetico at 12:30 P.M. on March 25, 1972, for operation at Vail. Between 3:10 P.M. on October 4 and 8:30 A.M. on October 13, Weyerhaeuser leased Burlington Northern #1504 for operation at Vail. The company also leased NW2 #668 from the Milwaukee in 1972. On December 15, the #481 broke down and Weyerhaeuser began to weigh its options, including rebuilding the #481 to 1500 hp, purchasing a new or used locomotive, or leasing a locomotive on a short- or long-term basis. Morrison-Knudsen estimated the rebuilding of #481 to cost $70,000. Weyerhaeuser also considered purchasing an Electro-Motive Division GP7 57E in Pennsylvania for $75,000, which was being offered by Whisler Equipment Company of St. Louis.

In an attempt to alleviate the power shortage at Vail, Weyerhaeuser transferred White River operation's Fairbanks-Morse H12-44 #1 to Vail in 1975. The locomotive was shipped first to Chehalis Western's Pe Ell shops for an overhaul and then renumbered 714. It is not clear why this engine was assigned the road number 714, because it was not delivered in 1971, nor was it the fourth diesel-electric locomotive on the Vail-McDonald roster. The locomotive experienced operating difficulties and saw only limited service before the arrival of the first of two rebuilt GP7s in 1976. In the interim, the company continued to rely on leasing motive power from the Burlington Northern and Milwaukee Road to move log cars north to South Bay. Locomotive leasing continued until 1976. Weyerhaeuser leased at least 15 locomotives from 1972–1976, including 10 Burlington Northern locomotives (#1504, #1627, #1632, #1860, #1871, #1882, and #1888) and five Milwaukee Road units (GP9 #286, SW1200 #616, #618, #619, and NW2 #668) to

Above: To support the new unloader at South Bay, Weyerhaeuser added a car spotter which operated like an incline. Since the unloader was now set at a fixed position, cars needed to be spotted at the unloader rather than the machine running along side the cars on the parallel track as did the two earlier unloaders. A steel cable would raise and lower the spotter car from an electric winch built by Westinghouse Electric. A small diesel engine on the spotter car ran a compressor which provided air for the car brakes. Notice the log car has extended stakes on the bunks, which would date this photograph after the late 1960s. This photo was taken in July 1977. —John Henderson

Weyerhaeuser #481 with caboose #800 sets a string of loaded log cars next to load binder rack, where the crew removes and stacks the binders and prepares the loads for placement into the waters of South Bay. —Lyle Spears

The electric log unloader picks up a car load of logs and prepares to set them gently into the booming grounds. —Lyle Spears

Weyerhaeuser #481 with caboose #800 enters the leg of the lower wye to turn the locomotive for the return trip to Vail with a string of empty log cars it will pick up after it leaves the wye. —Lyle Spears

Chehalis Western #684 enters Burlington Northern tracks as it leaves the Pe Ell transfer loop track with a string of ex-Northern Pacific four bunk steel log cars. —Lyle Spears

Chehalis Western #684 switches a string of empty wood skeleton cars with a string of empty Burlington Northern steel log cars at the Pe Ell interchange. —Lyle Spears

Left: Chehalis Western #684, along with Clyde crane #10, heads up a log recovery work train to retrieve logs from along the Milwaukee Road right-of-way between Chehalis and Western Junction. The train is captured here in Chehalis next to the Milwaukee Road's station just north of Chehalis Junction. —Lyle Spears

Clyde Locomotive crane #8 rests at Pe Ell. The crane would commonly be used in Chehalis Western work trains, headed by Burlington Northern motive power, to pick up logs which fell from log cars as they traveled along the Burlington Northern mainline. —Lyle Spears

Chehalis Western #299 log car was a converted SP&S 72' baggage car, photographed at Pe Ell in August 1971. —Lyle Spears

Chehalis Western #299, and #300, another converted SP&S 80' baggage car, rest at Pe Ell before being taken to South Bay. —Lyle Spears

Above: Weyerhaeuser Timber Company's White River Branch #1 was purchased to switch their White River Lumber Company mills in Enumclaw, Washington. The FM 120-44 was transferred to Vail in 1975 and re-numbered 714. —Jim Shaw, Frank W. Telewski Collection

Left: Chehalis Western #684 and a caboose rest on the rip track at Pe Ell. The locomotive shop door is open and work bay empty providing an good view inside the Pe Ell shop.
—Lyle Spears

Repainted, re-lettered with a modern Weyerhaeuser logo, and re-numbered 714, ex-White River Lumber Company #1 receives some mechanical attention. —John Henderson

Chehalis Western caboose #543 brings up the rear of a log train which has just arrived at Mile 10 siding on its way to the South Bay log dump and waits for a train with a string of empties to pass. Trainmaster Frank DeSordi directs the engineer of the passing train. Caboose #543 appears to be an ex-Milwaukee Road wood caboose.
—John A. Taubeneck

Left: Chehalis Western caboose #325 waits in the snow at Pe Ell.
—John A. Taubeneck

Below: Weyerhaeuser leased several locomotives during the early to mid 1970s to alleviate power shortages when the aging fleet of FM's were down for repairs. Here Milwaukee 619, a SW1200 switcher moves a string of empty wood skeleton log cars into the north end of the yard tracks at Vail. —John Henderson

Wooden skeleton cars required rebuilding after several years of service. Beginning in 1939, the old 42' PC&F cars were rebuilt with 44' sills manufactured at Everett and shipped to Vail. Here a skeleton car rests inside the shop building at Vail as part of a rebuilding program.
—John A. Taubeneck

supplement its power requirements. (See Appendix IV.)

By the mid-1970s, the supply of logs being pulled from the Pe Ell region began to dwindle, and the days of operation from Chehalis Western's second headquarters camp were numbered. However, second-growth timber that had been growing at Camp McDonald for over 30 years was nearing maturity for harvest. In response, Weyerhaeuser began to investigate reopening the old Chehalis Western right-of-way to gain access to the second growth. The relaying of the three miles of track over the old McDonald Line spelled the end of Pe Ell operations. The last train to run on the Chehalis Western from Pe Ell departed on December 23, 1975, ending 14 years of rail service at Pe Ell. Weyerhaeuser's camp at Pe Ell was eventually transferred to the Raymond operation and began to be managed within the company's Raymond-Aberdeen administrative area.

Chehalis Western caboose #711 was converted to a partial flat car similar to caboose #800. When the 711 was rebuilt, the old tongue and groove siding was replaced with plywood sheathing. —Peter J. Replinger

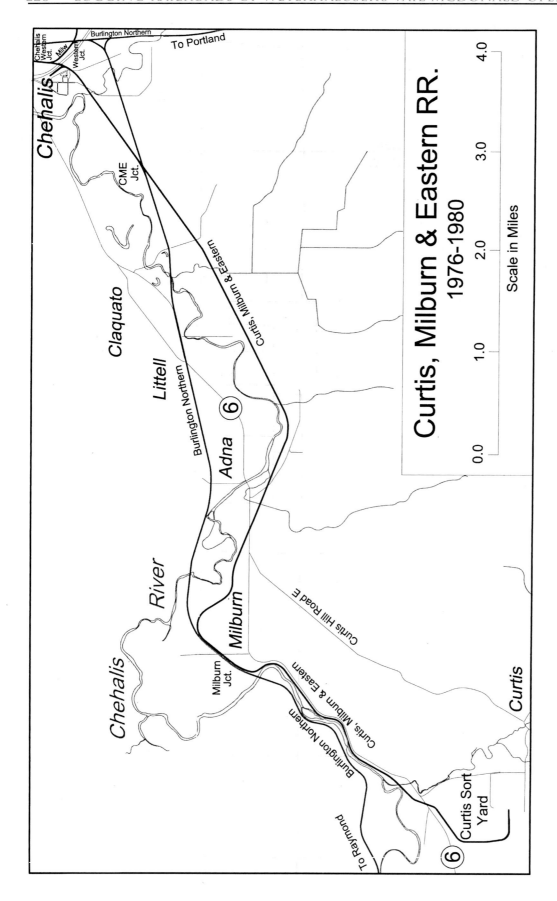

The new CM&E Ry. was a combination of the old Chehalis Western from Chehalis to Milburn, relaid track along the old Chehalis Western right-of-way from Milburn to Adna and a new track and yard forming the Curtis Sort Yard just west of the town of Curtis. —Drawn by Frank W. Telewski

CHAPTER 10
The Curtis, Milburn & Eastern: 1973-1980

Big plans were in store for the Vail-McDonald operation in the fall of 1973. Much of the McDonald Tree Farm had been reforested in the 1940s, and after 30 years of growth the trees were ready to be harvested. The older Everett mills had been designed to handle the large old-growth trees once common to the Puget Sound region and were not efficient at cutting the smaller second-growth timber that was rapidly becoming available from Weyerhaeuser's various tree farms. Everett Mill D, opened in 1965, and later Mill E, opened in 1972, were designed using technologies available at the time to mill the smaller, second-growth logs. However, within the short few years it takes to design, build, and put a mill into production, advances in technology that increased the efficiency of sawmilling made Mill E obsolete.

The rebuilding of the Chehalis Western tracks and bridges between Ruth and the interlocking diamond between the Burlington Northern and Chehalis Western one and a half miles west of Chehalis Junction required bypassing the line until the work was completed. In 1971 the two railroads signed a detour agreement and the CME Junction was created at the diamond. Photographed here on October 3, 1987, the bypass track has been disconnected from the two mainlines, but remains in place.
—Kristopher Johnson

During the 1970s, Weyerhaeuser had experimented with a new sawing technology known as "Chip-N-Saw." By the late 1970s, Weyerhaeuser Canada had installed a "Chip-N-Saw" mill during the renovation of its Vavenby, British Columbia, facilities. Later, the company installed the technology in its southeast mills, including the mill in Mountain Pine, Arkansas. These mills were specifically designed to maximize the use of smaller second-growth timber, which produced logs smaller than 16 inches in diameter, while increasing efficiency and decreasing the operating costs of the milling process. The mills produced chips rather than slab wood. The chips were transferred directly to wood chip hopper cars and sent to company pulp mills. The core of the log was then sawn into dimensional lumber.

To process McDonald's second-growth timber, Weyerhaeuser planned on building a modern sawmill and plywood mill near the town of Curtis, located west of Chehalis. This plan called for rail access to deliver logs to the mill and to move freight cars loaded with forest products to markets around the country, as well as to ship wood chips directly to company pulp mills at Everett, Longview, and Cosmopolis. The natural route for the railroad to follow was the original Chehalis Western roadbed, which had been abandoned over 20 years earlier.

Aerial view of the Curtis sort yard, the terminus for the new Curtis, Milburn & Eastern Railway.
—Washington Department of Natural Resources, Frank W. Telewski Collection

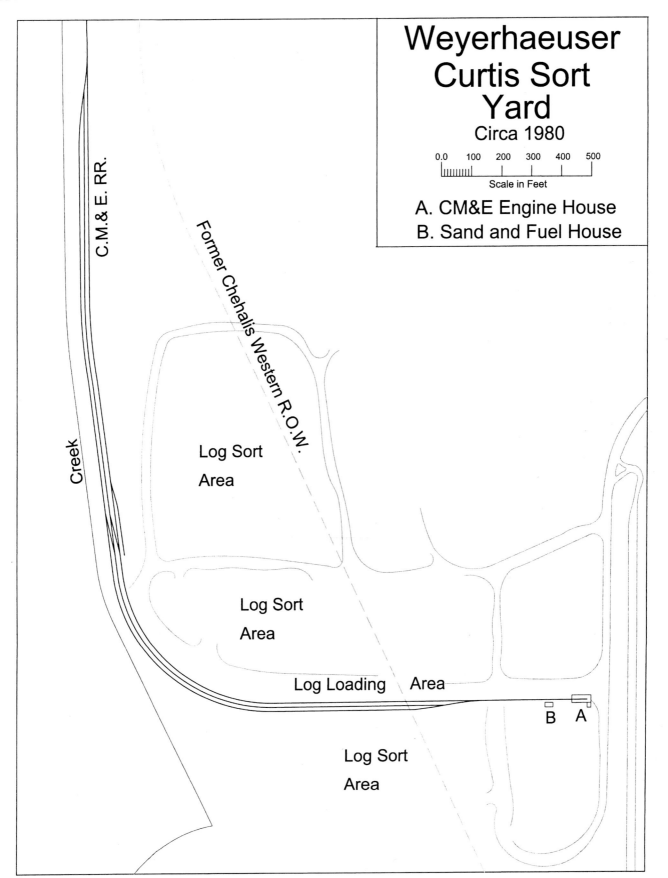

The Curtis Sort Yard consisted of a three track yard with cross-overs and a single spur track. The terminus of the railroad was a small locomotive shop which would house the now land-locked Alco, former CW 684, now CM&E 684.
—USGS Topographic Map, Washington DNR Aerial Photograph, Redrawn by Frank W. Telewski

The Chehalis Western abandoned former-Milwaukee Road bridge W.H. 42 crossing the south fork of the Chehalis River near Ruth when they abandoned the tracks to Camp McDonald in the early 1960s. In 1973, Weyerhaeuser hired the consulting firm of Noel Adams, P.E. & Associates to evaluate the bridge to determine if it could still serve the planned extension of tracks to Curtis for the CM&E RR. —Lyle Spears

This opportunity presented Weyerhaeuser with a dilemma. The original incorporation of the Chehalis Western no longer qualified it as a common carrier because the sun had set on various laws regulating railroads and their operation. Interstate common carrier status, issued by the Interstate Commerce Commission (ICC), would be required to move freight cars between the proposed mill and national rail access at Chehalis with the Milwaukee, Burlington Northern, and Union Pacific, and would also significantly reduce shipping costs for the company as an originating common carrier railroad set shipping charges. Also, a common carrier would more likely facilitate a grant of the running rights Weyerhaeuser coveted over the Milwaukee to access the Tacoma sort yard for export log shipping while maintaining existing running rights the company hoped to have grandfathered to a new common carrier. Finally, a common carrier would resolve some of the questions regarding commercial access to the old Atlas Powder site requested by the Burlington Northern.

On September 12, 1973, Weyerhaeuser incorporated the common carrier Curtis, Milburn & Eastern Railway Company. An application was filed for a certificate of convenience with the ICC to acquire and operate a railroad line in Lewis County that was presently owned by the Chehalis Western. Authorization was granted to acquire trackage rights and joint use of a line of railroad of the Chicago, Milwaukee, St. Paul & Pacific Railroad Company, and an order authorizing the Curtis, Milburn & Eastern Railway was filed to sell its securities without competitive bidding to the Weyerhaeuser Company, a common practice for wholly owned subsidiaries of larger companies.

Just like the Chehalis Western before it, the Curtis, Milburn & Eastern Railway was a wholly owned subsidiary of the Weyerhaeuser Company. The Chehalis Western would always retain ownership of the rail line from Chehalis Junction west to Milburn and the junction with the Burlington Northern. This required an agreement between the two Weyerhaeuser subsidiaries, providing running rights for the Curtis, Milburn & Eastern Railway over Chehalis Western tracks. The Curtis, Milburn & Eastern Railway would take ownership of the new tracks, which would run over the abandoned Chehalis Western right-of-way from Milburn west to Curtis. This required the relaying of three miles of track in 1975.

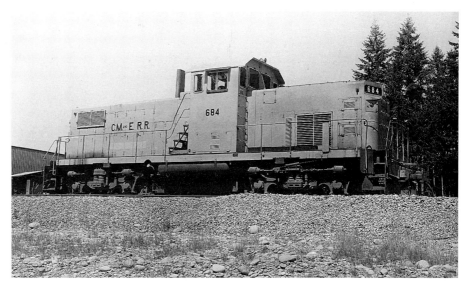

With the founding of the Curtis, Milburn & Eastern Railroad, Chehalis Western #684 was transferred to the new railroad and relettered for the C. M. & E. Railroad. —Jim Shaw, Frank W. Telewski Collection

At Curtis, a sort yard was established and plans were drafted for the construction of the new sawmill. A new sawmill and plywood mill designed specifically to handle second-growth timber delivered to Curtis would redirect traffic from South Bay and the Everett Mill complex. However, an economic slowdown, double-digit inflation, high interest rates, a significant reduction in new home construction, and a resulting decline in the wood products market during the mid-1970s put a freeze on the plans for the new Curtis Mills. The project was postponed in 1975 and eventually canceled in 1979. However, plans for the Curtis, Milburn & Eastern Railway, including the relaying of track and development of the Curtis sort yard, moved forward in the years prior to the final decision regarding the mill project.

Weyerhaeuser first began to examine reopening the abandoned Chehalis Western main line as early as March 1973, when the company hired Noel R. Adams, P.E. & Associates, Consulting Engineers, to evaluate bridge W.H. 42, which crossed the South Fork of the Chehalis River near Ruth. The 125-foot Howe Truss covered bridge was originally built by the Milwaukee Road around 1914. In 1938, the bridge had been moved to new treated piers after Weyerhaeuser purchased the line from the Milwaukee for the Chehalis Western. The bridge was inspected in 1945 and 1955 and only required minor repair in its 25 years of service to the logging railroad. When the Chehalis Western abandoned its line from Ruth to Camp McDonald and pulled up rails in the early 1960s, the bridge was left in place. But time had taken its toll on

Weyerhaeuser #765 is still relatively new when Peter Replinger captured it with a leased Union Pacific caboose at Vail in early 1977. The pile of new ties in the foreground will be used in the South Bay to Vail rail line restoration of 1976-77. —Peter J. Replinger

Curtis, Milburn & Eastern Railroad staff put the finishing touches on the oil and sand house at the Curtis sort yard. —Jim Whaley, Frank W. Telewski Collection

Curtis, Milburn & Eastern Railroad engine house at the Curtis sort yard. —Jim Whaley, Frank W. Telewski Collection

Curtis, Milburn & Eastern's sole locomotive, #684 pulls a string of loaded Milwaukee high stake steel log cars from Curtis to Chehalis Junction where a Milwaukee Road train will carry them to their final destination, either Western Junction for South Bay or on to the Tacoma Sort Yard for export. The switching of loads to the Milwaukee at Chehalis rather than the CM&E running to Western Junction was part of the WAM (Weyerhaeuser and Milwaukee) plan. —Jim Whaley, Frank W. Telewski Collection

During the brief life of both the CM&E and the WAM plan, it was common to see both the CM&E caboose (here still lettered for the Chehalis Western) and a Milwaukee Road bay window caboose bringing up the end of a train along the rails between Curtis and Chehalis Junction. —*Jim Whaley, Frank W. Telewski Collection*

Having just cleared a public road grade crossing, Curtis, Milburn & Eastern #684 heads towards Curtis with a string of empty Milwaukee Road steel log cars. Bringing up the end of the train are CM&E wood caboose and a Milwaukee Road bay window caboose. —*Jim Whaley, Frank W. Telewski Collection*

Ex-Chehalis Western #492 rests on a siding in the weeds at Vail on July 29, 1979. —*J. M. Seidl, Frank W. Telewski Collection*

Weyerhaeuser #776 and ex-Southern Pacific steel caboose #602 with a mixed train of old wood skeleton cars from the Camp 18 reload south of Vail and steel Milwaukee log cars it picked up at Western Junction from a WAM train delivers it loads to the South Bay unloader. —A. J. Schill, Frank W. Telewski Collection

the abandoned bridge, and Adams & Associates estimated the total cost of rehabilitation to be $86,048. By April, the company had decided the old bridge should be replaced with a wooden center-pier structure.

The need for bridge maintenance and repair extended beyond the abandoned bridges of the Chehalis Western. Eleven bridges remained in active service between Milburn and Chehalis. In anticipation of the repair work, the Burlington Northern prepared an agreement, which would allow the Chehalis Western to detour over the Burlington Northern's tracks from Milburn to the Burlington Northern–Chehalis Western interlocking diamond crossing, located 1.5 miles west of Chehalis. The detour agreement was dated February 2, 1971. In a memo dated July 31, 1974, Mr. Roy West notified corporate headquarters about the intent to replace the bridges' substructures below the bottom stringers. In this memo, Mr. West first proposed establishing a connection with the existing Burlington Northern track, where the two met at the diamond crossing. With an interchange point already in existence at Milburn, Chehalis Western trains from Pe Ell could remain on the Burlington Northern, bypassing the length of Chehalis Western track that required repairs.

Early in 1975, Weyerhaeuser secured permits from the Lewis County Planning Department to rebuild the 11 bridges between Chehalis and Milburn. However, operations out of Pe Ell ceased late in 1975, and after that time the Chehalis Western was no longer an operating railroad, because it had been replaced by the Curtis, Milburn & Eastern. With projected construction work on the river crossings delayed until 1978, the Detour Agreement had to be modified to include the Curtis, Milburn & Eastern. The Curtis, Milburn & Eastern secured use of the Burlington Northern's line between Milburn and Chehalis via an addendum to the original Detour Agreement. The Curtis, Milburn & Eastern agreed to take over the maintenance contract between the Burlington Northern and Chehalis Western that had been established in 1936 for the automatic interlocking 1.5 miles southwest of Chehalis. On December 29, 1978, the automatic interlocking diamond crossing between the Chehalis Western's tracks and the Burlington Northern was replaced by the Curtis, Milburn & Eastern as part of the maintenance agreement between the two railroads.

The last Chehalis Western train pulled out of Pe Ell in December 1975. With that movement, the Chehalis Western was retired to a paper railroad, only retaining ownership of the Chehalis-to-Milburn length of track. Train operations were transferred to the finished Curtis sort yard site on State Route 6, south of Adna, Washington, under the Curtis, Milburn & Eastern banner.

Second-growth timber from Camp McDonald began to move from the Curtis sort yard and reload to South Bay and Tacoma in January 1976. Logs were also hauled from Pe Ell by truck on the Curtis Haul Road, which linked the Pe Ell yard with the Curtis sort yard. A small engine facility was built at Curtis to service the #684, which was transferred from the Chehalis Western to the Curtis, Milburn & Eastern and was relettered for the new road, keeping the same road number. The #492 was transferred to Vail at the end of 1975, where it was put into service on work trains and was on standby service for log trains. It was never relettered for Weyerhaeuser but kept its Chehalis Western name, despite the fact that the railroad ceased to exist as an operating entity.

Although the Weyerhaeuser Company intended for the Curtis, Milburn & Eastern railroad to maintain the running rights the Chehalis Western had established in 1936 with the Milwaukee Road, the Curtis, Milburn & Eastern failed to reach an agreement for joint running rights. Instead, on December 20, 1973, it entered into an agreement whereby it was given joint interchange track rights on the Milwaukee Road in Chehalis. The Curtis, Milburn & Eastern hauled its trains to Chehalis and onto Milwaukee's interchange track, where the Milwaukee Road would replace power and crew for the run to Western Junction or on to the Tacoma sort yard. At Western Junction, the trains were met by Weyerhaeuser power for the run to South Bay. This was the core for what was called the Weyerhaeuser and Milwaukee plan, or WAM plan for short. The WAM plan required the Milwaukee Road to rebuild its aging fleet of steel, spring stake, skeleton log cars and gondolas used in log service into modern, four-bunk, high stake cars. The Milwaukee shops converted 200 spring stake log flats from the 59000–59499 and 59500–59599 series during the early to mid 1970s, and an additional 300 cars to high stake cars, mostly from 84000–90949 series gondolas. These cars were rebuilt with four bunks composed of seven-foot–high stakes. Steel log cars rebuilt earlier in the

Weyerhaeuser #765 approaches South Bay at low tide with a load of logs for the Everett Mills. —A. J. Schill, Frank W. Telewski Collection

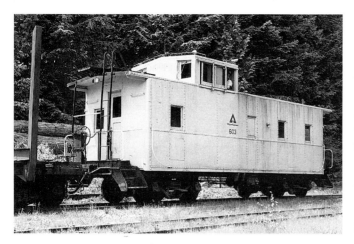 

Weyerhaeuser's steel cabooses #602 and #603, ex-Southern Pacific acquired in 1976, replaced the aging wood cabooses #711, #712, and #800 which had been in service since the late 1930s. —John Henderson

1960s and early 1970s had five-foot–high stakes on their bunks and were gradually modified to seven-foot–high by the Milwaukee Road shops. During the transition, the Milwaukee preferred to spot the shorter stake cars at Mineral and Western Junction.

WAM service started on January 4, 1976, at 11:00 P.M. By the fall of that year, four Milwaukee train crews and a trainmaster were dedicated to the service, and the addition of another train crew was planned for 1977. WAM 3 was the designation given for the train from Chehalis to Western Junction. The WAM 3 crew went on duty at 6:30 A.M. and would make two round trips between Chehalis and Western Junction per day, handling about 50 loads. Any Tacoma-bound loads in the first train were set out at Maytown for pickup by WAM 2 later in the evening. The crew for WAM 2 went on duty at 6:00 P.M. at Chehalis with approximately 50 loads, picked up about 20 loads at Western Junction and Skookumchuck, any loads left at Maytown by WAM 3, and delivered them all to the Tacoma Municipal Belt Line Railway at Old City Yard, Lincoln Avenue, Tacoma. WAM 1 would depart Tacoma at 11:00 P.M. and arrive back at Chehalis at 5:30 A.M. On average, WAM 1 would depart from Tacoma with 75 empties and pick up about 10 loads at Frederickson set out by WAM 4, which was handled by the Tacoma-Mineral Turn. The 10 loads and about 20 empties were set out at Western Junction, and the balance of empties were left on the siding at Chehalis with the Milwaukee caboose. The Curtis, Milburn & Eastern would in turn pick up the string of empties and Milwaukee caboose, add its caboose, and make the trip to the Curtis reload for another load of logs to meet WAM 3 and WAM 2 back at Chehalis the next day. Although the crews would change, the motive power used on WAM 1, 2, and 3 would remain the same.

WAM 4 traffic was always handled by the Tacoma-Mineral Turn, setting out about 10 loads for WAM 1 at Frederickson and taking the remainder to the Old City Yard in Tacoma. The Milwaukee proposed additional WAM service to transported logs from Weyerhaeuser's Mineral, National, Coal Creek, and Morton reloads and from Vail via Skookumchuck Junction to Weyerhaeuser's paper

An ex-Great Northern wood caboose used at Vail, but never assigned a road number, was one of the wood cabooses still in use in the 1970s. —John Henderson

mill in Cosmopolis, Washington. However, it is not clear whether this service was ever initiated by the Milwaukee. Since the Milwaukee Road would handle traffic over its own line, it insisted that the Curtis, Milburn & Eastern use Milwaukee Road's rebuilt fleet of steel, four-bunk log cars rather than the aging Chehalis Western wood skeleton cars, which no longer met Federal Railroad Administration (FRA) standards. After January, it was not uncommon to see both the Curtis, Milburn & Eastern caboose (ex-Chehalis Western wood caboose, ex-Great Northern wood caboose) together with a Milwaukee Road steel bay window caboose at the end of a string of log cars between Curtis and Chehalis. Since the aging Chehalis Western wood cars could no longer be used on the Curtis to Western Junction run, the remaining wood cars were transferred to Vail, where they would serve out their remaining years on the run from Vail to South Bay. They were finally retired in 1980.

With heavy traffic on the Vail to South Bay Line resulting from harvesting activity south of Vail and the delivery of logs by the Milwaukee Road at Western Junction, Weyerhaeuser was faced with a severe motive power shortage. The #481 was retired and scrapped in 1977 at the Purdy Company yard in Chehalis. The #492 and #714 weren't in much better operating condition, having been relegated to standby service only. Curtis, Milburn & Eastern's #684 was "land locked" west of Chehalis due to the WAM agreement.

To alleviate this problem and end its practice of leasing motive power from the Burlington Northern and Milwaukee, Weyerhaeuser purchased two rebuilt GP-7s from the Morrison-Knudsen Locomotive works. The first locomotive was rebuilt in 1976 from the ex-Norfolk and Western #2431, ex-Nickel Plate #431, originally built in July 1953, with EMD serial number 18599. Painted in school bus yellow-orange and black with silver trucks, fuel, and air tanks, it was assigned road number 765. The second GP-7, ex-Norfolk and Western #2436, was delivered by Morrison-Knudsen to Vail in 1977 with the same paint scheme as sister engine #765 and assigned road number 776. After the arrival of the second GP-7, FM's #492 and #714 were placed on surplus and eventually sold in 1980. Along with the new motive power,

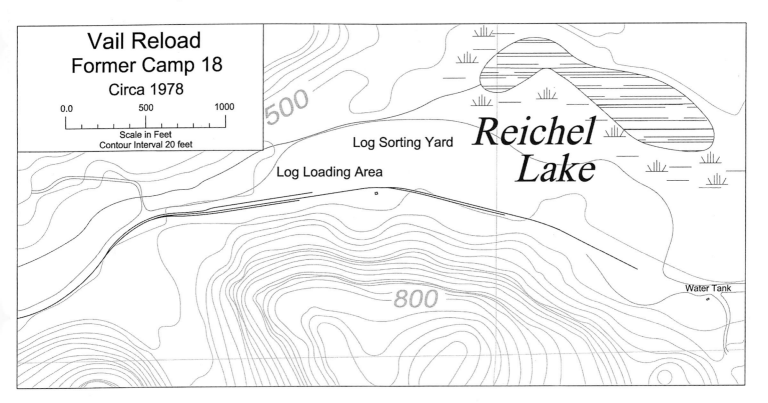

Vail reload, the former Camp 18 *circa* 1978. The old transfer machine, which used the spar and tail tree was removed and the old sidings were converted into spur tracks. —USGS Topographic Map, Washington DNR Aerial Photograph, redrawn by Frank W. Telewski

Weyerhaeuser purchased three steel cabooses from the Southern Pacific, two for Weyerhaeuser's Vail railroad and one for the CM&E without a number.

In 1976, rail traffic was relatively heavy on the Vail–South Bay main line. The section from Western Junction to South Bay saw the heaviest traffic, with both trains originating from the Vail sort yard at Camp 18 and trains handling the cars delivered by WAM trains at Western Junction and Skookumchuck. Typically, three trains ran northbound and three trains headed southbound Monday through Friday, between 8:00 A.M. and 5:00 P.M. A fourth north- and southbound train would run twice during the week. One north- and southbound train would also operate two Saturdays per month. From Western Junction south to the Vail reload, the traffic was lighter, with only two northbound log trains and one southbound returning with empties during the week, and one north- and southbound train on two Saturdays per month.

Speeder shack at the MP 13 gravel pit was made from a former filer's shack and also held the tools used by the section crew. —John A. Taubeneck

Besides handling log cars, the trains would on occasion pick up covered hopper cars of fertilizer at Wetico, bringing them to Vail and setting out empties on the return. The fertilizer was spread on Weyerhaeuser's timberlands as part of the high-yield forestry program. The increased traffic accelerated the wear on the old tracks between Vail and South Bay. Bids for rehabilitation of the entire main line were requested in January 1976, and the work was completed before the end of the year at a cost of $1.85 million. The work was conducted by an outside contractor, and Weyerhaeuser train crews delivered new and used #1 creosote ties to the job site. At this time, the ballast pit at milepost 13 was also upgraded with a rock crusher that converted river rock into crushed rock for ballast. The ballast produced by the crushers was 1-1/4×5/8 inches and was delivered by Weyerhaeuser trains in leased air dump cars.

Track maintenance also continued on the Curtis, Milburn & Eastern. In August 1976, the line took delivery of several Union Pacific air dump rock cars, which were loaded at the Segale gravel pit on the Milwaukee Road's line between Offutt Lake and Maytown. The gravel pit was originally established to supply fill for a new Milwaukee Road rail yard being built in Fife, just east of Tacoma. The gravel pit was opened earlier in the year when the Milwaukee Road built a 6,000-foot track off the main line, a 2,200-foot runaround track, and two spurs for loading. There was also a connection to the Burlington Northern tracks. The rock cars were picked up by a WAM train and delivered, along with a string of empty log cars to Chehalis. Curtis, Milburn & Eastern crews spread the gravel along its tracks.

Changes in the timber supply and markets led to the closure of three mills at Everett in the late 1970s. Weyerhaeuser opened Mill C, designed to cut old-growth hemlock, in 1924 and closed it in 1977. After 64 years of service cutting old-growth Douglas fir, Mill B was closed in 1979. Finally, the thermo-mechanical pulp mill, redesigned from a sulphite pulp mill built on the site of Mill A in 1936, was closed in 1980. This left the small log mill, Mill E, and the Kraft Pulp Mill in operation at the once-vast Everett Mill site. Despite the mill closures, South Bay was still busy receiving logs from Vail-McDonald and rafting them to Everett.

During the winter of 1978, Weyerhaeuser again dredged the South Bay log dump. To facilitate the dredging, Weyerhaeuser leased six side dump cars (908000, -03, -04, -06, -09, and -11) from the Union Pacific railroad. The cars were interchanged at Western Junction with the Milwaukee Road for weekend work on January 28 and 29. The dredged material was again dumped in the center of the upper wye, south of Woodward Bay.

Changes were in the future once more for the Vail-McDonald Railroads when the Milwaukee Road filed for reorganization with the Federal Bankruptcy Court in Chicago on December 19, 1977. On March 6, 1978, Weyerhaeuser purchased approximately three miles of Milwaukee's right-of-way and track from a point a half-mile east of Park Junction to Weyerhaeuser's reload at National. The purchase was processed through the bankruptcy court and was issued as a quitclaim deed.

Conditions on the Milwaukee deteriorated throughout the mid to late 1970s, especially after filing for reorganization, as the railroad applied a program of deferred maintenance. Increased derailments, speed restrictions imposed by slow orders over damaged track, and an increased frequency of equipment failures reduced reliability and negatively affected the WAM program. Mr. Roy West, woods manager for Vail-McDonald, initially suggested a rental agreement with the Milwaukee by which a Weyerhaeuser locomotive and crew would operate WAM 3. However, Mr. J. W. Stuckey, division manager for the Milwaukee, reassured Mr. West: "It is anticipated that we will have an improvement in our power situation in the near future due to a revised maintenance program being established on our property."

Conditions and equipment didn't improve significantly, and a pending embargo of train service by the Milwaukee as part of the reorganization plan threatened to halt the WAM trains. In anticipation of the embargo and the possibility that the Curtis, Milburn & Eastern would be ordered to run over Milwaukee tracks by the ICC in what is referred to as directed service, the Curtis, Milburn & Eastern placed an initial order with the Electro-Motive Division of General Motors Corporation (EMD) for the purchase of five new GP38-2s in April 1979. The purchase was part of a joint Milwaukee and Curtis, Milburn & Eastern–Weyerhaeuser program that would allow operation by the Curtis, Milburn & Eastern of WAM trains between Chehalis and Tacoma under ICC-ordered directed service. The large diesel-electric locomotives would provide the power required to haul log trains up and down the steep grade of Tacoma Hill. Details of

Another ex-SP caboose to serve at the Vail-McDonald operation was this Curtis, Milburn & Eastern caboose, which unlike its sister cabooses #602 and #603, was not assigned a road number. The caboose is resting at the end of the Chehalis reload track next to Interstate 5 that is just beyond the guardrail in the background.
—John A. Taubeneck

the purchase were worked out on November 29, 1979, as part of EMD order 796388. Delivery of the locomotives by EMD was tentatively scheduled for the second half of 1980, pending the submission of a purchase order.

Although the Milwaukee Road had faced reorganization before and survived, this time the consequences would be drastic, resulting in the abandonment of the Milwaukee Road lines from Montana to the Pacific in 1980. The new EMD locomotives purchased by the Curtis, Milburn & Eastern would not arrive until after abandonment. With the withdrawal of the Milwaukee, the WAM agreement ceased to exist, and logs stopped moving over the Curtis, Milburn & Eastern and Milwaukee to Western Junction and Tacoma. Weyerhaeuser was now forced to truck logs from the Curtis reload to the Everett Mill and Tacoma sort yard, while the company was involved in complex negotiations to purchase the Milwaukee Line from Chehalis to Tacoma. These actions led to the eventual abandonment of the Curtis, Milburn & Eastern as an operating railroad and the rebirth of the Chehalis Western in 1980.

Weyerhaeuser's two GP7s, #765 and #776 rest inside the 'roundhouse' at Vail. Although not truly a roundhouse with a turntable, on logging railroads, the engine shop was commonly called the roundhouse. This is a good study in contrast of the noses of these two engines. Note that the grab irons leading up the front of #776 were painted black and that the headlights were different on the two engines. —John A. Taubeneck

CHAPTER 11

End Of The Milwaukee Road As We Knew It: 1977-1980

Transportation troubles were on the horizon for Weyerhaeuser in early 1977. The company's ability to supply its mills and export market with logs and to move finished products from its numerous Pacific Northwest mills was threatened when the Milwaukee Road filed for reorganization with the Federal Bankruptcy Court in Chicago on December 19, 1977. This was not the first time the Milwaukee had filed for reorganization, but this time, with stiff competition from a strong Burlington Northern, the future was not very bright. As part of the reorganization, the Milwaukee proposed abandonment of its Puget Sound Extension. During the two years of bankruptcy hearings, the Milwaukee Road's Weyerhaeuser and Milwaukee (WAM) trains continued to move logs from the Curtis Milburn & Eastern's interchange at Chehalis to either Western Junction or the Tacoma sort yard as well as from Weyerhaeuser's various reloads to Tacoma, Skookumchuck, or the mills of Cosmopolis.

The loss of the Milwaukee's services would affect not only Weyerhaeuser but also hundreds of businesses who relied on the railroad company for transportation. In 1978, the Washington State Department of Transportation conducted a number of surveys to determine the economic

Weyerhaeuser's first diesel locomotive to serve at Vail, #481, is in the midst of scrapping on April 30, 1977 at the Purdy Company yard in Chehalis. —*Peter J. Replinger*

impact of a "possible Milwaukee abandonment" of lines west, including the use of state roads as alternative routes for truck transportation. One of these studies focused on the Morton Line, which served three mills in Morton and generated 2,419 carloads of traffic, and two log shippers at Mineral, one of which was Weyerhaeuser's reload, shipping 7,113 carloads of logs between July 1977 and June 1978. Between Chehalis and Tacoma, Weyerhaeuser shipped 27,496 carloads of logs in 1977 and 25,730 in 1978 via WAM trains.

The loss of these levels of rail traffic was unacceptable for Weyerhaeuser's operations, and by November 1978 the company began to investigate alternative ways to move logs from tree farm to mill or export ship. One possibility was the acquisition of the Milwaukee Road's line between Morton and Frederickson and the line from Chehalis to Frederickson to Tacoma by the Union Pacific. Another was for Weyerhaeuser itself to acquire the lines outright and operate under the Curtis, Milburn & Eastern should abandonment be approved by the Bankruptcy Court. By the fall of 1978, the Union Pacific had already conducted its own study to estimate the rehabilitation and scrap value of a number of Milwaukee lines it had considered for acquisition.

On November 28, 1978, Mr. Thomas B. Graves Jr., vice president of finance and administration of the Union Pacific Railroad, wrote to Mr. John G. Kauffman, vice president and director of transportation for Weyerhaeuser, regarding plans for acquisitions and shared estimates for rehabilitation and track scrap values of the Milwaukee Lines in question. Mr. Graves wrote:

"During our conversation yesterday, I indicated that Union Pacific would be more than happy to supply you with its rehabilitation cost estimates and estimated track scrap values for The Milwaukee Road lines from Tacoma to Chehalis and Morton. In connection I have attached a set of rehabilitation cost estimates for the track segments between Tacoma and Frederickson and Frederickson and Morton. Because we have concluded that the track segment between Frederickson and Chehalis would not be of interest to Union Pacific, since it generally parallels our line between Tacoma and Chehalis, we have not developed detailed rehabilitation estimates for this segment."

To develop an independent analysis of the condition of the Milwaukee's tracks, Weyerhaeuser contracted Harold E. Grier, a railroad track maintenance and management consultant from Concord, California, to conduct a survey of the rail lines. The agreement was signed on December 7, 1978, and Mr. Grier filed his first report to Forrest Savoy, manager of transportation engineering for Weyerhaeuser, on December 23rd. In general, he reported that ballast, ties, and rail were in deteriorating condition and that frequent derailments by the Milwaukee train crews only hastened the deterioration.

As part of the contract, Weyerhaeuser requested that Mr. Grier propose a design for a possible interchange between the Burlington Northern and Vail Line where the two crossed near East Olympia (formerly Chambers Prairie). Mr. Grier provided four possible plans for the interchange to Mr. Savoy on January 22, 1979. An interchange never existed at this location, even though some maps, such as Metsker's maps of Thurston County from the 1940s and 1950s, clearly show an interchange track between the two rail lines.[1] The construction of an interchange at this point would provide Weyerhaeuser with rail access to DuPont via the Burlington Northern's tracks.

Weyerhaeuser was also considering building a new log and wood products export facility at DuPont, located between Olympia and Tacoma on the south end of Puget Sound. The company purchased the old industrial site from E. I. DuPont de Nemours Company in January 1976, taking control of the property on July 1, 1977. DuPont used the facility to manufacture and ship explosives. The explosives were transported from manufacturing and storage areas to a dock via 16.91 miles of three-foot narrow-gauge railroad. The

---

[1] A common practice among map makers to prevent outright copying of their work was the incorporation of some minor error that would be characteristic of the original cartographer's work. Could it be that the phantom interchange track between the Northern Pacific and Vail main lines was one of Metsker's deliberate map maker's marks, or was it just an honest error? Metsker also failed to include the interchanges at Skookumchuck, Wetico, and Western Junction on his Thurston County maps.

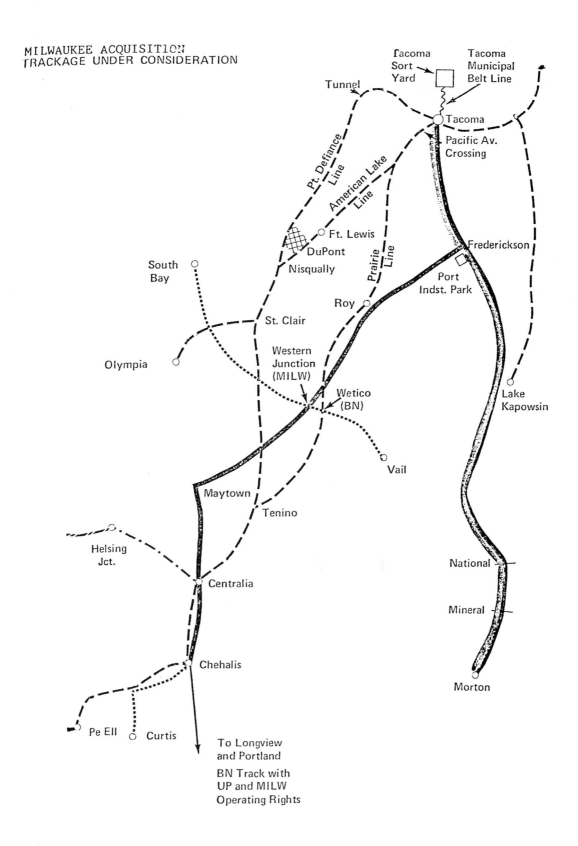

Milwaukee Road trackage purchased by Weyerhaeuser in 1980. —Weyerhaeuser Archives

acquisition of the DuPont property included the railroad, engine house, several cars, and a narrow-gauge 12-ton gas Plymouth locomotive (DuPont Powder Company #4, C/N 4352), which the company painted yellow and to which it added a Weyerhaeuser company decal.

This modern-day narrow-gauge Weyerhaeuser railroad never transported logs. Instead it was used to transport explosives stored on the site to the dock up until 1984. The plan called for the proposed new export facility at DuPont to be served by the Curtis, Milburn & Eastern and would replace the Tacoma sort yard and export facility. To ensure the success of the new export facility, the Chehalis Western, which superceded the Curtis, Milburn & Eastern in 1980, began to negotiate running rights with the Burlington Northern from the proposed interchange at East Olympia and the existing interchange at Wetico to DuPont. If access could not be provided over the Burlington Northern to DuPont, Roy West proposed building a rail spur "...from Greendale alongside the public road which bisects Ft. Lewis and crosses under the freeway just west of the DuPont exit and on into DuPont." Such a new spur would be 8.5 miles long and would have to cross the Burlington Northern's Prairie Line and American Lake Line west of the DuPont Interstate 5 exit. By early January 1980, Weyerhaeuser had successfully negotiated a trackage rights agreement with the Burlington Northern to run log trains from the existing interchange at Wetico to DuPont.

Pursuit of a resolution to the Milwaukee transportation question continued on March 14, 1979, when Weyerhaeuser Company officials met with officials from the Port of Tacoma to discuss a number of issues concerning the pending abandonment of Milwaukee Lines in and around Tacoma. The Port of Tacoma was served by the Tacoma Municipal Belt Line Railway (Muni-Belt), a switching road operating 25 miles of track and owned by the city of Tacoma. The Muni-Belt received cars from WAM trains from Chehalis, Skookumchuck, and Mineral, switching them to the Weyerhaeuser Tacoma sort yard for export ship loading. In the interim, the Union Pacific had already obtained a "right of first refusal" in acquiring the Milwaukee's Tacoma trackage. Such an acquisition by the Union Pacific would cut off the remaining segment of Tacoma to Chehalis Line from the Muni-Belt Line.

Both Weyerhaeuser and the Muni-Belt were faced with two major issues: what access would be available for interchange with the Muni-Belt across the length of Milwaukee's tracks in Tacoma should the Union Pacific acquire them, and should the Port of Tacoma and Weyerhaeuser enter into a joint venture to acquire and operate the Milwaukee Line from Tacoma to Fredrickson or from Tacoma to Chehalis. It was decided that Weyerhaeuser would contact the UP regarding trackage rights and interchange with the Muni-Belt and that the discussion should be a part of any reorganization. It was also decided that Weyerhaeuser would support the establishment of a Port and Weyerhaeuser team to consider alternatives to acquiring abandoned trackage; determine an organization that could gain access to federal funds for railroad rehabilitation; consider organization, management, and operating alternatives; and develop economic estimates for acquiring the alternate trackage, keeping in consideration all options: Morton-Fredrickson, Chehalis-Fredrickson-Tacoma, and Fredrickson-Tacoma. Finally, after the above decisions were made, the partnership would determine the steps and decide wether or not to enter negotiations with the Milwaukee Road.

In the meantime, despite continuing negotiations, the Milwaukee was moving ahead with plans to cease its western operations, which would result in the cancellation of the WAM plan. This was a major concern for Weyerhaeuser. In April 1979, R. E. Manning began to look at alternatives for moving both export logs bound for the Tacoma sort yard and domestic logs destined for the Everett Mills from the Vail-McDonald Tree Farm to South Bay, including the possible acquisition of the Milwaukee trackage. He presented this in a memo dated April 10 to Roy West, Weyerhaeuser's woods manager, in which he explained:

> *Under our current W.A.M. plan the Milwaukee hauls our logs on Milwaukee cars from Chehalis to Western Junction. When the Milwaukee folds as an entity we will have two courses of action open to us as follows: No. 1: Purchase the Milwaukee Railroad from Chehalis Junction to Skookumchuck Junction and haul with Milwaukee cars and our locomotive and crew. Try to get*

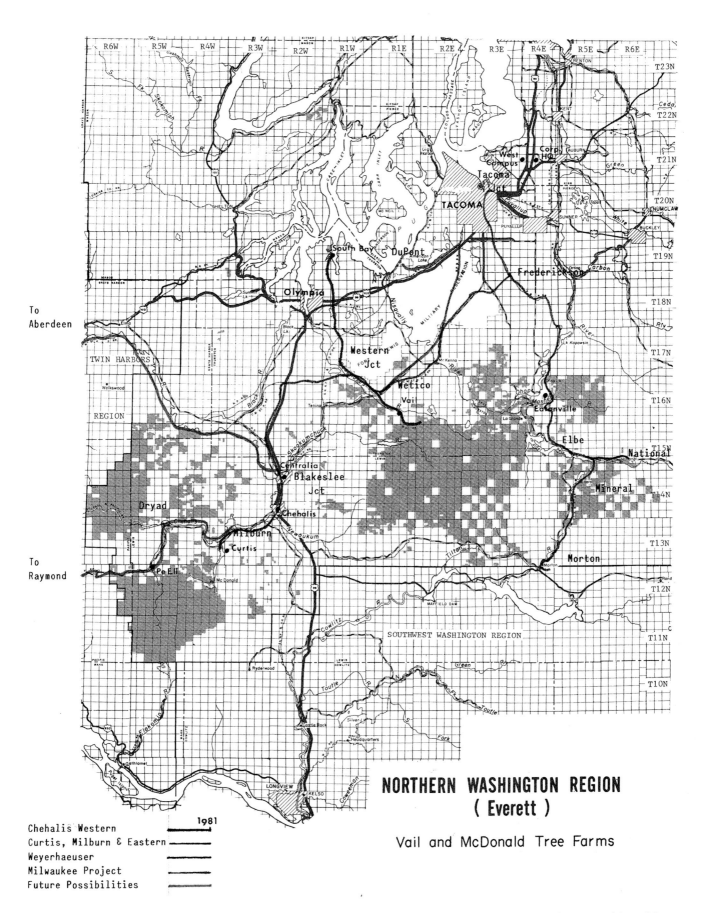

Weyerhaeuser woods, Curtis, Milburn & Eastern and Chehalis Western Railroads including rail lines considered for possible future purchase in 1981. —*Weyerhaeuser Archives*

this portion of our railroad as an extension of our logging railroad from Vail to Western Junction. No. 2. Haul with highway log trucks from Chehalis vicinity to some transfer point on our Vail to South Bay railroad. Having looked at several alternatives we think that a transfer point at the Mile 10 site is the best choice.

At this time, Weyerhaeuser began to investigate the possibility of an alternate truck plan. The logistics of converting from a rail operation to truck haul routes from the McDonald and Doty half of the tree farm to the Vail-South Bay main line were fraught with complications. One alternative was to haul via the Sleater-Kinney and Whitham Roads directly to South Bay. However, the route would go past North Thurston High School and South Bay Grade School, and Whitham Road was considered narrow and crooked for log truck traffic. A second choice was to access the Vail main line at the milepost 1.5 siding. However, since there was no truck access at the site, travel would again be required on Sleater-Kinney Road, and a variance from residential zoning would be required.

A similar problem existed for accessing the milepost 5 siding. A truck haul directly to Western Junction would require more use of county roads to avoid a 10-ton load-limited bridge over the Deschutes River at East Offut Lake. To develop milepost 10 as a transfer would require spreading 800 cubic yards of crushed rock and 800 cubic yards of topping rock, constructing a scale ramp, and grading and constructing a double bay ramp, scale shack, lights, and heating—at an estimated cost of $11,373. Mr. Manning stated with regard to the proposed reload: "The Mile 10 site is currently under study by Thurston County to be zoned residential. There is no zoning ordinance in effect now. If we start a transfer site there and zoning comes in, we would be allowed to continue under the grandfather clause. It will be several months before zoning occurs."

Also in April, Manning proposed moving the electric unloader at the Pe Ell yard to the Tacoma sort yard with the installation of a 75-foot trestle off the west end of the Tacoma sort yard wharf. This would facilitate the removal of export logs dumped into Puget Sound at South Bay and rafted to Tacoma, from the water to the shore at Tacoma sort yard for sorting and export loading. Alternatively, Mr. Manning suggested the construction of a marine railway to remove the logs from the water.

By June, most agencies, including the Interstate Commerce Commission (ICC), the Federal Railroad Administration, and the Office of Policy and Analysis involved in the restructuring of the Milwaukee Road, anticipated that the federal judge overseeing the restructuring and bankruptcy proceedings, Judge Thomas R. McMillen, would order a partial "embargo" of the Milwaukee Road, which would be limited to the western lines. An embargo would have effectively halted all Milwaukee Road traffic over the affected lines, opening up the possibility for other railroads to be directed to operate over those tracks. This would have established directed service by directed carriers operating over empty Milwaukee tracks. Directed service would provide a bridge between the rapidly deteriorating condition of service provided by the Milwaukee Road and the eventual carving up of the lines anticipated for abandonment. It was estimated that such a plan would provide an eight-month interim period for continued rail service.

In June 1979, Weyerhaeuser and the Milwaukee Road discussed the requirements, which would allow the Curtis, Milburn & Eastern to operate as a directed carrier over the Milwaukee Line. Mr. R. D. Richter, manager of rules for the Milwaukee Road, discussed the directed carrier provision with Mr. Tom Rasmussen, western transportation manager for Weyerhaeuser. Locomotive power requirements on the Chehalis to Tacoma Line, specifically the steep grade of Tacoma Hill, in anticipation of a federal order of directed service, were part of the discussion. Shortly afterward, the Curtis, Milburn & Eastern placed the order with the Electro-Motive Division of General Motors for five GP38-2s. The idea was to have the new locomotives operate the WAM trains between Chehalis and Tacoma under the Curtis, Milburn & Eastern once Milwaukee service was embargoed. On June 15, Mr. G. J. Barry, director of rules, safety, and training,

END OF THE MILWAUKEE ROAD AS WE KNEW IT: 1977-1980

EXHIBIT 1

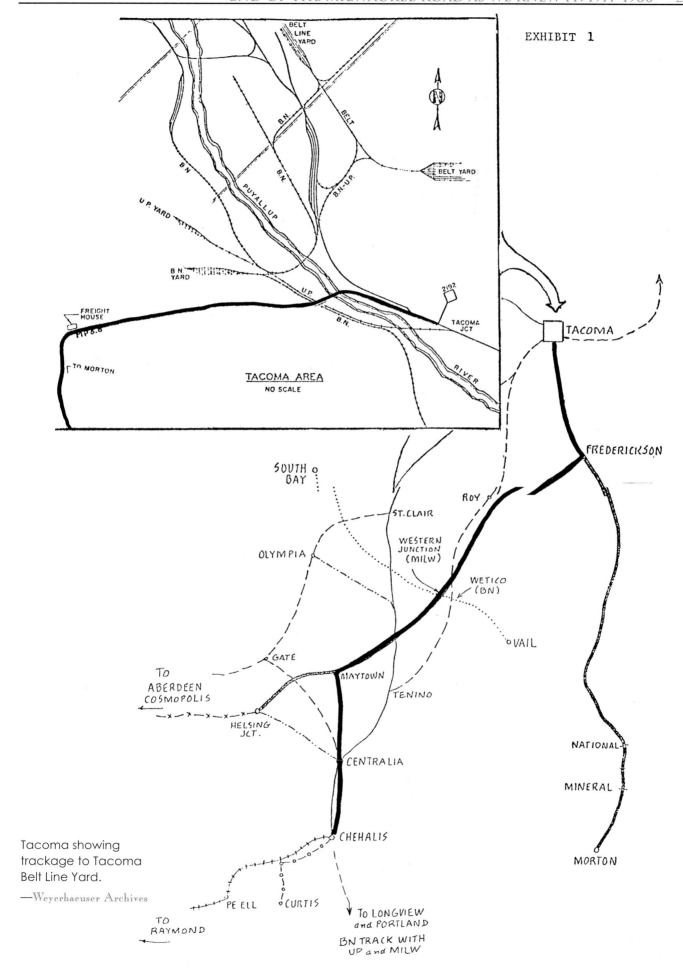

Tacoma showing trackage to Tacoma Belt Line Yard.
—Weyerhaeuser Archives

sent a letter to Mr. Forrest Savory to confirm the discussion. In his letter, he outlined the Milwaukee Road's concerns regarding directed service:

If the Court should reverse its decision and order directed service, we would like to include the following items in a plan of procedures to follow when that happens:

1. Current Milwaukee Road timetables to remain in effect, to identify the directed territories on the various subdivisions, with the directed carriers having authority to abolish or amend train schedules, etc., as desired.

2. Directed lines to be operated under the Consolidated Code of Operating Rules and, if compatible to the directed service, all Milwaukee Road safety rules, timetable special instructions, bulletins, etc., to remain in effect.

3. All train orders, clearances, track car lineups, etc., to be issued over the signature of the chief train dispatcher in charge of the dispatching office for the territory.

4. All compatible bulletins, notices, circular letters, etc., will remain in effect and future issues will be signed by the Milwaukee Road division manager who had been in charge of the territory, as instructed by the directed carrier.

5. The Milwaukee Road will continue reporting to the Interstate Commerce Commission and the various state agencies on serious derailments and personal injuries, highway/railroad crossing accidents, etc., on a division basis, on the directed lines. (The ICC has already requested that we do this.)

Roy West, woods manager for Weyerhaeuser, agreed with the first two points but questioned the validity of the last three based on the fact the Milwaukee Road would no longer be an operating entity west of Montana. Had federal Judge Thomas McMillen decided in mid-1978 to order a partial embargo of Milwaukee Road service over the western portion of the railroad, a temporary solution to Weyerhaeuser's transportation concerns would have been provided and the Curtis, Milburn & Eastern would have been appointed a directed carrier while the bankruptcy proceedings continued. However, such a court-ordered embargo was never issued since Judge McMillan ruled he did not have the authority to embargo the Milwaukee because the railroad was not in a "cashless" condition.

On July 23, a Milwaukee Road press release announced that Judge Thomas R. McMillen appointed Richard B. Ogilvie to replace, for health reasons, Stanley E. G. Hillman as trustee of the railroad. In the press release, Mr. Ogilvie announced "...the preliminary plan of reorganization which I shall file with the court by August 6." The Office of Rail Public Council in Washington D.C. issued a press release on July 25, stating it would help Washington shippers affected by the planned abandonment of 2,500 miles of track west of Miles City, Montana, by the Milwaukee Road. On August 8, the Washington State Department of Transportation (WSDOT) reported in its newsletter what had been anticipated for the better part of a year, confirming the worst for shippers of the Milwaukee Road:

The Trustee of the Milwaukee Road has announced his intention to file an abandonment application with the Interstate Commerce Commission (ICC) on or about August 8, 1979.... The ICC has served notice that they intend to consider the Milwaukee Road's application on an expedited schedule because of the Milwaukee Road's critical financial position. This expedited schedule calls for the ICC to issue its final decision on January 10, 1980.

The role of the WSDOT was, in part, to administrate the Local Rail Service Assistance Program:

> Monies available under this program are directed to be used in an 80 percent/20 percent federal/state (local) matching basis for projects which: 1. Rehabilitate light density rail lines to enable efficient rail freight service, 2. Construct new rail or rail-related facilities to improve rail freight service, 3. Acquire such lines to maintain existing or assure future rail service, 4. Subsidize continued rail operations, 5. Provide alternative means of transportation in a manner less expensive than continuing rail service.

On August 16, Mr. D. H. Byers of Weyerhaeuser's corporate law department, in coordination with the corporate transportation department, issued a company-wide memo informing all operating units that the company had filed a Petition to Intervene, which would allow the company to participate in the abandonment proceedings. Taking a united approach to the company's needs, the memo also instructed the individual units to "identify your location and include any comments, number of shipments handled by the Milwaukee or any other pertinent information concerning your operation if the abandonment is granted" and to forward this information on to the corporate transportation and law departments in order to coordinate the company's needs and response.

In response to the August 16 memo and in light of the August 8 official abandonment request, Mr. Roy West updated the evaluation of needs for the Vail-McDonald operation to ensure rail transportation of logs. Mr. West asked to consider several possibilities. One was the reinstatement of original running rights for the Chehalis Western from Chehalis to Western Junction negotiated with the Milwaukee Road in the 1930s. The Chehalis Western was relegated to a paper railroad after the founding of the Curtis, Milburn & Eastern, but it still owned 50 percent of the Vail main line and the original portion of the

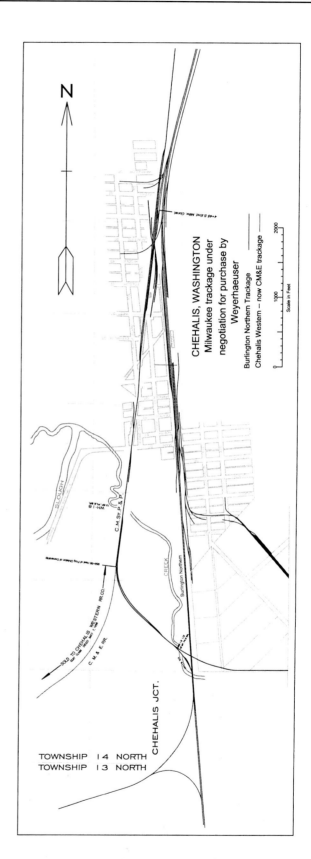

Milwaukee track being considered for purchase by Weyerhaeuser in Chehalis. —Weyerhaeuser Archives, redrawn by Frank W. Telewski

trackage from Chehalis Junction to Milburn, where the Curtis, Milburn & Eastern tracks originated. In fact, up to this time, the Curtis, Milburn & Eastern was still operating over Chehalis Western tracks to Chehalis with a trackage agreement between the two Weyerhaeuser railroads. In this scenario, the Chehalis Western would once again become an active railroad and would lease from the Curtis, Milburn & Eastern its Alco Century locomotive (#674) and grant interim running rights from Curtis to Milburn. This would also require the rental of several hundred Milwaukee Road steel log cars.

Other alternatives proposed by Mr. West included the acquisition of running rights for the Curtis, Milburn & Eastern from Chehalis to Western Junction using rented Milwaukee log cars or leasing the two Weyerhaeuser GP-7s (#765 and #776) at Vail to the Chehalis Western and having those locomotives pick up Curtis, Milburn & Eastern traffic at Chehalis. The new GP38-2s ordered by the Curtis, Milburn & Eastern in April 1979 would not be available until early 1981. A final alternative may, as Mr. West explained,

A small fleet of narrow gauge flat cars were used to transport explosives from manufacturing and storage facilities to the shipping dock at DuPont. —John Henderson

"...be the most effective of all because it only requires the reinstitution of the running rights of the Chehalis-Western from Western Junction to Chehalis, the rental of the Milwaukee cars, and the lease of a locomotive to the Chehalis Western by Weyerhaeuser, none of which have to be approved by any outside agency." He continued, "in case the Milwaukee is successful with their embargo we must be in a position to operate by rail from Curtis and put all production into South Bay. We have alternate plans for the movement of logs from Mineral by truck, which should be equal to our present rail cost."

The public collecting and filing of statements regarding the proposed abandonment by the Milwaukee proceeded as planned in September. On September 5, Mr. John F. Conrad, manager of the State Rail Branch of the Washington State Department of Transportation, provided his statement to the court. He had been evaluating the economic impact of the potential rail line abandonments in Washington State since January 1978. In his analysis, he focused on five areas that were identified as generating a significant amount of the Milwaukee's traffic but were without alternative rail service if operations were terminated. One of the five areas included in the analysis were the Chehalis Junction to Tacoma and Morton to Frederickson segments. One aspect of the analysis was the impact of increased truck traffic on existing state road and highway systems due to the loss of rail service. Mr. Conrad stated, "...we anticipate that impacts in some areas may be quite significant. This is particularly true on SR 7 which parallels the Morton-Frederickson line..." This traffic would include increased log truck traffic from the Mineral area due to the abandonment of Weyerhaeuser's Mineral reload as identified by Mr. West.

The statement by Mr. Conrad refocused attention on the Morton Branch, and in mid-September Tom Rasmussen met with shippers along the Morton Line who would be affected by the Milwaukee's abandonment. Companies and state agencies who participated in the meeting included the Port of Tacoma, Pacific Lumber and Shipping, Murray Pacific, Tubafor Mill, St. Regis, Washington State Department of Transportation, Washington State Department of Commerce and Economic Development, and Fred Tolan, a transportation consultant. The Champion Building Products representative from the Morton Mill was invited but could not attend. John Conrad, author of the state's statement to the hearing board earlier in the month, also represented the Washington State Department of Transportation. At the meeting, Weyerhaeuser representatives discussed the economics of purchasing, rehabilitating, and operating the Morton Line with allowances for an 80 percent federal subsidy and Weyerhaeuser's alternative cost options. The company discussed the joint venture capital required and net operating costs that non-Weyerhaeuser parties would have to provide for the operation to be viable. At this meeting, it was disclosed that the participation of a public body, such as the Port of Tacoma, was not required to access federal funding and that the Washington State Department of Transportation could administer federal funds directly to a Weyerhaeuser short line railroad.

The Washington State Department of Transportation announced the schedule of public hearings before the ICC regarding the Milwaukee abandonment in its Transpo Plan Newsletter of September 21. The hearings were scheduled to begin in Seattle on October 2. Mr. John G. Kauffman, vice president of transportation for Weyerhaeuser, provided his testimony to the ICC hearing on October 3, representing the entire interest of the company not only regarding the influence of the proposed abandonment of lines west, but also on the restructured core of the Milwaukee Road, given that the company was a major shipper over the lines the Milwaukee wished to keep intact. Not only did Weyerhaeuser have facilities in the Pacific Northwest, it also operated plants and shipped to distributors within the proposed Milwaukee core centered in the Midwest. Mr. Kauffman reported that in 1978 the company originated 490 carloads and received 3,400 carloads at its various facilities within the core railroad area. These numbers were much greater for the proposed area of abandonment: 39,000 carloads originated and 35,000 received in 1978.

At the hearing, Mr. Kauffman expressed the company's interest in "...playing a constructive role in trying to provide alternative rail service over two lines within Washington on which we contribute a significant portion of the traffic. The first is the Morton to Frederickson line, a 55 mile stretch of track serving seven shippers with an estimated annual volume of about 12,500 carloads." He testified that the Washington State Department of Transportation designated the Morton Line as an essential line in its Rail Plan and that the company was working with other Morton Line shippers to determine the economic feasibility of purchasing the line and operating it as a common carrier. Mr. Kauffman also stated that "should alternative rail service be feasible, we urge the Commission to provide the authorizations necessary to preserve continuity." Mr. Kauffman next focused on the 71-mile line between Chehalis and Tacoma: "Weyerhaeuser is the predominant shipper over this line, having originated approximately 25,000 carloads of traffic in 1978."

This portion of line was also designated essential in the Washington State Rail Plan because it would serve to reduce congestion, pollution, and wear and tear should traffic be forced to move by public highways, especially along the Interstate 5 corridor. Another concern addressed in Kauffman's testimony focused on the supply of rail cars for shippers in the Pacific Northwest, both for raw material movements, such as logs

Weyerhaeuser acquired this narrow gauge 12-ton Plymouth diesel locomotive (ex-DuPont #4) along with 17 miles of track when it purchased the DuPont Power Company property in 1976. —John Henderson

Another view of ex-DuPont #4 narrow gauge 12-ton Plymouth diesel locomotive now lettered for Weyerhaeuser Company photographed in April 1982. —John Henderson

and wood chips, and for finished products. This was a particular concern for the Washington mills at Everett, Snoqualmie, Raymond, Aberdeen, Cosmopolis, and Longview. He concluded his testimony with four points he believed the ICC should address:

> *1. Encourage competitive service where possible, 2. Insure that the timing of any abandonment is such as to allow for continuity of service where alternative service is being pursued, 3. Encourage alternative service where feasible by expediting any regulatory approvals required, 4. Condition abandonment upon the Milwaukee making available on a reasonable basis an adequate supply of cars and equipment for alternative service.*

Late in September, Judge McMillan decided the Milwaukee Road would be cashless by November and ordered the railroad to embargo all lines west of Miles City, Montana, on November 1. In response, Senator Warren Magnuson (Washington) immediately offered a rider to the Continuing Appropriations resolution, extending federal aid to the Milwaukee for an additional six weeks. The bill passed the Senate, but the House failed to pass a similar plan that would guarantee service for 30 days. In a separate ruling on October 3, the 7th District Court of Appeals reversed Judge McMillan's July decision, and in effect ordered the immediate embargo of the Milwaukee Road. This ruling allowed the ICC one week to implement directed service for essential portions of the Milwaukee. Directed service would then provide 240 days of continued operation, with government subsidization to provide an orderly transition and sale of viable portions of the railroad. Again, the possibility of the Curtis, Milburn & Eastern serving as the directed carrier along the

Explosive powder was stored and loaded in open-air covered platforms. Box car #506 is similar to #201, but has been rebuilt with plywood sides. —John Henderson

Chehalis-Tacoma tracks was raised. The arrangement for directed service already had the recommendation of the Milwaukee Road, with the Curtis, Milburn & Eastern trains operated by existing Milwaukee crews, equipment, and plant. Should the court call for implementation of directed service, the Curtis, Milburn & Eastern was ready to roll. An immediate embargo wasn't implemented, and November 1 remained the target deadline.

By early October, three scenarios became evident regarding the future of the Milwaukee Road and the line proposed for abandonment. These were outlined by Mr. Tom Rasmussen in an internal background paper distributed on October 4:

> *"We see some benefits and some drawbacks to all potential scenarios. We will remain willing to work with, and to follow the direction of, the Interstate Commerce Commission, the courts and the Congress. We hope that both interim and long-term solutions will be expeditiously sought, and be of least cost to the taxpayer—as well as least harm to Milwaukee employees."*

The three scenarios, from the Weyerhaeuser perspective, were as follows:

1. Federal funding such as that proposed in the Magnuson amendment would lead to a extension of six to eight months of operation of the Milwaukee in its present form.

2. Federal money would be infused into the Emergency Railroad Services Act (ERSA) and used to pay for directed service. This would include support for the Curtis, Milburn & Eastern, which would be directed, along with other railroads, to operate essential sections of the Milwaukee Road's western lines.

3. Some group or agency such as the Milwaukee employees group, which formed Save Our Railroad Employment (SORE), would investigate the possibility of an employee-owned company, or another single agency would directly operate the entire embargoed portion of the system.

All three scenarios had advantages and disadvantages, and there was no clear signal that any one of them would play out.

Throughout October, the clock ticked down to the November 1 embargo deadline. The western shutdown was due to take effect at 9:59 P.M., Seattle time, on October 31. In Chicago, the ICC had asked the federal judge to delay the embargo until November 6 so that Congress could have more time to possibly fund continued operation of the line's western portion (Tom Rasmussen's scenario 1). Both the House and Senate approved bills to continue operation; the Senate's bill specified a continuation of two months and the House's bill a continuation of one month.

The two chambers of Congress needed time reach an agreement and to send what would become known as Bill S.1905, the Milwaukee Railroad Restructuring Act, to President Jimmy Carter for his signature. Because the Transportation Department opposed any federal loan or grant to the Milwaukee, there was a strong chance of a presidential veto of the legislation. In the meantime, employees of the bankrupt railroad had already been given furlough notices, and the railroad was moving locomotives east; "otherwise, the company would have to pay other railroads to have the equipment removed," reported Wallace Abbey, director of corporate communications for the Milwaukee Road.

The federal judge refused to provide Congress with the few extra days to work out the legislation late in the evening of October 31. As a result, the deadline passed, the western lines were embargoed, and the WAM plan came to a halt. It was now up to the ICC to direct service, allowing the Burlington Northern to serve the Everett and Snoqualmie Mills and the Curtis, Milburn & Eastern to operate the WAM Plan with existing Milwaukee equipment and personnel (Tom Rasmussen's scenario 2). There was still a chance that Congress could provide funds to restart the whole system and keep it in operation until March 1980. In the

DuPont Power Company narrow gauge engine 8D, a Brookville locomotive rests on a siding at DuPont on April 13, 1982. —John Henderson

interim, Tom Rasmussen reported: "If the projected corrective action is taken by the 5th or 6th [of November], car supply and WAM Plan logs will not be significantly impacted. Further information will be provided as received."

On November 3, President Carter signed the Milwaukee Railroad Restructuring Act, providing a $10 million federal grant, followed by $75 million in federal loans, to restart and operate the entire Milwaukee Road system, effective immediately. The bill allowed one month for the development of the employee ownership plan (SORE), which had to be submitted to the ICC by December 1. The ICC decision was required by December 30, and the court decision to approve or reject was required by January 10, 1980. The bill included a provision for 20 days for labor-management negotiations on labor-protective provisions and 20 additional days for federal mediation if required. If the court or ICC were to reject the plan, an additional 60 days of federal funding was available, allowing for a period of time in which to conduct sales and transfers of equipment and lines. However, Section 18 of the Act suspended the ICC's authority to order directed service on the Milwaukee Road.

In essence, the Act was equivalent to Tom Rasmussen's scenario 1, federal funding to extend Milwaukee operation; provided for scenario 3, a possible group or agency taking over Milwaukee western lines; and eliminated scenario 2, which would have provided directed service via the Curtis, Milburn & Eastern. With the President's signature on the Act, the embargo was overruled and the Milwaukee Road once again began operating its own transcontinental and local trains in western states on Wednesday, November 7.

The legal ping-pong match between the courts and legislative branch continued through November. In a letter sent to the businesses along the Morton Branch, Tom Rasmussen wrote, "November 14, the federal court will consider the constitutionality of $75 million [in] additional federal loans that are subordinate to the creditors but not to stockholders.... If the judge rules against these loans, we could face another Milwaukee shutdown.... Should Congress reinstate directed service the C. M. & E. is fully prepared to handle the Morton line as a directed carrier." In the event the SORE plan failed, Mr. Rasmussen repeated Weyerhaeuser's interest in acquiring the Milwaukee trackage from Chehalis to Tacoma and from Morton to Fredrickson, believing it was the most economic way to operate a joint venture Morton Line. If the study undertaken by transportation consultant Fred Tolan proved feasible, Weyerhaeuser was prepared to make it available to a common carrier formed by the group. If it was not feasible, Weyerhaeuser would retain the line for possible future use.

An official plan to purchase the abandoned lines was presented to Weyerhaeuser senior management on October 10, 1979, "to insure competitive rail access to Tacoma and Dupont." As a result, Weyerhaeuser entered into negotiations with the Milwaukee Road to purchase what was essentially the 7th, 8th, 9th, and 10th subdivisions. On November 15, John Kauffman officially notified Richard Ogilvie, trustee for the Chicago, Milwaukee, St. Paul & Pacific Railroad Company, of Weyerhaeuser's initial interest in acquiring the assets from the Milwaukee Road, which would permit log transport from the Vail-McDonald Tree Farm to South Bay and Tacoma, including:

1. The right-of-way, track, and appurtenant structures commonly known as the Chehalis-Tacoma Line.

2. The right-of-way, track, and appurtenant structures commonly known as the Morton-Fredrickson Line.

3. 375 log cars for an aggregate purchase price of $3 million.

The small engine house at Dupont provided protection for the narrow gauge locomotives and a place to perform maintenance and repairs on the engines.

—John Henderson

Narrow gauge wood box car #201 was part of the aquisition of the DuPont facility by Weyerhaeuser in 1976. —John Henderson

Also in November, Tom Rasmussen contacted the Union Pacific to discuss Weyerhaeuser's concerns regarding access to the Municipal Belt Railway Yards and Tacoma interchange tracks of the Milwaukee Road via the Milwaukee trackage that Union Pacific proposed to acquire west of Tacoma Junction. The Union Pacific suggested any discussion regarding such matters be postponed until after the ICC rendered a decision on the SORE plan.

As required, the SORE plan was submitted to the ICC late in 1979. If approved, the employee-owned corporation would rescue 3,550 miles of the Milwaukee's western extension as the NewMil. But the ICC rejected SORE's NewMil plan based on financial considerations, and the western extension was slated for liquidation early in 1980.[2] A March 1 deadline for a second Milwaukee Road embargo now loomed. The failed attempt by SORE and Section 18 of the Milwaukee Railroad Reorganization Act, which excluded directed service, once again indicated rail shipment of logs would cease after February 28 with no immediate viable option other than truck hauls. Shortly after the final decision regarding the SORE plan had been issued, Weyerhaeuser and Milwaukee held a joint inspection of the railroad to inventory trackage and determine a net salvage value on January 16, 1980. A formal offer was presented to the Milwaukee Road on February 5 for 140 miles of track and a fleet of log cars.

Work on the joint venture to operate the Morton Line continued through the closing days of 1979 and into January 1980. Robert Nielsen, assistant secretary for Public Transportation and Planning, submitted some preliminary recommendations and cost estimates for the Morton Line to Fred Tolan, transportation consultant, on December 18. A formal meeting was held on January 16, during which a decision was reached by the shipper group not to operate a railroad and the group's activity was terminated. The decision was reached after a review of the economic analysis and issues by the shippers, Washington State Department of Transportation representatives, and the Northern Washington Region. The group had decided that "rail was unfavorable for both commercial products and logs: $100-150 higher (per railcar equivalent) than the trucking alternatives."

As stated earlier regarding the economic feasibility of operating the Morton Line and reiterated by Mr. Rasmussen in a January 22 memo, "as originally planned, we will continue to include the Morton Line in our acquisition negotiations with the Milwaukee, with the intention of mothballing." With the commitment to purchase the Morton branch, Weyerhaeuser indicated a willingness to work with anyone in a very coop-

---

[2] For an excellent review of the factors leading up to the demise of the Milwaukee Road's western extension and the Milwaukee Road itself, see Tod Jones's article: "What Really Happened." *CTC Board Railroads Illustrated*. Issue 257, March 2000.

erative way to keep the branch alive if it could be done economically in the future. This action would bank the line for possible future development by the company should the need and economic conditions change in favor of operation. Mr. Rasmussen continued, "The Milwaukee is expected to close down operations on March 1. We hope to conclude the acquisition by this time, but do not regard this date as a deadline because the Northern Washington Region is prepared to move logs without the railroad for a reasonable period of time."

On February 25, funding provided for in the Milwaukee Railroad Restructuring Act was running out, and the federal judge in charge of reorganization ordered the trustee of the Milwaukee Railroad to embargo the Milwaukee Lines west of Miles City, Montana, effective at midnight on February 29. The last Weyerhaeuser and Milwaukee Plan trains stopped running on February 28, 1980. All export logs from Pe Ell, Curtis, and Mineral were shipped via highway trucks to Tacoma. Pe Ell saw logs were trucked to Curtis, sorted, and stored in loose decks. All domestic saw logs, plywood logs, and pulp logs were trucked to the Vail reload for rail transport to South Bay. Export logs at Vail were also taken directly to South Bay. With a traffic rate of 20,000 to 25,000 log cars annually originating from Curtis alone, the transportation situation was critical to Weyerhaeuser's mill and export operations. A restoration of economical rail service was a priority for the company.

The Milwaukee had rejected Weyerhaeuser's first offer in January. The company made a second offer on April 30. This offer, reported to be in the vicinity of $4.4 million, was accepted, although it wouldn't be formally ratified by the bankruptcy trustee until August 20. The offer included the purchase of 140 miles of railroad and a fleet of 99 Milwaukee Road steel log cars.

As the details of the purchase were worked out, Weyerhaeuser needed to resolve the very important issue of who would operate over the purchased railroad. In early 1979, the question was moot:

Union Pacific GP9 #314 rests in the Vail yard next to the one of the shop buildings along with an ex-Milwaukee Road bay window caboose, recently acquired by Weyerhaeuser from the bankrupt railroad as part of the revitalization plan for the new Chehalis Western. The leased GP9 provided extra power during the transition period along with Union Pacific GP9 #139, prior to the arrival of the new fleet of GP38-2s from General Motors. —John A. Taubeneck

Weyerhaeuser's interstate common carrier Curtis, Milburn & Eastern would be expanded to operate from Chehalis to Tacoma. The railroad had already made plans to accommodate the long run to Tacoma when it set in motion the purchase of a fleet of new GP38-2s in April. However, the entire dynamic changed in November 1979 when the Milwaukee Railroad Restructuring Act was signed into law. Section 8 of the law stated that separated/furloughed employees of the Milwaukee Road, Conrail, and Rock Island had first right of hire by other rail carriers subject to ICC regulation who had purchased and planned to operate over former Milwaukee tracks. The provision to protect the furloughed railroad employees was set to expire on April 1, 1981.

In the interim, as an interstate common carrier regulated by the ICC, the Curtis, Milburn & Eastern would have to abide by the law if it operated trains to Tacoma. Section 8 was placed into the restructuring act to protect railroad employees, but in the case of Weyerhaeuser it actually threatened the jobs of Weyerhaeuser railroad employees operating trains out of Vail under the separate private Weyerhaeuser railroad at the time of the Milwaukee purchase. This included the train crews of GP-7s #765 and #776, as well as section crews who maintained the track from Vail to South Bay.

The original plan was for the Curtis, Milburn & Eastern to operate the entire system and the employees of the Curtis, Milburn & Eastern and Weyerhaeuser's Vail railroad to merge in IWA Local 3-130. Since the Vail crews were not employees of the Curtis, Milburn & Eastern, Weyerhaeuser would be required to give first right of refusal to former Milwaukee Road, Conrail, and Rock Island employees, quite possibly resulting in the laying off of the Vail train and section crews if the two Weyerhaeuser railroad operations were consolidated. In January 1980, officials associated with company transportation and the two railroad operations at Vail-McDonald discussed the various options and combinations of railroads that could be formulated to accommodate all current Weyerhaeuser railroad employees and operational concerns.

As an intrastate common carrier, the Chehalis Western, still a paper railroad, was not subject to the Milwaukee Reform Act, so all Weyerhaeuser railroad employees would be retained. Therefore, the final decision was to resurrect the retired Chehalis Western as an operating railroad and retire the Curtis, Milburn & Eastern. The official announcement of the acceptance of the offer to purchase the railroad segments was made to the Weyerhaeuser section crews, train crews, and Curtis, Milburn & Eastern employees by Roy West and Bob Pettit, trainmaster, in a letter on August 25. The letter read, in part: "Weyerhaeuser Company, through its logging railroad subsidiary the Chehalis Western Railroad Company, has formally agreed to purchase two segments of the railroad in Washington State from the Milwaukee Road. The transaction, which has been in negotiation for several months, is subject to Federal Court approval as part of the Milwaukee's bankruptcy reorganization." The federal court approved the purchase agreement on September 19.

Prior to the actual approval, Weyerhaeuser began to investigate the need for supplies required to upgrade the extremely deteriorated rail line. In its latter years, the Milwaukee Road had adopted a "deferred maintenance" plan that allowed the trackage to deteriorate. Early in January, company officials composed a list of basic small equipment that would be needed to operate the new railroad. The list included high rail equipment, speeders, cabooses, and track maintenance equipment. Many pieces of equipment were also purchased from the Milwaukee. Ties, rail, ballast, bridge timbers, and grade crossings all needed to be upgraded, repaired, or replaced. In many places, brush and overgrowth needed to be removed from the line of sight (sight lines) of locomotive engineers, especially at grade crossings. On June 11, 1980, B. A. Gammel of Gammel & Ollendick, suppliers of rail, ties, and track materials, mailed Mr. Forrest Savory, logistics manager, a list of quantities and cost of rail, plates, and bars.

Responding to internal pressure to get the new railroad up and running, Weyerhaeuser decided to take a risk and begin repair work before the actual closing of the sale. In a memo to Tom Rasmussen, dated four days before the federal judge's approval of the sale, Roy West wrote, "we should obtain an indemnifying agreement from the Milwaukee which would allow us to repair and use their tracks between Chehalis and Western Junction so we can possibly start the 27th of October when our first ties will be arriving." Actual repair work was reported to have begun on November 3, whereas the sale was officially closed on December 30, 1980. During July and August 1980, Weyerhaeuser's Vail train crew, headed by engineer Mr. James F. Barrett Sr., cautiously rode the rails with several Milwaukee officials in engine #776, recovering freight cars and equipment left by the Milwaukee Road after abandonment. Regular rail log traffic was initiated on the newly resurrected Chehalis Western railroad on November 18, with trains running between Chehalis and Western Junction.

The closing of the sale of the Milwaukee Road trackage to Weyerhaeuser's Chehalis Western on December 30 brought to an end the contract first struck between the two railroads back in 1936. Given its term of 50 years, the agreement would not have expired until 1986 had the Milwaukee Road not filed for abandonment of its western lines. The original agreement contained a provision for railroad abandonment. Article VI stated: "Nothing herein contained shall prohibit either company from abandoning its line of railroad, the use of which is by this agreement granted to the other company, but before either party shall abandon its said line it shall first give six (6) months' notice in writing to the other party of its intention to do so and shall secure any and all public authority which may be required for such abandonment..." The rest of Article VI is written with the specifics of the Chehalis Western's lines from Western Junction to the Skookumchuck Quarry and the segment from Chehalis Junction to Ruth.

It appears that the Milwaukee Road was more concerned with the longevity of the Chehalis Western than vice versa. Certainly, logging railroads were not known to last for an extended period of time, and the Milwaukee Road probably feared losing access to the Skookumchuck Rock Quarry once the supply of logs was exhausted from the Vail-McDonald operation. Unforeseen in the 1930s, the revolution of tree farming provided a renewed supply of logs, which would keep the logging railroad operating for many years to come. Although the 1980 purchase didn't exactly follow the letter of the 1936 contract, in the end one railroad exercised its contractual option to purchase the abandoned lines of the other. What was unprecedented in railroad history was that a logging railroad would outlast an established transcontinental railroad and eventually absorb a significant section of its tracks for its own use in the last quarter of the 20th century.

CHAPTER 12

The Chehalis Western: 1980-1992

The Chehalis Western officially returned to an operating railroad, but this transition required an investment of over $19 million to purchase the Milwaukee and to support construction and track restoration work, most of which was handled by the Alco Century #684 during the middle part of 1980. To complete the details of the operation, the Chehalis Western established a trackage agreement with the Curtis, Milburn & Eastern, granting Chehalis Western trains running access over the Curtis, Milburn & Eastern's tracks to the Curtis reload. This agreement was necessary because both railroads were separate companies, even though both were wholly owned subsidiaries of the Weyerhaeuser Company. The agreement was established on December 19, 1980. It specified that the Chehalis Western would pay the Curtis, Milburn & Eastern the sum of $8.16 per loaded car carried over the Curtis Line, and in return the Curtis, Milburn & Eastern would contract to maintain the track in its existing condition.

Alco Century #684 rejoins the roster for the Chehalis Western after the collapse of the Milwaukee Road's western extension and retirement of the Curtis, Milburn and Eastern. Still in C.M.&E. lettering, the engine was photographed at Western Junction in 1983 along with Chehalis Western #765 and an ex-Southern Pacific caboose used by the C.M.&E.

—Jim Shaw, Frank W. Telewski Collection

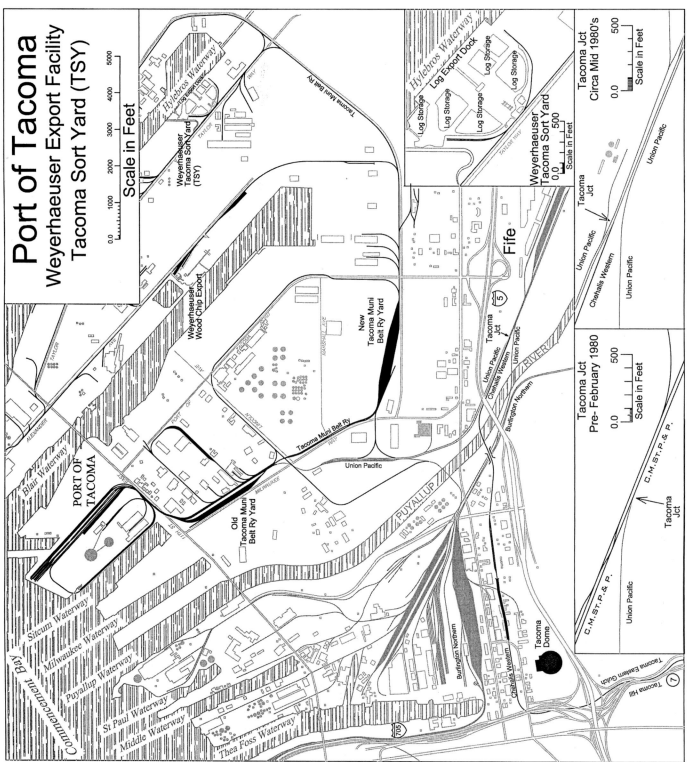

Rail lines accessing the Port of Tacoma, showing the location of Tacoma Junction and Weyerhaeuser's Tacoma Sort Yard and export facility. —USGS Topographic Maps, USGS Aerial Photographs, redrawn by Frank W. Telewski

Weyerhaeuser #765 pulls a train of former Milwaukee Road steel log cars through Vail on its way to South Bay on May 7, 1980. The Milwaukee Road ceased operation in Washington on February 28, 1980, bringing to a close the WAM plan trains. Weyerhaeuser purchased a fleet of the steel log cars from the Milwaukee along with the tracks from Chehalis to Tacoma and the Morton Branch on December 30, 1980. —A. J. Schill Photographer, Frank W. Telewski Collection

Weyerhaeuser #765 arrives with its train of loaded former Milwaukee Road steel log cars at South Bay, having moved to the rear of the train to push it out to the unloader on May 7, 1980. —A. J. Schill Photographer, Frank W. Telewski Collection

Thus, the Curtis, Milburn & Eastern was retired to a paper railroad and its only motive power, the Alco Century #684, was transferred to Western Junction. Coast Engine & Equipment Company overhauled the diesel engine #684 in February 1980, readying it for service on the new Chehalis Western. Weyerhaeuser's two GP-7s stationed at Vail would also be called into service on the new Chehalis Western, but would remain lettered for Weyerhaeuser Company until 1982. Prior to the arrival of a fleet of GP38-2s, originally ordered by the Curtis, Milburn & Eastern in April 1979, Mr. Roy West, General Manager of the Chehalis Western, investigated options for additional motive power on the Chehalis Western, especially for train service to the Tacoma sort yard.

Weyerhaeuser purchased the Milwaukee Road #X283 Jordan spreader for use in restoring the tracks from Chehalis to Tacoma. Photographed at Vail on August 28, 1980, the X283 would require rebuilding and conditioning before it could be placed in service. Notice the FM 12-44 in the background, possibly #714 or #492. —John Henderson

One option was leasing two U-25s or two GP-7s from Morrison-Knudsen Company, the other was a loan of three Baldwin S-8s, which were in storage at Weyerhaeuser's Klamath Falls operation in Oregon. Neither option was required, because the GP-38s arrived before track renovation was complete between Western Junction and Tacoma.

In addition to the Milwaukee trackage and a fleet of 99 45-foot steel log cars per the September 11, 1980, purchase agreement, the new Chehalis Western also acquired a Milwaukee Road Jordan spreader (X283)—rebuilt in October 1981 by the Western Washington Forest Industries Museum under the guidance of Jack Anderson—and four Milwaukee Road bay window cabooses. The railroad also purchased two covered hopper cars from the Southern Pacific on April 22, 1981, (Chehalis Western #595 and #596) to serve as sand cars at the Western Junction shop and placed an order with Pacific Car & Foundry on June 24 for three new International Car Company 30-foot, 50-ton Wide Vision Cupola cabooses (#s 597–599), which were delivered in September 1981.

To complete the extensive repair work required to safely operate trains, the Chehalis Western also acquired a fleet of ballast cars and side dump cars, some from Weyerhaeuser's Oregon, California & Eastern. The line purchased two 30-cubic-yard air-operated side dump cars built by Austin-Western (#1585 and #1611) from Garrett Railroad Car & Equipment in New Castle, Penn., on July 7, 1982. The ballast cars were built by Morrison-Knudsen and included some rebuilt salt cars originally from the Genesee & Wyoming railroad. The railroad acquired a small fleet of railroad maintenance equipment, including a Canron Rail Alignment vehicle, a Fairmont Tamper, and four ex-MILW patrol speeders. A used Pettibone crane was purchased, as well as a Wellman-Ohio diesel electric locomotive crane with a 37½-ton capacity (built in 1959 and reconditioned in 1975), from the Ontario Locomotive and Industrial Railway Supplies Inc. in November 1982. In keeping with the spirit of a logging railroad, the Chehalis Western shops built their own

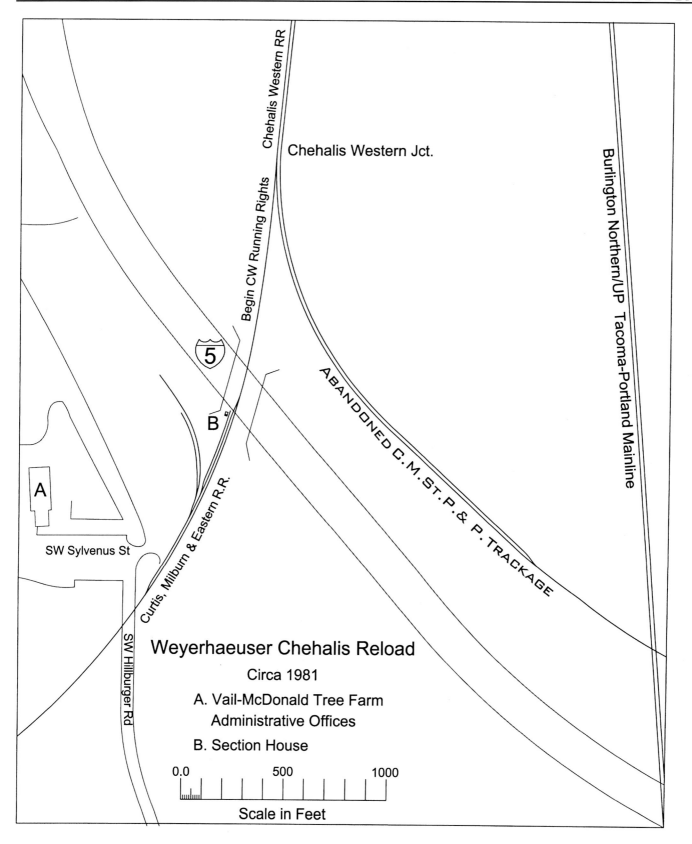

Chehalis reload after the rebirth of the Chehalis Western *circa* 1981. —USGS Topographic Maps, USGS Aerial Photographs, redrawn by Frank W. Telewski

In addition to purchasing a Jordan spreader, Weyerhaeuser also purchased several other pieces of Milwaukee rolling stock and equipment to supply its new Chehalis Western. Ex-Milwaukee Road ribside bay window cabooses #991944 and #991931 rest on a yard track at Vail on August 28, 1980. They would see limited use on the logging railroad and were soon replaced by newer Pacific Car and Foundry (PACCAR) wide vision cupola cabooses in September 1981, although the bay window cabooses would remain at Vail until at least April 1982. —John Henderson

spike driver from an old speeder and equipped it with an air compressor, which drove the speeder and supplied two air jack hammers hung on booms that were used to drive the spikes. To support the railroad, the Chehalis Western also built a modern locomotive and car maintenance shop and servicing facility that included a three-stall steel shop building at Western Junction.

The entire railroad maintenance operations moved from both Vail and the small Curtis, Milburn & Eastern shop at Curtis to Western Junction in June 1981. With the transfer of rail operations to the shops

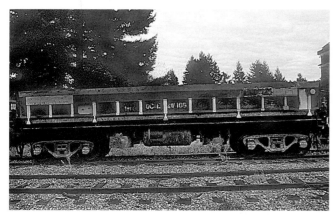

Ex-Oregon, California and Eastern side dump car #109 was never relettered for the Chehalis Western. —Frank W. Telewski

A string of ballast cars in the Chehalis Western fleet of maintenance-of-way equipment. —Frank W. Telewski

New tracks are laid as part of the restoration work on the old Milwaukee Road tracks and construction of the new shop facility at Western Junction in early 1981. —John A. Taubeneck

at Western Junction, the old Vail shops were completely converted to truck maintenance. However, before the Western Junction shops were completed, bad order Milwaukee log cars and other rail equipment were brought to the Vail shops for repairs and rebuilding. Although both Weyerhaeuser GP-7s were used extensively on the Chehalis Western, the units weren't relettered for the line until 1982. The ex-Curtis, Milburn & Eastern # 684 Alco was assigned to work train duty.

In September 1981, the Chehalis Western acquired 65 to 70 truckloads of track materials, including seven miles of 100-pound relay rail, plates, bars, and anchors. The materials originated from the salvage of the Milwaukee Road main line and came at a substantial savings, allowing the Chehalis Western to meet its original budget forecasts. The material was shipped directly to Western Junction and stored at the south end of the service facilities until it was used. The Chehalis Western continued restoring the old Milwaukee Road tracks into 1982, in what was referred to as the 1982 Milwaukee Project Rehabilitation Program.

In August 1982, the Chehalis Western contracted Sperry Rail Service to inspect its rail restoration using Sperry Detector car #123, which was delivered at Tacoma Junction. During the first two years of the Milwaukee Project Rehabilitation Program, the Chehalis Western replaced 65,000 ties, spread 100,000 cubic yards of ballast along 65 miles of track, and tamped and aligned the track. Crews laid a total of 10.4 miles of new track, including the new yards and storage tracks at Western Junction, completely restored grade-crossing signals in 1981, by 1982 had improved all grade crossings, and cleared sight lines, ditching, and drainage. In 1981, seven miles of the Curtis, Milburn & Eastern track was relaid using 100-pound rail, the entire line was ballasted and tamped, and the grade crossings and associated signals were upgraded. The Chehalis Western completed ditching and drainage in 1982. With a rehabilitated main line, the Chehalis Western maximum speed limit did not exceed 35 mph. In a bulletin issued by the Chehalis Western to all train crews, an operating speed of 25 mph was set.

Log car availability was critical to the success of the Chehalis Western. As early as October 25,

1979, Mr. Roy West expressed concern about a possible shortage of log cars, in particular the replacement of the aging wood skeleton cars. An appropriation request filed on December 12 clearly outlined the need for 535 log cars to maintain the flow of logs from the Vail-McDonald Tree Farm. From December 27–30, 1979, Mr. Forrest Savory conducted an inspection of the Milwaukee log car fleet, with the assistance of Mr. D. Guarnaccia from Weyerhaeuser's Klamath Falls

Chehalis Western's Canron Rail Alignment vehicle #501. —Frank W. Telewski

operation and Mr. F. Kauffman from the Purdy Company, a railroad salvage company. A total of 422 cars were deemed operational, and 58 were deemed bad order cars.

In January 1981, the Chehalis Western had on hand 89 of the original 99 cars purchased from the Milwaukee Road, which were serviceable, and leased an additional 94 Milwaukee log cars from U.S. Steel (series 58195–58494). Weyerhaeuser purchased 65 ex-Burlington Northern (Northern Pacific and Great Northern) steel log cars located at the St. Regis Lake Kapowsin facility on August 8, 1980. This brought its total fleet of steel log cars to 248. The Burlington Northern cars were marooned at the Lake Kapowsin facility when a railroad bridge on the Burlington Northern line was washed out in a storm. In order to place the cars in service on the Chehalis Western, Mr. West ordered the cars lifted onto flatbed trucks and transported to Chehalis Western tracks.

The Chehalis Western also offered to purchase an additional 31 heavily damaged (heavy bad order) Milwaukee cars at Tacoma, which were originally designated for scrap, as well as 92 Milwaukee cars owned by Continental Illinois Leasing (series 58700–58799). Using parts from the 10 bad order cars from the original purchase of 99 and the 31 cars at Tacoma, Chehalis Western crews were able to rebuild enough operational cars to increase the fleet to 267. With a large, serviceable fleet of steel log cars, Weyerhaeuser retired its fleet of 146 aging Pacific Car & Foundry wood skeleton cars that could no longer meet Federal Railroad Administration safety standards. On September 24, 1981, 28 of the wood cars were donated to the new tourist railroad and museum at Mineral Lake, the Mount Rainier Scenic Railroad.

Chehalis Western's Fairmont Tamper #526. —Frank W. Telewski

The Chehalis Western's proposed expanded service to ship logs to Twin Harbors and Longview required additional log cars. Mr. West estimated a total of 648 cars would be needed to serve the Tacoma sort yard, South Bay,

Twin Harbors, and Longview. The calculation was based on the number of cars shipped daily times the number of days required to turn around a car, from loading to unloading and back to loading. South Bay had a turnaround time of a day and a half, handling 64 cars per day. Tacoma sort yard could handle 106 shipments per day, with a three-day turnaround. Twin Harbors, with 20 cars per day, and Longview, with 15 cars per day, both required interchanging with other railroads—hence the need for a five-day turnaround. To meet the increased demand for log cars, Mr. West suggested the Chehalis Western lease or purchase 90 cars owned by First Pennsylvania Banking and Trust Company (series 58800–58899). Eventually, the Chehalis Western leased an additional 180 cars from U.S. Steel Credit Corporation (series 58195–58494) and 85 cars from Schuler Industries, and purchased an additional eight Burlington Northern cars. By the end of 1983, the Chehalis Western's steel log car fleet totaled 722.

With the large fleet of log cars, the Chehalis Western embarked on a new way of sorting and storing logs. Originally, the storage and sorting of logs by species, type, and destination was once conducted exclusively at the Vail and Curtis reloads and at the booming grounds in South Bay. By the mid-1980s the Chehalis Western used log cars for sorting and storage. Logs of the same species and type were loaded onto a car at the reloads, and the loaded cars were brought to Western Junction for sorting by type and species and classified for domestic use or export. The Chehalis Western used the sidings along the former Milwaukee Line, at Vail, and at Western Junction to organize and store log shipments destined for the various Weyerhaeuser operations. Carloads were grouped on the sidings according to the type and quality of logs held in the log car bunks. The different classes of timber were then selected car by car to fill specific orders for

Chehalis Western's new International Car Company Wide Vision Cupola caboose #598 poises for it builder's photograph. —PACCAR Photograph, Barrett Family Collection.

Two of Chehalis Western's three International Car Company Wide Vision Cupola cabooses at Western Junction. —Frank W. Telewski

The Mount Rainier Scenic Railway

The collapse of the shipping consortium appeared to doom the Morton to Frederickson branch of Weyerhaeuser's Milwaukee Road purchase to a "mothballed" future. However, one of the shippers saw an opportunity in it. L. Tom Murray Jr., Murray Pacific Corporation of Mineral, had a dream of developing a logging museum and tourist railroad that would showcase the proud steam era. George H. Weyerhaeuser and the Weyerhaeuser Company supported the founding of the Western Washington Forest Industries Museum, both financially and in granting trackage rights. Many Weyerhaeuser employees who had worked on the Vail-McDonald railroad volunteered to assist in preparations for opening day. Work on the museum continued through the early months of 1981.

The Mount Rainier Scenic Railway, the rail-operating branch of the Western Washington Forest Industries Museum, began running tourist trains on June 28. The inaugural ribbon-cutting ceremonies and run, highlighting a restored Heisler, was set for Friday, July 3. Unfortunately, on June 26 the Heisler, while hauling passenger coaches from Mineral to Elbe, experienced mechanical problems when a bearing burned out and one of the cylinder heads cracked. Weyerhaeuser locomotive #776 was on standby and provided assistance in hauling the train of passenger coaches up to Elbe. The diesel locomotive continued in service for the first weekend of tourist train operations. A 1928 Climax was available at Mineral, but didn't have the power of the Heisler and wasn't capable of hauling as many cars. However, it was available for backup power for the July 3 ribbon cutting and was placed in service when Washington State Governor John Spellman led dignitaries on the first ride on the steam-powered train from Elbe to Mineral and back. One of Weyerhaeuser's GP-7s carrying a volunteer crew waited along the tracks near Mineral, just in case assistance was needed.

The Mount Rainier Scenic Railroad continued to grow, and in 1982 Mr. Tom Murray expressed interest in expanding the trackage at the Mineral shops to support the repair and servicing of the museum's railroad equipment. Having secured permission to build an extension off Weyerhaeuser's reload track, a small truck repair shop building was moved to the site and used as the locomotive shop. Over the course of the 1980s, the roster of operating locomotives grew to include ex-Port of Grays Harbor #5, 1924; Porter 2-8-2; ex-Hillcrest Lumber Company #10, 1928; 3-truck Climax; ex-Kinzua Pine Mills #91, 1930; West Coast Special Heisler; ex-Hammond Lumber Company #17; Alco 2-8-2T; and ex-Pickering #11 Pacific Coast Shay. At the start of the 21st century, the Mount Rainier Scenic Railroad still offers excursion rides behind these historic logging locomotives.

---

mills or export. The entire system was computerized, and the location of each car and its contents were documented in the database held at Western Junction. When trains were assembled, one train would take domestic loads to South Bay for the Everett Mills, and another train would take the export loads to the Tacoma sort yard.

Track restoration dominated activity during 1980, and a minimum of 40,000 ties were laid that year. Rail service was restored between Curtis and Western Junction, and the first log train made its run on November 18. As restoration of the tracks from Western Junction to Tacoma neared completion in January 1981, the Chehalis Western had access to only three locomotives, Weyerhaeuser's two GP-7s and the aging ex-Curtis, Milburn & Eastern Alco Century. Earlier, in April 1979, the Curtis, Milburn & Eastern had placed an order with EMD for the purchase of five new GP38-2s as part of a joint agreement with the Milwaukee, which would allow the Curtis, Milburn & Eastern to operate WAM trains between Chehalis and Tacoma. In early 1980, after a series of internal corporate discussions, Weyerhaeuser decided to purchase only four locomotives. The final purchase order for the four locomotives was submitted to EMD in March 1980. General Motors EMD delivered these four locomotives to Vail on February 9, 1981.

Because the locomotives were originally purchased by the Curtis, Milburn & Eastern and delivered after the Curtis, Milburn & Eastern was retired as an operating railroad, they arrived painted yellow and black without any lettering. The lack of lettering was only temporary. Shortly after they had arrived at the Vail shops, the locomotives were lettered for the new Chehalis Western. They were delivered with road numbers 817, 818, 819, and 810, in accordance with the numbering policy established in 1948 when the first diesel locomotive was purchased for the Vail-McDonald operation. These four locomotives represented the 7th, 8th, 9th, and 10th locomotives in operation, all purchased in 1981. To maintain consistency in using only three digits when numbering locomotives, the Chehalis Western decided to drop the second "1," so the 10th locomotive's number was 810 rather than 8110.

The main purpose of the Milwaukee purchase and restoration work on the line to Tacoma was to provide access to Weyerhaeuser's Tacoma sort yard and the export log market. Weyerhaeuser was committed to moving export logs to the Tacoma sort yard early in 1981 at a projected level of 84 cars per day. With service about to begin to the sort yard, Weyerhaeuser issued a press release on February 24 to inform the public that regular train service would be in operation on the rail line and that "people residing near this track and/or accustomed to the inactive crossings are advised that log trains will once again be running, and appropriate railroad safety procedures should be observed."

A train composed of locomotives #817 and #818, 42 loaded former Milwaukee Road steel log cars, an ex-Milwaukee bay window caboose, and a crew headed by engineer James Barrett Sr. and his son, Scott Barrett, conductor, made the inaugural run to the Tacoma sort yard on March 2, 1981. James Barrett had begun working for Weyerhaeuser in 1936 and had served on many of the original steam locomotives, including #110, #111, and #120. He had moved on to the Fairbanks Morse locomotives when they first arrived in the late 1940s and then operated the GP-7s when they arrived at Vail in the mid-1970s. An employee with Weyerhaeuser's Vail logging railroad and Chehalis Western when it first operated out of Camp McDonald, he was the second of three generations of Barretts to work for Weyerhaeuser's Vail-McDonald Tree Farm railroads. Lawrence Barrett, Jim's father, worked at Vail from the late 1920s to the late 1940s as a fireman on the steam locomotives. Such family connections were not uncommon at many of Weyerhaeuser's logging operations.

Shortly after the delivery of the new locomotives from EMD, the Chehalis Western operated one train out of Chehalis and two from Vail to Western Junction. The new GP38-2s were capable of being MUed (multiple unit), or joined together, to operate as a single engine with only one crew. The first train with three locomotives, #817, #818, and #819, MUed and carrying 84 loads and an ex-Milwaukee Road bay window caboose, made the run to Tacoma with engineer Ernie Kell and Rick Nelson on June 22, 1981. The locomotives were frequently operated in this configuration to handle from 84 to 126 car trains on the steep grade of Tacoma Hill. The remaining GP38-2 would work the run from Curtis to Western Junction, while the GP-7s, occasionally MUed, handled traffic between South Bay and Vail (including switching at Western Junction). After their arrival in September 1981, the three new Wide Vision Cupola cabooses replaced the aging ex-Milwaukee Road bay window cabooses in train service.

South Bay–bound traffic was disrupted twice in 1980–81. The first time, traffic was interrupted for 10 days when 11 bents of the Woodward Bay bridge were destroyed in a July 1980 fire. A contractor rebuilt the trestle. The second time occurred late in

Chehalis Western #590 is a Wellman-Ohio locomotive crane acquired from Ontario Locomotive and Industrial Railway Supplies, Inc. in November 1982.
—Frank W. Telewski

March 1981 because of a tug boat strike, which required that Everett-bound logs be shipped via the Burlington Northern at a rate of 30 cars per day. By the end of 1981, a total of 12,724 carloads of logs had been delivered to the Tacoma sort yard and 20,135 to South Bay, bound for Everett's Mill E.

Concern over running rights and supplying service to other rail customers affected by the Milwaukee abandonment also surfaced on the other end of the railroad, in Chehalis. In early 1981, both the Burlington Northern and Union Pacific were switching industries over the Chehalis Western's recently purchased Milwaukee trackage. In a memo to Tom Rasmussen, Roy West made a request:

In order to provide us with a proper legal position on these activities I would suggest that we get some type of agreement which allows these railways to switch over Chehalis Western tracks to service these industries. At the same time, we should endeavor to acquire an interchange agreement with maintenance based on usage by the Curtis, Milburn & Eastern, the Chehalis Western and the major common carriers.

As a result, on April 11 the two lines established an agreement to facilitate switching across approximately 4,000 feet of former Milwaukee track in Chehalis. With the restoration of the Milwaukee Line to Tacoma completed, several industrial customers, mostly in the Tacoma industrial area at Frederickson, filed requests for switching service with the Chehalis Western. The Union Pacific and Burlington Northern had rejected a proposal that they supply the service, and in January 1981, the Chehalis Western began to explore in detail the number of customers and amount of traffic that would be generated between the industries and the Muni-Belt yard, or Union Pacific interchange, at Tacoma Junction.

Weyerhaeuser's #2000 tank car was a water car with a 20,000 gallon capacity. —Frank W. Telewski

One of the major concerns regarding the ability of Chehalis Western to switch industries along the former Milwaukee tracks focused on its common carrier status. The Chehalis Western was a private logging railroad classified as an intrastate common carrier. As such, it was restricted to handling traffic originating and terminating within the state of Washington. If the Chehalis Western were to start handling cars originating in or destined for other states, it would either have to be reclassified as an interstate common carrier or file with the ICC (Interstate Commerce Commission) for an exemption. At the time, the decision was not to pursue changing the Chehalis Western's status or filing for an exemption with the ICC. However, the question of the Chehalis Western providing service to other industries along the line would recur throughout the life of the railroad.

Although Weyerhaeuser purchased the Morton Line with the initial intent to mothball it, the stipulation of the purchase and maintaining the title to the railroad branch's right-of-way required that Weyerhaeuser's Chehalis Western run one train a year over the tracks and conduct minimal maintenance on the track and roadbed. Shortly after the acquisition of this branch, Tom Murry of Murry Pacific approached Weyerhaeuser about using a portion of the railroad for a logging railroad museum and tourist railroad. To facilitate both needs, Weyerhaeuser set to restoring the tracks from Frederickson to Mineral.

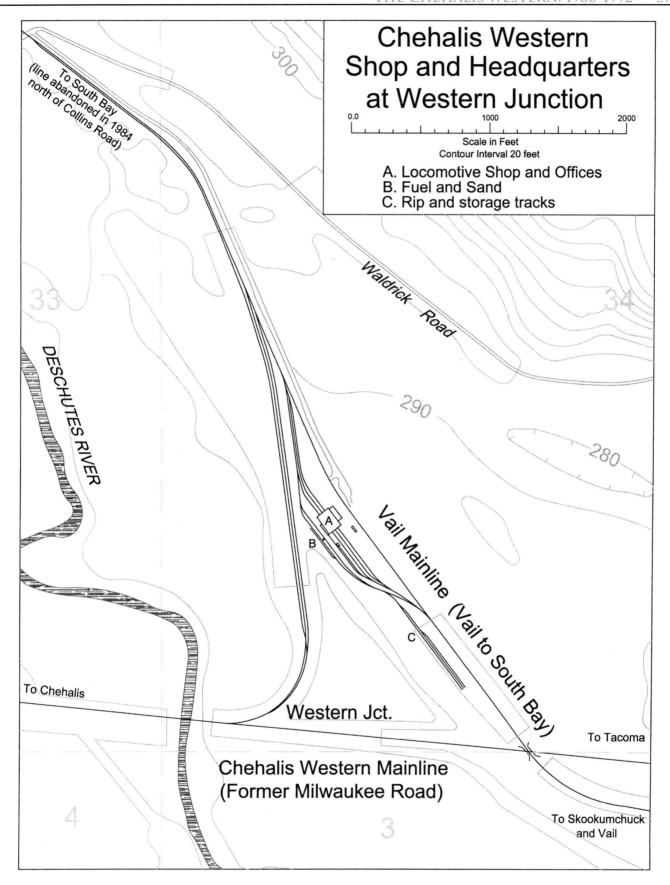

Track layout of Chehalis Western new shops and headquarters at Western Junction. —USGS Topographic Map, USGS Aerial Photograph, Washington DNR Aerial Photograph, redrawn by Frank W. Telewski

Weyerhaeuser purchased two ex-Southern Pacific covered hopper cars for sand service at their new locomotive facilities at Western Junction. They were numbered 595 and 596. —Frank W. Telewski

Opposite page: Aerial view of the Chehalis Western's shop facilities at Western Junction as they appeared in the mid 1980s. —Washington Department of Natural Resources, Frank W. Telewski collection

In April 1981, the Chehalis Western had begun to re-channel the Nisqually River upstream from the existing railroad bridge near Park Junction and part of its track restoration program. In the fall of 1981 three trestles in the Morton area were vandalized, including two near Hobie Road east of the Morton-Elbe Highway and the third about three miles south of Hobie Road between Morton and Mineral. The timbers of all three trestles were cut with a chain saw. An arson fire set on another Morton Line trestle over the Little Mashell River and Box Car Canyon on February 4, 1982, forced the Mount Rainier Scenic Railroad to curtail its summer excursions. Since the Chehalis Western used the line twice a year to ferry cars from the Tacoma sort yard storage and also to maintain the commitment of the original purchase agreement to retain possession of the right-of-way, Weyerhaeuser agreed to rebuild the bridge later in the year, reestablishing the rail connection from Fredrickson to Morton.

During the second quarter of 1981, a revitalized and expanded Chehalis Western began to evaluate its operation and set priorities for negotiations regarding service and running rights in conjunction with the Burlington Northern and Union Pacific. The number one issue was reestablishment of the running rights agreement with the Burlington Northern between Milburn and Pe Ell, and the establishment of a spur at Doty, an issue last raised with the Burlington Northern in August 1980. In 1980, Weyerhaeuser had investigated reactivation of the 1943 trackage rights agreement with the Burlington Northern (an agreement originally negotiated with the NP and grandfathered after the merger) between Milburn and Pe Ell for the Chehalis Western. Mr. Earl J. Currie, vice president of Burlington Northern, wrote Mr. Rasmussen in response to the request: "You are aware an increase in the contract mileage rate was under discussion when the Chehalis Western Operation between Pe Ell and Milburn ceased. It will be necessary to review the basic contract in light of current circumstances before a commitment can be made with respect to contract terms." A year later and still without a commitment from the Burlington Northern, Roy West stated the need for running rights over the Burlington Northern in a memo to Tom Rasmussen: "This, of course would serve the Doty block which will come on stream with second growth within the next five years."

Although Weyerhaeuser's plan to build a modern saw mill at Curtis never came to fruition, the company did build a new mill at Raymond on the site of an older company mill. The Raymond facility began cutting lumber in 1981. The new mill was equipped with laser and computer technology, which permitted the cutting of dimensional lumber from logs less than 12 inches in diameter, perfect for processing smaller, shorter rotation, or thinned second-growth timber being harvested across the holdings of the Vail-McDonald Tree Farm. The Chehalis Western projected that an annual volume of 400 log cars could be directed to Raymond. To facilitate the movement of logs west to Raymond, the Chehalis Western continued expanded negotiations with the Burlington Northern to include running rights to Weyerhaeuser's new mill located on the mouth of the Willapa River.

The railroad was also interested in securing running rights over the Union Pacific from Blakeslee Junction in Centralia to its mills at Cosmopolis and Aberdeen. Access to the Twin Harbors, as the Chehalis Western referred to Cosmopolis and Aberdeen, would have provided the Chehalis Western with the ability to transport second-growth timber directly to company mills on the mouth of the Chehalis River. The mills at Twin Harbors included a modern bleached sulfite mill that produced absorbent, specialty, and dissolving pulps at Cosmopolis and a Chip-N-Saw mill in Aberdeen.

In June 1981, the Chehalis Western began negotiating with the Union Pacific for running rights from Blakeslee Junction to the mills in Twin Harbors. At the time, the only major concern was that the run to the mills be entirely on Union Pacific trackage. "There seems to be a very strong indication that we could acquire these running rights in a timely fashion as long as we do not have to go on the Burlington Northern to get the logs into the mill," Roy West reported on June 1. Eventually, log cars were shipped to Twin Harbors as well as to the modernized Weyerhaeuser mills at Longview. But the Chehalis Western never secured running rights over the Union Pacific. Instead, the log cars were interchanged with the Union Pacific at Blakeslee Junction for transport to Twin Harbors.

A 1983 transportation agreement between the Chehalis Western and Burlington Northern facilitated shipping logs on Chehalis Western cars to Longview. The Burlington Northern would receive the Longview-bound cars from the Chehalis Western at Chehalis and transport them south to Rocky Point for inter-

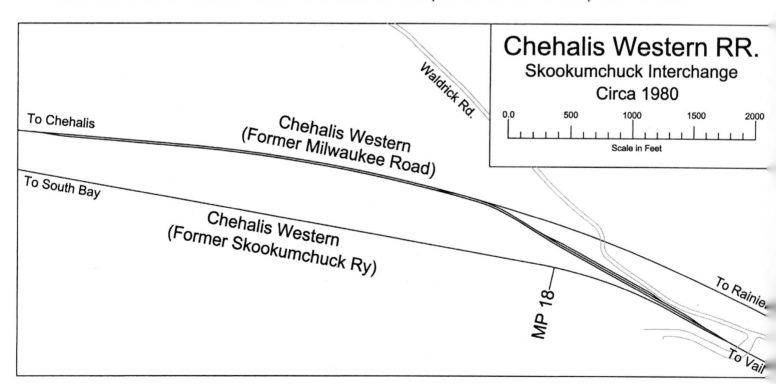

Track layout of Skookumchuck after the rebuilding of the former Milwaukee rail line by the Chehalis Western in 1981. —Drawn by F. W. Telewski

Sign off Waldrick Road directs visitors to the offices and maintenance shops of the Chehalis Western Railroad at Western Junction.— Frank W. Telewski

change with Weyerhaeuser's Columbia and Cowlitz Railway, which in turn would take the cars to the Longview mills. The agreement was established for a minimum volume of 2,000 cars per year.

In February 1983, the Burlington Northern informed Weyerhaeuser that the Raymond Line was a candidate for abandonment. Weyerhaeuser considered purchasing the line for its Chehalis Western Railroad but decided the annual operating cost, estimated to be over $1,000 per car, would be too high. On March 31, 1983, after discussions with Weyerhaeuser's transportation department, the Burlington Northern decided not to abandon the line. Outbound cars containing finished lumber from the Weyerhaeuser Mill were shipped over the Burlington Northern, but inbound log cars were never sent to the Raymond Mill. Instead, second-growth timber from the Doty and Pe Ell regions was trucked directly to the Raymond Mill. Eventually, the Raymond Mill would have to rely completely on truck transport, because the Burlington Northern abandoned the Raymond branch in the 1990s.

The issue of common carrier service to the industries between Tacoma and the Fredrickson industrial area resurfaced in 1983 when the Willamina & Grand Ronde Railroad Company contacted Weyerhaeuser about acquiring the length of track to restore rail service between Morton and Fredrickson. The Willamina & Grand Ronde had met with representatives of the potential shippers, including North Pacific Plywood, Brazier Forest Products, Cowlitz Stud, and Champion International, each of whom expressed a renewed interest in rail service. By the end of the year, the offer had become public and was addressed in an article in the *Seattle Business Journal* on January 16, 1984. The *Journal* reported that, "the two may strike a deal" that would restore rail freight service along the Morton Line. Mr. M. Root, vice president of the Willamina & Grand Ronde, requested a five-year lease from Weyerhaeuser for a 6.6-mile length of track south of Fredrickson, with an option to either lease or buy the entire route between Frederickson and Morton.

The proposal to restore freight service to the entire line remained on hold until Mr. Root could determine how many of the former shippers could be lured back to rail service. Weyerhaeuser officials were reportedly studying Root's plan and considering other options, including an original plan to offer service via the Chehalis Western. The short 6.6-mile length of track would initially serve three industries: North Pacific Plywood, located two miles south of Frederickson Junction; Brazier Forest Products in Spanaway; and Fors Farms feed mill of Midland. Some old issues resurfaced from Root's proposal: one was the labor contract with the International Woodworkers of America (IWA), which stipulated that the union had rights to all jobs on the Chehalis Western Line. The IWA contract called for all Chehalis Western trains to operate with four-man crews. Although Mr. Root expressed a willingness to hire IWA workers, he wanted to run three-man train crews. If Weyerhaeuser proceeded with its plans to develop the DuPont site as a port for log export bypassing Tacoma, the portion of the old Milwaukee Line from Morton to Tacoma could become available to Mr. Root.

Once again, the Chehalis Western and Weyerhaeuser raised the possibility of the Chehalis Western providing service to the industries south of Tacoma, but the issue of interstate versus intrastate common carrier status still wasn't resolved. One complication was the possibility that the ICC would provide an exemption of the intrastate Chehalis Western handling interstate freight. The issue centered on the freight rate charged by the Chehalis Western, which, because it was an intrastate common carrier, could not offer shippers "through rates." These rates could be offered only by interstate common carriers. Shippers would have to pay the Chehalis Western for handling each car and would still need to pay the full interstate freight fare when the cars were delivered to the cross-country carrier. Weyerhaeuser rejected the "Willamina" proposal in 1984 and again began to investigate how it could offer service to the Fredrickson shippers.

On February 15, 1985, Robert Pettit, rail superintendent for the Chehalis Western, distributed a letter to the industries along the Chehalis Western's right-of-way. The letter stated the Chehalis Western's interest in applying for an exemption from the ICC so that the private railroad could provide inbound and outbound rail car service to the affected industries. It also asked any interested parties to complete the petition form and return it to the Chehalis Western for filing with the ICC. A total of 12 shippers and receivers supported the Chehalis Western's petition, which was filed with the ICC on May 28. The petition specifically sought an exemption to operate as a feeder or switching line in the state of Washington. The ICC recognized the Chehalis Western as a subsidiary of Weyerhaeuser Company operating as a toll logging railroad wholly within the state of Washington. The Chehalis Western estimated the volume of common carrier traffic to be about 1,400 carloads per year.

View of the three stall engine house also housed the railroad office and dispatcher. — Frank W. Telewski

After reviewing the status of the Chehalis Western and interpreting the laws as they pertained to common carrier status, the commission granted the railroad the exemption on August 28. The decision was published in the *Federal Register* on October 4 and became effective on November 4, 1985. In April 1986, the Chehalis Western notified the Union Pacific of the award of the ICC exemption to operate as a feeder, or switching line and requested the establishment of an interchange agreement at Tacoma and Blakeslee Junctions for non-Chehalis Western cars.

The year 1984 was the second highest traffic year for the Chehalis Western, second only to 1981. Supplying logs to four locations kept the train crews busy, and the total flow of rail cars jumped 18 percent to a high of 32,200 for that year. Shipments of logs to Twin Harbors and Longview picked up in 1984, with a total of 2,500 cars interchanged to supply the mills at the two locations. Although the number of cars brought to South Bay had declined by almost 50 percent from a high of 20,135 five carloads in 1981 to only 9,791 in 1983, traffic heading north out of Western Junction increased by 10 percent in 1984.

In the midst of the heavy rail traffic, the Chehalis Western initiated inspection and repair of two bridges on the Chehalis-Curtis Line late in 1984. These bridges, designated WH-42 and WH-20, were inspected by the Osmose Company Railroad Division and Ken Lentz, senior project manager for the Chehalis Western. Bridge inspections were also conducted on the Morton branch in 1985.

Rail traffic volume on the Chehalis Western, 1981–1985, by number of cars hauled.

Destination	1981	1982	1983	1984	1985*
TSY	12,742	15,932	17,219	18,900	18,450
South Bay	20,135	14,037	9,791	10,800	8,520
Other**	951	93	271	2,500	4,600
Total	33,810	30,062	27,281	32,200	31,570

* Projected traffic volume.

**Includes cars bound for Twin Harbors and Longview Mill complexes.

Early in 1984, the Chehalis Western projected 1985 rail traffic would be brisk. However, the domestic economic slowdown began to affect the Chehalis Western's operations by late 1984. In the early 1980s, mortgage interest rates approached 20 percent, and new home construction, the single largest market for lumber, had fallen to a level not seen since the height of the Great Depression. In response, the company undertook a reorganization plan that reduced the number of employees from 48,000 to less than 39,000 in three years. Production at unprofitable western lumber operations were curtailed, and some mills were sold or closed altogether. Such was the fate of the Everett Mill complex when Weyerhaeuser announced it was closing Mill E, the last sawmill in Everett, on October 5, 1984. The end of sawmilling at Everett eliminated the need for South Bay. As a result, the line from Western Junction to South Bay was abandoned in the third quarter of 1984. Only five months earlier and apparently unsuspecting of the future closure of the Everett Mill, the Chehalis Western had invested in rebracing the South Bay unloader dock and rebuilding the trestle's fire suppression system, and had been considering upgrading the grapple capacity of the log unloader. Due to reduced demands for lumber, a smaller volume of logs once bound for Everett Mill E was diverted to the Aberdeen Chip-N-Saw Mill. Subsequently, in 1985 rail traffic on the Chehalis Western dropped.

The Lacey Planning Department filed a request with the Chehalis Western on August 9, 1985, for access to the South Bay Line as a switching track, which would provide access to a proposed industrial business park adjacent to the Yelm Highway and the Chehalis Western track. Once again, any switching of non–log-related traffic was dependent on the ICC waver for common carrier status awarded in November. The rails remained intact on the segment from Lacey south to Western Junction until 1991, possibly in the hope that the DuPont export facility would become reality, in which case the line would provide a more direct link with the Burlington Northern main line rather than having to ship via Wetico. If left intact, the line could also service the Lacey industrial park.

On November 13, 1985, the city of Olympia inquired about the abandonment of the line to South Bay. The city was planning on improving Pacific Avenue from Interstate 5 east beyond the railroad trestle, which spanned the interstate with the addition of vehicular lanes and sidewalks. Because the line was abandoned, the city was given permission to remove the trestle. The State of Washington Department of Natural Resources acquired the South Bay booming grounds and 6.5 miles of right-of-way from South Bay to Lacey in 1988 and established a state park. Shortly thereafter, the Chehalis Western removed the rails and ties from the abandoned segment of the old rail line originally built in 1927. The Thurston County Parks and Recreation Department acquired the abandoned right-of-way linking Lacey to Stedman Road from the Chehalis Western in 1991. Shortly thereafter, the Chehalis Western removed the rails and ties and converted the old roadbed into a recreational trail.

Another abandonment occurred in 1985. The Burlington Northern initiated abandonment proceedings for the west end of the 5th Subdivision (Northern Pacific's old Prairie Line) from Roy to Tenino Junction. This included the interchange track with the Chehalis Western at Wetico. The line wasn't abandoned

Chehalis Western #684, still lettered for its former owner, the Curtis, Milburn & Eastern, is serviced at Western Junction's new fuel track. —Jim Shaw, Frank W. Telewski Collection

Relics from a by-gone era of steam railroading, tender-water tank cars #211 and #215 and two old riveted 10,000 gallon water tank cars #000 and #527 rest on a yard track behind former Milwaukee Road steel log cars #59807 and #59601 at Western Junction. The four cars were held in reserve in case fire broke out along the rail line. —Frank W. Telewski

until after 1992, and the rails were lifted shortly thereafter. The right-of-way was assumed by the Port of Olympia, which established interim trail use and rail banking.

The year 1985 was critical for the future of the Chehalis Western. Almost overnight, the fortunes of the railroad became uncertain. Besides the risk inherent in the slow domestic lumber market in the Puget Sound region at the time and the closure of the South Bay Line, Weyerhaeuser's plans to build an export facility at DuPont were moving slowly. At DuPont, Weyerhaeuser had removed most of the original 17 miles of three-foot narrow-gauge track, leaving only 2.54 miles running from the engine house to the dock. The last train of dynamite was shipped on February 22, 1984, as the company prepared to develop the site. Meanwhile, environmental groups challenged the development plans in the courts.

On March 7, 1985, the Washington State Supreme Court upheld the Shoreline permit issued by the city of DuPont for Weyerhaeuser's export facility. With all the necessary state and federal permits in hand, the project could move forward. Weyerhaeuser was required to begin construction within two years and to complete it within five years of the date of issue. However, in June 1985 the company began to reevaluate plans to develop DuPont in light of the slowing domestic and export markets. It decided to abandon plans for the export facility in September, citing significant changes in transportation economics and reduced volumes of export logs and product since the DuPont project was first proposed in the mid-1970s. The company decided to rely on the existing product export facilities at Longview and log export from Tacoma. In the last half of 1985, the DuPont property was transferred to the Weyerhaeuser Real Estate Company Land Management Division, and in subsequent years, the land was developed as the master planned community of Northwest Landing.

With the reassessment and eventual abandonment of plans to develop an export facility at DuPont, Weyerhaeuser also began to reassess the future of the Chehalis Western. Originally, the company had envisioned the Chehalis Western servicing the DuPont export facility not only with logs but also with wood chips and finished products from its mills in Longview, Aberdeen, Cosmopolis, and Springfield. The proposed volume of traffic justified the railroad's existence, even with the loss of the Everett Mills. With all these negative factors in hand, company officials began to consider dissolving the Chehalis Western in June 1985.

The economic woes of the 1980s continued to plague Weyerhaeuser's domestic timber and lumber operations. In 1986, the company had entered into negotiations with the two unions for a new contract that included a proposed wage cut of up to $4 per hour as a way to stabilize its economic losses. The proposal, in part, resulted in a six-week strike by the International Woodworkers of America and the Lumber Production and Industrial Workers unions. The union International Woodworkers of America went on strike, resulting in a shutdown of Weyerhaeuser's operations, including the Chehalis Western. The strike was resolved late in July when members of the IWA voted to accept the new contract in which a $4 cut in wages and benefits was replaced by a profit-sharing plan. Although Local 3-130 of Raymond, which included the more than 200 loggers from the Vail-McDonald Tree Farm, voted 516-17 to reject the contract, it was ratified by a 2-to-1 margin. With the strike resolved, Chehalis Western trains once again began delivering logs to the export facility in Tacoma.

The slow domestic economy of the mid-1980s also had a serious impact on the Chehalis Western's plans to operate as a common carrier. For the 19 months the Chehalis Western held its ICC exemption, permitting it to engage in common carrier service, the railroad never published any tariffs nor held itself out as a carrier for hire. In March 1987, the Chehalis Western decided to reconsider its award of exemption by the ICC to offer switching service to industries along its right-of-way. In a letter to Mr. Joseph Dettmar, deputy director of Rail Section for the ICC, Chehalis Western's vice president, John G. Kauffman, explained regarding common carrier status:

> *However, economic conditions have prevented the Chehalis Western from ever servicing these shippers. Since no change in these conditions is foreseeable in the near future, the Chehalis Western has decided to relinquish the exemption it obtained in Finance Docket No. 30680 and seek a determination from the Commission's staff that the Chehalis Western was not a common carrier during the period it held, but did not act upon, the exemption.*

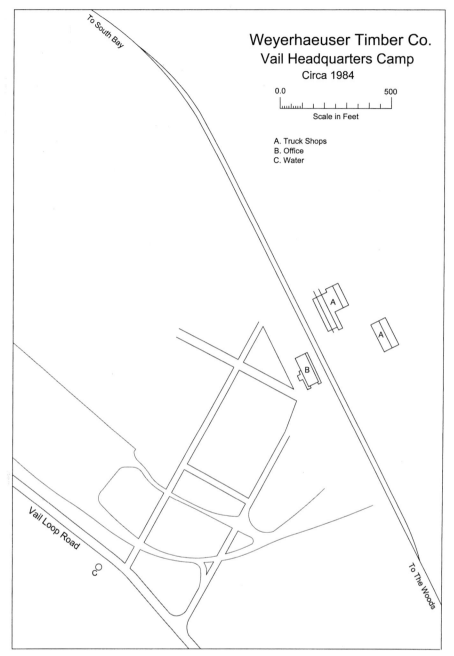

After the shops at Western Junction were build, most of the trackage at Vail was abandoned as the former locomotive and car shop buildings were converted to serve the logging truck fleet. —Drawn by Frank W. Telewski

The commission responded in April that because the Chehalis Western never held itself out to the public as a common carrier, it never was a common carrier and as such was never subject to Commission regulation. The ICC concluded the Chehalis Western did not become a carrier merely because the Commission had granted the requested exemption.

Ex-Weyerhauser Company #776, relettered for its new owner, Chehalis Western, waits at the Curtis Reload for its log train. —Jim Shaw, Frank W. Telewski Collection

In 1987, a second steam tourist railroad was created, this time on the western end of the Chehalis Western. That year the Chehalis-Centralia Railroad Association leased the Cowlitz, Chehalis & Cascade's #15 from the city of Chehalis, which had been on display in Chehalis since 1955. The Association moved the 90-ton Baldwin Locomotive Works Mikado to the Mount Rainier Scenic Railroad shop at Mineral for restoration. After a 32-year slumber and two years of work, #15 was ready to be fired and came back to life on April 29, 1989. The engine made two runs to Tacoma and back to Mineral that spring and on Saturday, May 20, headed an excursion trip over the Chehalis Western's tracks from Tacoma to its home tracks in Chehalis. In tourist service, the train ran over the Chehalis Western and Curtis, Milburn & Eastern tracks on summer weekends from Chehalis to Ruth.

Meanwhile, the volume of log traffic on the Chehalis Western continued to decline toward the end of the 1980s. The Burlington Northern still delivered covered hopper cars of fertilizer at Wetico, which the Chehalis Western transferred to Vail, and gondolas of scrap metal, much of it from the salvage of the South Bay Line in 1987 and 1988, were shipped out of Vail and Western Junction. Additional rail traffic was generated when Weyerhaeuser transformed the Curtis saw log reload into a pole yard. Pole-length logs carried on log cars, empty bulkhead flat cars, and empty gondola cars were delivered to Curtis by the Chehalis Western. At Curtis, Weyerhaeuser converted the logs to telephone poles and shipped them via the Chehalis Western in loaded gondola and bulk-head flat cars to Chehalis. At Chehalis, the loaded cars were interchanged with the Burlington Northern.

During late 1987 and early 1988, the Chehalis Western ran three to five weekday trips from Western Junction to Tacoma, arriving with a load of logs between 8:00 A.M. and 9:00 A.M. and departing with a string of empties around noon. By 1989, the trackage from Western Junction to Chehalis had been all but mothballed. Traffic along this length of track was limited to an occasional train picking up or setting out stored log racks at Maytown and Centralia, and the movement of a locomotive to and from the Curtis Pole Yard. The Western Junction to Tacoma train crew went on duty at 6:00 A.M., taking a string of empty cars south to the Vail reload. After setting out the empties, the crew picked up a string of loaded cars and headed for Tacoma, arriving between 10:30 A.M. and 11:30 A.M. After exchanging loads and empties and taking a lunch break, the crew and train departed Tacoma by 1:00 P.M., returning to Western Junction by 2:30 P.M.

As the traffic slowed, Weyerhaeuser began to redistribute its motive power to other company railroads. The Chehalis Western's #810 and #819 were sold to Weyerhaeuser's Golden Triangle railroad in Columbia, Mississippi. GP-7s #765 and #776, no longer needed for the South Bay run, were sold to Weyerhaeuser's Columbia and Cowlitz Railroad in Longview in 1988. By the summer of 1991, the Chehalis Western rarely operated on weekends but still made runs during the week. At the close of 1991, the railroad had shipped only 4,000 loads, down from over 30,000 loads six years earlier.

In 1991, the Chehalis Western did move a few cars not related to its logging operations. The Boeing Aircraft Company was building a new plant south of Frederickson at milepost 15 on the Chehalis Western Line, which required rail shipments of anodization tanks. Boeing expressed concern that if the tanks were not delivered by rail, they would have to be cut up for truck shipping and welded back together at great expense to the company. The Chehalis Western and Boeing negotiated an agreement by which Boeing could contract a third party to service its facility but not to act as a common carrier. In other words, the third party could serve the Boeing plant but could not offer its services to any other industry along the right-of-way. This arrangement would provide rail service without directly involving the Chehalis Western, while not establishing common carrier service on the Chehalis Western Line. Although the Chehalis Western had never exercised its exemption to serve as a common carrier, the railroad did agree to move several of the tanks from Tacoma Junction to the plant site in August and September while Boeing awaited a decision from the ICC on its requested exemption to hire a third-party rail carrier to handle future shipments.

Chehalis Western #776 passes Maytown on its way to Western Junction in June 1982 running on former Milwaukee trackage with a string of loaded ex-Milwaukee Road steel log cars from the Curtis Reload. Note that the log cars have not yet been relettered CWWR. At Western Junction, the loads will be sorted for domestic and export markets, domestic logs will then be taken to South Bay, whereas the export logs will be shipped to the Tacoma Sort Yard. —Jim Shaw, Frank W. Telewski Collection

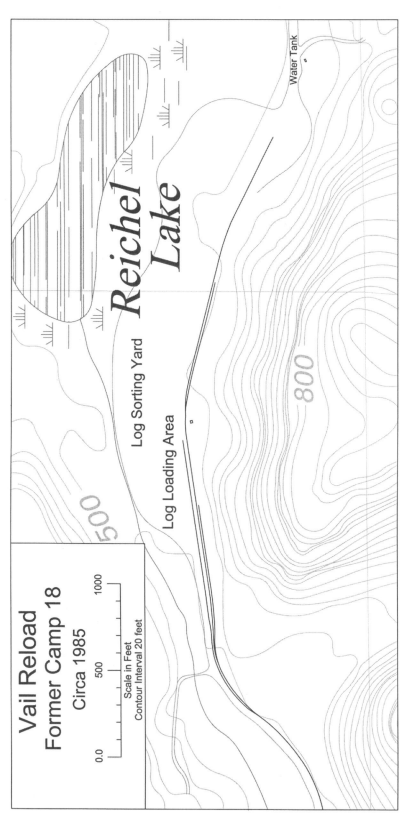

Shortly after the re-establishment of the Chehalis Western in 1981, the tracks at the Camp 18 reload south of Vail were restored and the layout altered a little to facilitate car loading. —USGS Topographic Map, Washington DNR Aerial Photograph, redrawn by Frank W. Telewski

The tanks were delivered to Tacoma Junction on flat cars, half a tank to a car. A Chehalis Western log train with empty cars returning from the Tacoma sort yard would pick up the flat cars at Tacoma Junction and set them out for Boeing at Frederickson before continuing on to Western Junction. Boeing required rail shipments of additional tanks after September and also was interested in using the rail connection to move finished aircraft components from the new plant once construction was completed. The ICC granted the exemption to Boeing on October 10, 1991, and eventually Boeing contracted with Railink Inc. of Midlothian, Virginia, to supply switching service to its plant in the absence of the Chehalis Western.

As mentioned earlier, the Chehalis Western sold the remaining portion of the South Bay Line from Lacey south to Stedman Road to Thurston County on April 26, 1991, for use as a recreational trail. As a result, the rails and ties were finally taken up along this 8½-mile length of track, beginning on November 11 and completed by March 1992. Several rail crossing issues needed to be resolved as part of the final abandonment plan of the rail line. Most notable among these were the Yelm Highway railroad overcrossing and the undercrossing of the Burlington Northern Tacoma to Portland main line, referred to by the Burlington Northern as Bridge No. 33.1 near Kyro, Washington, south of Lacey and north of East Olympia.

In accordance with the original agreement drafted between Weyerhaeuser and the Northern Pacific dated May 25, 1927, Weyerhaeuser was responsible for the restoration of the Northern Pacific, and now the Burlington Northern, railroad embankment and tracks to the condition they were in prior to bridge construction. As such, Weyerhaeuser agreed to construct a 12-foot culvert for the recreational trail under the Burlington Northern main line and fill in the

Originally ordered for the Curtis, Milburn and Eastern in April 1979, the four GP38-2s arrived without lettering, as the CM&E was no longer an operating railroad when they were delivered on February 9, 1981. Here #819 and #810, the last two locomotives in the order, are seen resting in the Vail yard. —John A. Taubeneck

Chehalis Western's new fleet of GP38-2s receive service at the fueling and sanding facility at Western Junction in June 1985. —Lyle Spears

Weyerhaeuser Company #765 and #776 were relettered for the Chehalis Western in 1982. Here they are captured MUed (Multiple Unit) together hauling a string of empty log cars to the Vail Reload on a November day in 1984.
—Jim Shaw, Frank W. Telewski Collection

Chehalis Western #'s 817, 818 and 819 MUed climb Tacoma Hill with a string of empty log cars on April 15, 1983.
—J. M. Seidl, Frank W. Telewski Collection

Chehalis Western bulkhead flat car #15402 sets behind the shop building at Western Junction with a load of freight trucks. Note the reporting marks are CWRR, not CWWR, the official AAR reporting marks. Chehalis Western #684 is in the background. — Lyle Spears

Chehalis Western GP38-2 #817 plus at least one other unidentified GP38-2 back a loaded train of ex-Milwaukee Road steel log cars into the Tacoma Beltline's yard beyond Lincoln Avenue Junction in Tacoma. This engineer had to back his train over Union Pacific tracks from Tacoma Junction in order to reach the Tacoma Beltline's tracks. From here, the Beltline will deliver the loads to Weyerhaeuser's Tacoma Sort Yard, located on the Port of Tacoma's Hylebros Waterway for export. —John A. Taubeneck

existing bridge as part of the sale contract with the county.

What appeared to be a simple task rapidly increased in complexity. A trestle caught fire at 1:00 A.M. on July 30, 1991, and by 8:30 A.M. the bridge and trestle supporting the Burlington Northern main line were completely destroyed. Four boys had started a campfire that spread to the trestle. As a result, some 50 freight trains per day had to be rerouted, and Amtrak passengers had to be bussed between Portland and Seattle.

The Burlington Northern quickly set out to restore the rail line by filling in the old bridge without the proposed culvert and billed Weyerhaeuser for the work. This left Weyerhaeuser's proposal to install the necessary recreational undercrossing unresolved, which resulted in its request to the Burlington Northern to install the culvert as stipulated in the sales agreement with Thurston County. The issue remained unresolved until May 1993, when the Burlington Northern, citing concerns of disrupted rail traffic, liability, and the fact that another public road undercrossing existed within 900 feet of the original trestle, denied Weyerhaeuser permission to install the culvert undercrossing.

A Chehalis Western computer car inventory report from May 4, 1992, provides an interesting perspective into the operation and rail traffic during the twilight years of this once giant logging railroad. Of a total of 510 log cars reported in service, 264 loads, 232 empties, and 14 bad ordered cars were on the rip track at Western Junction. Fifty of the cars were loaded on May 1, 21 on April 30, and the remainder as early as February 26. Loads were stored at Western Junction (91 loads), the spur track that once led to South Bay

Hostling the power, the term applied to servicing locomotives, at Western Junction after a long workday. Chehalis Western #s 765, 776 and 817 line up at the fuel track as #684 waits behind caboose #597. —Jim Shaw, Frank W. Telewski Collection

Chehalis Western #776 rests at Western Junction. — Lyle Spears

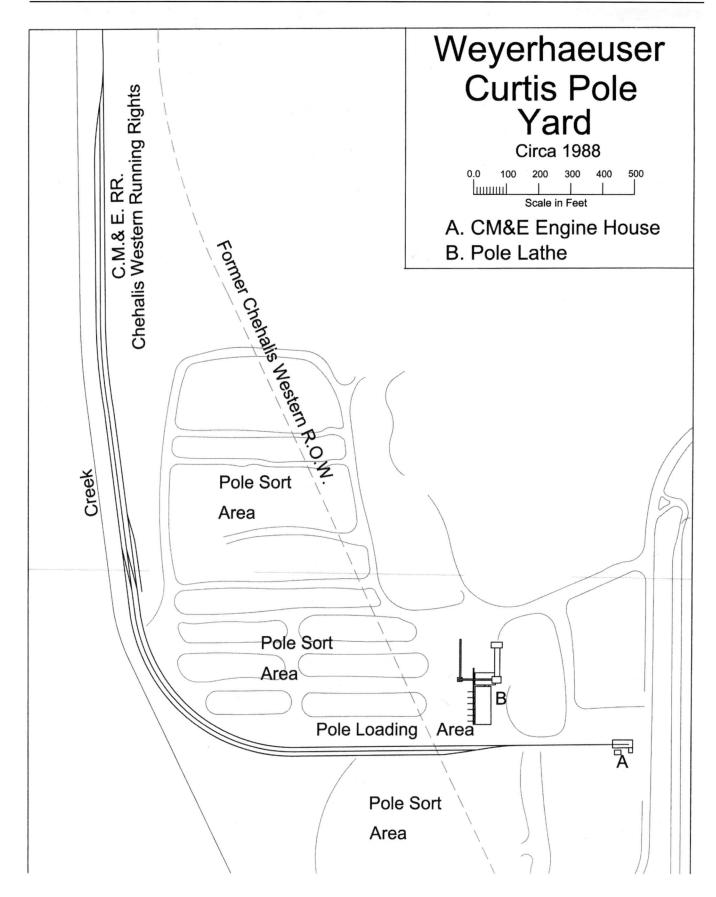

Curtis Pole Yard. In the late 1980's, Weyerhaeuser converted the Curtis Sort Yard into a pole yard and manufacturing facility. The track layout did not change, however this map indicates the location of the pole lathe. —Drawn by F. W. Telewski from Aerial photographs

(69 loads), Vail (13 loads), Rainier siding (36 loads), Essex siding (26 loads), and the Greendale siding (29 loads) and were sorted by grade and species. Forty-two cars were unloaded at the Tacoma export facility/Tacoma sort yard on May 1; the remainder of the empties were in transit. The fleet of log cars was reduced by 216 from a total of 722 in the inventory for 1984. All of the original cars purchased from U.S. Steel, Continental Illinois, and the First Pennsylvania Bank were still in service, but the original fleet of some 108 log cars owned by the Milwaukee Road was reduced to only 45 cars. Also, there was no evidence of the 72 cars purchased from Burlington Northern on the 1992 roster. However, between 1984 and 1992 there was the addition of five cars numbered 1102, 1005, 1009, 1010 and 1011 to the roster which rounded out the fleet to 511 cars.

The slowdown in log traffic spelled doom for the once energetic railroad, and the last regular log train made the run to Tacoma on July 1, 1992.

At the Curtis Pole Yard, pole-length logs were loaded onto the pole lathe which would strip the bark and put a smooth surface on the length of the pole. Notice the former Curtis, Milburn & Eastern engine house in the background and a steel log car loaded with pole-length logs. —Weyerhaeuser Archives

Left: A pole is manufactured at Curtis. Finished poles rest in the foreground ready for loading onto railcars. —Weyerhaeuser Archives

Below: A loader removes finished poles for sorting. An empty steel Chehalis Western log car and an idler flat car rest on the rail in the background. —Weyerhaeuser Archives

Right: Finished poles are ready for loading. —Weyerhaeuser Archives

Blakeslee Junction was the connection with the Union Pacific's line to Grays Harbor, the Burlington Northern's line to Hoquiam and the Chehalis Western. —Kristopher Johnson

Chehalis Western work train headed up by #776 waits for the Union Pacific's Hoquiam Turn to pass at Blakeslee Junction. It's October 8, 1987 and the western end of the Chehalis Western sees less activity after the closure of the Curtis sort yard and reload. On this day, the Chehalis Western work train picks up scrap from along the line, which is loaded into gondolas. —Kristopher Johnson

By the time this photograph was taken in June 1990, Weyerhaeuser had redistributed most of the Chehalis Western's power to its other subsidiaries. This required using the 684, still lettered here for the Curtis, Milburn & Eastern, once again in log train service. Notice the idler flat car behind the engine, protecting it from the longer-than-car-length load of pole logs which will be delivered to Curtis.

—Jim Shaw, Frank W. Telewski Collection

CHAPTER 13

Requiem for a Logging Railroad Giant: 1992-1995

Trees take time to grow and there were times when demand exceeded local supply. Both domestic and export markets and demands also changed over time. As the supply of export logs to the Tacoma Sort Yard dwindled, and second growth logs from the McDonald-Pe Ell-Doty region were redirected away from South Bay to Raymond by truck, the Chehalis Western saw a significant reduction in rail traffic. Weyerhaeuser began to consider its options for the future of its once giant logging railroad and began to dismantle the former Milwaukee portion of the Chehalis Western when it donated the line from Graham to National and Morton to the City of Tacoma in 1990. This included approximately 50 miles of track, including that operated by the Mt. Rainier Scenic Railway. Log and pole shipments from Curtis ceased in early 1992 and the railroad leased the tracks of the former Curtis, Milburn & Eastern to the Centralia-Chehalis Railroad Association to operate as a tourist railroad using former Cowlitz, Chehalis & Cascade 2-8-2 #15. Regular log train service on the entire Chehalis Western ended on July 1, 1992. Railink Inc., of Midlothian, Virginia continued to handled the private, non-common-carrier Boeing contract switching between Tacoma Junction and Frederickson, operating two trains weekly, switching about 10 inbound cars per month up to 1994. The City of Tacoma was interested in acquiring the Chehalis Western and in April 1993 selected the Tacoma Eastern Railway Company to operate the trackage recently acquired and that which they hoped to acquire from Weyerhaeuser in the future.

Weyerhaeuser held a meeting at Western Junction in January 1994 to review the status of the dissolution of the Chehalis Western and associated logging railroad facilities which once served the Vail-McDonald Tree Farm. Company officials addressed several issues at the meeting, including security at the Western Junction shops, rail service to the Frederickson Boeing plant, the sale of railroad lands, interchange issues with the Union Pacific and Burlington Northern, locomotives and equipment, harvest of timber along right-of-way and on Western Junction property, options for the Vail and Curtis, Milburn & Eastern lines and the eventual sale of the Chehalis Western line. The Union Pacific had requested use of the Chehalis Western line for their emergency standby use should their line to Tacoma become blocked. The agreement between the Union Pacific and Weyerhaeuser was formalized on November 1, 1994, granting the UP non-exclusive rights "for the sole purpose of moving and storing rail cars on a temporary basis." The Union Pacific was not allowed to act as a common carrier over the Chehalis Western's tracks and paid Weyerhaeuser $600 every month for the privilege of using the tracks. Both the #817 and #818 were still stored at Western Junction in January 1994 and required being run every two weeks to keep them in serviceable condition. Annual maintenance was also still required and the #817 needed work on its front trucks before it could be sold. The truck was sent to the railroad shop at Longview where the shop crew replaced the old worn wheels with new wheels. Three options were being considered for the two remaining GP38-2s, transfer to Weyerhaeuser's Texas, Oklahoma and Eastern; sell them on the market; or lease to the Southern Pacific. In April, the two GP38-2s were transferred to the Texas, Oklahoma and Eastern along with spare parts, including several modules and radiator cores in stock at Western Junction.

In October of 1992, the Chehalis Western was idle, having run its last regular log train three months earlier. All's quiet at Western Junction on this autumn day. Chehalis Western #818 is visible inside the shop building in the right hand stall, its sister engine, #817 is directly behind it, while Chehalis Western #684 is at the fueling and sanding rack. —Frank W. Telewski

The last log trains ran over Chehalis Western tracks from the period of May to July of 1994 when the last remaining locomotive, old Alco #684, was used to move a quarter-million feet of logs harvested along the right-of-way to a truck reload at Western Junction. A contractor was hired to operate the train and skid logs to the track using an LS 98 crane on an old Pacific Car & Foundry bull car. The logs were yarded to the track by the use of a cable and grapple from the crane in the area of rail access. The crane then loaded the logs onto the log cars.

With the dissolution of the once vast logging railroad empire, both new and old concerns needed attention. One was rail access to the old Skookumchuck Quarry. In 1994, the south jetty at Westport had worn down under the constant pounding of the Pacific Ocean surf and there was interest in extracting more rock from the quarry. The original agreement to keep open rail access expired when the Milwaukee Road abandoned the western railroad lines in 1980. By 1994, the Vail line from Western Junction south to the Vail Loop Road was also up for abandonment and sale to Thurston County for their Rails to Trails rail banking program. One possibility considered by the Quarry's owners in the end of January 1995 involved securing rail access to the quarry by the extraction of a private rail line from Rails to Trails. Late in the 1990s the quarry was re-opened and rock was extracted for jetty construction, however the rock was removed by truck, not by rail.

Another concern was the liquidation of the Curtis, Milburn & Eastern line from Milburn to Curtis Yard, and the Chehalis Western's line from Chehalis Junction to Milburn, originally purchased from the Milwaukee Road in 1936. The Centralia-Chehalis Railroad Association had been operating their steam excursion train over these rail lines since 1989 and had just been awarded an extension in their contract to use the railroad for the 1994 season. Among the options was the possibility to donate the line to the Railroad Association, sell the line to the Chehalis Port or Lewis County Economic Development, or sell the rail line and Curtis yard to Northwest Hardwoods. Eventually, in 1996, Weyerhaeuser sold the Curtis, Milburn & Eastern trackage to the Port of Chehalis. On May 5, 1998, the Port of Chehalis announced that the Curtis Pole Company had leased the former Curtis sort and reload yard from Weyerhaeuser. The Centralia-Chehalis Railroad Association continued to operate their trains along the railroad into 2002.

A cut of empty steel log cars were stored on sidings and along the mainline. Here, a string of empty cars were set out on the former Milwaukee Road line near Rainier.
—Frank W. Telewski

With no rail log traffic from the woods to Tacoma, the extensive logging railroad served no purpose and was an expense to maintain even in its limited service to Boeing, limited logging along the right-of-way, and for providing an emergency route and car storage to the Union Pacific. Weyerhaeuser Company was interested in wrapping up the liquidation of the rail operation within the first six months of 1994 and considered scrapping the Chehalis to Tacoma line if no buyer stepped forward. The only line that would be kept was the stretch, which served the Boeing facility at Frederickson, main-

Engine 684 wasn't relettered for the Chehalis Western (CWWR) until after 1990. Here it rests inside the locomotive shop building at Western Junction in the early 1990s. —Frank W. Telewski

Originally built in 1927, and added on to over the years, the shop buildings at Vail once used to maintain steam engines, then diesel locomotives, were used to maintain trucks and other logging equipment after 1981. In 1992, the buildings still supported truck logging, but the their future was uncertain. Eventually, these buildings were razed in the mid 1990's. —Frank W. Telewski

taining access to the aircraft manufacturer's facilities. In the interim, the Chehalis Western tracks were used as temporary storage for the fleet of steel log cars which originated from the shut down of Weyerhaeuser's Klamath Falls logging railroad and the Weyerhaeuser common carrier, Oregon, California and Eastern in Oregon in the mid-1990.

After a period of time Weyerhaeuser entered into final negotiations with the City of Tacoma to purchase the Chehalis Western railroad, including the shops at Western Junction. Negotiations with the City of Tacoma to complete the purchase of properties of the Chehalis Western were well under way by August with a purchase agreement between the two parties signed on August 12, 1994. The sale closed in early 1995. The City of Tacoma entered into a 20 year lease with the Tacoma Eastern Railway Company to operate over the retired Chehalis Western lines and to use Western Junction as their service facilities on December 6, 1994. The Tacoma Eastern, with AAR reporting marks TE, planned to offer both freight and passenger excursion service. One plan called for the establishment of regular passenger service from Tacoma to Mt. Rainier National Park, transferring passengers from the train to bus at National. Passenger service failed to materialize. However, on February 1, 1995, the Tacoma Eastern officially began common carrier rail freight service over the former Chehalis Western Railroad. The first revenue train operated on February 26, 1995. During the transition from the Chehalis Western to the Tacoma Eastern, the operation of the Mt. Rainier Scenic Railroad was not significantly effected.

The Centralia-Chehalis Railroad Association operates a tourist railroad using former Cowlitz, Chehalis & Cascade #15 over the former Chehalis Western and Curtis, Milburn and Eastern tracks west of Chehalis. —Frank W. Telewski

In 2000, the centennial year of the Weyerhaeuser Company, the Vail-McDonald Tree Farm still bustled with activity. However, little remained of the once vast logging railroad empire, which served these extensive company landholdings. With the rails removed from the Vail line, Weyerhaeuser dismantled the three wooden railroad shop buildings in the mid 1990s, leaving only the original office and company store as the last building remaining from the original company town of Vail. The original steel water tower still stood overlooking the yard, which marshaled trucks rather than trains. The log dump at South Bay fell victim to arson and by the end of the decade, the large unloader was dismantled and scrapped along with the majority of the dump's trestle. The Skookumchuck right-of-way could still be followed as a county trail to the Vail town site. The shop buildings and service facility at Western Junction remained intact and operated by Coast Engine and Equipment Co. (CEECO) as a locomotive and car service facility and was joined by American Oriental Express in 2002. Chehalis Western's Alco #684 was still operational on stand-by service and still lettered CWWR at Western Junction in 2002. The original Chehalis Western right-of-way from Chehalis Junction west to Milburn, and the track relayed on the original Chehalis Western right-of-way to the Curtis reload were still intact. The company shops at Pe Ell, the relocation for the Chehalis Western in the 1960s still stood and also supported truck logging operations and maintenance for the Raymond operation. The only

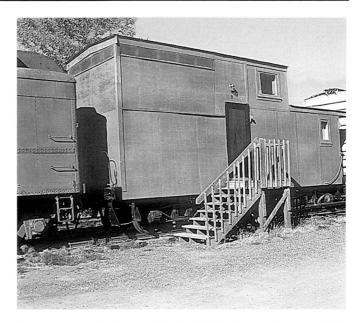

Barely recognizable, ex-Chehalis Western caboose #711 was converted into a hot tub room for the Caboose Hotel at Elbe. —Frank W. Telewski

Weyerhaeuser's old truck scaler's office at Mineral was overgrown by alders, blackberries and Scotch broom in 1999. However, scaler's tickets dated February 28, 1980 still littered the floor, the last day a Milwaukee WAM plan log train left the Weyerhaeuser Mineral reload. —Frank W. Telewski

Weyerhaeuser's caboose #602, a former Southern Pacific steel caboose, now resides next to the old Northern Pacific Railroad station in Issaquah, Washington. —Frank W. Telewski

Weyerhaeuser's #110 was restored by the Black Hills Central Railroad, Hill City, South Dakota in 2000. Here it takes on water at Hill City in June 2001 in preperation for a tourist trip. —Frank W. Telewski

Hidden behind plantings, chain link fencing and barbed wire to protect it, Weyerhaeuser #100, ex-Hetch Hetchy #5 and an original Vail four wheel bobber caboose on static display in a Sutherlin, Oregon city park. —Jeff Johnstone

sign of the Chehalis Western's second home aside from the original shop buildings at Pe Ell was the roadbed for the loop track and the rusting remains of the log loader. Rails embedded in the concrete floor and the locomotive service pit could still be seen inside the shop building.

The Weyerhaeuser reload and scale buildings at Mineral could still be found engulfed by young alder and fir trees, scaler's tickets still littered the scale house floor dated February 26, 1980, the last day of rail operations via the Milwaukee Road. Many pieces of railroad equipment used by the logging railroads of the Vail-McDonald operation could be found at the Mt. Rainier Scenic Railway including the steel ballast and brush-snow plow cars built at Vail, several Chehalis Western wood skeleton cars and two original Vail wood skeleton cars. Chehalis Western caboose #711 was added to the Caboose Hotel at Elbe and the #800 was dismantled

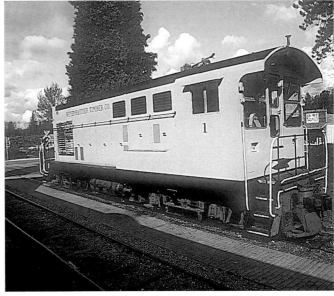

The Puget Sound Railway Historical Society acquired Vail's #714, ex-White River #1, in 1987 and restored to its original paint and lettering, placing it into tourist railroad service at their Northwest Railway Museum in Snoqualmie Falls, Washington. —Frank W. Telewski

The remaining bents of what was once the twin bridges, trestles which supported Branch 2 and a siding just above the switchback on the way to Camp 4 at Siding 8. Locomotives would have turned at the wye just below the bridges and then run around the train to be headed back in the proper direction. —Frank W. Telewski

Built in the late 1920s, a few bents and pilings are all that remains of a trestle on the LD line along Porcupine Ridge of the Vail Tree Farm in August 2001. Log trains powered by the likes of the 5 spot Pacific Coast Shay, or the Baldwin semi-saddle tank Mallets #110 and #111 would cross this trestle on their way to and from Spike Camp and LD Camp in the late 1920's and early 1930s. —Frank W. Telewski

The remains of an old tank car, which once provided water along the rail lines, lies rusting on the side of a logging road which was once the 40 line at Vail. —Frank W. Telewski

and slated for restoration at the Mt. Rainier Scenic Railway's Mineral shop during the summer of 2000. Only two steam locomotives were known to have survived into the new century. The #110 Baldwin mallet was restored to service by the Black Hills Central Railroad, Hill City, South Dakota, and the #100 was placed on static display in a city park in Sutherlin, Oregon along with one of the original Vail 4-wheel cabooses retired from service on Weyerhaeuser's Sutherlin logging railroad. The #714, ex-Weyerhaeuser White River Branch #1, Fairbanks-Morse H10-44 diesel locomotive was restored to service by the Puget Sound Railway Historical Association and used in excursion service on their Snoqualmie Valley Railroad, Snoqualmie Falls, Washington.

In the woods above Vail and Camp McDonald, most of the old railroad right-of-way has been converted into log truck and fire roads as diesel rigs now move logs from the tree farm to the mills where once steam locomotives and wood skeleton log cars traveled. Shooflies bypassed old trestles, a few bents could still be observed standing amongst the second and third growth timber. Most of the Skookumchuck High Bridge had long since decayed, but a few bents still existed on the southwestern rim of the steep canyon. One original wood water tank still remained on what was once the 12 line, providing a source of water for fire trucks. An old water tank car lay by the side of the road of what was once the 40 line below the old Camp 3 site on the 40 line. Once converted for use as a water tank during the waning days of steam, it is now a rusty orange reminder that trains once ruled these woods roads. Another tank car tank rests on top of a hill and still serves as a water tank for fire trucks. Most of the steel was pulled and sold for scrap, although the occasional spike and tie plate, and sometimes even a section of rail still can be found along the old railroad grades. The R&L crews removed most of the old ties from the right-of-ways in the 1940s and 1950s, however in places, usually old camp sites or skidder sides, the remains of a decomposed tie could still be found, some with spikes still protruding. Scattered through the woods are miles of old skidder cable and the occasional rusty tool left by a woodsman. Most of the camp sites can be identified by the remains of camp debris, including stoves, tubs, steel frames of cots, wire wrapped wood pipes, iron pipe, the occasional locomotive spark arrestor, and in some places old china used to feed the hundreds of hungry loggers and trainmen who worked deep in the woods. At the site of Camp 2 on the 42 line could be found the remains of a large intact skidder sled, with some boiler firebricks scattered around.

An old length of rail left behind in the woods at Vail was forged in 1888. One-hundred-eleven years old when photographed in 1999, the length of rail is a clear reminder to future Weyerhaeuser loggers that trains once ruled the woods and the sound of steam locomotives and the felling of large trees thundered through the forests. —Frank W. Telewski

The tree farms of Thurston and Lewis Counties still grew trees at the start of the 21st Century, and the Weyerhaeuser Company was still a major

Left: Where locomotives once ran exclusively, diesel trucks now handle all of the log traffic at Vail and McDonald. Following the old Vail Mainline, the driver of Weyerhaeuser log truck 585 stops to check his rig before leaving the tree farm via Vail. —Frank W. Telewski

Below: When the Skookumchuck watershed was first opened up by logging railroads in the late 1920s, the concepts of modern silviculture and tree farming were in their infancy. This view is along Porcupine Ridge along the LD line. At the end of the 20th century, the practice of tree farming was a well established means of stewardship ensuring a continuing supply of timber from previously cut over lands. —Frank W. Telewski

employer in the region during it's 100th anniversary, with no sign of giving up on their productive forest lands or the people who care for them throughout the seasons. Thousands of men and women worked to support the Vail-McDonald operation, through good times and bad, wind, fire and snowstorm, flood and drought, keeping the supply of logs rolling. The times had changed and the rails no longer ruled the woods. However, some 75 years after the first steam trains began to roll into the hills south of Vail, if you were to be very quiet while standing on a mountain top of the Vail-McDonald Tree Farm, maybe, just maybe you could still hear the echo of a distant steam whistle carried on the wind.

Appendix I

Vail-McDonald Camp Locations

Camp	Locations
Camp 1	Vail Company Town, Bunk Houses, Houses, School 1927-1980 Shops (1994)
Camp 2	Skookumchuck MILW interchange[1] 1927 LD Camp 1927-28 5 miles above Vail[2], Camp Cars, 150 men, Bert Gillespie, '28; Art Grandstrom, '29 Foreman LD10, 1929-1932, 13 miles above Vail[3] Br2@2H, 1932-1935 50 Line, 6/1935-1938[4] 42 Line, 1938-1945
Camp 3	Miller Hill LB, 1927-1930, Bob Douglas, '29 Foreman LD28-Spike Camp, 1930-1934 50 Line, 6/1935-1937[5] 40 Line, 1937-1945
Camp 4	1927-1928, 2.5 miles above Vail[6], 20 8-man houses, dinning hall, 110 men, Brad Fox, '28; Jack Peacock, '29 Foreman, location unknown 1929-1930, 20 8-man houses, dinning hall, six camp cars, location unknown LD28-Spike Camp, 1930-1933, 30 8-man houses, dinning hall, six camp cars B2-Siding 8, 1933-1941, Becomes an R&L Camp 44 Line, 1941-1945
Camp 5	LD Camp, 1927-1934 or 38? Branch 10, 1938-1950
Camp 6	LD28-Spike Camp, 9/2/28-1934, Fire 9/26/1930[7], approx 11 miles SE of Vail[8], 2G leg of wye at head of Branch 2, Switchback 1931[9]-193?, Became Boom-Stick camp Camp McDonald, 1938-1948
Camp 7	LD line on Porcupine Ridge, 1929-1934 50CSpur, 1934-1935, Camp McDonald, 1940-1948
SouthBay	80 men (1928-1936), Boom office and dump (1985)

[1] Thurston County Independent, 2/24/28 p.1
[2] Thurston County Independent, 2/3/28 p.1
[3] Thurston County Independent, 6/2/33 p.1
[4] Thurston County Independent, 6/8/34 p.1
[5] Thurston County Independent, 6/8/34 p.1
[6] Thurston County Independent, 2/3/28 p.1
[7] Thurston County Independent, 9/26/30 p.1
[8] Thurston County Independent, 8/31/28 p.1

Appendix II
Rolling Stock and Equipment

At best, this is only a partial listing of rolling stock and equipment used at Vail and Camp McDonald. It is difficult to reconstruct a comprehensive list, as we were not able to locate any inventory lists of equipment by road numbers. Car numbers were collected directly from photographs and limited records of acquisition. Woods equipment had reporting marks of WTCo (pre-1959) or WCo after 1959. Chehalis Western Equipment was lettered for the Chehalis Western (CW) or CWWR after 1980. A limited number of rolling stock was relettered for the Curtis, Milburn and Eastern from 1976 to 1980. Rolling stock was verified either from photographs, original purchase orders from Pacific Car and Foundary (PC&F) records or from inventories held at Weyerhaeuer Company Archives, Tacoma, Washington.

Equipment Register- Weyerhaeuser Vail/MacDonald

Car #	
000	10,000 gal water car (1960's-1990's?)
001	PC&F style tank car 10,000?
1	Crew Car, ex-NCL wood car used at Camp McDonald
2	Crew Car, ex-NCL wood car used at Camp McDonald
76	Crew Car, ex -NCL steel car used at Camp McDonald
52	PC&F swivel bunk in 1-200 series
1-200	42' PC&F skeleton log cars 7/27/1927 Order #28035
100	56' PC&F 4 truck moving car (1/21/29) used for High Lead Unit #1?
142	PC&F swivel bunk in 1-200 series
201-400	42' PC&F skeleton log cars purchased 1938?
291	42' PC&F skeleton log cars w/ swivel bunk
302	42' PC&F skeleton log car
401	40' PC&F Moving flat car w/steel deck United Commercial Co
402	40' Flat Car, United Commercial Company
402	40' Flat Car, United Commercial Company
403	40' Flat Car, United Commercial Company
404	40' Flat Car, United Commercial Company
405	40' Flat Car, United Commercial Company
406	40' Flat Car, United Commercial Company
407	40' Flat Car, United Commercial Company
412	40' PC&F Moving flat car w/steel deck
414	40' PC&F Moving flat car w/steel deck
418	40' PC&F Moving flat car w/steel deck
419	40' PC&F Moving flat car w/steel deck
430	40' flat car (purchased 1936 total of 14 cars)

431	40' flat car (purchased 1936)
436	40' flat car (purchased 1936)
449	44' PC&F Skeleton log car
450-505	44' PC&F Skeleton log cars ?
506	44' PC&F Skeleton log car
501	8,000 gal tank car (oil?)
503	8,000 gal tank car (oil?)
504	8,000 gal tank car (oil?)
508	8,000 gal tank car (oil?)
512	10,000 gal tank car
513	8,000 gal tank car (oil?)
514	8,000 gal tank car (oil?)
516	10,000 gal tank car
518	10,000 gal tank car PC&F type with elevated walkway (water?)
519	10,000 gal tank car
521	10,000 gal tank car PC&F type with elevated walkway (water?)
522	10,000 gal tank car PC&F type with elevated walkway (water?)
523	10,000 gal tank car (water?)
527	10,000 gal tank car (water?)
529	10,000 gal tank car (water?)
531	10,000 gal tank car (water?)
532	10,000 gal tank car (water?)
534	10,000 gal tank car
535	10,000 gal tank car
538	10,000 gal tank car (water?)
540	10,000 gal tank car (water?)
543	10,000 gal tank car (water?)
543	Wood Caboose, 8 wheel ex-MILW, also used by CW
550-583	PC&F Logger's Ballast Car (wood)
581	Brush/ballast car- snow plow (scratch built January 1951)
587	Steel ballast car (scratch built August 1949)
600	PC&F Motorized Dump car
601	PC&F Motorized Dump car
602	Steel Caboose, 8 wheel, ex-SP purchased 1976
603	Steel Caboose, 8 wheel, ex-SP purchased 1976
605	Flat car for Burro crane
700	Snow Plow
701	Wood Caboose
702	Wood Caboose, 8 wheel

703	Wood Caboose, 4 wheel PC&F (1 of 4)
704	Wood Caboose, 4 wheel PC&F (1 of 4)
707(?)	Crew car, ex-NP Pullman #707 (used until Nov 11, 1941)
709	Wood Caboose
711(?)	Crew car, ex-NP Pullman #711 (used until Nov 11, 1941)
711	Wood Caboose, 8 wheel PC&F ex-CW
712	Wood Caboose, 8 Wheel PC&F?
714(?)	Crew car, ex-NP Pullman #714 (used until Nov 11, 1941)
718	Crew car, ex-Puget Sound Electric Railway #504 (used until Nov 11, 1941)
719(?)	Crew car, ex-NP Pullman #719 (used until Nov 11, 1941)
###	Crew car, ex-Northwest Traction #50 (used until Nov 11, 1941)
721	Crew car, ex-Northwest Traction #54 (used until Nov 11, 1941)
###	Crew car, ex-Northwest Traction #76 (steel car) (used until Nov 11, 1941)
723(?)	Crew car, ex-NP Pullman #723
730	Wood Caboose, 4 wheel PC&F (1 of 4)
733(?)	Crew car, ex-NP Pullman #733
741	Crew car, ex-Oregon Electric Interurban Ry. #69
742	Crew car, Combine, ex-Oregon Electric Interurban Ry. #63?
743	Crew car, ex-Oregon Electric Interurban Ry. #68?
744	Crew car, 1880 open platform Barney & Smith wood coach, ex-NP #981
745	Crew car, ex-Oregon Electric Interurban Ry. (#103?)
747	Crew car, ex-Oregon Electric Interurban Ry. (#104?)
748	40' steel flat car
800	Wood Caboose, 8 wheel PC&F ex-CW
940	4 bunk steel log car
2000	Steel tank car (Water) 20651 gal WTCX reporting marks
###	24 wheel lidgerwood carrying car
###	Wood Caboose, 8 wheel, steel gang
No #	Wood Caboose, 8 wheel ex-GN, wrecked and scrapped shortly after purchase
2	Wood Caboose, 8 wheel ex-White River Lumber Co. #2, appears to have kept lettering
150	Tender water car
No #	25 Ton American locomotive crane
No #	South Bay Incline car
xx	Burro crane
1	Washington Iron Works Tree Rig skidder 2-26-28 #4040 S-1-14+10×12; #4035 DL-10×12 w/54' 4 truck PC&F skidder car (#100)
2	Washington Iron Works Tree Rig skidder 7-24-28 #4081 S-1-14+10×12; #4082 DL-10×12 w/56' 4 truck PC&F skidder car
3	Washington Tower skidder (largest of the skidders at Vail) 1-20-32 #4262 S-13.5×14+10.25; #4264 L-12.5×12; #4263 U-12.5×12; #4265 GL-4×6

4	Lidgerwood Tower Skidder (ex-Siler) purchased 4-36.
5	Lidgerwood Tower Skidder
5 (2nd)	Diesel donkey
6	Washington Iron Works skidder diesel purchased 1949
7	Lidgerwood skidder
8	Tower skidder (in use by 6-37)
	S-15.5×14, in use at Longview, WA by 5-19-40
8	Clyde Ironworks locomotive crane C/N 304 ex-Simpson Timber, (Vail 1942)
9	Clyde Ironworks locomotive crane C/N 303 ex-Mud Bay #1, Mt. Rainier Scenic #21 (Vail 1941)
10	Clyde Ironworks locomotive crane C/N 305 ex-White River #946
11	Clyde Ironworks locomotive crane
xx	Ohio Logger's Special crane 25 ton C/N 3813 (12/12/27)
xx	Ohio Logger's Special crane 25 ton C/N 3814 (12/31/27)
xx	Ohio Locomotive crane 20 ton C/N 3786
xx	Browing Locomotive Crane Model 7DT C/N 957
xx	Speeder (Gibson Model G4 3/35)
19	Speeder
20	Speeder
25	Speeder (Vail, Skagit Iron & Steel Model 6-60, C/N 114 8/9/28)
28	Speeder
29	Speeder
30	Speeder (Skagit Steel & Iron Model 6-40 C/N 203 2/22/37)
31	Speeder (Vail, Skagit Steel & Iron Model 4-25 C/N 205)
32	Speeder
xx	Speeder Trailer (Vail, Skagit Steel & Iron, #14 model 6-40 9-4-40)
xx	Speeder (Skagit Iron & Steel Works C/N 207 Model 4-25)
xx	Speeder (Skagit Iron & Steel Works C/N 211 Model 6-40)
35 (1st)	Speeder (Gibson cupola type)
35 (2nd)	Speeder (Skagit Steel & Iron Model 6-40, similar to #30)
36	Speeder (Gibson in use 1942)
37	Speeder (Gibson)
42	Speeder- Gibson Heavy Duty Model L4/Model LO 525, 110-H.P. BUDA Gas engine (McDonald, WTCo, not CW)
43	Speeder- Gibson Heavy Duty Model L4/Model LO 525, 135-H.P. BUDA Gas engine (McDonald, WTCo, not CW)
44	Speeder- Gibson Heavy Duty Model L4/Model LO 525, 135-H.P. BUDA Gas engine (McDonald, WTCo, not CW)

45 (McDonald,	Speeder- Gibson Heavy Duty Model L4/Model LO 525, 135-H.P. BUDA Gas engine WTCo, not CW)
xx	Speeder trailer- Gibson
62	Speeder trailer- Gibson
66	Speeder trailer- Gibson
55	Speeder
513	Fairmont Speeder
530	Speeder (Fairmont?)
533	Speeder (Fairmont?)
XX	#40 Sheffield Speeder (ex-Siler)
XX	#40 Sheffield Speeder (ex-Siler)

Leased cars WTCo/CW

25320	UP caboose
122015	NP Log Flat (leased 1975)
122064	NP Log Flat (leased 1975)
122067	NP Log Flat (leased 1975)

Equipment Register- Weyerhaeuser Chehalis Western (CW reporting marks, Pre 1976)

50	Speeder $709.40
000	Tank Car, water
207	Four bunk skeleton log car
211	Tender water car (ex-CW 211 2-8-2)
215	Tender water car (ex-CW 215 2-8-2)
231	44' PC&F skeleton log car
299	log car ex- SP&S 72' baggage car
300	log car ex- SP&S 80' baggage car
325	Wood Caboose, 8 wheel ex-NP?
527	Tank Car, water
543	Wood Caboose, 8 wheel ex-MILW
711	Wood Caboose, 8 wheel PC&F (wrecked and rebuilt between 1960 and 1963)
712	Wood Caboose, 8 wheel PC&F ex-WTCo, ex-NP?
717	44' PC&F skeleton log car
724	44' PC&F skeleton log car
738	44' PC&F skeleton log car
742	44' PC&F skeleton log car
746	44' PC&F skeleton log car
800	Wood Caboose, 8 wheel PC&F (wrecked and rebuilt)

801-850	44' PC&F skeleton log cars (purchased 1/39)
851-946	44' PC&F skeleton log cars, (96 total cars purchased 5/11/39)
865	PC&F swivel bunk in 851-946 series
851	44' Canadian steel frame skeleton cars (22 total listed in 1967 inventory)
940	All steel four bunk skeleton log car
942	44' PC&F skeleton log car four bunk car

Equipment Register- Curtis, Milburn & Eastern

325	Wood Caboose, 8 wheel
No #	Steel Caboose, 8 wheel, ex-SP purchased 1976

CWWR Reporting marks (Post 1980)

X283	Jordan Spreader, ex-MILW (at Mineral 7/99)
44	Speeder
109	Air side dump car lettered OC&E, not CWWR
110	Air side dump car
111	Air side dump car
419	Hi-Railer crew cab pickup ex-MILW 220
433	M-K salt Car (Still at Western Jct 7/99)
500	Hi-Railer pick-up truck ex-MILW 1471
501	Canron rail alignment w/flat (Still at Western Jct 7/99)
505	Hi-Railer utility type truck
507	Hi-Railer flat bed truck-crane
513	Fairmont Speeder
515	Ballast regulator-spreader
521	Ingersol Rand generator
525	Speeder crane
526	Fairmont Tamper
530	Speeder
533	Speeder
546	Salt Car
547	Salt Car
548	Ballast Car
549	M-K Ballast Car
550	M-K Ballast Car
551	Salt Car
552	M-K Ballast Car
553	M-K Ballast Car

590	Wellman-Ohio Locomotive Crane (ex-BN log flat 634381 as tender) (Still at Western Jct 7/99)
592	Air side dump car
593	Air side dump car
595	PS-2 covered hopper car (Sand) ex-SP 401041
596	PS-2 covered hopper car (Sand) ex-SP 401865
597	International widevision caboose
598	International widevision caboose
599	International widevision caboose
940	Steel Skeleton log car w/4 bunks
1001	60' Steel flat car- 4 bunk flats (converted WTCX flat cars)
1002	63' Steel flat car- 4 bunk flats (ex-BN bulkhead flat car, bulkheads removed at Longview)
1005	60' Steel flat car- 4 bunk flats (converted WTCX flat cars)
1009	60' Steel flat car- 4 bunk flats (converted WTCX flat cars)
1010	63' Steel flat car- 4 bunk flats (ex-BN bulkhead flat car, bulkheads removed at Longview)
1011	61' Steel flat car- 4 bunk flats (ex-GN #161082)
1545	Air side dump car
2431	50' gondola
13564	50' gondola
15402	Bulkhead Flat car (incorrect reporting marks CWRR)
65680	Flat car
9919XX	Ex-Milwaukee Road bay window, ribsided caboose
9919XX	Ex-Milwaukee Road bay window, ribsided caboose
991931	Ex-Milwaukee Road bay window, ribsided caboose
991944	Ex-Milwaukee Road bay window, ribsided caboose

Servicable Wood skeleton cars as of 9/25/80 Total # of cars 146

Purchased ex-MILW steel 50 ton high-stake log cars 9/25/80, list based on 1992 inventory as is short some 138 cars owned by the Milwaukee Road.

Series	**Owner**	**Built**	**Rebuilt**	**Total in CW Fleet**
58195-58494	(U.S. Steel Credit Corp)	1948-52	1976	274

Rebuilt 1976 from ex-MILW steel skeleton log flats series 59000-59499, bunk height above top of bunk 7' 2 1/8".

58195	58202	58211	58218	58225	58234
58196	58205	58212	58219	58226	58235
58197	58206	58213	58220	58227	58237
58198	58207	58214	58221	58228	58238
58199	58208	58215	58222	58230	58239
58200	58209	58216	58223	58231	58241
58201	58210	58217	58224	58233	58242

58243	58286	58328	58370	58415	58457
58244	58288	58329	58371	58416	58458
58245	58289	58330	58372	58417	58459
58246	58290	58331	58373	58418	58460
58247	58291	58332	58375	58419	58461
58248	58292	58333	58376	58420	58462
58249	58293	58335	58377	58421	58463
58250	58294	58336	58379	58422	58464
58251	58295	58338	58380	58423	58465
58252	58298	58339	58381	58424	58466
58253	58299	58340	58382	58425	58467
58254	58299	58341	58383	58426	58468
58255	58300	58342	58384	58427	58469
58256	58301	58343	58385	58428	58470
58257	58302	58344	58386	58429	58471
58259	58303	58345	58387	58430	58472
58260	58304	58346	58388	58431	58473
58261	58305	58347	58389	58434	58474
58262	58306	58348	58390	58435	58475
58263	58307	58349	58392	58437	58476
58264	58308	58350	58393	58438	58477
58265	58309	58351	58394	58439	58478
58267	58310	58352	58396	58440	58479
58268	58311	58353	58397	58441	58481
58270	58312	58355	58398	58442	58482
58271	58313	58356	58400	58443	58483
58272	58314	58357	58401	58444	58484
58273	58316	58358	58402	58445	58485
58274	58318	58359	58404	58446	58486
58275	58319	58360	58405	58447	58487
58276	58320	58361	58406	58448	58488
58277	58321	58362	58407	58449	58489
58278	58322	58363	58408	58450	58490
58279	58323	58364	58409	58451	58491
58280	58323	58365	58410	58452	58492
58281	58324	58366	58411	58453	58493
58283	58325	58367	58412	58454	58494
58284	58326	58368	58413	58455	
58285	58327	58369	58414	58456	

Series	Owner	Built	Rebuilt	Total in CW Fleet
58495-58499	(1st Sec. Bank of Utah) ex-MILW ? series	1948	?	2

58497

58499

Series	Owner	Built	Rebuilt	Total in CW Fleet
58500-58504	(Milwaukee Road)	1948-49	12/1975	3

50 Ton Log Flat, Equipped with barber S2 trucks from Hiawatha Box cars, superior drop shaft hand break, MILW DRG B-6850, bunk height above top of bunk 7' 2 1/8".

Rebuilt 1975 from ex-MILW 59000-59499 series steel skeleton log flats

Non. Cap.	110000
Axle Cap.	177000
LT. WT	37800
LD. LMT	139200

58500

58502

58504

Series	Owner	Built	Rebuilt	Total in CW Fleet
58505-58699	(1st Sec. Bank of Utah)	1948-49	1976	3

Rebuilt 1976 from ex-MILW 59000-59499 series steel skeleton log flats, bunk height above top of bunk 7' 2-1/8".

58505

58663

58699

Series	Owner	Built	Rebuilt	Total in CW Fleet
58700-58799	(Continental Illinois Leasing)	1948-49	1976	92

Rebuilt 1976 from ex-MILW 59000-59499 series steel skeleton log flats, bunk height above top of bunk 7' 2 1/8".

58700

58701

58702

58703	58706	58709	58712	58715	58718
58704	58707	58710	58713	58716	58719
58705	58708	58711	58714	58717	58720

APPENDIX II

58721	58737	58752	58766	58779	58792
58722	58738	58753	58767	58780	58793
58723	58739	58754	58769	58781	58794
58724	58740	58755	58770	58782	58795
58725	58741	58756	58771	58784	58796
58726	58742	58758	58772	58785	58797
58728	58744	58759	58773	58786	58798
58729	58745	58760	58774	58787	58799
58730	58746	58761	58775	58788	
58731 *no CWWR*	58747	58762	58776	58789	
marks	58748	58763	58777	58790	
58732	58750	58764	58778	58791	
58734	58751	58765			
58735					

Series	**Owner**	**Built**	**Rebuilt**	**Total in CW Fleet**
58800-58899	(1st Penn. Banking & Trust) ex-MILW ? series	1945-49	1973	90

58800	58817	58834	58851	58867	58885
58801	58818	58835	58852	58868	58886
58802	58819	58836	58853	58870	58887
58803	58820	58837	58854	58871	58888
58804	58821	58839	58855	58872	58889
58805	58822	58840	58856	58873	58890
58806	58823	58842	58857	58874	58891
58807	58824	58843	58859	58875	58892
58808	58825	58844	58860	58876	58893
58809	58826	58845	58861	58878	58894
58810	58827	58846	58862	58879	58895
58811	58828	58847	58863	58881	58896
58812	58829	58848	58864	58882	58897
58814	58830	58849	58865	58883	58898
58815	58833	58850	58866	58884	58899

Series	**Owner**	**Built**	**Rebuilt**	**Total in CW Fleet**
58900-58999	(Milwaukee Road)	1945-49	1972	6

50 Ton Log Flat, Equipped with barber S2 trucks from Hiawatha Box cars, superior drop shaft hand break, MILW DRG B-6850. Stake height increased from 5' 0" to 7' 2-1/8" on 35 cars 4/1974.

Rebuilt 1972 from ex-MILW 84000-90949 series gondolas

Non. Cap.	110000
Axle Cap.	177000
LT. WT	40200
LD. LMT	136800

58900

58918

58950

58969

58998

58999

Series	**Owner**	**Built**	**Rebuilt**	**Total in CW Fleet**
59600-59621	(Milwaukee Road)	1952	1967	2

Side sills, bunks and side stakes applied at Tacoma 1964

Rebuilt 1967 from ex-MILW 59500-59599 steel skeleton logging flats, stake height 5' above bunks.

Non. Cap.	110000
Axle Cap.	177000
LT. WT	40000
LD. LMT	137000

59600

59601

Series	**Owner**	**Built**	**Rebuilt**	**Total in CW Fleet**
59622-59649	(Milwaukee Road)	1948-49	1967	1

Side sills, bunks and side stakes applied at Tacoma 1964

Rebuilt 1967 from ex-MILW 59000-59499 steel skeleton logging flats, stake height 5' above bunks.

Non. Cap.	110000
Axle Cap.	177000
LT. WT	39000
LD. LMT	138000

59647

Series	**Owner**	**Built**	**Rebuilt**	**Total in CW Fleet**
59650-59674	(Milwaukee Road)	1952	1967	1

Side sills, bunks and side stakes applied at Tacoma 1965

Rebuilt 1967 from ex-MILW 59500-59599 steel skeleton logging flats, stake height 5' above bunks.

Non. Cap.	110000
Axle Cap.	177000
LT. WT	40000
LD. LMT	137000

59656

Series	**Owner**	**Built**	**Rebuilt**	**Total in CW Fleet**
59675-59774	(Milwaukee Road)	1945-49	1969-70	15

Rebuilt 1969 from ex-MILW 84000 & 86000 series gondolas, bunk height 6' 2 5/16" from top of floor, 5' above top of bunk. Height increased to 7' 2 1/8" on 23 cars 4/1976

Non. Cap.   110000
Axle Cap.   177000
LT. WT   40200
LD. LMT   136800

59676	59686	59705	59721	59759
59678	59691	59709	59727	59768
59680	59697	59711	59746	
59684				

Series	**Owner**	**Built**	**Rebuilt**	**Total in CW Fleet**
59775-59874	(Milwaukee Road)	1945-49	1970-71	7

Barber S2 trucks from Hiawatha Box cars

Rebuilt 1970-71 from ex-MILW 84000-90949 series gondolas, bunk height 6' 2 5/16" from top of floor, 5' above top of bunk. Height increased to 7' 2 1/8" on 70 cars 4/1976

Non. Cap.   110000
Axle Cap.   177000
LT. WT   40200
LD. LMT   136800

59796	59848	59863
59807	59855	59864
59834		

Series	**Owner**	**Built**	**Rebuilt**	**Total in CW Fleet**
59875-59974	(Milwaukee Road)	1945-49	1970	10

Barber S2 trucks from Hiawatha Box cars

Rebuilt 1970 from ex-MILW 84000-90949 series gondolas, bunk height 6' 2 5/16" from top of floor, 5' above top of bunk. Height increased to 7' 2 1/8" on 72 cars 4/1976

Non. Cap.   110000
Axle Cap.   177000
LT. WT   40200
LD. LMT   136800

59878	59900	59911	59926	59940	59974
59894	59902	59923	59936	59952	

Purchased ex-BN(NP, GN) steel log cars located at the St. Regis Lake Kapowsin facility 8/29/80 Total # of cars 65

632806	ex-BN (Purchased from Block Steel Industries, $1,000)
632808	ex-BN (Purchased from Block Steel Industries, $1,000)
632842	ex-BN (Purchased from Block Steel Industries, $1,000)
632869	ex-BN (Purchased from Block Steel Industries, $1,000)
633103	ex-BN (Purchased from Block Steel Industries, $1,000)
633116	ex-BN (Purchased from Block Steel Industries, $1,000)
633162	ex-BN (Purchased from Block Steel Industries, $1,000)
633449	ex-NP #120XXX, BN 633449 41' (Purchased from Smith Brothers, $1000 each)
633462	ex-BN (Purchased from Block Steel Industries, $1,000)
633492	ex-BN (Purchased from Block Steel Industries, $1,000)
68504	ex-GN (Purchased from Block Steel Industries, $1,000)
122091	ex-NP (Purchased from Block Steel Industries, $1,000)
xxxxxx-xxxxxx	54 cars total, ex-BN (Purchased from Smith Brothers, $1000 each)
634381	ex-BN log flat used at crane tender
655887	Flat car
833449	ex-BN 41' log flat
990391	Steel bay window caboose ex-MILW
991931	Steel bay window caboose ex-MILW
991935	Steel bay window caboose ex-MILW
991944	Steel bay window caboose ex-MILW
###	Double Brush/ballast car steel, scratch built, similar to 581
no#	Speeder flatcar w/tank
no#	Speeder flatcar
no#	Speeder flatcar

Appendix III
Steam Locomotives at Vail-McDonald including the Chehalis Western 1927-1953

No.	Type	Builder	C/N	Date	Cyl.	Driver	Pounds	Weight	PSI	Cost
1	2T Shay	Lima	2030	11-11-07	11×12	32"	100,000	22,600	200	
	Stillwater Lbr. Co. #1 Stillwater, WA									
	Cherry Valley Log. Co. #1 (2nd) Stillwater, WA									
	WTCo #1 V-M 1927 (bell put on diesel #481 in 1948)									
2(1st)	3T Shay	Lima	3090	08-12-20	13.5×15	36"	189,000	35,000	200	$27,922
	Cherry Valley Log. Co. #2 Stillwater, WA									
	WTCo #2 V-M 1927 (here summer 1938)(out of service with bad boiler 09-42)									
	M. Block & Co. Seattle, WA (sold for scrap at Vail 08-17-43 $1,000)									
	scrapped 11-43									
2(2nd) see #102(2nd)										
3(1st)	2T Shay	Lima	2671	09-09-13	12×12	36"	110,000	23,900	200	
	Cherry Valley Log. Co. #3 Stillwater, WA									
	WTCo #3 V-M 01-15-28 $7000									
	WTCo #3 Klamath Falls, OR 11-16-28									
3(2nd) see #102(2nd)										
4(1st) see #104										
4(2nd)	3T	Heisler	1573	11-28	18.25×16	40"	198,000	43,600	200	
	M. B. Log. Co. #4 Markham, WA									
5(1st)	2T Shay	Lima	486	02-26-95	10×12	29.5"	64,000	14,070		
	Mosher & McDonald #2 Monroe, WA									
	Cherry Valley Log. Co. #2 later #5 Monroe and Stillwater, WA									
	WTCo #5 V-M									
	WTCo. #5 Longview, WA 01-01-28									
	scrapped 01-37									
5(2nd)	3T Shay	Lima	3316	02-16-28	13×15	36"	184,800	38,200	200	$26,730
	BC Forest Products, Ltd. #4 Youbou, BC 01-47									
	scrapped 10-59									
6	3T Shay	Lima	3253	03-14-24	12×16	36"	172,400	30,350		$25,245
	Siler Log. Co. #2 (2nd) Cathcart, WA (used by Hyman-Michaels to scrap line)									
	WTCo. V-M 04-36 $7,000 (stored at Vail as surplus equipment 10-15-36, most likely never relettered to WTCo.)									
	North Bend Tbr. Co. #6 North Bend, WA 03-37 $7,217									
	M. Bloch & Co. (D) Seattle, WA 08-42									
6	2-6-6-2T	BLW	57601	03-24	17&26×24	44"	220,000	37,600	200	$40,927
	Clemons Log. Co. #6 Melbourne, WA									
	WTCo #6 Mel 1936 (still here 01-18-46)									
	WTCo #6 V-M (here 10-14-46) In transit to Longview?									
	WTCo #111 Longview, WA (1946?)									

No.	Type	Builder	C/N	Date	Cyl.	Driver	Pounds	Weight	PSI	Cost
99	2-6-2T	Porter	5030	03-12	15×20	44"	96,000	15,600	180	

Campbell Lbr. Co. #6 Redmond, WA (for sale 06-28-27)
Siler Log. Co. #? Cathcart, WA (most likely)
WTCo #99 V-M 04-36 $2,000
Believed scrapped durring WWII

| 100 | 2-6-2 | Alco/Cooke | 62965 | 1921 | 18×24 | 48" | 127,500 | 24,800 | 180 | |

Hetch Hetchy RR #5 Groveland, CA
WTCo #100 V-M 1935 (still here 06-30-48)
WTCo #100 Sutherlin, OR 1948
City of Sutherlin, OR (display) 1961

| 101 | 2-8-2 | BLW | 39787 | 1913 | 20.5×28 | 48" | 175,000 | 35,500 | 170 | |

Cherry Valley Log. Co. #101 Stillwater, WA
WTCo #101 V-M (tender enlarged vertically)
Listed for sale 06-50 tender only on inventory 01-01-53

| 102(1st) | 2-8-2 | BLW | 37496 | 1912 | 18×24 | 44" | 139,000 | 27,000 | 180 | |

Twin Falls Log. Co. #102 Yacolt, WA
Clarke County Tbr. Co. #102   A 1917
WTCo #102(1st) V-M 03-08-27 $11,500.00
WTCo #102 (later #1) K Falls (here by 10-12-28)
scrapped 1950

| 102(2nd) | 2-8-2T | BLW | 53146 | 04-20 | 16×22 | 41" | 124,500 | 21,100 | 180 | |

Simpson Log. Co. #2(3rd or 4th) Shelton, WA
WTCo #2(2nd) later #102(2nd) 1936 #3(2nd) V-M
City of Prineville Ry #5 Prineville, OR 03-41 (tender from COP #2 added)
scrapped 1945

| 102(3rd) | 2-8-2 | BLW | 57705 | 03-24 | 19×24 | 44" | 152,480 | 30,000 | 180 | |

Siler Log. Co. #3 Cathcart, WA
WTCo. #102 V-M 04-36 $12,000
(only steam loco on inventory 01-01-53)
(tender used with diesels as water car #150)
(tender to fire car #150 still at Vail 12-74)

| 103 | 2-8-2 | BLW | 37539 | 1913 | 20.5×28 | 48 | 173,000 | 42,500 | 170 | |

Twin Falls Log. Co. #101 Yacolt, WA
Clarke County Tbr. Co. #101 Yacolt, WA 1917
WTCo #101 Longview 08-12-25 $12,500 (likely never relettered)
Clarke County Tbr. Co. #101 Yacolt, WA
WTCo #103 V-M 05-01-27 $9375.00 (tender extended vertically)
Red River Lbr. Co. #103 Westwood, CA 1943
Fruit Growers Supply Co. #103 Westwood, CA 1944
Fruit Growers Supply Co. #103 (to #3(2nd) 1951) Susanville, CA (1945/50)
scrapped 1956

| 104 | 2-8-2 | BLW | 52192 | 08-19 | 18×24 | 44" | 140,800 | 27,040 | 180 | |

Cherry Valley Log. Co. #4 Stillwater, WA
WTCo #4 later #104 V-M
WTCo #2 K Falls 1929
scrapped 1950

APPENDIX III

No.	Type	Builder	C/N	Date	Cyl.	Driver	Pounds	Weight	PSI	Cost
105	2-8-2	BLW	35781	1910	18×24	44"	136,000	24,000	160	$12,500

Port Blakely Mill Co. (Blakely RR) #1 (3rd)   Kamilche, WA
Stimson Mill Co. #1   Kamilche, WA   1916
Siler Log. Co. #5   Cathcart, WA
WTCo. #105   V-M   03-36   (photographed here 1952)

110	2-6-6-2T	BLW	60561	08-28	17&26×24	44"	222,000	37,500	200	

Rayonier Inc. #110   Hoquiam, WA   1954   (tender from 2-8-2 #101 added)
Promontory Chapter National Ry Historical Society   Salt Lake City, UT   1968
Wasatch Railroad Museum & Foundation   Heber City, UT   1971
Nevada State RR Museum   Boulder City, NV   1993
Black Hills Central RR   Hill City, SD   1998

111	2-6-6-2T	BLW	60811	05-29	16&16×24	44"	263,250	46,900	210	

(here 12-12-29)
(may have been used at Longview in mid-1930s)
tender added and tanks cut down for service out of Camp McDonald after 1938
Canadian Forest Products, Ltd. #111   Woss, BC   1946 $30,000   (oil tank removed)
scrapped 03-61   (tender frame converted to snow plow)

112	2-6-6-2T	BLW	62065	1937	18&28×24	44"	247,000	42,500	200	

WTCo #112   Longview, WA?
WTCo #112   V-M   (here 1939)
Kosmos Tbr. Co. #12   Kosmos, WA   1950
U. S. Plywood Corp. #12   A   1953
Harbor Plywood Corp. #12   Chelatchie Prairie (Amboy), WA   1954 (last ran 1957)
International Paper Co.   A   (never relettered or ran)
scrapped 10-59

114	2-6-6-2T	BLW	60343	1928	18&28×24	44"	245,000	42,500	200	$40,065

Clemons Log. Co. #8   Melbourne, WA
WTCo #114   V-M   1936
WTCo #114   Longview, WA   1948   (still here 2-24-50)

120	2-6-6-2	BLW	61904	1936	20&31×28	51"	293,000	59,600	225	

WTCo #120   V-M
Chehalis Western RR #120   1941
WTCo #120   Longview, WA   1949 $27,402.59
Columbia & Cowlitz RR #120   Longview, WA   1954 (not lettered for C&C)   (still here 11-12-54)
Rayonier Inc. #120   Hoquiam, WA   1954 $10,000   (last ran 1961)
scrapped 1969

Leased

4	3T	Climax	1589	11-21	15.25×16	36"	160,000	35,200	200	

Simpson Log. Co. #4(3rd)   Shelton, WA
used at   V-M   1937   (lettered for Simpson #4)
#?   Willapa Harbor Lbr. Mills Shay in 09& 10-38 for construction at Camp McDonald.

Chehalis Western RR   Curtis (Camp McDonald), WA 1936-1992

No.	Type	Builder	C/N	Date	Cyl.	Driver	Pounds	Weight	PSI	Cost
120	2-6-6-2	BLW	61904	1936	20&31×28	51"	293,000	59,600	225	

WTCo #120   Vail-McDonald
CW RR #120   1941
WTCo #120   Longview. WA   1949 $27,402.59
Columbia & Cowlitz RR #120   Longview, WA   1954 (never lettered for C&C) (still here 11-24-54)
Rayonier Inc. #120   Hoquiam, WA   1954 $10,000   (last ran 1961)
scrapped 1969

| 211 | 2-8-2 | BLW | 41739 | 10-14 | 24×30 | 57" | 249,900 | 47,670 | 185 | |

Atlanta Birmingham & Atlantic #102
Atlanta Birmingham & Coast RR #211   Atlanta, GA
CW RR #211   11-38 $5000   (listed for sale 06-50)

| 215 | 2-8-2 | BLW | 41743 | 10-14 | 24×30 | 57" | 249,900 | 47,670 | 185 | |

Atlanta Birmingham & Atlantic #106
Atlanta Birmingham & Coast RR #215   Atlanta, GA
CW RR #215   11-38 $5000   (listed for sale 06-50)

Tenders from #211 and #215 became fire cars #215 and #211 respectivly at Vail. Now at Western Forest Industries Museum (Mt. Rainier Scenic RR) Mineral, WA.

Steam Locomotive	1927	1928	1929	1930	1931	1932	1933	1934	1935	1936	1937	1938	1939	1940	1941	1942	1943	1944	1945	1946	1947	1948	1949	1950	1951	1952	1953
#1 2T Shay 2030		██																									
#2 3T Shay 3090		█████████████████																									
#2(2nd) 2-8-2T 53146 see #102																											
#3 3T Shay 2671	█																										
#3(2nd) 2-8-2 53146								████████																			
#4 3T Heisler 1573			████████████																							
#5 3T Pacific Coast Shay 3316																			█████								
#6 3T Shay 3253										█																	
#6(2nd) 2-6-6-2T 57601																				█							
#99 2-6-2T 5030											█████████						????										
#100 2-6-2 62965																						████					
#101 2-8-2 39787					██																						
#102 2-8-2 37496					█																						
#102(2nd) 2-8-2 see 2nd #3																											
#102(3rd) 2-8-2 57705										█████																████	
#103 2-8-2 37539																█											
#104 2-8-2 52192										████████																	
#105 2-8-2 35781																							█				
#110 2-6-6-2T 60561		████████████████████																									
#111 2-6-6-2T 60811		█████████████														????											
#112 2-6-6-2T 62065																						█					
#114 2-6-6-2T 60343										██████																	
#120 2-6-6-2 61904														███													
Leased Locomotives																											
#4 3T Climax											█																
#? Shay												███															
Chehalis Western																											
#211 2-8-2 41739												█████████											███				
#215 2-8-2 41743												█████████											███				
#120 2-6-6-2 61904														████████								█					

Appendix IV

Weyerhaeuser-Vail; Chehalis Western; and Curtis Milburn & Eastern Diesel Locomotives

Weyerhaeuser: Vail, Washington 1948-1982

No.	Builder	Type	C/N	Built
481	Fairbanks-Morse	H10-44	10L60	4-48

Scrapped April 1977

No.	Builder	Type	C/N	Built
714	Fairbanks-Morse	H12-44	10L437	8-51

Ex- Weyerhaeuser Timber Company, White River Branch, #1, Enumclaw, Washington
Rebuilt by Milwaukee Road, Tacoma Shops 1971
To Weyerhaeuser Company, Vail, 1975
To Pacific Transportation Services, #121, Tacoma, Washington 1982
Leased to Continental Grain Company, Tacoma, Washington 1982
Leased to Puget Sound Historical Association, Snoqualmie, Washington 1987 and Relettered Weyerhaeuser Timber Company White River Branch #1.

No.	Builder	Type	C/N	Built
765	EMD	GP7	18599	7-53

Ex-NKP, #431
To Norfolk & Western, #2431
To Morrison-Knudsen (Remanufacturer), Boise, Idaho for rebuilding
To Weyerhaeuser Company, #765, 1976
To Chehalis Western, #765, 1981
To Columbia & Cowlitz, #701 (2nd), Longview, Washington, 1989
Rebuilt by Weyerhaeuser, Renumbered Columbia & Cowlitz #702 (2nd) 1998

No.	Builder	Type	C/N	Built
776	EMD	GP7	18604	7-53

Ex-NKP, #436
To Norfolk & Western, #2436
To Morrison-Knudsen (Remanufacturer), Boise, Idaho for rebuilding
To Weyerhaeuser Company, #776, 1977
To Chehalis Western, #776, 1981
To Columbia & Cowlitz, #700 (2nd), Longview, Washington, 1989
To National Railway Equipment Co., Chicago 1998
To Lake County Railroad #700, Lakeview, Oregon 1998

Weyerhaeuser: Leased Locomotives, Vail, Washington 1972-1976 (BN delivered to Wetico, MILW delivered to Skookumchuck)

No.	Builder	Type	C/N	Built
286	EMD	GP9	25281	5-59

Chicago, Minneapolis, St. Paul & Pacific #286
Weyerhaeuser Leased
To Wilson, Dealer, Des Moines, IA 12-82
To Farmrail, August 1984

Appendix IV

No.	Builder	Type	C/N	Built
616	EMD	SW1200	18760	1-54

ex-Chicago, Minneapolis, St. Paul & Pacific #1639
Chicago, Minneapolis, St. Paul & Pacific Renumbered #616
Weyerhaeuser Leased
Chicago, Minneapolis, St. Paul & Pacific Renumbered #704

No.	Builder	Type	C/N	Built
618	EMD	SW1200	18762	1-54

ex-Chicago, Minneapolis, St. Paul & Pacific #1641
Chicago, Minneapolis, St. Paul & Pacific Renumbered #618
Weyerhaeuser Leased
To STMA #502 May 1980

No.	Builder	Type	C/N	Built
619	EMD	SW1200	18763	1-54

ex-Chicago, Minneapolis, St. Paul & Pacific #1642
Chicago, Minneapolis, St. Paul & Pacific Renumbered #619
Weyerhaeuser Leased
To DRI&NW #619 September 1975

No.	Builder	Type	C/N	Built
668	EMD	NW2	00845	6-39

ex-Chicago, Minneapolis, St. Paul & Pacific #1650
Chicago, Minneapolis, St. Paul & Pacific Renumbered #668
Weyerhaeuser Leased 3-24-72
Chicago, Minneapolis, St. Paul & Pacific scrapped January 1981

No.	Builder	Type	C/N	Built
1504	EMD	GP7	11053	11-50

ex-Great Northern #604
Burlington Northern #1504
Weyerhaeuser Leased 10-4-72 to10-13-72
Burlington Northern rebuilt to GP10 Burlington Northern #1404 February 1975

No.	Builder	Type	C/N	Built
1627	EMD	GP7	14094	4-51

ex-Northern Pacific #553
Burlington Northern #1627
Weyerhaeuser Leased 8-17-75
Burlington Northern retired September 1982

No.	Builder	Type	C/N	Built
1632	EMD	GP7	15690	3-52

ex-Northern Pacific #558
Burlington Northern #1632
Weyerhaeuser Leased 9-15-75
Burlington Northern retired October 1982

No.	Builder	Type	C/N	Built
1860	EMD	GP9	20371	6-55

ex-Northern Pacific #234
Burlington Northern #1860
Weyerhaeuser Leased 2-3-75
Rebuilt to Burlington Northern GP28M #1535:1 January 1993

No.	Builder	Type	C/N	Built
1871	EMD	GP9	21093	2-56

ex-Northern Pacific #248
Burlington Northern #1871
Weyerhaeuser Leased 1-5-75
Burlington Northern retired October 1982

No.	Builder	Type	C/N	Built
1882	EMD	GP9	21431	2-56

ex-Northern Pacific #259
Burlington Northern #1882
Weyerhaeuser Leased 12-10-74
Burlington Northern retired August 1991

No.	Builder	Type	C/N	Built
1888	EMD	GP9	21222	7-56

ex-Northern Pacific #265 wo/dynamic
Burlington Northern #1888
Weyerhaeuser Leased 3-26-72 (still in Northern Pacific paint scheme)
Burlington Northern retired February 1989

Chehalis Western: Camp McDonald (1949), PeEll (1961-1976), Western Junction (1980-1994)

No.	Builder	Type	C/N	Built
492	Fairbanks-Morse	H10-44	10L148	5-49

To Pacific Transportation Services, #122, Tacoma, Washington 1982
Leased to Continental Grain Company, Tacoma, Washington 1982
Scrapped May 1987

493	Fairbanks-Morse	H10-44	10L149	6-49

Scrapped August 1974

684	Alco	C415	6003-01	5-68

To Curtis, Milburn & Eastern, #684, December 1975
To Chehalis Western, #684, 1990
To Tacoma Eastern, #684, Western Junction, Washington 1995 (never relettered or painted)

765	EMD	GP7	18599	1953

Ex-NKP, #431
To Norfolk & Western, #2431
To Morrison-Knudsen (Remanufacturer), Boise, Idaho for rebuilding
To Weyerhaeuser Company, #765, 1976
To Chehalis Western, #765, 1982
To Columbia & Cowlitz, #701 (2nd), Longview, Washington, 1989
Rebuilt by Weyerhaeuser, Renumbered Columbia & Cowlitz #702 (2nd) 1998

776	EMD	GP7	18604	1953

Ex-NKP, #436
To Norfolk & Western, #2436
To Morrison-Knudsen (Remanufacturer), Boise, Idaho for rebuilding
To Weyerhaeuser Company, #776, 1977
To Chehalis Western, #776, 1982
To Columbia & Cowlitz, #700 (2nd), Longview, Washington, 1989
To National Railway Equipment Co., Chicago 1998
To Lake County Railroad #700, Lakeview, Oregon 1998

817	EMD	GP38-2	796388-1	1-81

Originally ordered for Curtis, Milburn & Eastern #817, received without lettering
Lettered for Chehalis Western #817
To Texas, Oklahoma & Eastern, #D-27, De Queen, Arkansas, 1994

818	EMD	GP38-2	796388-2	1-81

Originally ordered for Curtis, Milburn & Eastern #818, received without lettering
Lettered for Chehalis Western #818
To Texas, Oklahoma & Eastern, #D-28, De Queen, Arkansas, 1994

819	EMD	GP38-2	796388-3	1-81

Originally ordered for Curtis, Milburn & Eastern #819, received without lettering
Lettered for Chehalis Western #819
To Golden Triangle Railroad, #819, Columbus, Mississippi, December 1989

| 810 | EMD | GP38-2 | 796388-5 | 1-81 |

Originally ordered for Curtis, Milburn & Eastern #810, received without lettering
Lettered for Chehalis Western #810
To Golden Triangle Railroad, #810, Columbus, Mississippi, December 1989

Chehalis Western: Leased Locomotives, McDonald 1949-1961, PeEll, Washington 1962-1976; Western Junction 1980-1994

No.	Builder	Type	C/N	Built
139	EMD	GP9	19140	2-54

Union Pacific #139
Chehalis Western Leased 1-7-81
Union Pacific retired February 1983
Scrapped by Joseph Simon & Sons, Tacoma, Wash., August 1984

| 314 | EMD | GP9 | 23670 | 7-57 |

Union Pacific #314
Chehalis Western Leased 1981
Sold to Santa Fe 11-81, rebuilt to ATSF yard slug 104, completed on 2-26-82
Renumbered Burlington Northern Santa Fe 1104, 2-89
Renumbered Burlington Northern Santa Fe 3953, 2-00

| 1630 | EMD | GP7 | 15688 | 3-52 |

Ex-Northern Pacific #556
Burlington Northern #1630
Chehalis Western Leased 12-17-75
Burlington Northern retired April 1978

| 1637 | EMD | GP7 | 19034 | 12-53 |

ex-Northern Pacific #563
Burlington Northern #1637
Chehalis Western Leased 11-21-75
Burlington Northern retired September 1982

| 1846 | EMD | GP9 | 20307 | 6-55 |

Ex- Northern Pacific #220
Burlington Northern #1846
Chehalis Western Leased 12-10-74
Burlington Northern retired June 1985

| 8080 | Whitcomb | 80 Tons | 60220 | 3-43 |

Ex-US Army Transportation Corps. #8080
To Weyerhaeuser Timber Company, #8080, Longview, Washington, September 1947
To Chehalis Western, #8080, (for only a short period of time in the late 1940's or early 1950's)
To Weyerhaeuser Timber Company, #8080, Sutherlin, Oregon
To Port of Grays Harbor, #10 Aberdeen, Washington, 1958
To Port of Vancouver, #3, Vancouver, Washington, 1973
To Cliff Koppe Metals, Inc., Vancouver, Washington, 1990
Scrapped 1990

Curtis, Milburn & Eastern: Curtis, Washington 1976-1980

No.	Builder	Type	C/N	Built
684	Alco	C415	6003-01	5-68

Ex-Chehalis Western #684
To Curtis, Milburn & Eastern, #684, December 1975
To Chehalis Western, #684, January 1980
To Tacoma Eastern, #684, Western Junction, Washington 1995 (never relettered or repainted)

Diesel Locomotive	1948	1949	1950	1951	1952	1953	1954	1955	1956	1957	1958	1959	1960	1961	1962	1963	1964	1965	1966	1967	1968	1969	1970	1971	1972	1973	1974	1975	1976	1977	1978	1979	1980	1981	1982	1983	1984	1985	1986	1987	1988	1989	1990	1991	1992	1993
#481 FM 10-44	━	━	━	━	━	━	━	━	━	━	━	━	━	━	━	━	━	━	━	━	━	━	━	━	━	━	━	━																		
#714 FM 10-44																											━	━	━	━	━	━	━													
#765 GP7																													━	━	━	━	━													
#776 GP7																													━	━	━	━	━													
Chehalis Western RR																																														
#492 FM 10-44																									━	━	━	━	━	━	━	━	━													
#493 FM 10-44																									━	━	━	━	━	━	━	━	━													
#684 Alco 415																						━	━	━	━	━	━	━	━	━	━	━	━													
#765 GP7																																━	━	━	━	━	━	━	━	━	━					
#776 GP7																																━	━	━	━	━	━	━	━	━	━					
#817 GP38-2																																			━	━	━	━	━	━	━					
#818 GP38-2																																			━	━	━	━	━	━	━					
#819 GP38-2																																			━	━	━	━	━	━	━					
#810 GP38-2																																			━	━	━	━	━	━	━					
Curtis, Milburn & Eastern Ry																																														
#684 Alco 415																															━	━	━	━												
Leased Locomotives																																														
#139 GP9 Union Pacific																															▪															
#286 GP9 Milwaukee Road																																	▪													
#314 GP9 Union Pacific																														▪																
#616 SW1200 Milwaukee Road																															▪															
#618 SW1200 Milwaukee Road																																▪														
#619 SW1200 Milwaukee Road																																▪														
#668 NW2 Milwaukee Road																																	▪													
#1504 GP7 Burlington Northern																																	▪													
#1627 GP7 Burlington Northern																													▪																	
#1630 GP7 Burlington Northern																													▪																	
#1632 GP7 Burlington Northern																													▪																	
#1637 GP7 Burlington Northern																														▪																
#1846 GP9 Burlington Northern																													▪																	
#1860 GP9 Burlington Northern																													▪																	
#1871 GP9 Burlington Northern																														▪																
#1882 GP9 Burlington Northern																														▪																
#1888 GP9 Burlington Northern																																▪														

Appendix V

Bridge Data on Vail Operation Logging Railroad from 1940

List of Bridges from end of Main Line to Camp 4 via Branch 2, Spur 40 and Spur 44:

Branch 2 Bridges

Bridge No.	Length	Max. Ht.	Built	Remarks
31.42	420ft	96ft	1927	1940 New bridge built
32.02	234	42	1928	1940 New bridge built
33.51	364	61	1929	June
33.66	286	80	1929	July
34.56	286	52	1929	Dec.
35.05 TT	301	53	1930	1941

New bridge built on B4 Switchback

35.19	286	52	1930	March
36.01	301	67	1930	May-April
36.10	151	50	1930	May
39.14	361	66	1931	R & L CAMP

Spur 40 Bridges

2.07	271ft	58ft	1934	
3.09	271	50	1934	
4.09	406	90	1935	
4.53	181	70	1935	
4.60	226	54	1935	
4.79	211	52	1935	
4.87	301	75	1935	
5.85	406	70	1935	
6.05	256	60	1935	
7.03	301	71	1936	
7.14	226	67	1936	
7.74	256	50	1936	
8.80	226	54	1936	
9.08	301	67	1936	

CAMP 2

Bridge No.	Length	Max. Ht.	Built	Remarks
9.60	286	67	1936	
9.72	241	67	1936	
12.71	241	78	1937	

CAMP 3

Bridge No.	Length	Max. Ht.	Built	Remarks
14.82	376	100	1937	East of Camp 3 up Newaukum River
15.06	211	53	1937	
16.12	271	61	1937	Camp 3

Spur 44 Bridges

Bridge No.	Length	Max. Ht.	Built	Remarks
0.35	256	55	1937	
1.09	331	81	1938	Nov. - Oct.
1.87	241	78	1938	Nov. - Dec.
3.61	256	73	1939	Aug. - July
3.95	226	70	1939	Aug.

CAMP 4 Mile 61.46
Vail, Dec. 7-43
R.L.A.

Appendix VI

Bridges and Stations Along the Chehalis Western Mainline

June 14, 1937

E.H.B.
Chehalis Western rechained stations are on typed sheets attached. Please put this stationing on blue print profile which we have in spur files.
Brady's profile (which will be profile #2) starts at station 516+42.2. The west end of bridge No. WH 44 is station 510+83.2, so that your profile #2 starts 558= west of this point. Do what you can on profiles without the notes. Will try to bring notes back with me.
RLA

Notes on Milwaukee railroad chaining starting at Chehalis Junction, going West.

Bridge No. WH 20 East end at stat.	26+86.5
Bridge No. WH 20 West end at stat.	30+38.0
Mile post No. 1 set at stat.	52+80.0
Milwaukee - N.P.R.R. crossing	76+22.0
Bridge no. WH 22 East end at stat.	77+15.0
Bridge no. WH 22 West end at stat.	77+95.0
Mile post No. 2 set at stat.	105+60.0
Bridge No. WH 24 East end at stat.	122+50.7
Bridge No. WH 24 West end at stat.	122+62.0
Bridge No. WH 26 East end at stat.	125+50.0
Bridge No. WH 26 West end at stat.	129+73.7
Bridge No. WH 28 East end at stat.	140+26.6
Bridge No. WH 28 West end at stat.	141+03.8
Mile post No. 3 set at stat.	158+40.0
Point of switch for East end of AJOY@ passing track	173+49.3
Point of switch for West end of AJOY@ passing track	179+62.1
Bridge No. WH 30 East of stat.	183+53.5
Bridge No. WH 30 West of stat.	184+01.6
Bridge No. WH 32 East of stat.	204+67.0
Bridge No. WH 32 West of stat.	205+94.2
Mile post No. 4 set at stat.	211+20.0
Bridge No. WH 34 East of stat.	219+98.5
Bridge No. WH 34 West of stat.	221+10.0
Bridge No. WH 36 East of stat.	242+84.3
Bridge No. WH 36 West of stat.	243+30.0
Mile post No. 5 set at stat.	264+00.0

Bridge No. WH 38 East of stat.	273+93.6
Bridge No. WH 38 West of stat.	274+58.0

WEST ADNA SPUR. Headblock, switch points & frog have been removed but the rest of the track has been left.

Approximately where headblock was	290+34.0
Last rail which was left on siding	291+25.0
Approximate end of spur	297+22.0
Mile post No. 6 set at stat.	316+80.0
Bridge No. WH 40 East of stat.	320+68.8
Bridge No. WH 40 West of stat.	321+13.2

About 1500 feet of track has been taken up here

Right rail ends at stat.	345+52.4
Left rail end at stat.	345+69.5
Both rails begin at crossover to N.P. at stat.	360+91.8
Point of switch for crossover to N.P. at stat.	369+38.3
Mile post No. 7 set at stat.	369+60.0
Point of switch for crossover to N.P. at stat.	384+87.8
Mile post No. 8 at stat.	422+40.0
Point of switch for passing track, East end	430+73.0
Point of switch for passing track, West end	443+00.4
Mile post No. 9 set at stat.	475+20.0
Point of switch for ARUTH@ passing track East end	477+81.6
Point of switch for industry track, East end	479+78.0
Point of switch for industry track, West end	484+07.3
Point of switch for ARUTH@ passing track West end	490+57.9
Bridge No. WH 42 East end at stat.	490+85.8
Bridge No. WH 42 West end at stat.	501+69.3
Post set at stat.	510+00.0
Bridge No. WH 44 East end at stat.	510+39.3
Bridge No. WH 44 West end at stat.	510+83.2
0-00 Weyerhaeuser Tbr. Co. R.R. survey going South	516+41.2
Post set at stat.	520+00.0
Mile post No. 10 set at stat.	528+00.0
Bridge No. WH 46 East end at stat.	528+20.9
Bridge No. WH 46 West end at stat.	528+31.3
Post set at stat.	540+00.0
Post set at stat.	550+00.0
Left rail ends at stat.	576+29.0
Right rail end at stat.	576+46.3

Mile post No. 10.92 set at the end of the rails.

Deed to	576+37.3

References

INTRODUCTION

J. H. Hauberg, 1975. *Weyerhaeuser & Denkmann: Ninety-Five Years of Manufacturing and Distribution of Lumber*, Rock Island, IL.

W. G. Hoar, 1968. *History Is Our Heritage*. White Birch Printing Inc, Shell Lake, WI; R. C. Brown, 1982.

Rails into the Pines, The Chippewa River and Menomonie Railway, printed by Chronotype Publications, Rice Lake, WI. R. C. Brown, Publisher.

R. H. Hidy, F. E. Hill & A. Nevins, 1963. *Timber and Men: The Weyerhaeuser Story*, MacMillan Company, NY.

American Lumberman, May 8, 1915, p. 39.

CHAPTER 1

Agreement between Thurston County and Weyerhaeuser Timber Company to secure crossings of county roads by the Skookumchuck Railway, September 20, 1926, Barrett Family collection.

CHAPTER 2

F. R. Titcomb to L. R. Crosby, December 27, 1926, January 15, 1927, January 19, 1927, January 21, 1927, February 21, 1927, April 22, 1927, July 16, 1927, WTCo. Letterpress Correspondence. Weyerhaeuser Archives.

F. R. Titcomb to Pacific Car & Foundry Co., November 21, 1927, WTCo. Letterpress Correspondence. Weyerhaeuser Archives.

Thurston County, Washington, 1924, by Charles F. Metsker, with Skookumchuck Railroad Line added. Map collection, Weyerhaeuser Archives.

L. R. Crosby to G. S. Long, January 13, 1927, December 9, 1927, WTCo, Incoming Correspondence, Skookumchuck Operation. Weyerhaeuser Archives.

Minot Davis to F. R. Titcomb, February 21, 1929, WTCo. Incoming Correspondence, Skookumchuck Operation. Weyerhaeuser Archives.

Two early photos identified as Camp 4 by Clark Kinsey show two different camps. Several attempts have been made by the authors to verify the early locations of Camp 4 in the Vail woods prior to Camp 4 at Spike Camp on Porcupine Ridge. Robert Gehrman, formerly with Vail Reforestation and Land Department, believes a Camp 4 was located west of the peak of Miller Hill. James F. Barrett, former Vail-McDonald railroad employee who began working at Vail in 1935, said that there was only one camp on Miller Hill (Camp 2). James Barrett's father, Lawrence Barrett, worked on Miller Hill and is the source of his information. Additionally, Mr. Barrett also cites timekeeper Leo Riley, who came from Cherry Valley when the operation moved to Vail. Mr. Riley also ran the 1 spot when he wasn't working as a timekeeper and related to Mr. Barrett that there was just one camp on Miller Hill.

James F. Barrett Sr., interview with.

Skookumchuck Operation, Map No. 0-5, Secs. 20-21-28-29~T.15N., R.2E., Weyerhaeuser Company, Vail, Wash. (no date)

Vail Annual Forestry Report-Progress Map, 1944; Map collection, Weyerhaeuser Archives.

Alexander Retires in *Weyerhaeuser Magazine*, October 1951 3(9):2. Weyerhaeuser Archives.

Logger Fatalities Large. September 1924. *The Timberman*, 25(11):153.

W. J. Ryan to Pacific Car & Foundry Co., July 5, 1927, WTCo. Letterpress Correspondence

J. S. Ober to Pacific Car & Foundry Co., August 30, 1928, WTCo. Letterpress Correspondence. Weyerhaeuser Archives.

Southwestern Washington. December 1927, *The Timberman*, 29(1W):202.

Completing Logging Road. September 1927, *The Timberman*, 28(11):203

Olympia News, January 6, 1928, p. 1; February 3, 1928, p. 1; February 24, 1928; p. 1.

The Daily Olympian, February 1, 1928, p. 1

Morning Olympian, February 3, 1928, p. 1; February 19, 1928 p. 1.

R. A. Pettingill to A. D. Orr, December 31, 1927. WTCo. Incoming Correspondence, Skookum Chuck Operation. Weyerhaeuser Archives.

F. R. Titcomb to L. R. Crosby, June 23, 1927, Letterpress Correspondence. Weyerhaeuser Archives.

Cedar Poles Removed from Skookumchuck Operation, October 15, 1928 to July 29, 1929, WTCo. Incoming Correspondence, Skookumchuck Operation, 1928. Weyerhaeuser archives

Great Northern Freight Car Diagrams, December 13, 1937. Frank W. Telewski collection.

Delegates visit Weyerhaeuser Operations at Vail. November 1929, *The Timberman*, 31(1):150.

Thurston County Independent, August 31, 1928; July 13, 1928; November 8, 1928; February 24, 1928; November 1, 1929.

Logging a Million Feet of Timber Daily at Vail. *West Coast Lumberman*, October 1929.

John Taubeneck, November 11, 1996 notes.

CHAPTER 3

W. J Ryan to R. L. Alexander. September 19, 1930, WTCo. Letterpress Correspondence. Weyerhaeuser Archives.

John Labbe Collection, note (AR-1930, 1931).

M. Davis to Hofius Steel & Equipment, November 11, 1930, WTCo. Letterpress Correspondence. Weyerhaeuser Archives.

Logging Railroad Extensions, November 1930, *The Timberman*, 32(1):137

Vail Track Main Line and Woods Lines Engineers Notebook. Barrett Family collection.

F. R. Titcomb to R. A. McDonald, August 22, 1931, WTCo. Incoming Correspondence, Skookumchuck Operation. Weyerhaeuser archives.

R. A. Pettingill to Mr. Obenour, WTCo, Incoming Correspondence, Skookumchuck Operation. Weyerhaeuser archives. November 5, 1931; November 27, 1931; November 22, 1932

Shut Down Dates, Skookumchuck Operation, Dec. 1930 thru 1931, WTCo. Incoming Correspondence, Skookumchuck Operation. Weyerhaeuser Archives

Thurston County Independent, July 4, 1930; September 11, 1931; July 1, 1938; April 1, 1932; December 18, 1936; September 21, 1928; August 2, 1929; September 26, 1930; August 24, 1934; May 17, 1935; July 26, 1935; July 22, 1938; August 11, 1939; January 24, 1930; September 21, 1930; September 31, 1930; November 21, 1930; January 29, 1937; February 25, 1938; November 10, 1933; June 2, 1933; July 14, 1933; June 8, 1931; November 17, 1933; March 3, 1939; June 24, 1938; July 22, 1938

E. J. Murnen to W. H. Peabody, November 18, 1930, RG#1 WTCo. Letterpress Correspondence. Weyerhaeuser Archives.

West Coast Lumberman [1931, 59(10):58.], [1932, 59(2):18.], [1933 60(8):24], [1933, 60(8): 24]

S. J. Obenour to Hon. Sam C. White. September 27, 1930, WTCo. Letterpress Correspondence. Weyerhaeuser Archives.

G. S. Long to R. A. McDonald. November 3, 1930, WTCo. Letterpress Correspondence. Weyerhaeuser Archives.

J. S. O. to Superintendent of Railway Services, July 6, 1933, WTCo, Incoming Correspondence, Skookum Chuck Operation. Weyerhaeuser Archives.

Bulldozer in Road Grading. August 1933, *The Timberman*, 34(10):75.

CHAPTER 4

Vail Track Main Line and Woods Line Engineer's Notebook. Barrett Family collection.

Thurston County, Washington, 1924, by Charles F. Metsker, with Skookumchuck Railroad Line added. Map collection, Weyerhaeuser Archives.

Weyerhaeuser Timber Company Section Map-Cruiser Report Section 30, TWP 15N, R2E, Weyerhaeuser Company, Vail, Washington.

James F. Barrett, Sr., interview with.

Donald Clark Papers, University of Washington, Manuscript Section, Box 735.

Thurston County Independent, July 29, 1934; April 20, 1934; May 10, 1935; May 17, 1933; June 8, 1934; July 12, 1935; July 26, 1935; August 2, 1935; August 23, 1935; May 16, 1941; June 20, 1941; May 8, 1936; November 27, 1936; June 5, 1936; June 19, 1936; September 9, 1936; September 25, 1936; February 25, 1938

Robert M. Gehrman, Springfield, Ore. October 15, 2000, telephone interview with Frank W. Telewski.

West Coast Lumberman, 1939 66(5):56i.

W. J. Ryan to C. H. Ingram, July 29, 1940; C. H. Ingram Papers, Vail-McDonald Operation. Weyerhaeuser Archives.

C. H. Ingram from W. J. Ryan, July 29, 1940; C. H. Ingram Papers, Vail-McDonald Operation.

CHAPTER 5

The Common Carrier Status of the Chehalis Western Railroad, Roger Henselman, May 21, 1958. Weyerhaeuser Archives.

Agreement between the Chehalis Western and the Chicago, Milwaukee, St. Paul & Pacific Railroads, March 17, 1936. Barrett Family collection.

Chicago, Milwaukee, St. Paul & Pacific Railroad Co. Joint Time Table No. 2, Rocky Mountain Division and Coast Division, December 1, 1974. Barrett Family collection.

Building Logging Railroads, March 1936, *The Timberman*, 37(5):89; Articles of Incorporation, Chehalis Western Railroad Company, Minute Book No. 1. Weyerhaeuser Archives.

Agreement, February 29, 1936, Chehalis Western Railroad Company, unprocessed records, 99-101. Weyerhaeuser Archives.

Tenino Journal, April 30, 1915, p. 1.

Tenino News, April 29, 1915, p. 1.

Tenino Independent, April 28, 1999, pp. 7–10; April 5, 1989, Vol. 66, No. 45. From an interview with George Hales, Scott Barrett.

Thurston County Independent, March 4, 1932; January 18, 1935; July 19, 1935; August 2, 1935; August 9, 1935; September 13, 1935; September 27, 1935; March 20, 1936; May 20, 1938; July 15, 1938

Columbia Construction Co. Skookumchuck Rock Quarry Railroad map, December 13, 1935. George Hales Family collection.

George Hales, transcript of interview by Scott Barrett, October 12, 1986.

Data from photo album. George Hales Family collection.

James F. Barrett, Sr., interview with.

Agreement, February 29, 1936, Chehalis Western Railroad Company, unprocessed records, 99-101. Weyerhaeuser Archives.

James H. Whaley, 1976. "Weyerhaeuser's New Shortline," *Pacific Rail News*, 16(12):10-11.

CHAPTER 6

Building Logging Railroad, *The Timberman*, March 1936, Vol 37(5):89

Articles of Incorporation, February 28, 1936, Chehalis Western Railroad Company Minute Book No. 1, Weyerhaeuser Archives.

Lewis County Railroad, April 1937, *The Timberman*,Vol 38(6):114.

Current events in Douglas fir region:Weyerhaeuser's Operations. *The Timberman*, October 1938, Vol. 39(12):86

Camp McDonald. April 1939, *The Timberman*,Vol 49(6):14-15.

W. J. Ryan to M. Davis, May 10, 1938 with hand written note from R.A. McDonald. Public Affairs,Railroad Locomotives 1926-1947, Weyerhaeuser Archives.

H. A. Gibson to R. A. McDonald, October 27, 1938, Public Affairs, Railroad Locomotives 1926-1947, Weyerhaeuser Archives.

W. J. Ryan to R. A. McDonald, April 15, 1938, Public Affairs, Railroad Locomotives 1926-1947, Weyerhaeuser Archives.

C. S. Perry, Supt. Motive Power, Atlanta, Birmingham and Coast Railroad Company to the Chehalis Western Railroad, November 29, 1938, Public Affairs, Railroad Locomotives 1926-1947, Weyerhaeuser Archives.

The Common Carrier Status of the Chehalis Western Railroad, Roger Henselman, May 21, 1958, Weyerhaeuser Archives.

McDonald Annual Forestry Report-Logging Progress, 1943, Map Collection, Weyerhaeuser Archives.

W. J. Ryan to C. H. Ingram, July 29, 1940, C. H. Ingram Papers, Vail-McDonald Operations, Weyerhaeuser Archives.

Agreement between the Northern Pacific, Weyerhaeuser Timber Company, and Chehalis Western Railroad, December 9, 1943, Chehalis Western Railroad Company unprocessed records 99-101. Weyerhaeuser Archives.

C.M.ST.P.&P.R.R. Condensed Profile, Washington Division, January 1976, Frank W. Telewski Collection.

Minot Davis to H. D. Smith, Traffic Department, November 1, 1943, C.H. Ingham Papers, Weyerhaeuser Sales Company-Traffic, Weyerhaeuser Archives.

A. L. Raught, Jr. to Minot Davis, February 15, 1944, C.H. Ingham Papers, Vail Operation, Weyerhaeuser Archives.

CHAPTER 7

Logmania. *West Coast Lumberman*, 1935, 62(11): 40b-40h.

J. A. Wahl to A. L Raught Jr., July 15, 1948, C. H. Ingram Papers, Vail Operation. Weyerhaeuser Archives.

Pick Up the Whole Load! in *Weyerhaeuser News*, No. 9. 1944

A. L. Raught Jr. to J. A. Wahl, April 6, 1945; November 19, 1946, C. H. Ingram Papers, Vail Operation. Weyerhaeuser Archives.

Old Camp Three Opened for Tree Planting Crew in *Weyerhaeuser Magazine*. April 1954, 6(4):1. Weyerhaeuser Archives.

Manager's Report for 1947, Vail-McDonald Branch Collection. Weyerhaeuser Archives.

Last Trestle Goes in *Weyerhaeuser Magazine*, October 1954, 6(10). Weyerhaeuser Archives.

The Common Carrier Status of the Chehalis Western Railroad, Roger Henselman, May 21, 1958. Weyerhaeuser Archives.

Cats, Locie Visited in *Weyerhaeuser Magazine*, December 1950, 2(6):14. Weyerhaeuser Archives.

The Lumberman, 77(12)52-56, 100-104.

West Coast Lumberman, [1943, 70(6)], [1944, 71(12):36–38.], [1946, 73(10)78], [1951, 58(10):54-55,117]

Pictorially Speaking in *Weyerhaeuser Magazine*, August 1950, 2(4):15. Weyerhaeuser Archives.

REFERENCES 339

Manager"s Report for 1947, Vail-McDonald Operation. Weyerhaeuser Archives.

Vail-McDonald: The woods are different now. *Weyerhaeuser Magazine* 3(11):5-7, December 1951.

Weyerhaeuser Magazine. February 1952, 4(2):1. Weyerhaeuser Archives.

A Look at Randle in *Weyerhaeuser Magazine*. December 1952, 4(12):1. Weyerhaeuser Archives.

Manager's Report, Weyerhaeuser Timber Company, Vail-McDonald Operation, January 1952. Barrett collection.

Doty Blow down in *Weyerhaeuser Magazine*. May 1952, 4(5):2. Weyerhaeuser Archives.

Termination Agreement, Chicago, Milwaukee, St. Paul & Pacific and Chehalis Western, December 27, 1951, Chehalis Western Railroad Company unprocessed records, 99-101, Weyerhaeuser Archives.

Indian Henry in *Weyerhaeuser Magazine*, July 1952 4(7):1. Weyerhaeuser Archives.

Pulp Wood Shipped in *Weyerhaeuser Magazine*, April 1953, 5(4):4. Weyerhaeuser Archives.

The Vail-McDonald Tree Farm in *Weyerhaeuser News*, June 1956, 32:20-21.

Reload Built at Chehalis in *Weyerhaeuser Magazine*. January 1954 6(1):1. Weyerhaeuser Archives.

Vail Builds Buses in *Weyerhaeuser Magazine*, October 1950, 2(5):14. Weyerhaeuser Archives.

Bridges Rebuilt in *Weyerhaeuser Magazine*, February 1951, 3(1):15, September 1951, 3(8):2, November 1952, 4(11):2. Weyerhaeuser Archives.

Around Camp M in *Weyerhaeuser Magazine*, March 1951, 3(2):2. Weyerhaeuser Archives.

Movable Spar Tree in *Weyerhaeuser Magazine*, October 1951, 3(9):2. Weyerhaeuser Archives.

Fir seed is harvested for reforesting. *Thurston County Independent*, September 29, 1939, p. 1; Fir planting to be tried above Vail. *Thurston County Independent*, October 6, 1939, p. 1.

Flying Seeder in *Weyerhaeuser Magazine*, March 1950, 2(2):1.Weyerhaeuser Archives.

Spring Planting in *Weyerhaeuser Magazine*, June 1951, 3(5):1. Weyerhaeuser Archives.

Large Tree Plant in *Weyerhaeuser Magazine*, June 1952, 4(6):2. Weyerhaeuser Archives.

Students Aid Planting in *Weyerhaeuser Magazine*, April 1953, 5(4):3. Weyerhaeuser Archives.

Crews Planting Trees in *Weyerhaeuser Magazine*, December 1953, 5(12):2. Weyerhaeuser Archives.

Vail-McDonald Depreciation Schedule, 1953, Controller, Weyerhaeuser Archives.

CHAPTER 8

The Vail-McDonald Tree Farm in *Weyerhaeuser News*, June 1956, 32:20-21.

More Than Two Million Trees Planted on Vail-McDonald Tree Farm in 1954 in *Weyerhaeuser Magazine*, February 1955, 7(2):1. Weyerhaeuser Archives.

Train Crew Spots Lost Youth in *Weyerhaeuser Magazine*, March 1954, 6(3):2. Weyerhaeuser Archives.

Number 34 Yarder in *Weyerhaeuser Magazine*, April 1956, 8(4):1. Weyerhaeuser Archives.

Seed Plant in Operation in *Weyerhaeuser Magazine*, December 1954, 6(12)1; Seed for Reforestation in *Weyerhaeuser News*, June 1957, 35:22-23.

Wood Products Division Annual Report, 1961, Everett, Wash. Branch Collection. Weyerhaeuser Archives.

Bundling Machines Busy in *Weyerhaeuser Magazine*, May 1954, 6(5):1. Weyerhaeuser Archives.

New Log Catcher Installed in *Weyerhaeuser Magazine*, June 1955, 7(6):1. Weyerhaeuser Archives.

Wood Products Division Annual Report, 1961, Everett, WA Branch Collection, Weyerhaeuser Archives.

The Daily Chronicle, "Log Train and Truck Collide," June 9, 1959.

CHAPTER 9

Wood Products Division Annual Report, 1961, 1962, 1963, 1964, 1965 Everett, WA Branch Collection, Weyerhaeuser Archives.

W. L. Bush to F.G. McGinn, November 4, 1970. James Barrett Collection.

W. L. Bush to D. L. Carlson, General Superintendent, Tacoma Municipal Belt Line Railway, August 26, 1971. James Barrett Collection.

F. G. McGinn to W. L. Bush, November 27, 1970, February 29, 1972. James Barrett Collection.

C.M.St.P.&P. Condensed Profile, Washington Division. January 1976. Frank W. Telewski Collection.

R. B. Hornberger, Distribution Manager, International Car Company to Weyerhaeuser Company, December 15, 1972. James Barrett Collection.

K.A. Knutson, Burlington Northern to F. Disordi, Chehalis Western, November 22, 1974. James Barrett Collection.

Weyerhaeuser Log Scale Ticket #'s 485499 and 485826, Mineral Yard dated February 26, 1980. Frank W. Telewski Collection.

W. L. Bush to G. H. Weyerhaeuser and R. C. Vincent, May 5, 1967, June 27, 1967. James Barrett Collection.

R. L. Merklen, Burlington Northern to W. L. Bush, March 13, 1972; R.L. Merklen, Burlington Northern to W. L. Bush, June 5, 1972. James Barrett Collection.

R. A. Beulke, Burlington Northern to R. A. Gosline, Manager of Rail Transportation, Weyerhaeuser Company. July 9, 1973, July 30, 1973, January 27, 1975. James Barrett Collection.

R. West to J. P. Tessier, December 29, 1972; M.F. Muir, Whisler Equipment Co. January 11, 1973. James Barrett Collection.

CHAPTER 10

First Meeting of Directors, September 12, 1973, Curtis, Milburn & Eastern Railroad Company, Minute Book. Weyerhaeuser Archives.

Curtis log yard operations start. *Daily Chronicle*, January 5, 1976, p. 1.

R. E. Manning to D. Gasaway, January 6, 1975. James Barrett collection.

Status Review, Chehalis Railroads, January 27, 1984, Chehalis Western Railroad unprocessed records 99-101. Weyerhaeuser Archives.

J. W. Wicks to R. A. West, June 9, 1978. James Barrett collection.

Agreement, Milwaukee Road and Curtis, Milburn & Eastern, December 20, 1973, Chehalis Western Railway Company unprocessed records, 99-101. Weyerhaeuser Archives.

Nighswonger, D. 2000. *Milwaukee Road Color Guide to Freight and Passenger Equipment, Volume 2*. Morning Star Books, Scotch Plains, NJ.

Anonymous, 1976. WAM Plan is... *Milwaukee Road Magazine*, 66(7&8):1-5.

Notice C-141, Chicago, Milwaukee, St. Paul & Pacific Railroad Company, Tacoma, December 31, 1975. Allan Miller collection.

Anderson, N. E. 1976. Morrison-Knudsen locomotive rebuilding activities in 1976. *Pacific News*. 17(4):6-15.

Washington Bulletin B No. 12, January 29, 1976, C.M.St.P.&P, Tacoma, Wash.

Quitclaim Deed, November 30, 1978, Chehalis Western Railroad Company unprocessed records, 99-101. Weyerhaeuser Archives.

J. W. Stuckey to R. A. West, February 10, 1978. James Barrett collection.

EMD Order 796388, November 29, 1979. Electro-Motive, Division of General Motors Corp. La Grange, Ill., Chehalis Western Railroad Company unprocessed records, 99-101. Weyerhaeuser Archives.

CHAPTER 11

Robert S. Nielsen, State of Washington Dept. of Transportation to Mr. William Bush, Weyerhaeuser Company, September 18, 1978. James Barrett paper collection.

Mr. Graves, Vice President-Finance and Administration, Union Pacific Railroad to Mr. Kauffman, Vice President-Director of Transportation, Weyerhaeuser Company, November 28, 1978. James Barrett paper collection.

T. E. Rasmussen, Burlington Northern Trackage Rights to DuPont, January 7, 1980. James Barrett paper collection.

Meeting notes with Port of Tacoma, March 14, 1979. James Barrett paper collection.

R. E. Manning to R. West, April 10 & 11, 1979. James Barrett paper collection.

R. A. West to T. Rasmussen, July 10, 1979. James Barrett paper collection.

Background paper-Milwaukee Railroad, October 4, 1979. James Barrett paper collection.

Chicago, Milwaukee, St. Paul & Pacific Railroad Company news release, July 23, 1979. James Barrett paper collection.

Office of Rail Public Council press release, July 25, 1979. James Barrett paper collection.

Transpo Plan Newsletter, Washington State Department of Transportation. August 8, 1979. James Barrett paper collection.

D. H. Byers to Distribution List, August 16, 1979. James Barrett paper collection.

Roy West to J. R. Callahan et al., February 9, 1981, Chehalis Western Start-Up to Tacoma. James Barrett paper collection.

Roy West to Bob Dowdy, August 17, 1979. James Barrett paper collection.

T. E. Rasmussen to R. A. Dowdy et al., September 17, 1979. James Barrett paper collection.

Testimony of John G. Kauffman before the Interstate Commerce Commission, Docket No. AB-7, October 3, 1979, Seattle, Wash. James Barrett paper collection.

Tacoma News Tribune, October 30 & 31, 1979.

The Milwaukee Road, Tom Rasmussen, November 11, 1979. James Barrett paper collection.

T. Rasmussen to F. H. Tolan et al., November 12, 1979. James Barrett paper collection.

T. B. Graves Jr. to T. E. Rasmussen, November 30, 1979. James Barrett paper collection.

R. S. Nielsen to F. Tolan, December 18, 1979. James Barrett collection.

Report on Morton Line Meeting, January 16, 1980. Chehalis Western Railroad Company unprocessed records, 99-101. Weyerhaeuser Archives.

T. E. Rasmussen to G. H. Weyerhaeuser and H. E. Morgan, January 22, 1980. James Barrett collection.

Status Review Chehalis Railroads. January 27, 1984, Chehalis Western Railroad Company unprocessed records, 99-101. Weyerhaeuser Archives.

Roy West, memo. February 26, 1980. James Barrett paper collection.

The Journal, Morton, Washington, August 28, 1980; September 17, 1980.

Mr. F. A. Savory to R. A. West et al. January 7, 1980, Chehalis Western Railroad Company unprocessed records, 99-101. Weyerhaeuser Archives.

R. A. West and B. Pettit to employees, August 25, 1980. James Barrett Paper collection.

The Chronicle, September 9, 1980; October 31, 1980.

B. A. Gammel to Forrest Savory, June 11, 1980. James Barrett paper collection.

R. A. West to T. E. Rasmussen, October 20, 1980. James Barrett paper collection.

CHAPTER 12

R. A. West, December 19, 1980. James Barrett paper collection.

R. A. West note to the rail file. January 4, 1980, Chehalis Western Railroad Company unprocessed records, 99-101, Weyerhaeuser Archives.

F. A. Savory to R. A. West, Interim locomotives for Chehalis Western system, April 18, 1980, Chehalis Western Railroad Company unprocessed records, 99-101, Weyerhaeuser Archives.

Garrett Railroad Car & Equipment, New Castle, Penn., sales invoice, July 7, 1982, James Barrett paper collection.

Ontario Locomotive and Industrial Railway Supplies Inc. sales invoice, November 19, 1982. James Barrett paper collection.

Tenino Independent, May 27, 1981.

Mr. R. West to Ms. Claudia Biermann, Railway Car Purchase. October 25, 1979, Chehalis Western Railroad Company unprocessed records, 99-101, Weyerhaeuser Archives.

Appropriation Request Supporting Data, Rail Car Purchase, December 14, 1979, Chehalis Western Railroad Company unprocessed records, 99-101, Weyerhaeuser Archives.

Mr. F. A. Savory to T. E. Rasmussen, *et al.*, January 7, 1980, Chehalis Western Railroad Company unprocessed records, 99-101, Weyerhaeuser Archives.

Forrest Savory to Dennis Bloch, August 29, 1980; Forrest Savory to Larry Smith, August 29, 1980. Frank W. Telewski collection.

Memorandum of Conference covering Milwaukee/CM & E Railroad Five (5) GP38-2 Locomotives EMD Order 796388, Electro-Motive, Division of General Motors Corp. La Grange, Ill. November 29, 1979, Chehalis Western Railroad Company unprocessed records, 99-101, Weyerhaeuser Archives.

Roy West to Bob Pettit and Forrest Savory, January 16, 1980, CM&E/MILW Railroad Locomotives Project Approval Summary, Chehalis Western Railroad Company unprocessed records, 99-101, Weyerhaeuser Archives.

Roy West to J. R. Callahan, *et al.*, February 9, 1981. James Barrett paper collection.

Weyerhaeuser press release, February 24, 1981. James Barrett paper collection.

Roy West to Tom Rasmussen, January 8, 1981; April 29, 1981. James Barrett paper collection.

T. E. Rasmussen to T. P. Rogers, April 11, 1980. James Barrett Paper collection.

The Chronicle, November 25, 1981.

E. J. Currie to T. E. Rasmussen, August 13, 1980. James Barrett paper collection.

Interoffice communication from F. A. Savory to R. A. West, September 24, 1981. James Barrett collection.

Letter from L. F. Bouy, Automation Industries, Inc., Sperry Rail Service Division, to R. J. Pettit, July 16, 1982. James Barrett collection.

B. Pettit to All Train Crews, May 14, 1983. James Barrett paper collection.

M. Root to G. Weyerhaeuser, February 8, 1983. James Barrett paper collection.

Interstate Commerce Commission Decision Finance Docket No. 30680. Chehalis Western Railroad Company exemption from 49 U.S.C. Subtitle IV. August 28, 1985.

B. L. Skrivseth to A. L. Shoener, April 2, 1986. Chehalis Western Railroad Company unprocessed records, 99-101, Weyerhaeuser Archives.

Status Review: Chehalis Western Railroad, January 27, 1984. Chehalis Western Railroad Company unprocessed records, 99-101, Weyerhaeuser Archives.

Sensel, J. 1999. *Traditions Through the Trees*. Documentary Book Publishers and Weyerhaeuser Company.

Seattle Times, "Lumber Mill in Everett to Shut Down"; p. 1. October 5, 1984.

Jerry Herman to Vern Schmidt, August 9, 1985, Chehalis Western Railroad Company unprocessed records, 99-101, Weyerhaeuser Archives.

The Olympian, "County Buys Abandoned Railroad Line"; August 1, 1991.

S. O. Jones to G. R. Harder, October 3, 1984. James Barrett paper collection.

John Mohr to Sidney Strickland, December 15, 1992. State of Washington Utilities and Transportation Commission.

Seattle Times, "Weyerhaeuser Strike Blazing a Trail"; July 20, 1986; *The Olympian*, "Woodworkers May Ratify Contract"; July 25, 1986; *The News Tribune*, Woodworkers Don't Agree Strike's Over"; July 26, 1986; *The Olympian*, "Weyerhaeuser Workers Accept Cuts"; July 26, 1986.

The Olympian, "Weyerhaeuser Workers Accept Cuts"; July 26, 1986.

John G. Kauffman to Mr. Joseph Dettmar, March 19, 1987. Chehalis Western Railroad Company unprocessed records, 99-101, Weyerhaeuser Archives.

Northwest Railfan, January 1988 (Issue #16), May 1989 (Issue #20).

Baird, R. 1992. The last days of the Chehalis Western. *Railfan & Railroad* 11(8):60-67.

Verified notice of exemption of the Boeing Company-Acquisition of certain rights, and operations on trackage of Chehalis Western Railway Company before the ICC. Finance Docket No. 31916, July 26, 1991.

Interstate Commerce Commission Decision, Finance Docket No. 31916. The Boeing Company, Acquisition and Operation Exemption, Chehalis Western Railway Company, October 10, 1991,

The Olympian, "Boys' Campfire Starts Trestle Blaze"; July 31, 1991. Section C, p. 1.

Don Wallace to Peter P. Magnone, May 25, 1993. Chehalis Western Railroad Company unprocessed records, 99-101, Weyerhaeuser Archives.

Baird, R. 1992. "The last days of the Chehalis Western"; *Railfan & Railroad*, 11(8):60-67.

CHAPTER 13

Baird, R. 1992. The last days of the Chehalis Western. *Railfan & Railroad* 11(8):60-67.

E.M. Berntsen to D. Clairmont, September 14, 1994, Chehalis Western Railroad Company unprocessed records, 99-101, Weyerhaeuser Archives.

L. Gilliam, Texas to V.N. Schmidt, July 12, 1994. James Barrett Paper Collection.

Resolution No. 32844, City of Tacoma, December 6, 1994. James Barrett Collection.

Tacoma Eastern Railway brochure "We're the new kid on the block..." March 6, 1995. James Barrett Collection.

Index

Dates of Operation

1924–1929 (Skookumchuck Operation years), 1–28

1927–1929 (Vail Operation camps), 29–58

1930–1934 (Great Depression and Vail Operation years), 59–106

1934–1942 (Skookumchuck Crossing years), 71–106

1934 (Chehalis Western Operation and Columbia Construction Quarry), 107–120

1937–1945 (Chehalis Western Operation and Camp McDonald), 121–148

1943–1953 (Vail-McDonald Operation transition years), 149–178

1954–1961 (Vail-McDonald Operation years), 179–196

1961–1975 (Pe Ell years), 197–242

1973–1980 (Curtis, Milburn & Eastern years), 229–242

1977–1980 (Milwaukee Road Operation years), 243–262

1980–1992 (Chehalis Western Operation years), 263–296

1992–1995 (operational decline years), 297–306

A

Accident and wrecks, 42, 62, 65–66, 77, 83, 89–90, 93–94, 186–189, 196

Adams, Noel R., 233–236

Adams & Associates, 236

Alco locomotives, 81, 205, 252, 263, 269, 329

Alexander, Robert, 35–36

Allen Engineering Company, 19

Allis-Chalmer diesel tractors, 149

Allis-Chalmer loggers, 87

Altshool, John, vi

American Locomotive Company, 88–89, 205

American Oriental Express, 301

Amundsen, Ed, 133

Anderson, Jack, vi

Atlanta, Birmingham & Coast, 121–125

Atlas Powder Company, 213

B

B. C. Forest Products, 161

Bagley, Arthur, 77

Baldwin Locomotive Works, 40–43, 75, 82–83, 93–95, 285–286

Ballast cars and pits, 19, 174–175, 269

Barrett, James F., iv, 53, 136, 209, 262, 273

Barrett, Jim, v–vi

Barrett, Lawrence, 53

Barrett, Rosalie F., iv–vi

Barrett, Scott, 75, 123

Barrett, Susan, vi

Barrett family, 28, 58, 67–69, 79, 157

Barry, J. G., 248, 250

Beaber, Rick, vi

Bell-Nelson Mill, vi, xii–xiii

Beulke, Richard, 213

Bibliography, 335–343

Black Hills Central Railroad, 302–304

Blankenship, F., 77

Blomquist, Chris, vi

Blum, Gina, vi

Blumauer logging railroad, 111

Bobbers, 100

Bob's Photo, 205

Boeing, 287

Boire, Lisa, vi

Brandstrom, Alex J. F., 154

Bridges and trestles, 13–18, 71–106, 130, 138, 157–158, 171, 184, 206–209, 232–233, 236–237, 248, 280–281, 303, 331–334

Brown, Edward, 65–66

Brown, Kenneth S., 1–2

Buckets, 88

Bucklin, G. R., 167

Buckskin ties, 19

Bucyrus-Erie shovels, 32

Bunk houses, 85–88

Burlington Northern, 10, 200, 212–215, 222, 229, 233–236, 244, 277–278, 285–287, 298–306

Bush, William L., 212–213

Butler, William, 77

Butt rigging signal codes, 57

Byers, D. H., 251

C

Caboose Hotel, 303

Cabooses, 97–100, 125–128, 133, 160–161, 176, 185, 189–193, 219–227, 235– 241, 263, 268, 271, 301–303

Campbell, Verne, 77

Camps

    Camp 1, 307

    Camp 2, 19, 60, 74–84, 88, 307

    Camp 3, 60–68, 77–88, 98, 304, 307

    Camp 4, 68, 71–78, 94, 102–104, 307

    Camp 5, 77, 80, 88, 307

    Camp 6, 129, 134–139, 307

    Camp 7, 60, 75, 77, 134–135, 144, 307

    Camp 18, 155, 161, 189–190, 236, 239–240

    Camp McDonald, 81–88, 96, 103, 121–148, 166, 191, 237, 307

    Camp Randle, 167–169

    CCC camps, 62–65

    Cherry Valley Camp, 64, 71, 81

    LD Camp, 303, 307

    locations (listings and maps), 69, 79, 307

    R&L Camp, 76

    Skookumchuck Camp, 2

    South Bay Boom Camp, 78, 307

    Spike Camp, 66, 68, 71, 74, 307

    Vail Headquarters Camp, 26, 166, 284

    Vail Operation camps (1927–1929), 29–58

Canfield, Floyd, vi

Canron Rail Alignment vehicles, 270

Cargo arches, 149–151

Carlson, William, v

Cars (rolling stock and equipment listing), 308–320

Carter, James E., 257

Cascade Contracting Company, 112

Caterpillar diesel engines, 20–25

CCC (Civilian Conservation Corps) camps, 62–65

CEECO (Coast Engine and Equipment Company), 301

Centralia-Chehalis Railroad Association, 299–300

Champion Building Products, 253

Chapman, Charles S., 172

Chatwood, Sr., Bob, vi

Chehalis Western Operation years

    1934, 107–120

    1937–1945, 121–148

    1980–1992, 263–296

Cherry Valley Logging & Railway Company, 23, 36

Cherry Valley Timber Company, 36

Chicago, Burlington & Quincy, 213

Chicago, Milwaukee, St. Paul & Pacific Railroad, 108–120

Chip-N-Saw mills, 230–234, 278

Chippewa River and Menomonie Railway, ix

CIO-International Woodworkers of America, 82

Circular saw mills, vii, ix

Civilian Conservation Corps (CCC) camps, 62–65

Clark, C. A., 167

Clark, Donald, 67

Clark, E. T., 150

Clark, John, 164–166

Clarke County Timber Company, 36, 38

Clemons Lumber Company, 2, 82, 95

Clemons Tree Farm, 172

Climax, 83, 95, 323

Clyde Iron Works cranes, 42, 192, 208, 222

Coast Engine and Equipment Company (CEECO), 301

Coast Lumber Company, ix

Cochran, Allen, 88–89

Collins, Jack, 133

Columbia Construction Company, 108–120

Columbia Construction Quarry, 107–120

Columbus Day Storm, 204–206

Company stores, 20–26

Conklin, Robert P., 150, 152

Conrad, John F., 252

Continental Illinois Leasing, 270

Cookhouses, 74, 135

Cowlitz River Valley Historical Society, vi

Cox Brothers, 139

Cranes, 60, 88, 137, 187, 192, 201–208, 222, 273

Crescent Springs Railroad, ix

Crosby, Harry Lillis, 2

Crosby, Harry Lowe (Bing), 2

Crosby, Helen (Kate), 2

Crosby, Lloyd R., xiii, 2, 23–24, 27, 31, 41, 71, 152

Crumley, Ralph, 77

Cummings, George, vi

Cummings, John R., vi, 176, 186–189, 209

Curtis, Milburn & Eastern years (1973–1980), 229–242

Curtis Pole Company, 299

D

Davis, Minot, xiii, 83, 107–108

Decline of operation years (1992–1995), 297–306

Depression years (1930–1934), 59–106

DeSordi, Frank, 225

Dibble, Hawthorne & Moor, 112

Diesel loaders, 152

Diesel locomotives (listing), 326–330. *See also* Locomotives

Diesel tractors, 149–151

Dispatchers, 123

Dog houses, 125

Donkey engines, 50–51, 69, 82, 105

Dumps (log), 6–8

Duplex loaders, 87

DuPont Company. *See* E. I. DuPont de Nemours Company

DuPont Powder Company, 246

E

E. I. DuPont de Nemours Company, 244–248

Economic histories, 61

Ehrengart, William M., 54, 122

Electro-Motive Division (EMD)/General Motors locomotives, 239–242, 326–329

Embargo activities, 248–256

EMD (Electro-Motive Division)/General Motors locomotives, 239–242, 326–329

Engine houses, 234, 280

Equalizing tower skidders. *See* Tower skidders

Equipment and rolling stock (listing), 308–320

Erndart, William, 42

Essena, Ray, 184

Everett mills, 3, 23, 27, 39–70, 81–82, 109, 179, 209–210, 237, 242

Exhibit Y, 146

F

Fairbanks-Morse (FM) locomotives, 162–163, 328

Fairfield, John, 77

Fairmont Tampers, 270

Farrow, Al, 39, 44, 84, 90–91, 93, 95, 118, 125–126, 130, 144, 161

Federal Railroad Administration, 248, 270

Filberg, Robert J., 150–152

Fires and fire-fighting equipment, 62, 89–90, 93–94, 132–134, 164, 291–294

Floods, 181

FM (Fairbanks-Morse) locomotives, 162–163, 328

Ford trucks, 20

Fournier, Milt, 181, 185

French, Mr., 60

Froner, Milton, 188–189

Fuller, William, 77

G

Gas shovels, 82

Geared locomotives, 60

Gehrman, Bob, vi

General Motors Corporation EMD (Electro-Motive Division) locomotives, 239–242, 326–329

General Petroleum Corporation, 12

George, King, 183

George (timekeeper), 103

Georgia Car & Locomotive Company, 124–125

Gibson, H. A., 124

Gibson speeders, 104, 124, 145

Gonzaga University, 2

Grandstrom, Arthur, 54

Graves, Jr., Thomas B., 244

Great Depression and Vail Operation years (1930–1934), 59–106

Great Northern, 42, 238–239

Green River Lumber Company, 65

Greenwood, Michael, v

Grier, Harold E., 244

Guarnaccia, D., 270

H

Hales, George, vi, 107–108, 111–112, 114–117

Hales family, 107–108, 111–112, 114–117

Hansen, Henry, 88–89

Hansen, Martin E., v, vi, 40, 43–44, 84, 90–91, 93, 95–98, 100, 118, 122, 130, 137, 143–144, 154, 161

Harbor Plywood, 184

Harrington, W. L. (Dick), 63, 65

Hart Construction, 10–11, 130, 168, 171

Haunreiter, Ed, 181

Henderson, John, vi, 41, 127, 176, 201, 207, 210, 216, 218, 225–226, 238, 254–255, 257–260, 266, 268

Hercules Sandstone Company, 111

Hetch Hetchy Railroad, 81, 88, 302

Hewitt Land Company, 89

High lead signal codes, 57

Hill, Harold A., 95–98, 118, 123–124, 126, 129, 131, 133, 136, 139, 143, 146–147

Historical sources, 335–343

Hofius Steel & Equipment Company, 23, 41

Hoot owl shifts, 62

Huff, Bob, 143

Hussey, Richard, vi, 104–105

I

ICC (Interstate Commerce Commission), 122, 124–125, 160–161, 232, 241, 243–261, 280–285

International Car Company, 212

International Woodworkers of America (IWA), 279–285

Interstate Commerce Commission (ICC), 122, 124–125, 160–161, 232, 241, 243–261, 280–285

IWA (International Woodworkers of America), 279–285

J

Jammers, 1–3, 10–12. *See also* Unloaders

Jewel, Jeff, vi

Johnson, Albert, 11–12

Johnson, Bob, vi

Johnson, Kristopher, vi, 229, 295

Johnston, Jeff, vi

Jordan spreaders, 266, 268

Junk, Merle, 163

K

K & K Timber Company, 42

Kaiser, Henry J., 114

Kauffman, F., 270

Kauffman, John G., 244, 252–253, 284

Keithahn, George, 83

Kell, Ernie, 273

Kell, Harry, 189

Kell, John, vi

Kelsey, Melvin, 83

Kern Contracting Company, 112

Kinsey, Clark, 6, 13, 20, 23–26, 29, 31, 33–34, 37, 48–50, 53, 56, 59–60, 64, 66, 71, 75–76, 80

Kinsey, Darius, 38, 40, 43, 45, 51, 73–74, 81, 83–84, 86–88, 92–94, 96–97

Kinsland, Ed, 83

Kosmos Timber Company, 164, 170–171

Kraft pulp mills, 241

L

Labbe, John T., v–vi, 100, 125–126, 128

Labor unrest, 82

Lambertson, Frank, 20, 25, 76–77, 83

Larsen, Charles, 89

Larsen, Ivar, 77

Larson, Lars, 77

Larson, Louis, 77

Larson, Ludwig, 77

Lawson, T., 100

Lentz, Ken, vi

LeRoy, Paul, vi, 158

Lidgerwood spar skidders, 82, 92–94, 141

Lima Locomotive Works, 39, 45

Lindstrom-Handforth Lumber Company, 32–34

Linemen, 105

Link-Belt Company, 214

Loaders, 152

Local Rail Service Assistance Program, 251

Locomotive signal codes, 57

Locomotives

    #1, 38, 60, 224–225, 304, 321

    #2, 38, 60, 82, 321

    #3, 38, 91, 321

    #4, 60, 95, 254, 321, 323

    #5, 38, 60, 88, 91, 321

    #6, 83, 321

    #8, 82–83

    #10, 187

    #15, 300

    #25, 82

    #99, 82, 90, 161–162, 322

    #100, 81, 88, 90, 95, 130, 143, 302, 322

    #101, 60, 76, 158, 161–163, 322

    #102, 82, 91, 93, 176, 322

    #103, 60, 76, 322

    #104, 322

    #105, 76, 82, 130, 143, 323

    #110, 60, 80, 84, 88, 95, 130, 302–303, 323

    #111, 60, 78, 83–84, 144, 303, 323

    #112, 130, 144, 162–163, 323

    #114, 82–83, 95, 130, 323

    #120, 75–76, 82–83, 95, 126, 129–130, 154, 323–324

    #139, 329

    #150, 162–163

    #211, 121–122, 124–126, 161–163, 324

    #215, 122, 124–126, 129, 131, 158, 162–163, 324

    #282, 280–281

    #286, 326

    #314, 260, 329

    #415, 205

    #481, 158, 184–185, 219–220, 243, 326

    #492, 160, 181–182, 205, 235, 239, 328

    #493, 160, 181–182, 185–186, 205, 328

    #616, 327

    #618, 327

    #619, 226, 327

    #668, 327

    #674, 252

    #684, 206, 221–222, 224, 233–235, 239, 263, 269, 296, 299, 328

    #714, 225, 239, 304, 326

    #765, 233, 237, 242, 252, 265, 286, 289, 291, 328

    #776, 242, 252, 285–286, 289, 291, 295, 326, 328

    #810, 288, 329

    #817, 289–291, 328

    #818, 289, 328

    #819, 288–289, 328

    #1504, 327

    #1627, 327

    #1630, 212, 329

    #1632, 327

    #1637, 212, 329

    #1680, 327

    #1846, 212, 329

    #1871, 327

    #1888, 328

    #8080, 329

    Alco, 81, 205, 252, 263, 269, 329

    American Locomotive Company, 88–89, 205

    Baldwin Locomotive Works, 40–43, 75, 82–83, 93–95, 285–286

    Climax, 83, 95, 323

    diesel (listing), 326–330

    Fairbanks-Morse, 162–163, 328

    geared, 60

    General Motors Corporation EMD, 239–242, 326–329

    Georgia Car & Locomotive Company, 124–125

    listings (steam and diesel), 321–324, 326–330

    locomotive cranes, 32, 187, 192, 273

    Mikado, 91, 93, 96, 124–125, 143, 285–286

    MK, 239

    Plymouth narrow gauge, 246, 254, 257–258

    Porter, 82

    rod, 60, 76

    saddle-tank, 76–78, 96

    Shay, 82, 96, 111, 114, 119, 122, 143, 160, 321–324

    speeders, 82

steam (listing), 321–324
tandem diesel, 141
Whitcomb, 329
Loftus, Louis, 77
Log dumps, 6–8
Log load transfer machines, 202–203
Loggers Special cranes, 31
Logmania problem, 150–152
Logos, 83–84, 104
Long, George S., xii–xiii, 24, 41, 171
Longview mills, 108–109
Lorenz, Bob, 118

M

Machine shops, 24–25, 76, 134, 168–169, 276, 279, 298–300
Mack trucks, 159–160
Malone, Roe, 54
Manning, R., 167, 246, 248
Maps
    Camp 2, 80
    Camp 3, 85
    Camp 4, 73
    Camp 5, 88
    Camp 18, 155
    Camp Doty, 147
    Camp McDonald, 123
    camps and spurs, 79
    Chehalis Reload, 182, 267
    Chehalis Western interchange (Milwaukee Road), 1–6
    cruiser's section, 4–5
    Curtis, Milburn & Eastern, 228
    Curtis Pole Yard, 292
    Curtis Sort Yard, 231
    deliberate errors, 244
    Everett Branch mileage diagram, 195
    Everett harbor, x
    Harbor Plywood Corporation, 178
    McDonald, 142
    McDonald dispatch, 123
    Metsker maps, 244
    Mile 13 ballast pit, 175
    Mile 18 transfer, 148
    Mile 21 gravel pit, 99
    Milwaukee acquisition, 245
    Milwaukee track purchase, 251
    Mineral reload, 207
    Morton reload, 170
    Pe Ell Headquarters, 196
    reciprocal use, 110
    Skookum Chuck engineering map, 30
    Skookum Chuck gravel pit spur, 11
    Skookum Chuck interchanges, 9, 12, 278
    Skookum Chuck (Vail) mainline, xx
    Skookum Chuck (Vail) progress, 28, 58, 67, 101, 153
    South Bay, 216
    South Bay boom camp, 78
    South Bay log dump and boom, 8, 126
    Tacoma area, 249
    Tacoma Sort Yard, 205, 224, 233, 264
    tie mill logging, 21
    Vail and McDonald tree farms, 247
    Vail Headquarters, 22, 166
    Vail Reload, 239, 287
    Western Junction, 165, 275
Marion steam shovels, 114
McAbee, Charles, v
McClean (contractor), 130
McClure, Dennis, vi
McClure, Don, 181
McClure, Doug, 185
McDonald, A. S., 133–134
McDonald, Ronald A., xv, 27, 41–42, 54, 60, 63, 77, 103, 122, 133–134
McDonald and Vail logging railroads
    1924–1929 (Skookumchuck Operation years), 1–28
    1927–1929 (Vail Operation camps), 29–58
    1930–1934 (Great Depression and Vail Operation years), 59–106
    1934–1942 (Skookumchuck Crossing years), 71–106
    1934 (Chehalis Western Operation and Columbia Construction Quarry), 107–120
    1937–1945 (Chelalis Western Operation and Camp

McDonald), 121–148
1943–1953 (Vail-McDonald Operation transition years), 149–178
1954–1961 (Vail-McDonald Operation years), 179–196
1961–1975 (Pe Ell years), 197–242
1973–1980 (Curtis, Milburn & Eastern years), 229–242
1977–1980 (Milwaukee Road Operation years), 243–262
1980–1992 (Chehalis Western Operation years), 263–296
1992–1995 (declining years), 297–306
bridges and stations
Chehalis Western Operation, 333–334
Vail Operation, 331–332
camp locations (Vail-McDonald), 307–320
locomotives. *See also* Locomotives
    diesel (1948–1994), 326–330
    steam (1927–1953), 321–324
overviews, v–xix
reference resources, 335–343
McDonald camp, 121–148
McGinn, F. Gregg, 212
McKay, Charles, 54
McMillan, George, 77
McMillen, Thomas R., 250–251, 255
McNiven, Scott, 181
Merrill, Lee, 160
Merrill & Ring Lumber Company, 114
Merritt, Jack, 88–89
Metsker maps, 244
Mikado locomotives, 91, 93, 96, 124–125, 143, 285–286
Milich, Frank, 83
Miller, Alan, vi
Miller, Neil, 133
Miller Hill, 39, 74
Mills
    Bell-Nelson, vi, xii–xiii
    Chip-N-Saw, 230–234, 278
    circular saw, vii, ix
    Everett, vii–xii, 3, 23, 27, 39–70, 74, 81–82, 109, 179, 209–210, 229, 237, 240–242
    Kraft pulp, 241
    Longview, 108–109
    Port Blackely, 81–82
Milwaukee Railroad Restructuring Act, 256–257
Milwaukee Road Operation years (1977–1980), 243–262
MK (Morrison-Knudsen) locomotives, 239
Moholt, Megan, v, vi
Morgan, Davis, 133
Morning Olympian, 42
Morrison-Knudsen (MK) locomotives, 239
Morsen, Bert, 89
Mt. Rainier, 6
Mt. Rainier Scenic Railroad, vi, 272, 300, 304
Murray, Jr., Tom, 31, 272–274
Murray Pacific, 274
Mutual Lumber Company, 23, 65

N

Narrow gauge equipment
    cars, 252–253, 259
    engine houses, 258
    locomotives, 246, 254, 257–258
National Pole Company, 42
National Railroad Adjustment Board, 125
Nelson, Arthur, 42
Nelson, Jr., Bert, 77
Nelson, Rick, vi, 273
Nelson, Suzanne, vi
Neson, Fred, 77
Neuman, Francis, vi, 46, 76, 140, 163, 167
Nielson, Robert, 259
Noel R. Adams, P.E. & Associates, 233–236
Noonan, Joseph, 83
Norfolk and Western, 239
North Bend Timber Company, 82
Northern Pacific, xii, 10, 19–24, 75, 109–111, 137, 197, 213, 221, 291
Northwest Aluminum Company, 213
Northwest gas shovels, 82
Northwest Hardwoods, 299
Northwest Railway Museum, 303
Northwest Traction, 98
Numbered locomotives. *See* Locomotives

O

Obenour, Mr., 62–63

Office of Policy and Analysis, 248

Ogilvie, Richard B., 250, 258–259

Ohio locomotive cranes, 32

Ohio Loggers Special cranes, 31

Oil and sand houses, 234

Olsen, Al, 160

Onstad, A. H., 3, 10–11

Operation years
- 1924–1929 (Skookumchuck Operation years), 1–28
- 1927–1929 (Vail Operation camps), 29–58
- 1930–1934 (Great Depression and Vail Operation years), 59–106
- 1934–1942 (Skookumchuck Crossing years), 71–106
- 1934 (Chehalis Western Operation and Columbia Construction Quarry), 107–120
- 1937–1945 (Chehalis Western Operation and Camp McDonald), 121–148
- 1943–1953 (Vail-McDonald Operation transition years), 149–178
- 1954–1961 (Vail-McDonald Operation years), 179–196
- 1961–1975 (Pe Ell years), 197–242
- 1973–1980 (Curtis, Milburn & Eastern years), 229–242
- 1977–1980 (Milwaukee Road Operation years), 243–262
- 1980–1992 (Chehalis Western Operation years), 263–296
- 1992–1995 (operational decline years), 297–306

Operational decline years (1992–1995), 297–306

Oregon Electric Interurban Railway, 41, 100

Overviews, v–xix

Ozanich, John, v

P

PACCAR, Inc., 41, 127, 271

Pacific Car & Foundry (PC&F) cars, 19, 41, 65, 100, 127, 132, 194, 197, 204, 207, 210, 227, 266

Pacific Logger's Congress, 44–45, 57

Pacific Northwest Forest Experiment Station, 154

Pallett, Bob, vi

Pallett, Colleen Hales, vi

Panush, Mr., 133

PC&F (Pacific Car & Foundry) cars, 19, 41, 65, 100, 127, 132, 194, 197, 204, 207, 210, 227, 266

Pe Ell years (1961-1975), 197–242

Pearson and Larson Company, 19, 27

Pettingill, R. A., 61–63

Pettit, Robert (Bob), vi, 280

P&H diesel shovels, 32

Pile drivers, 41

Plymouth narrow gauge locomotives, 246, 254, 257–258

Pole yards, 293–294

Porcupine Ridge, 74

Port Blakely Mill Company, 81–82

Porter locomotives, 82

Price, W. H., 172

Prouty, Andrew Mason, 35

Puget Sound Electric Railway, 98

Puget Sound Railway Association, 303

Purdy Company, 243

Q

Quarries (Columbia Construction Quarry), 107–120

Quinhill, Ora, 189

R

Radio communications, 163

Rail alignment vehicles, 270

Railink, Inc., 297–306

Railroad Brotherhoods, 109, 125–126

Railroad Contracting Company, 19

Rails to Trails, 299

Railway Mail Service, 66, 68

Rainier Historical Society, 6, 23, 46, 76, 104, 140, 163, 167

Ransey, Faller Melbourne, 83

Rasmussen, Tom, 256–262

Raubeneck, John A., 260

Raught, Jr., A. L., 157

Reference resources, 335–343

Reforestation and Land (R&L) Department, 76–77

Reichel, Harold L. (Buck), 163, 167

Reloads, 167

Replinger, Peter J., vi, 26, 34, 144, 204, 226, 233, 243

Riley, Leo, 53

Rivera, Diana, vi

R&L (Reforestation and Land) Department, 76–77

Roberts, Emory J., 100

Rod locomotives, 60, 76

Rogers, Vance, 88–89

Rogers ballast cars, 19, 41, 144

Roher, Landis, vi

Rolling stock and equipment (listing), 308–320

Root, M., 279

Ryan, Walter J., xiii, 41, 122, 152

S

Saddle-tank locomotives, 76–78, 96

Sand and oil houses, 234

Sand cars, 81

Sante Fe, 60

Sauk River Lumber Company, 150

Savory, Forrest, 250

Scaler's offices, 301

Scheel, Hans Peter, 111

Scheel, Walter G., 27

Schill, A. J., 236–237, 265

Schmelzer, Ken, vi, 61, 174, 176, 193–194, 210, 215

Schmidt, Antone, 83

Seidl, J. M., 235

Sensa, Joe, 42

Shaw, Jim, vi, 286–287, 291, 296

Shays, 82, 96, 111, 114, 119, 122, 143, 160, 321–324

Shelby, H. D., 83

Shell Lake Lumber Company, ix

Shops (machine), 24–25, 76, 134, 168–169, 276, 279, 298–300

Shovels, 12, 60, 82, 88, 112, 114, 116

Siler Logging Company, 81–82, 91–92

Simpson Logging Company, 82, 93, 95

Skagit Steel & Iron Works speeders, 64

Skid shacks, 37, 68, 80

Skidders, 12, 52–53, 56, 60–61, 63–66, 76, 82, 87, 92–94, 104, 141, 180, 197

Skinny's Curve, 77

Skookumchuck Crossing trestle, 71–106

Skookumchuck Operation years (1924–1929), 1–28

Smith, J. L., 19

Smith-Layman, 87

SORE plan, 256–260

Sound Timber Company, ix, xii

Southern Pacific, 160–161, 238, 277

Spar skidders, 82, 92–94, 141

Spears, Lyle, vi, 180–181, 189–192, 202–203, 206, 208, 216, 219, 232, 288, 291

Speeders, 39, 59, 64, 82, 87–88, 97, 104, 124, 145, 176, 191, 240

Spreaders, 266

Spurs, 11, 74–79, 94, 117–119, 130–141, 303

Star Route Mail Service, 66, 68

Stations

    Chehalis Western Operation, 333–334

    Vail Operation, 331–332

Steam jammers, 1–3, 6, 10–12, 176–177

Steam locomotives (listing), 321–324. *See also* Locomotives

Steam shovels, 12, 60, 112, 114, 116

Steam unloaders. *See* Steam jammers

Sterling trucks, 159–160

Stillwater Lumber Company, 39

Stock market crash (1929), 39–70

Stolp, Otto, 42

Storms, 201–206

Strong & McDonald, 19, 35, 129–130

Swanson, Gunner, 149

Swivel bunk cars, 215

T

Tampers, 270

Tandem diesel locomotives, 141

Taubeneck, John A., vi, 225–227, 240–242, 269, 288, 290

Taylor, James, 77

Telephone lines, 105

Telewski, Frank W., 6, 8–9, 12, 22, 28, 39, 58, 67, 69, 72–73, 78–80, 85, 88–89, 95, 99, 101, 106, 113, 115, 124, 126, 146–147, 153, 155, 157, 162, 165, 170, 175–176, 185–186, 196, 198, 205, 207, 211, 220–224, 228, 230–239, 251, 263–280, 282–287, 289, 291–292, 296, 298–305

Telewski, Fred F., iv

Telewski, Jill Grimes, vi

Telewski, Madeline E., iv

Tenino County Independent, 32

Thurston County Board of Commissioners, 2

Thurston County Historical Society, v *Thurston County Independent,* 35, 60, 68, 112

Timberman,The, 3, 8, 44, 54–55, 57, 135, 141

Titcomb, F. R., 2, 8, 24, 31, 41, 60–61, 82

Toby, Fred, vi

Tolan, Fred, 259

Tower skidders, 51, 61, 63–66

Tractors (diesel), 149–151

Transfer machines, 202–203

Transition years (1943–1953), 149–178

Tree farms, 166, 189–190, 267, 306

"Tree Growing Company," 171–173

Tree rig skidders, 52–53, 56, 60–61

Trestles. *See* Bridges and trestles

Truck scaler's offices, 301

Turvey Logging Company, 112

Typhoon Frieda, 201

U

Union Pacific, 124, 240, 244, 259, 274, 278, 298–306

United Commercial Company, 41

United States Steel Corporation, 8, 23

University of Washington Libraries, v, 33, 66–67, 75

Unloaders, 177, 209, 211, 214, 218, 220. *See also* Jammers

Upington, G. M., 2, 27

U.S. Army Corps of Engineers, vi, 8

U.S. Department of War, 8

V

Vail, Billy, 27

Vail and McDonald logging railroads

    1924–1929 (Skookumchuck Operation years), 1–28

    1927–1929 (Vail Operation camps), 29–58

    1930–1934 (Great Depression and Vail Operation years), 59–106

    1934–1942 (Skookumchuck Crossing years), 71–106

    1934 (Chehalis Western Operation and Columbia Construction Quarry), 107–120

    1937–1945 (Chehalis Western Operation and Camp McDonald), 121–148

    1943–1953 (Vail-McDonald Operation transition years), 149–178

    1954–1961 (Vail-McDonald Operation years), 179–196

    1961–1975 (Pe Ell years), 197–242

    1973–1980 (Curtis, Milburn & Eastern years), 229–242

    1977–1980 (Milwaukee Road Operation years), 243–262

    1980–1992 (Chehalis Western Operation years), 263–296

    1992–1995 (declining years), 297–306

Vail-McDonald Operation

    1954–1995, 179–196

    1992–1995 (transition years), 149–178

Vail Operation

    1927–1929 (camps), 29–58

    1930–1934, 59–106

Vincent, Ralph, 150–151, 167

Vincent, Rowland C., 213

Vorn, Richard, 42

W

Wahl, John, 157–159, 162–163, 167

WAM (Weyerhaeuser and Milwaukee) plan, 243–261

Ward, John P., 149

Ward, Ted, vi, 102, 132, 134–136

Washington Department of Natural Resources, 230

Washington Forest Fire Association, 133

Washington Iron Works skidders, 52–53, 56, 60–61, 63–66, 76, 92

Washington State Department of Transportation (WSDOT), 243–255

West, Roy, vi

West Coast Lumberman, The, 20, 45, 55, 138, 141

West Coast Lumberman's Association, 172

West Coast Preserving Company, 168

West Fork Logging Company, 31

Weyerhaeuser, Frederick, vii–xii

Weyerhaeuser, George H., 213, 272

Weyerhaeuser, Jr., J. P., 83, 107, 109, 125

Weyerhaeuser and Denkmann, vii–ix

Weyerhaeuser and Milwaukee (WAM) plan, 243–261

Weyerhaeuser Archives, 2–3, 8–22, 24–25, 29–31, 36–38, 47–51, 56, 58–60, 64, 67–71, 80, 101, 113, 121–124, 126, 129, 131,

133, 136, 139, 146–147, 149–152, 157, 159–160, 164, 168–169, 171, 179, 183–184, 187, 196, 199–200, 214, 216–217, 251, 293–294

Weyerhaeuser News, 137

Weyerhaeuser's Vail and McDonald logging railroads

    1924–1929 (Skookumchuck Operation years), 1–28

    1927–1929 (Vail Operation camps), 29–58

    1930–1934 (Great Depression and Vail Operation years), 59–106

    1934–1942 (Skookumchuck Crossing years), 71–106

    1934 (Chehalis Western Operation and Columbia Construction Quarry), 107–120

    1937–1945 (Chelalis Western Operation and Camp McDonald), 121–148

    1943–1953 (Vail-McDonald Operation transition years), 149–178

    1954–1961 (Vail-McDonald Operation years), 179–196

    1961–1975 (Pe Ell years), 197–242

    1973–1980 (Curtis, Milburn & Eastern years), 229–242

    1977–1980 (Milwaukee Road Operation years), 243–262

    1980–1992 (Chehalis Western Operation years), 263–296

    1992–1995 (declining years), 297–306

    bridges and stations

        Chehalis Western Operation, 333–334

        Vail Operation, 331–332

    camp locations (Vail-McDonald), 307–320. *See also* Camps

    locomotives. *See also* Locomotives

        diesel (1948–1994), 326–330

        steam (1927–1953), 321–324

    overviews, v–xix

    reference resources, 335–343

Whaley, Jim, vi, 234–235

Whatcom Museum of History and Art, v–vi, 51, 73–74, 81, 83–84, 86–88, 92–94, 96–97

Whistle signal codes, 57

Whitcomb locomotives, 329

White, Sam C., 66

White River Lumber Company, 225

Willamette diesel loaders, 152

Willamina & Grande Ronde Railroad Company, 279

Willapa Harbor Line, 197–228

Williams, Wilmer O., 83

Wilson, Jeff, vi

Wolff, Clarence, 189

Woods, Bill, 103–104

Works Projects Administration (WPA), 65

WPA (Works Projects Administration), 65

Wrecks and accidents, 42, 62, 65–66, 77, 83, 89–90, 93–94, 186–189, 196

WSDOT (Washington State Department of Transportation), 243–255

Y

Y (exhibit), 146

Yarders, 87

Years of operation

    1924–1929 (Skookumchuck Operation years), 1–28

    1927–1929 (Vail Operation camps), 29–58

    1930–1934 (Great Depression and Vail Operation years), 59–106

    1934–1942 (Skookumchuck Crossing years), 71–106

    1934 (Chehalis Western Operation and Columbia Construction Quarry), 107–120

    1937–1945 (Chelalis Western Operation and Camp McDonald), 121–148

    1943–1953 (Vail-McDonald Operation transition years), 149–178

    1954–1961 (Vail-McDonald Operation years), 179–196

    1961–1975 (Pe Ell years), 197–242

    1973–1980 (Curtis, Milburn & Eastern years), 229–242

    1977–1980 (Milwaukee Road Operation years), 243–262

    1980–1992 (Chehalis Western Operation years), 263–296

    1992–1995 (operational decline years), 297–306